THE HUNGRY STEPPE

THE HUNGRY STEPPE

Famine, Violence, and the
Making of Soviet Kazakhstan

Sarah Cameron

CORNELL UNIVERSITY PRESS   **ITHACA AND LONDON**

Cornell University Press gratefully acknowledges receipt of subventions from the Department of History and the College of Arts and Humanities at the University of Maryland—College Park. Publication of this book was also made possible, in part, by a grant from the First Book Subvention Program of the Association for Slavic, East European, and Eurasian Studies.

First published 2018 by Cornell University Press

Printed in the United States of America

Library of Congress Cataloging-in-Publication Data

Names: Cameron, Sarah I., 1977– author.
Title: The hungry steppe : famine, violence, and the making of Soviet Kazakhstan / Sarah I. Cameron.
Description: Ithaca [New York] : Cornell University Press, 2018. | Includes bibliographical references and index.
Identifiers: LCCN 2018007700 (print) | LCCN 2018008082 (ebook) | ISBN 9781501730443 (pdf) | ISBN 9781501730450 (epub/mobi) | ISBN 9781501730436 | ISBN 9781501730436 (cloth ; alk. paper)
Subjects: LCSH: Famines—Kazakhstan—History—20th century. | Famines—Soviet Union—History—20th century. | Nomads—Sedentarization—Kazakhstan—History—20th century. | Collectivization of agriculture—Kazakhstan—History—20th century. | Soviet Union—History—1925–1953.
Classification: LCC DK908.8618 (ebook) | LCC DK908.8618 .C36 2018 (print) | DDC 958.45084/2—dc23
LC record available at https://lccn.loc.gov/2018007700

For Arnd

Өлі риза болмай, тірі байымайды

Until the spirits of the dead are honored, the living will not prosper

—Kazakh proverb

Contents

Explanatory Note

The peoples and places in this book underwent numerous changes in nomenclature during Russian imperial and Soviet rule. In the imperial period, Russian sources referred to the steppe as the "Kirgiz steppe." Similarly, they referred to the steppe's nomadic inhabitants as "Kirgiz," even though these peoples referred to themselves as "Qazaq." By the early Soviet period, Russian sources began to refer to the steppe as the "Kazak steppe" and the nomadic peoples that inhabited it as "Kazaks." In 1936, Moscow adopted a different spelling for the republic and its titular nationality, referring to them as "Kazakhstan" and "Kazakhs." For simplicity's sake, I refer to the peoples that are at the heart of this book as "Kazakhs." I use the term "Kazakh steppe" to refer to the steppe prior to the advent of Soviet rule and the term "Kazakhstan" to refer to the republic during Soviet rule and after independence. In citing published works, I have kept the spelling used in the original. I have adopted the term "The Hungry Steppe" as the title of this book although the phrase technically refers only to a portion of the region that I am studying. The Hungry Steppe, also known as the "Betpak-Dala" (or "Ill-Fated Steppe"), is an immense plateau located in the heart of Kazakhstan, just south of the city of Karaganda.

The place that would become known as Kazakhstan began to assume its territorial form under Soviet rule. It was known first as the Kirgiz Autonomous Soviet Socialist Republic (ASSR) before it was renamed the Kazakh ASSR in 1925. As an ASSR, Kazakhstan was a constituent part of a federal republic, the Russian Soviet Federative Socialist Republic (RSFSR). In 1936, the republic gained union republic status, becoming known as the Kazakh Soviet Socialist Republic (SSR). Throughout these shifts in administration, I refer to the republic simply as "Kazakhstan." For Russian-language materials, I have used the Library of Congress transliteration system. For Kazakh-language materials, I have used the system in Edward Allworth, *Nationalities of the Soviet East* (1971). The Kazakh language underwent several changes in script during the period that this study surveys. In the interest of consistency, all Kazakh terms have been transliterated from the Cyrillic, which is the script in use in Kazakhstan as of the publication of this book. I have transliterated the names of places and people according to these systems, except in a handful of cases where an English spelling has become standard (i.e., Kazakh president Nursultan Nazarbayev) or an exact transliteration seemed needlessly cumbersome (thus, the Kazakh nomadic encampment is rendered as "aul" rather than "auïl"). I have transliterated Kazakhs' names from Kazakh, but place names from Russian. In cases where I could not be certain whether an individual was Kazakh, I transliterated his or her name from the source language. All web links are current as of April 2018. I have translated the titles of all archival files, except when the source language would help the reader to find the document in a published collection.

The maps contained in this book were created by Nathan Burtch using Arc-GIS 10.4.1 for Desktop, which is created by Esri Inc. Terrain data from "Global Multi-Resolution Terrain Elevation Data 2010 (GMTED2010)" earthexplorer.usgs.gov and river data from ESRI, "World Major Rivers," *Data and Maps for Arc-GIS* (2016) were used directly to create the maps. City locations were also created directly using latitude and longitude information from Wikipedia. But in other cases, the data used in the creation of these maps represent an estimate, as there is no definitive source for the period that these maps depict. Approximate water body data were derived from Yuri Bregel, "The Principal Geographic Features and Provinces [map]," *An Historical Atlas of Central Asia* 2003), 3 and ESRI, "World Water Bodies," *Data and Maps for ArcGIS*. Approximate vegetation zone data were derived from Lammert Bies, "Cartography" [map] (2003); Bregel, "The Principal Geographic Features and Provinces"; George J. Demko, "Natural Regions of Kazakhstan [map]," *The Russian Colonization of Kazakhstan, 1896–1916* (1969), 12; and "Global Multi-Resolution Terrain Elevation Data." Approximate administrative boundaries were derived from Bregel, "The Principal Geographic Features and Provinces"; Map Trust of the Moscow Department of Public Works, "Map of the Asiatic Part of the USSR [map]" (1935); and "United Nations Environment Program," http://ede.grid.unep.ch/. Approximate railroad boundaries were derived from Bregel, "The Principal Geographic Features and Provinces."

Maps

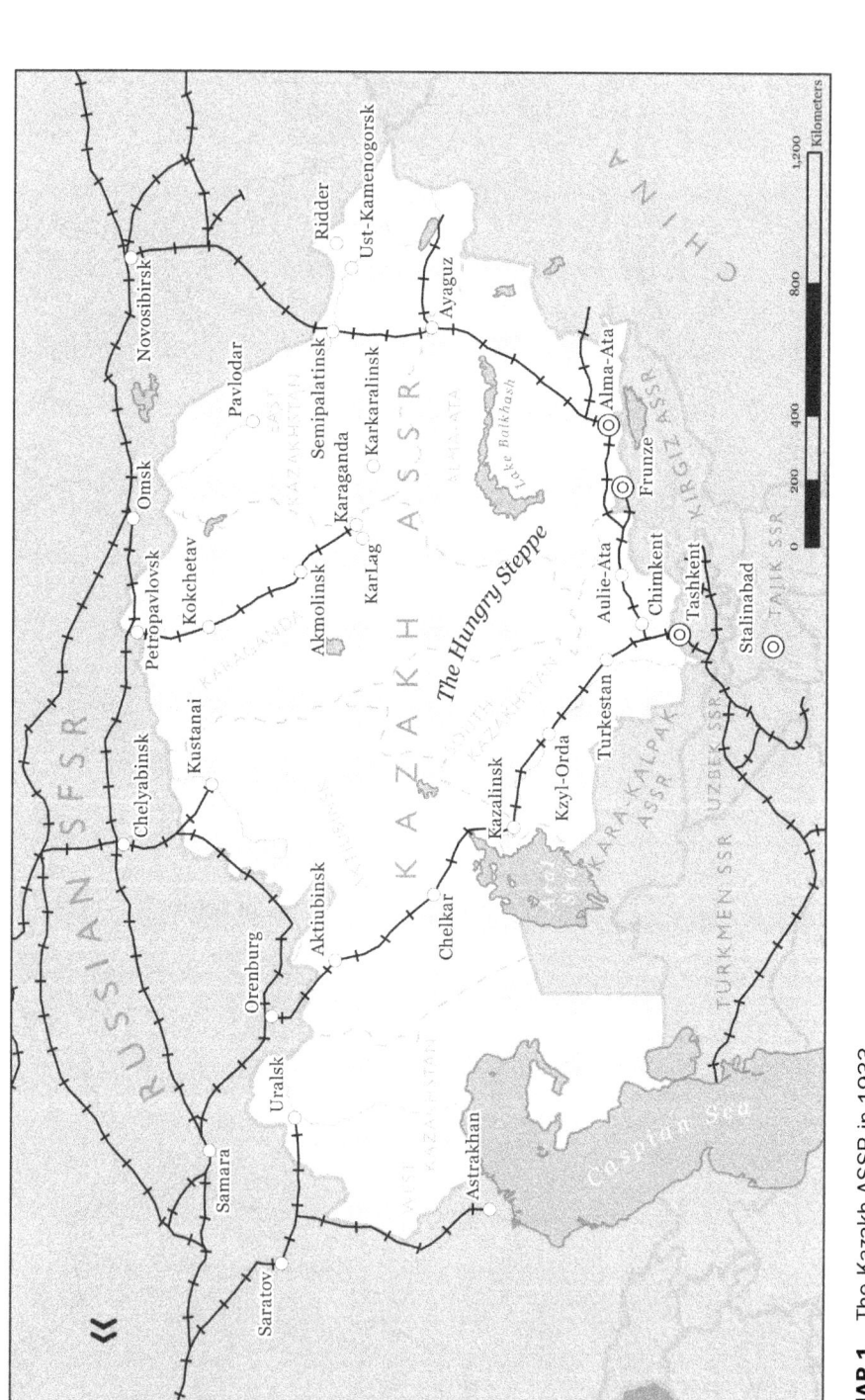

MAP 1 The Kazakh ASSR in 1933

THE HUNGRY STEPPE

Introduction

"I was still a child but I could not forget this," said Zh. Äbïshülï, recalling the Kazakh famine of 1930–33. "My bones are shaking as these memories come into my mind." Officials with the Soviet regime had stripped Äbïshülï's family of their livestock and grain, and starving people were fleeing in every direction. His father's relatives fled Soviet Kazakhstan entirely, escaping across the border to China. For those who remained, Äbïshülï saw, hunger became a "silent enemy." He remembered the *arba*, or horse-drawn cart that collected the bodies of the dead, dumping them in mass burial grounds on the outskirts of settlements. Many years after the Kazakh famine of 1930–33, Äbïshülï would fight on the front lines for the Red Army during World War II. Nonetheless, he believed that, "Surviving a famine is not less than surviving a war."[1] Another famine survivor, Nŭrsŭltan Äbdïghanŭlï, then a seven-year-old boy, saw several family members die of hunger before his eyes in the fall of 1932. Other relatives perished in a mountain valley as they fled to Kirgizia. In early 1933, "the real black clouds of hunger came," Äbdïghanŭlï recalled. His family moved south to Uzynaghash, where his father took a position as the head of a district inspectorate commission. Though Äbdïghanŭlï's grandmother had warned him to stay hidden under blankets during the journey—children could be kidnapped and eaten by the starving—Äbdïghanŭlï peeked out from underneath them and saw corpses scattered across the ground, hints of the horrors that lay beyond.[2]

As such recollections suggest, the period 1930–33 was a time of almost unimaginable sorrow in Soviet Kazakhstan, also known as the Kazakh Autonomous

Soviet Socialist Republic (the Kazakh ASSR). A massive famine claimed the lives of 1.5 million people, a quarter of the republic's inhabitants, and ravaged a territory approximate in size to continental Europe.[3] The crisis upended lives and families, and left a trail of devastation in its wake. As hunger set in, over a million starving refugees from Kazakhstan flooded neighboring Soviet territories such as Kirgizia, Uzbekistan, the Middle Volga and Western Siberia, as well as China (especially the western province known as Xinjiang) creating a regional crisis of unprecedented proportions.[4] Some never returned to Kazakhstan, and today significant populations of Kazakhs, many descendants of those who fled during the famine's course, remain in Xinjiang, Russia, Uzbekistan, and Kyrgyzstan.[5] Others fled within Kazakhstan, and by the disaster's end, more than half of the republic's remaining population had altered their district of residence.

Prior to the famine, most Kazakhs practiced pastoral nomadism, migrating seasonally along predetermined routes to pasture their animals, including sheep, horses, and camels.[6] This practice had been the predominant way of life in the steppe for more than four millennia.[7] It was an adaptation to the scarcity of good pastureland and water. It was also a crucial source of identity, one that had often determined who was "Kazakh" and who was not in the steppe region.[8] But the famine forced Kazakhs to become sedentary, or abandon the economic practice of nomadism. Not only did this spark a sweeping shift in the steppe's economic practices, it also transformed Kazakh culture and identity.

For those who survived, the famine years were deeply traumatic. "Today, I tell people I don't remember the famine," said D. Äuelbekov, who got, in his words, "a taste of starvation," living through the famine as a young child.[9] In one of the most striking results of the famine, Äuelbekov and other Kazakhs who survived became a minority in their own republic. For the remainder of the Soviet period, Kazakhs would occupy a curious position in Kazakhstan, at once the titular nationality and at the same time an ethnic minority. Moscow's population policies, which would bring waves of settlers into the republic in the decades after the famine, would further contribute to Kazakhs' minority status.[10] Only by the 1989 census did Kazakhs outnumber Russians (39.7 to 37.8%) and it was not until the 1999 census, eight years after the Soviet collapse, that Kazakhs constituted more than 50 percent of the population in Kazakhstan, by then an independent country.[11]

In its staggering human toll, the Kazakh famine was certainly one of the most heinous crimes of the Stalinist regime. Yet the story of this famine has remained largely hidden from view, both in Kazakhstan and in the West. This book seeks to tell that story, asking two interrelated questions: What were the causes of the Kazakh famine of 1930–33? And how does this famine, an event long neglected in narratives of the Stalin era, alter our understanding of Soviet modernization and nation making? It begins with the disaster's roots in the last decades of the Russian empire and concludes with the republic's slow road to economic recovery in the postfamine years of the mid-1930s. It argues that the Kazakh famine of 1930–33 was the result of Moscow's radical attempt to transform a group of Muslim, Turkic-speaking nomads known as "Kazakhs," and a particular territory, Soviet Kazakhstan, into a modern, Soviet nation. It finds that through the most violent means the Kazakh famine created Soviet Kazakhstan, a stable territory with clearly delineated boundaries that was an integral part of the Soviet economic system, and forged a new Kazakh national identity.

But the nature of this state-driven modernization was uneven. In many respects, Moscow failed to achieve its goals. Though the crisis embedded nationality as the primary marker of Kazakh identity, a goal of Moscow's "nation-building" efforts, it did not eliminate alternate forms of Kazakh identity entirely. Kazakhs' allegiances to various clans—transformed by the famine and divorced from their original origins in the system of pastoral nomadism—continued to exert an important influence in the postfamine years. Though Moscow sought to make Kazakhstan into a meatpacking center to rival Chicago, the regime's radical program of state-led transformation actually sparked the total collapse of the republic's livestock economy.[12] By the fall of 1933, over 90 percent of the animals in the republic had perished, a striking turn of events for what had been the Soviet Union's most important livestock base.[13] It would take more than three decades for Moscow to restore the republic's sheep and cattle numbers to their pre-famine levels.[14] Ultimately, neither Kazakhstan nor Kazakhs themselves became integrated into the Soviet system in precisely the ways that Moscow had originally hoped. The scars from the disaster would haunt the republic throughout the remainder of the Soviet era and shape its transformation into an independent nation in 1991.

How did the story of the Kazakh famine, one of the most dramatic consequences of Stalinist modernization, become marginalized? It is in part because collectivization, the event that triggered devastating famines in Ukraine, Kazakhstan, the Volga Basin, and the Don and the Kuban regions has been presented primarily as a story of peasants. In 1929, Josef Stalin launched the First Five-Year Plan, a radical scheme to help the Soviet Union industrialize and "catch up" to the capitalist West. The collectivization of agriculture was at the heart of this modernization scheme. By forcing rural people to give up their land and livestock and enter collective farms, Moscow sought to tighten control over the food supply and boost the Soviet Union's production of meat and grain, particularly wheat. Through the institution of the collective farm, Moscow worked to sever local institutions and networks and firmly implant Soviet power in the countryside, an area that the Bolsheviks had long struggled to control.

A large and distinguished body of literature has detailed this assault, focusing almost exclusively on the Soviet peasantry.[15] There are good reasons for this scholarly focus: the vast majority of people in the Soviet Union were peasants. On the eve of the October 1917 revolution, the peasantry accounted for more than 85 percent of the population, the industrial proletariat just 3 percent.[16] Though the Bolsheviks had seized power in the name of the "working class," they found themselves the inheritors of a predominately peasant state. Throughout the years of the New Economic Policy (1921–28), the "peasant question" would preoccupy the Bolsheviks like no other, as they struggled to ensure a steady supply of grain from the countryside to the cities, confronted the threat of widespread peasant rebellion, and debated how best to incorporate this ideologically suspect group into state structures. Launched by Stalin in the midst of a food supply crisis, a shortage of grain on state markets, collectivization was an attempt to bring this recalcitrant group to heel.

But the focus on the peasantry has obscured other facets of collectivization. At the margins of the former Russian empire, in places like the Russian Far North where hunter-gatherers predominated, or in the Russian Far East, home to a significant population of fisherman and hunters, or in Kazakhstan, Kirgizia, Turkmenistan, Kara-Kalpakia, Buriat-Mongolia, and Kalmykia, all of which had majority pastoral nomadic populations, the Bolsheviks confronted ways of life that were clearly not peasant in their orientation.[17] If we broaden the story of collectivization to encompass these areas, then it is clear that the Soviet Union was not just a European power but an Asian one too. Collectivization was not only about the regime's attempt to increase the production of grain but also about the struggle to transition from a system of long-distance animal herding to a network of meatpacking combines and slaughterhouses.[18] Like other powers during the interwar period, the Soviet Union sought to bring arid regions dominated by nomadic societies further under state control.[19]

Particularly in the West, the stories of the Soviet collectivization famines have focused largely on Ukrainians.[20] There are several reasons for this emphasis. On the most basic level, more Ukrainians died during the collectivization famines than any other nationality. Scholars estimate that somewhere between five and nine million people died due to famine during collectivization.[21] Ukrainians, who were the majority ethnic group in Ukraine as well as an important ethnic group in the Kuban region, suffered acutely. In Ukraine alone, somewhere between 2.6 and 3.9 million people (Ukrainians and those of other ethnicities) are believed to have died due to famine.[22] In absolute terms, Ukraine was the center of famine during the collectivization period.

In the West, the issue of the Ukrainian famine has been buoyed by the Ukrainian diaspora. For many Ukrainians, the famine has come to serve as a crucial event in the creation of a national memory. Much of the scholarship on the Ukrainian famine has focused on the question of whether the crisis was used by Stalin to punish Ukrainians as an ethnic group, and the debate surrounding this question has frequently turned polemical, inflamed by ideological divisions as well as present-day political tensions between Ukraine and Russia.[23] Some Ukrainians have called upon the international community to recognize their famine as a genocide, and they have demanded retribution from Russia for their suffering.[24] To bolster the claim that the famine was used by Stalin to punish Ukrainians as an ethnic group, some scholars have sought to emphasize the "uniqueness" of Ukrainians' suffering, downplaying or even neglecting to mention the horrors endured by other groups, such as the Kazakhs, during the same period.[25]

But the charged debate over the Ukrainian famine has eclipsed other aspects of the story. The Don Cossacks and the Volga Germans also suffered disproportionally from famine.[26] Pockets of the Russian heartland, such as the province of Saratov, had high rates of famine mortality. In Kazakhstan, famine deaths were sharply ethnicized: though Kazakhs constituted just under 60 percent of the republic's total population on the eve of the famine, some 90 percent of those who died in the Kazakh famine were Kazakhs.[27] The famine claimed the lives of more than a million Kazakhs, approximately 40 percent of all Kazakhs in the republic.[28] Ultimately, the Kazakhs would lose a greater percentage of their population due to famine than even the Ukrainians.[29]

Inside the Soviet Union, the story of the Kazakh famine, like other crimes of Stalinism, was suppressed. In the immediate aftermath of the disaster, authorities in Moscow charged the republic's party secretary Filipp Goloshchekin, whom they had removed from office at the height of the famine in early 1933, with committing "distortions" and "errors" during his tenure as the republic's leader. Goloshchekin was a colorful figure. An "old Bolshevik" (one of a small number of Bolsheviks who had joined the party prior to the October 1917 revolution) who had originally trained as a dentist, he came to his post in Kazakhstan with an impressive array of revolutionary credentials. He was rumored to have been in the small circle of party cadres who carried out Vladimir Lenin's orders to execute the tsar and his family.[30] He was renowned for his toughness and intense devotion to the Bolshevik cause, reportedly even going so far as to tell a cadre who pleaded for the release of his father from prison, "Communists don't have fathers."[31] In 1941, some years after being dismissed from his post in Kazakhstan, Goloshchekin was shot as part of the purges, meeting a fate shared by many others who had joined the party in its early years.[32]

Criticism of Goloshchekin's leadership continued in subsequent decades, while the famine itself remained officially unacknowledged.[33] During preparations for the 1937 census, the first conducted after the famine, officials noted the dramatic drop in the republic's Kazakh population. But they covered up the existence of a famine by arguing that such losses could be explained solely by the departure of many Kazakhs to neighboring republics to work during the period 1930–33, and this account, that missing Kazakhs had simply "migrated" away, became the predominant explanation for the republic's sharp demographic shift.[34] In his 1956 "secret speech," Stalin's successor, Nikita Khrushchev, condemned Stalin for many crimes, but he failed to mention the collectivization famines. Nŭrziya Qajïbaeva, who lived through the Kazakh famine as a young girl, recalled these decades: "It wasn't safe to speak about the famine openly; the Party and the authorities disapproved of it. Newspapers, books, schools and institutes never touched upon this problem."[35] In the intervening years, families discussed the hardships they had suffered privately, while authors wove the story of the famine into Kazakh-language novels and short stories.[36]

In Kazakhstan, public analysis of the famine began in the late 1980s and early 1990s, as scholars "discovered" the republic's horrifying loss of life.[37] In the decade that followed the republic's transformation into an independent nation in 1991, discussion of the disaster dominated both scholarly and popular media. In 1992, Nursultan Nazarbayev, Kazakhstan's president, himself a holdover from the Soviet period, authorized an investigation, and this commission ruled it a genocide.[38] This outpouring of interest in the 1990s led to the publication of a number of important studies, but many of the works produced offered only a slightly revised version of the Soviet explanation for the famine: they depict Goloshchekin as appropriating brutal policies from Stalin and intensifying them further, working to punish Kazakhs as an ethnic group.[39] The famine began to be referred to as "Goloshchekin's genocide." In part, the continuing fixation with Goloshchekin was fueled by anti-Semitism: Goloshchekin was a Jew, born to a family of humble origins in Vitebsk *guberniia* (province) in the Russian empire's western borderlands.[40] In an effort to intensify the perception of evil, several works by Kazakhstani authors relied on anti-Semitic tropes to depict Goloshchekin's behavior during the famine.[41]

Until recently in the West, there were few scholarly investigations into the Kazakh famine, and even its basic events and causes were not well known.[42] The reasons for this silence are many. During the 1920s and 1930s, few foreign travelers visited Kazakhstan. In Ukraine, the Welsh journalist Gareth Jones brought the horrors of the Ukrainian famine to the attention of the West, but in Kazakhstan there was no similar figure on the ground to chronicle the story.[43] Some fifty years later, the Ukrainian famine returned to view with the publication of the British historian Robert Conquest's seminal work, *Harvest of Sorrow*, in 1986. As Cold War tensions heightened, the US Congress set up a commission to investigate the Ukrainian famine.[44] An active Ukrainian diaspora then kept the story alive, endowing institutes and centers for Ukrainian studies across North America. But there was no comparable movement among the much smaller Kazakh diaspora. As a result, the Kazakh famine, unlike many other crimes of Stalinism, was not incorporated into a Cold War narrative about the Soviet Union. As this book discusses in greater detail in a concluding chapter, after an explosion of interest in the 1990s, the current Kazakh government has largely turned away from public discussion of the famine, further reducing the likelihood that the story would be picked up in the West.

Other factors, such as the lingering influence of evolutionary theory, which holds that the disappearance of mobile peoples and their transformation into settled societies is part of the inevitable outgrowth of modernity, may also explain the relative silence. When the Kazakh famine is mentioned in the scholarly literature, it is often referred to as a "miscalculation," a "misunderstanding of cultures," or as an event that can be attributed to "Moscow's shameful neglect" of the repercussions of its policies, depictions that would seem to downplay the disaster's violent nature.[45] Arguably, the persistent but mistaken notion that the collectivization of the Kazakhs was not a violent act—or at least not *as* violent as Stalinist crimes committed against settled societies—may be one of the reasons that the famine has been neglected for so long by scholars in the West. If the starvation of the Kazakhs was a problem that originated in part from "natural" causes, then historians of Soviet history should first turn their attention to unearthing those crimes that stemmed purely from human causes.

More recently, an international group of scholars—the French scholar Isabelle Ohayon, the Italian scholar Niccolò Pianciola and the German scholar Robert Kindler—have published books on the Kazakh famine.[46] Drawing on a rich range of archival materials and using divergent approaches, including social, political, and economic history, they have made important contributions to the understanding of the famine's major events, causal factors, and effects on Kazakh society. Ohayon's study offers what she calls a "social history" of the sedentarization of the Kazakhs under Soviet rule: she focuses specifically on the catastrophic effects of forced settlement on Kazakh society, rather than on central decision making.[47] Pianciola's book, by contrast, is grounded in economic history, an approach he uses to analyze the transformation of two pastoral nomadic societies, the Kazakhs and the Kirgiz, under Russian imperial and Soviet rule.[48] Finally, Kindler's study examines the role of violence in the Kazakh famine, scrutinizing, in Kindler's words, how different actors used violence to generate "order."[49] Though these scholars disagree over the extent to which Moscow anticipated the full dimensions of the crisis, all contend that Moscow sought to use the famine as a means of incorporating the Kazakhs into the party-state.[50]

This book supports this basic conclusion, but it seeks to revise the understanding of both the famine itself and this period in Soviet history by exploring the specific form that the incorporation of the Kazakhs was supposed to take. It focuses on Soviet nation making and Soviet modernization.[51] It traces the frequent tensions that occurred between these two projects as Moscow sought to make the Kazakhs into a Soviet nation and guide the republic into Soviet modernity, and it analyzes their outcome, which saw immense human suffering and the republic's total economic collapse but also the creation of a Kazakh national identity. Engaging with the field of environmental history, an area previously unexplored by scholars of the Kazakh famine, it contextualizes the disaster in the longer history of the steppe's agrarian transformation. While previous studies of the famine by Western scholars have relied solely on Russian-language sources, this study incorporates both Kazakh and Russian-language sources, permitting greater insight into the disaster's devastating consequences for Kazakh society.

Though the story of the Kazakh famine has long been sidelined, it is in fact a crucial lens through which to view the transformations of the Stalin era. By turning to a region outside the Soviet Union's west, this study places the issue of Soviet modernization in a new light.[52]

In Kazakhstan, the very scope of the Soviet modernization project—to transform not just peasants but *nomads* into factory workers, a far greater "leap" through the Marxist-Leninist timeline of history—was strikingly different from areas further west. World War I played a crucial role in transforming European Russia, politicizing the millions of Russian peasants who served and laying the groundwork for the advent of mass politics, but the imprint of this conflict played out quite differently in the Kazakh steppe: Kazakhs, like other Central Asian men under Russian imperial rule, were specifically excluded from active combat for most of the war, and the steppe was distant from the front lines.[53] Further complicating Moscow's modernizing aims, Kazakh culture was primarily an oral culture rather than a literary one. Illiteracy rates in the Kazakh *aul*, or nomadic encampment, were above 90 percent.[54] Though immense, the republic was sparsely populated, and it had little existing infrastructure such as dirt roads or telegraph connections.[55] Newspapers and other materials from Moscow reached Alma-Ata, the republic's capital, thirty to forty days after they were printed, and postmen could travel three to four hundred kilometers across the steppe by camel to deliver a piece of mail.[56]

In Kazakhstan, the timing and tempo of Moscow's modernization project would also be distinct: In 1928, eleven years after the October 1917 revolution had transformed European Russia, Goloshchekin declared that the Kazakh aul had yet to undergo the October revolution. He announced the onset of a Little

October, an October-style revolution from above, which he claimed would belatedly bring about far-reaching social change in the steppe. Party members rationalized that extraordinary speed was needed to help the Kazakhs catch up to settled groups, and, as the First Five-Year Plan began, Kazakhstan's party committee proposed to settle and collectivize the Kazakhs simultaneously.[57]

But Moscow's program of state-driven modernization sought to remake not only Kazakh society but also the Kazakh steppe itself. The environment of the steppe, like other arid and semiarid zones, was highly unstable. Rainfall patterns varied dramatically from year to year. The distribution of good quality soils shifted regularly, with some soils becoming highly salinated over time. The dry winds that swept over the steppe, known as *sukhovei*, periodically altered the shape and size of the region's bodies of water. Not only was this landscape unfamiliar to Soviet experts—it did not have clear parallels in the categories of analysis that they imported from European Russia—but its ecological instability posed a challenge to Marxist-Leninist ideas of economic development, which were predicated on the notion of constant and ever-increasing yields. Due to the steppe's unpredictable weather, the harvest from these lands might be plentiful one year and disastrous the next.

This ecological instability would bedevil those who sought to transform the steppe into an agrarian region. Under Russian imperial rule, the first wave of Russian and Ukrainian peasants that dared to settle there suffered through such terrible deprivations due to poor harvests that the Governor-Generalship of the Steppe temporarily closed the Kazakh steppe to further colonization. In the early Soviet period, experts, pointing to this history, warned of the dangers of settling the Kazakh nomads and expanding agricultural settlement further into the steppe. But the Central Committee decided that the possibility of getting an excellent grain harvest one year was worth the risk of a catastrophic harvest the next. In the summer of 1931, the Central Committee lost this gamble with human life, as a devastating drought intensified the famine first sparked by collectivization in the winter of 1930–31. Moscow never adjusted its grain procurement targets for this ecological instability, and Kazakhs had to make up the shortfall, intensifying the effects of the famine that had already begun.

Today, Kazakhstan is one of the world's leading exporters of wheat, which is the country's most important agricultural commodity.[58] After the Soviet collapse, some village households in southern Kazakhstan turned to mobile pastoralism, but the livestock sector currently plays a far smaller role in the country's economy than grain.[59] This dramatic shift in land use patterns—from pastoral nomadism to settled agriculture—began under the Russian empire and was dramatically accelerated by the Stalinist regime during collectivization. But despite the assertions of many Soviet experts that Soviet power would "conquer" nature, bending it to socialist ends over the course of the First Five-Year Plan, Moscow, like other states that sought to transform the drylands, struggled to remake the Kazakh steppe as it wished.[60] In the postfamine years, agriculture would continue to be a difficult enterprise in the region: Crop failures, among other factors, brought Nikita Khrushchev's Virgin Lands program (1954–60), which aimed to expand the amount of cultivated land in northern Kazakhstan and other regions, to a halt.[61] The 1960s and 1970s saw repeated droughts, sandstorms, and poor harvests.[62] As the history of the Kazakh steppe demonstrates, Soviet power was not monolithic. Rather, in this arid region, as in other areas of the Soviet periphery, environmental factors shaped the nature of development.[63]

The case of the nomadic Kazakhs illustrates the extraordinary importance that Moscow placed on its nation-making project, even as it underscores its destructive power. Due to a combination of practical and ideological considerations, the Bolsheviks chose to solve the "nationality question" (*natsional'nyi vopros*), or how they might manage the ethnic diversity of the peoples of the former Russian empire, by selectively supporting it. Moscow granted various forms of nationhood—including national territories, languages, and cultures to certain groups—and sought in turn to mold these groups into cohesive Soviet nationalities.[64] Over time, this wide-ranging project came to encompass efforts such as the establishment of native educational institutions, the training and promotion of native cadres, the standardization of national languages, the delineation of national borders, and the crafting of national histories.

But these nation-making efforts, which came to be known as "nationality policy" (*natsional'naia politika*), were less a rigidly defined course of action than a working set of ideas and assumptions about Soviet nationhood that shifted in emphasis over the course of the Soviet period. The broad outlines of the policy were elaborated in resolutions passed at the Twelfth Party Congress and a special Central Committee conference in 1923. Stalin periodically clarified or revised points relating to nationality policy in his speeches, arguing that Soviet nations should be "national in form, socialist in content."[65] But these documents did not provide a detailed blueprint for how these nation-making efforts would be implemented.[66] Nor could they possibly anticipate every conflict that would result from the attempt to form nations, which were inherently particularistic, within the rubric of socialism, an approach that promised universality. In important ways, the project of Soviet nation making hinged on local initiative and popular participation.

The idea that Kazakhs formed a nation came to the steppe in the late nineteenth century. After the October 1917 revolution, a small group of settled Russophone Kazakhs formed a political party known as Alash Orda and declared a Kazakh autonomous state based in the city of Semipalatinsk in the steppe's northeast. In 1919, the members of Alash Orda surrendered to the Bolsheviks, and they forged an uneasy alliance with the regime, seeking to use the Bolsheviks' promises of national rights to promote their own ideas of autonomy.[67] But for most Kazakhs, nationality was not an important organizing principle of their everyday life on the eve of Soviet rule: Nŭrziya Qajïbaeva, for instance, remembered that her family had heard of Kazakh political parties such as Alash Orda in 1917 but noted that "their ideas and way of life were incomprehensible to the common nomad Kazakhs."[68] Rather, being "Kazakh" was closely linked to being a nomad, a way of life that precluded an attachment to a "nation" grounded in territory. The term "Kazakh" was a mixed social and ethnic category, one that denoted an ethnicity but also a way of life, pastoral nomadism.[69]

Though nationality was a concept antithetical to nomadic life, Moscow went to extraordinary lengths to form Kazakhs into a nation, seeking to engage, mobilize, and transform Kazakhs even in the republic's most remote corners.[70] But this project confronted many challenges, most notably the fact that culture and economics in the Kazakh steppe were closely intertwined. Because most Kazakhs practiced pastoral nomadism, the fate of the practice under Soviet rule was at once an economic question (was nomadism the most efficient use of the steppe's landscape?) and a national question (should nomadism, a defining element of Kazakh identity, be promoted as part of a Kazakh "national culture"?). Though initially Moscow pursued a contradictory approach, supporting pastoral nomadism in some respects but undermining it in others, by 1928 "national" and "economic" goals had aligned. Pastoral nomadism was declared economically inefficient and a practice at odds with the development of Kazakh national culture.

This feature reframes the long-running debate over the Ukrainian famine. Most scholarship on the Ukrainian famine can be divided roughly into two opposing camps, "nationality" and "peasantry."[71] Scholars holding the latter view argue that the Soviet collectivization famines were part of a broader assault on a social category, the peasantry, and they conclude that Ukrainians suffered disproportionately not due to any specific intent to punish them as a group, but rather because most Ukrainians were peasants.[72] Scholars holding the former view, by contrast, point to Ukrainians' historically troubled relationship with the regime, and they see nationality, or Stalin's specific intent to punish Ukrainians, as instrumental in creating the horrifying death toll.[73]

In Kazakhstan, as in Ukraine, there was a clear overlap between national and social identities. Most Kazakhs were nomads, while in Ukraine, most Ukrainians were peasants. The "nationality" vs. "peasantry" debate assumes that Moscow used these two categories, national and social, to pursue different goals. Either Moscow sought to use famine as a weapon to punish Ukrainians as a national group or Moscow sought to use famine to punish peasants. But as the Kazakh case reveals, national and social categories were not necessarily in opposition to one another but might serve overlapping, mutually reinforcing goals. During the refugee crisis, Goloshchekin and other top officials did not refer to starving Kazakhs as refugees (*bezhentsy*) but rather as *otkochevniki* (literally, nomads who are moving away), a group in the throes of moving to a "higher" stage of national development, settled life. By framing the refugee crisis as an important moment of national transition, albeit one that required extra vigilance to ensure that Kazakhs progressed to the next stage, officials used the language of both Soviet economic policy and Soviet nationality policy to legitimize assaults on starving Kazakhs.

In taking a more complete view of Soviet efforts at nation formation, we also get a clearer view of the ways that these attempts could be both progressive and profoundly destructive at the same time. The regime's use of violence against national groups did not always signal a shift away from Soviet nation making. Rather, it sometimes represented an attempt to consolidate national identities, bringing the nature of these identities into line with the regime's political goals. At the height of the famine, for instance, thousands of starving Kazakhs were slaughtered by the regime as they attempted to flee across the Sino-Kazakh border to Xinjiang, a place historically and culturally linked to the Kazakh steppe and an important part of many Kazakhs' seasonal migration routes. Though this assault was sparked by many concerns, including Moscow's fears that refugees could connect with enemies of the Soviet regime in China, Soviet authorities used a central tenet of Soviet nation making, that nationality was connected to territory, to justify and support their murderous actions.[74]

The literature has framed the regime's commitment to nation making as separable from core Bolshevik policies, such as industrialization and collectivization, with the understanding that Moscow used its nationality policy as a palliative, or "soft-line," measure to present core policies in a more attractive light.[75] But in Kazakhstan, officials did not necessarily see such distinctions, believing economic questions and "the national question" to be closely intertwined with one another.[76] Nor were Moscow's nation-making efforts always greeted eagerly by Kazakhs themselves, as the "soft-line" categorization would suggest. As this book explores, the Kazakh famine took its peculiarly destructive shape not in spite of the Soviets' nation-making efforts but partly because of them.

Kazakhs' transformation into a new Soviet nation was not just imposed from above. Rather, it was participatory, and this book stresses the ways that Kazakhs themselves shaped Soviet Kazakhstan's eventual integration into state structures. Their participation in the nation-making project was not limited to such tasks as standardizing a national language or creating a national history.[77] This book finds that Moscow empowered Kazakhs themselves to carry out some of the most destructive assaults on their own society, entrusting them with determining who should be a considered a *bai* (a nomadic "exploiter") and who should not, as well as how to impose grain and meat procurements at the local level.[78] Though institutions heavily dominated by outsiders from European Russia, such as the Red Army, did play an important role in many violent attacks on Kazakhs, the OGPU (secret police) sought to diversify the army's rank and file, believing that further Kazakh participation would make such assaults more "effective."[79] By encouraging and inviting Kazakh involvement in the local-level implementation of these campaigns, Moscow successfully drove a wedge into Kazakh society, shattering old allegiances and sowing violent conflict in the aul.

But the notion of nationality was also a powerful tool, one that Moscow could not always control as it wished. Once released, the language of "national rights" or "national territories" could be claimed by different actors to promote goals that did not always align with those of the regime. Empowered by the regime's nation-making efforts to conduct local-level campaigns of violence, many native cadres used the considerable flexibility given to them by the regime to manipulate these campaigns in accordance with their own interests. As the conflict over resources accelerated during the famine, some groups used the language of nationality to justify their assaults on others, and the regime fought to control the widening swath of violence. Indeed, the enormous struggle that Moscow encountered in trying to contain some of the unintended effects of its nation-making efforts would seem to contradict the idea that it could pull back the policy at will.

What were the causes of the Kazakh famine? The primary cause was similar to that of the other Soviet collectivization famines, forced collectivization, which included debilitating meat and grain procurements. But as a pastoral famine, as opposed to a famine among settled societies, the Kazakh famine had features that distinguished it from those that afflicted the Soviet Union's west. Due to the enormous pressure for grain, local cadres forced Kazakh nomads, a population that consumed grain but did not ordinarily grow it, to meet onerous grain requisition requirements.[80] To fulfill these requirements, Kazakhs flooded markets with their livestock. In a feature characteristic of pastoral famines, the terms of trade for livestock worsened: grain became very expensive, while animals were very cheap, forcing Kazakhs to sell off even more of their livestock.[81] Onerous meat procurements further impoverished Kazakh pastoralists, depriving them of their means of existence—seasonal migrations with their animal herds—while the closure of republican, provincial, and district borders prevented Kazakhs from reaching the pastures necessary to feed their animals. Though the major cause of the Kazakh famine was Stalin's policies, the legacies of Russian imperial rule must be considered an important contributing factor. Intense peasant settlement of the Kazakh steppe during the late nineteenth and early twentieth centuries prompted shifts in nomads' migration routes and consumption patterns, making Kazakhs more susceptible to famine.

Moscow's official sedentarization policy was not a major cause of the Kazakh famine.[82] The regime devoted few resources to the official program of sedentarization, and the program quickly foundered. But the heavy meat and grain procurements that accompanied collectivization accomplished what the official policy of sedentarization failed to do, forcing Kazakhs to abandon nomadic life due to utter and total destitution. Once famine began in the winter of 1930–31, other factors became important in the crisis, including a drought in the summer of 1931, which amplified the effects of Kazakhs' impoverishment.[83]

Finally, the steppe's relative underdevelopment magnified the effects of the disaster. Focused on implementing a breakneck program of state-driven modernization, Moscow ignored warnings from medical experts who, noting the republic's lack of modern medical services, urged the party to devote more resources to public health services and vaccination programs.[84] As famine broke out, diseases such as typhus, smallpox, tuberculosis, and cholera began to spread. These diseases were induced by hunger, but they were also exacerbated by other famine-related phenomena, such as massive population movement and unsanitary conditions.[85] Many Kazakhs would die from these diseases, which would play a far greater role in the Kazakh famine than in the famines in the Soviet Union's west. There the level of modern medical services was higher, and most famine victims succumbed to actual starvation.[86]

Did Stalin intend to cause the Kazakh famine? It is clear that the regime's broader goal was to transform Kazakhs and Kazakhstan radically, with little regard for the tremendous loss of life incurred in the process. Soviet agricultural experts, many of whom would later be imprisoned or shot, warned of the risks of forcibly settling the Kazakh nomads and expanding the republic's agrarian frontier into drought-prone regions. Stalin received news of Kazakhs' suffering at several crucial points, in late 1930 with the first onset of hunger; in January 1931 as the second collectivization drive began; and again in late 1932 during the height of the Kazakh refugee crisis. Once famine had begun, Moscow took steps that worsened Kazakhs' misery, including imposing devastating meat and grain procurements on the republic, expelling starving Kazakhs from cities, slaughtering thousands of Kazakh refugees as they attempted to flee across the border to China, and "blacklisting" districts in the republic (a severe penalty that included a total ban on trade and deliveries of food).

Moscow's sweeping program of state-led transformation clearly anticipated the cultural destruction of Kazakh society, and, as I discuss in the conclusion, there is evidence to indicate that the Kazakh famine fits an expanded definition of genocide. But there is no indication that Stalin planned the famine on purpose or sought to destroy all Kazakhs. Many of the famine's central events, from the massive outflow of refugees to the dramatic drop in the republic's livestock levels, were counterproductive to the regime's interests and were unanticipated consequences of the collectivization campaign. Once famine began, the needs of other groups in the republic, such as peasants and workers, whose labor in fields and factories was crucial to the fulfillment of the First Five-Year Plan, were prioritized over starving Kazakh nomads.[87] Very belatedly, Moscow issued limited food aid to the republic, although little of this relief reached starving refugees.

But while Stalin did not foresee the full scope of the crisis, the case of the Kazakh famine should upend some of our assumptions about Stalinism and Stalinist violence. In Kazakhstan, the nature of the Stalinist state often appears different from the way it does in the Soviet Union's west, characterized at times by its frailty or even absence rather than its coercive strength. Though the literature has stressed the central place of the Soviet Union's west in the genealogy of Stalinist violence, this book shows that the spectrum of violence under Stalin was broader than previously believed.[88] The Soviet east also generated important techniques of social control, and practices of population management were exchanged between east and west. While Stalin initiated the brutal policies that sparked the Kazakh famine, he does not appear to have tracked developments in the republic with the same attention he devoted to major grain-growing regions like Ukraine. According to his visitors' book, Stalin met with Goloshchekin just twice during the latter's tenure as the republic's party secretary, and few within Stalin's inner circle appear to have had detailed knowledge of the republic.[89] As collectivization began, İzmükhan Küramïsov, who served as Goloshchekin's deputy from 1929 to 1931, joked that some officials in Moscow could not even locate Kazakhstan on a map. Others, he noted, regularly confused "Kazakhs" and "Cossacks."[90]

Similarly, the case of the Kazakh famine should challenge some of our existing ideas about Stalinist hierarchies. Soviet society is often viewed through the lens of a hierarchy of suffering, in which Gulag prisoners are believed to have suffered the most.[91] But starving Kazakhs were expelled from their land at the height of the famine to make room for the construction of a forced labor camp, Karaganda Corrective Labor Camp (KarLag) in central Kazakhstan, and they died from hunger and disease outside the gates of this camp while prisoners labored within. Rather, the Kazakh famine is a reminder of the crude, heartbreaking way that so many Soviet citizens died under Stalin's rule—not in the confines of the Gulag or in the mass shootings of the Great Terror of 1937–38—but in ditches and abandoned villages from hunger sparked by collectivization.[92]

Why didn't Kazakhs resist? And why did local officials continue to implement such destructive policies? As this book details, many Kazakhs did rebel. Kazakhstan, like other famine-stricken regions, saw massive revolts during collectivization, which Moscow struggled mightily to subdue. The motivations of local officials were varied. Some were coerced into cooperation by fear and intimidation. Others sought to use a career in the Communist Party as a method of personal advancement. Still others were convinced of the righteousness of the Communist cause, as the case of Shapïq Shokin (Shafik Chokin), a Kazakh who rose from extreme poverty to become president of Kazakhstan's Academy of Sciences, illustrates. As a teenager, Shokin worked as a plenipotentiary for the regime, confiscating grain and other goods from Kazakh households during the famine. His service earned high praise from his superiors, and he subsequently enrolled in the Central Asian State University in the name of V. I. Lenin (SAGU) in Tashkent, Uzbekistan. There he encountered Kazakh refugees dying from hunger in the city streets. Nonetheless, Shokin later recalled, "If someone had told me then that the famine was an affair of my hands, I would not only have not believed it, but I would have considered it an insult, vile slander." He concluded, "I was certain: We were bringing not only a new system but a new, more just vision of life."[93]

This study relies on Russian and Kazakh-language primary and secondary sources culled through extensive field research in Kazakhstan and Russia, including work with archival documents at former Communist Party and state archives in Almaty and Moscow, as well as regional archives in Almaty and Semipalatinsk. It also incorporates a wide range of published primary sources, including newspapers, ethnographic accounts, and agricultural journals. Many of the materials, including collections from the former Communist Party archives in Kazakhstan (now known as the Presidential Archives) and Kazakh-language sources, have been little utilized by Western scholars.[94] These sources shed light on a number of underexplored aspects of the Kazakh disaster. Archival sources reveal that Stalin knew of Kazakhs' suffering at several key moments in the famine, and they highlight the extremely brutal manner in which the regime treated starving Kazakh refugees. The use of Kazakh-language secondary sources opens up a dialogue on the famine with Kazakhstani scholars, many of whom publish exclusively in Kazakh rather than in Russian, while the use of Kazakh-language primary source materials, such as oral history accounts, brings to light the voices of famine survivors, who are otherwise difficult to find in archival sources or memoir accounts.

The last point is an important one, and it raises some of the key methodological differences between researching the Kazakh famine and some of the other crimes of the Stalinist regime, such as the Gulag system, the special settler system, or even the Ukrainian famine. In the Kazakh famine, a far greater percentage of those who suffered were illiterate, and some of the sources that historians typically rely on to get at the ground-level perspective, such as petitions, are much more difficult to find. In the case of the Ukrainian famine, there were numerous efforts to collect oral history accounts of the disaster, spurred in part by the congressional investigation into the Ukrainian famine in the 1980s.[95] By contrast, in the Kazakh case, such efforts were more limited and generally began much later, meaning that there were far fewer survivors still around.[96] By the time they were interviewed, many of these survivors, who were small children during the disaster, were very elderly, making it more difficult for them to recall the famine's events.[97] While the fall of the Soviet Union has brought to light numerous memoirs, diaries, and letters by survivors of the Ukrainian famine or the Gulag system, there has been no similar outpouring of materials by survivors of the Kazakh famine.[98] In part this reflects the fact that due to lower literacy rates fewer Kazakhs could write down the story as it unfolded, but it also may be indicative of a broader reticence about the famine in Kazakhstan today. Nonetheless, wherever possible, this book seeks to include sources that were written by Kazakhs themselves.

In incorporating Russian imperial and Soviet archival documents and ethnographic studies, this book pays careful attention to the challenges inherent in analyzing nomadic life through the eyes of the sedentary world. The settlement of the Kazakh nomads was a phenomenon that many Russian imperial and Soviet officials believed to be evolutionarily "correct," part of the onward march of history, and it was a prospect that many of them welcomed. These officials tended to portray the Russian empire or the Soviet state as the sole agent of change in nomadic life, as a "modern" settled society came into contact with a "backward" nomadic society. But prior to the Soviet state's launch of forced collectivization in 1929–30, ecological and economic factors played an important role in sparking some of the changes to nomadic life that these observers detailed. Moreover, some of the shifts that occurred prior to collectivization, such as Kazakh nomads' increasing reliance on agriculture, were not new but rather had long been a part of the steppe's history as nomads adjusted their practice of pastoralism to political and ecological change. In seeking to understand Kazakh nomadic life, the book analyzes the very categories that these officials created, such as "seminomadic," for what they might reveal about nomadic life, as well as Russian imperial and Soviet views of the nomadic world.

This book proceeds chronologically through the major events and causal factors of the Kazakh famine. Chapter 1 examines the Kazakh steppe under Russian imperial rule. It finds that a period of massive peasant colonization of the Kazakh steppe during the late nineteenth and early twentieth centuries sparked far-reaching changes to nomadic life and to the ecological profile of the steppe itself. It concludes that these changes made Kazakhs more prone to famine, intensifying the effects of the Soviet regime's brutal collectivization policies. Chapter 2 examines the period 1921–28, scrutinizing how Soviet officials and ethnographers struggled to fit Kazakh nomads and the environment of the steppe into their Marxist-Leninist worldview. By 1928, prompted by broader shifts across the Soviet Union, this period of fluidity ended: pastoral nomadism was portrayed both as economically backward and as an impediment to Kazakhs' further development as a Soviet nation. Chapter 3 examines Moscow's initial assault on Kazakh nomadic life under the auspices of "Little October," a belated October-style social revolution begun in 1928. It shows how Moscow invited and encouraged Kazakh participation in this campaign, a strategy that successfully began to unravel Kazakh society from within. Chapter 4 scrutinizes the launch of forced collectivization in the period 1929–31, showing how it was accompanied by a broader assault on nomadic culture and practices. It reveals that Moscow repeatedly ignored warnings about the dangers of expanding the republic's agrarian frontier into drought-prone regions. By the winter of 1930–31, famine had begun. Chapter 5 reveals Moscow's struggle to control the Sino-Kazakh border during the period 1931–33, as hundreds of thousands of starving Kazakhs sought to flee across the border to Xinjiang. In stark contrast to less coercive methods of border control in the Soviet Union's west, Soviet border guards began to shoot those who fled, a choice that escalated tensions with Republican China. Chapter 6 examines the refugee crisis during the years 1931–33, an event that was both sparked by and in turn accelerated the republic's economic collapse. It shows how the events of the crisis started to embed ideas of nationality at the local level, although not always in the ways that Moscow would have hoped. Only in 1934 did the famine finally come to an end in part through a certain amount of luck (including excellent weather and a good harvest that year), as well as renewed attention by a variety of state agencies in Moscow to problems, such as the spread of disease. The conclusion examines the republic's development in the postfamine years. It also considers the question of genocide and what the case of the Kazakh famine tells us about other Soviet collectivization famines. The epilogue explores how the famine has been memorialized and remembered in postindependence Kazakhstan.

THE STEPPE AND THE SOWN

Peasants, Nomads, and the Transformation
of the Kazakh Steppe, 1896–1921

During the late nineteenth century, more than 1.5 million peasants from European Russia settled the Kazakh steppe, dramatically altering this region and the lives of the pastoral nomadic peoples who lived there.[1] In the span of just twenty years—the peak of peasant settlement was the period 1896–1916—the Kazakh steppe, dominated by Muslim, Turkic-speaking peoples since the fifteenth century, became transformed into a multiethnic, multiconfessional society. Parts of the Kazakh steppe were no longer predominately Kazakh, at least in terms of their ethnic makeup: by 1916, in Akmolinsk province, Slavic settlers constituted 59 percent of the population; Kazakhs, 34 percent. In certain northern *uezdy* of Akmolinsk province, such as Omsk, the change was even more striking: there Slavic settlers composed 72 percent of the population; Kazakhs, 21 percent.[2]

In addition to these demographic changes, the arrival of these settlers altered the steppe's environmental profile. Most settlers were grain farmers, and they brought large swaths of the steppe under cultivation. By 1916, the northern section of the Kazakh steppe had become one of the Russian empire's key grain-producing regions, and many pastoral nomads had been displaced from their traditional pasturelands. In a historic shift, this territory, a place long synonymous with pastoralism, a practice defined by the herding and management of animals, was now a mixed economic region, one populated by large numbers of settled, agrarian peoples in addition to pastoralists.

The settlement of the Kazakh steppe by Slavic peasants was part of a broader migration of Slavic peoples to Siberia, the Russian Far East, and Central Asia during the late nineteenth century.[3] In the aftermath of the emancipation of the serfs in 1861, many peasants, known as *samovol'tsy*, or "self-settlers," came illegally, seeking fertile lands to farm and relief from the poverty and land hunger that characterized peasant life in parts of European Russia. By 1889, St. Petersburg, seeking to regulate this flow of migrants and convinced of the civilizing role that Slavic settlers could play in these regions, issued the Resettlement Act. This act, which marked the first central government effort to coordinate this migration, codified settlement as official state policy, setting up settlement programs in European Russia, Western Siberia, and the provinces of Akmolinsk, Semipalatinsk, and Semirech'e. In 1893, construction on the Trans-Siberian railroad began, and one of the last remaining obstacles to large-scale peasant colonization of these regions, the arduous trip across European Russia by oxen and cart, was erased.

Russian imperial officials anticipated that peasant settlement would encourage Kazakhs to abandon their nomadic way of life for a settled one, a goal that St. Petersburg had pursued to varying degrees since the rule of Catherine the Great.[4] The spread of agriculture, it was believed, would "civilize" native peoples and make the lands in these regions more "productive."

But as this chapter reveals, though Kazakhs' pastoral nomadic practices began to shift in response to this wave of peasant settlement, it was not always in the ways that St. Petersburg might have hoped. Though most nomads began to reduce their mobility, they also adopted other strategies, such as trade and the rental of their pasture lands, to maintain their nomadic way of life and adapt to the changing social, political, and environmental circumstances of life on the steppe. World War I and the destruction brought by the Russian Civil War dealt a particularly devastating blow to nomadic life, but the predictions of many Russian imperial officials that nomadism, an "anachronism," would soon give way to settled life did not come to pass.[5] In 1924, as the new Soviet state began to divide the region up into national republics, pastoral nomadism remained the predominant way of life for most Kazakhs.[6]

In a pattern that foreshadowed elements of the Soviet state's battle to make the Kazakh steppe into an agrarian region, settlers endured devastating droughts, frosts, and hunger. They struggled to adapt their agricultural practices to the steppe's environmental conditions. Though there was a lot of land in the Kazakh steppe, much of it was very arid, salinated, or otherwise unsuitable for farming. A focus on quantity—the overall amount of "surplus" land in the Kazakh steppe—concealed the complexity of this landscape and the ways that fertile lands were regularly interspersed with poor quality soils. After several years of poor harvests, the Governor-Generalship of the Steppe temporarily closed the steppe to further colonization in 1891.[7] Though many settlers chose to remain, ultimately some 20 percent of all settlers who came during this period of intense peasant colonization would return to European Russia.[8]

The legacies of this period and the particular imprint that it left on pastoral nomads, Slavic settlers and the steppe itself help explain the scale of the Kazakh famine of 1930–33, which led to the death of 1.5 million people, the vast majority of them Kazakhs. Though the available data do not allow a full investigation of ecological change in this period—the systematic collection of temperature and precipitation data in the Kazakh steppe began only in the late nineteenth century—other materials, including archival sources and ethnographic accounts, illustrate important shifts in the relationship among humans, animals, climate, and environment.[9] Due to this intense period of human and animal growth, observers note that some water sources were drying up and the fertility of various soils had become exhausted. As both nomads and Slavic settlers adapted to the changing circumstances of life on the steppe, these two ways of life developed close economic linkages, particularly a grain and livestock trade. Kazakhs began to change their diet, shifting away from a diet based on meat and milk products to one in which grain played a larger role. It is likely that they began to consume less food overall, increasing their vulnerability to famine.[10]

As researchers have shown, both abrupt change and slower-moving structural processes can combine to produce a famine.[11] The Soviet regime's sweeping program of state-driven transformation was the most important cause of the Kazakh famine of 1930–33, and it is doubtful that famine would have broken out anywhere in Kazakhstan without the regime's violent assault on nomadic life. But the legacies of Russian imperial rule—principally changes induced by massive peasant colonization of the Kazakh steppe during the late nineteenth and early twentieth centuries—were an important contributing factor.[12] These changes, which were both seen and unseen by Soviet officials, contributed to a general sense by the early Soviet era that the steppe's economy was in state of crisis, and that only a radical fix, forced settlement of the Kazakh nomads, could make the area economically productive. Ultimately the changes that began under Russian imperial rule would intensify the scale of the Kazakh famine, amplifying the effects of the Soviet regime's brutal policy changes.

This chapter begins by situating pastoral nomadism in the broader sweep of Central Eurasian history.[13] It explains the basic features of this way of life and the ways that nomads regularly adapted to political and ecological shifts. It then traces how the Kazakhs and the Russian empire first came to interact, a process that culminated in the Russian empire's conquest of the Kazakh steppe in the nineteenth century. It examines pastoral nomadic life on the eve of peasant settlement, revealing the close relationship between

pastoral nomads' practices and the environment of the steppe. Finally, it analyzes how the arrival of peasant settlers then began to alter various features
of this relationship.

Pastoral Nomadism and Central Eurasia

The practice of pastoral nomadism has a long history in the steppe zone of Central Eurasia, dating back at least four millennia.[14] In the middle of the first millennium BCE, the Scythians, a northern Iranian people, migrated into the western
steppe, becoming the region's first known nomadic empire. The Greek historian
Herodotus famously documented the inner workings of this empire, focusing
on the Scythians' mastery of mounted warfare and their development of systems
of trade.[15] Later, Islamic geographers named the steppe for the nomadic peoples
who lived there: in the beginning of the eighth century AD, the steppe was known
as "The Steppe of the Ghuzz," in reference to the Oghuz Turks. By the eleventh
century, the territory was referred to by a Persian name, "Dashti-i Qïpchaq," or
the Steppe of the Qïpchaqs. Though the Qïpchaqs ceased to be the dominant
ethnic group in the steppe after the Mongol conquest, this name remained in use
until the nineteenth century, when the territory became known as "the Kirgiz
steppe" (*Kirgizskaia step'*).[16] It was during the Soviet period that the territory
became known as "the Kazakh steppe," a name it retains today. As these naming
practices suggest, the history of the steppe is, in many eyes, synonymous with
nomadism, and it conjures up images of mounted, raiding warriors who wandered free from the trappings of settled life.

But as researchers have shown, the history of pastoral nomadism in Central Eurasia is far more complex than an image of wandering, raiding warriors
would seem to suggest. Throughout the centuries, nomadism did tend to be the
predominant economic activity in the steppe zone, with sedentary populations
concentrated in oases or irrigated river valleys. But archeologists have found evidence dating from the Bronze Age (3000–1000 BCE) to indicate that there were
significant variations in economic activities across the steppe zone, with some
pastoral nomadic communities intensifying their focus on herding, while others placed more emphasis on hunting.[17] Scholars have shown that some farming, including the cultivation of drought-resistant crops such as spring wheat,
millet, and oats, was practiced as a supplementary activity in economic zones
dominated by nomads, from the Neolithic Age to the modern era.[18] These studies have challenged the idea that the steppe could support only long-distance
animal herding. By contrast, they have proven that the environmental constraints
on settled agriculture in this region were neither precise nor immutable.[19] These

findings and others have prompted a rethinking of what pastoral nomadism in Central Eurasia actually was and how it changed over time.[20]

The term "pastoral nomadism" can be challenging to define. Pastoralism refers to an economic practice, the herding and supervision of animals. Pastoralists raise their animals on the open range, in contrast to ranchers who generally provide hay or fodder for their animals and stable them in pens or sheds.[21] Nomadism might be defined roughly as a strategy, or the regular movement of people from place to place in a deliberate, rather than an aimless, manner.[22] Thus, pastoral nomads were those groups of people who carried out repeated, purposeful migrations to pasture their animal herds, such as sheep, camels, and horses. Most regularly incorporated other activities, including trade, hunting, and seasonal agriculture, to supplement their practice of pastoralism. Due to the need to migrate with their animal herds, pastoral nomads generally lived in a dwelling that could be collapsed and transported easily, such as a tent or a yurt (*kiïz uy*).[23]

It is important to note that pastoral nomads' strategies were not timeless and unchanging.[24] As researchers have shown, pastoral nomads regularly altered their practices according to opportunities and risks.[25] Environmental changes, such as shifts in temperature or precipitation, might cause some pastoral nomads to migrate seasonally, rather than year-round. Social and political changes, such as the intrusion of new peoples or shifts in political structures, might prompt them to increase or decrease their reliance on other economic strategies, such as agriculture or hunting.[26] Moreover, pastoral nomadism was not solely an ecological adaptation; it could also serve as a political strategy. During times of crisis, threatened groups could retreat to utilize marginal environments.[27]

During the late nineteenth and early twentieth centuries, as the steppe came under intense Slavic peasant colonization, Russian imperial officials witnessed important shifts in pastoral nomadic life, changes that seemed to confirm their idea that they were in a unique historical moment, whereby pastoral nomadism would disappear under the onward march of modernity. The settlement of the Kazakh nomads was a phenomenon that many Russian imperial officials believed to be evolutionarily "correct," and it was also a prospect that many of them welcomed.[28] When they observed nomadic life, they tended to see the Russian empire as the sole agent of the changes that they witnessed. A host of shifts, it was believed, including pastoral nomads' increasing reliance on agriculture, could be attributed to Kazakhs' increased proximity to a settled (and presumably more cultured) society.

But as this chapter explores, the Russian empire was not the only agent of change in the Kazakh steppe. Kazakhs were not passive in the face of massive peasant settlement. Ecological and economic factors also played a role in determining the nature of the changes that Russian imperial observers witnessed.[29]

Nor were many of the shifts that they witnessed unique. Many had long been an integral part of the region's history. In Central Eurasia, the dividing line between the pastoral nomad and the sedentary agriculturalist was often far less distinct than in other regions of the world.[30] Pastoral nomads' practice of agriculture or the decision to shorten their yearly migrations—strategies that observers generally labeled as "semi-nomadism"—did not necessarily signal that these peoples were transitioning to settled life. Forms of semi-nomadism could be long-lasting and stable. Though some ecological, social, and political factors might cause groups to settle, others might cause groups to nomadize, with semi-nomads or settled groups taking up nomadic life.[31]

The Encounter between the Kazakhs and the Russian Empire

The use of the term "Qazaq" as a form of self-identification dates to the late fifteenth century. During 1459–60, Janibek and Kirey, sons of Barak Khan of the White Horde of the Mongol empire, broke away from Abu'l-Khayr, khan of the Uzbeks. Abu'l-Khayr had been weakened by his defeat at the hands of the Oirats (western Mongols), and Janibek and Kirey used this opportunity to move their supporters, a group of pastoral nomadic tribes of Turkic and Mongol origins, to Semirech'e. They became known as the "Özbek-Qazaqs." The first term was reference to the khanate they had left behind, the Uzbeks (Özbeks), while the latter term, "qazaq," was a Turkic term used to refer to those individuals and groups who had abandoned their clan or ruler to live the life of a vagabond or adventurer.[32] Over time, a number of Abu'l-Khayr's followers left to join this rival polity. By the sixteenth century, the Kazakh khanate, as it became known, was the dominant force in the central and eastern steppe, and the descendants of Janibek, Kirey, and their supporters were known simply as "Qazaqs."

According to popular tradition, in the late sixteenth century the Kazakh khanate split into supratribal confederations, each of which was known as a "horde" (*zhüs*). Over time, the Elder (*ulu*) Horde came to control Semirech'e, the Middle (*orta*) Horde the central steppe and southwestern Siberia, and the Little (*kishi*) Horde the west of the steppe.[33] Each of these hordes was ruled independently by a khan, or military ruler, though particularly influential khans, such as Khan Tauke (1680–1718), could bring all three hordes under their command. Customarily, these khans were part of the Chinggisid nobility, those peoples who claimed descent from Janibek, Kirey, and, by extension, Chinggis Khan, the founder of the Mongol empire, himself. The Chinggisids formed part of the khanate's small aristocratic elite, who were collectively known as "white bone" (*aq süiek*), while commoners were known as "black bone" (*qara süiek*).[34]

Russia's formal entrance into the politics of the steppe had begun in the mid-sixteenth century, with the Muscovite state's conquest of the Tatar khanates of Kazan and Astrakhan. Pushing further into the steppe, Russia extended its power into the North Caucasus, across the Ural Mountains to the east and, eventually, under Catherine the Great, to the khanate of Crimea on the Black Sea in 1783.[35] Settlement of the steppe belt by Slavic peasants followed, with the arrival of these peasant-farmers intensifying in the eighteenth century. But as the Russian empire's frontier advanced, frequent conflicts between these Slavic settlers and the nomadic peoples of the steppe, including Bashkirs, Kalmyks, and Kazakhs, erupted.[36] In the Kazakh steppe, as in other parts of the Russian empire, St. Petersburg set up a defensive perimeter to prevent nomads from conducting raids on agricultural settlements. Known as the Siberian Line, this perimeter would largely define the southern frontier of Slavic settlement in the Kazakh steppe until the mid-nineteenth century.[37]

During the eighteenth century, the Russian empire began to engage more deeply in the affairs of the Kazakh steppe south of the Siberian Line, though many details of this relationship were left undefined. By the nineteenth century, for reasons ranging from economic interests to geostrategic competition, the Russian empire began to tighten its hold over the Kazakh steppe.[38] Though the Russian's conquest of the Kazakh steppe was not done without protest— most notably, the immense Kenesarï Qasïmŭlï revolt (1837–47), centered on the lands of the Middle Horde—by the late nineteenth century, the Russian empire's incorporation of the lands of the three Kazakh hordes was complete. In 1822, St. Petersburg approved the Statute on the Siberian Kirgiz (Kazakhs), which formalized the status of Middle Horde Kazakhs as Russian subjects and reorganized the administration of the Middle Horde, eliminating the position of the khans. In 1844, St. Petersburg issued the Regulation for the Administration of the Orenburg Kazaks, which declared the territory of the Little Horde to be part of the Russian empire. The lands of the Elder Horde were brought under Russian rule last, following the Russian conquests of Tashkent (1865), Samarkand and Bukhara (1873), and Kokand (1876).[39]

Through a series of rulings, St. Petersburg established the principle of state ownership of the lands of the Kazakh steppe. The Provisional Statute on Administration in Ural'sk, Turgai, Akmolinsk, and Semipalatinsk Provinces (1868) declared the lands in these regions, which roughly corresponded to the territories of the Middle and Little Hordes, to be state property. The 1891 Steppe Statute, which came to include all these territories, plus Semirech'e, part of the traditional pasturelands of the Elder Horde, built on this principle of state ownership. Article 120 of this statute further stipulated that lands considered to be in "excess" of nomads' needs, known as *izlishki*, could be appropriated by the state.[40] With the principle of state ownership established, St. Petersburg began to demarcate the lands of the Kazakh steppe. The 1868 Provisional Statute created internal borders, including *oblasti* (provinces), *uezdy* (districts), and *volosti* (cantons), in the lands of the steppe. In 1881, in the Treaty of St. Petersburg, the Russian empire and the Qing empire agreed on the demarcation of an international border, dividing Kazakhs living in Chinese Turkestan from Kazakhs living in Russian Turkestan. These newly drawn boundaries (local, regional, international) did not halt Kazakhs' seasonal migrations across borders, but they impeded them, marking the beginning of far-reaching changes to Kazakhs' nomadic way of life.

Kazakhs and Pastoral Nomadism

One of the most eminent scholars of nomadism, the late Kazakhstani ethnographer Nŭrbolat Masanov, has characterized Kazakhs' practice of pastoral nomadism as an ecologically determined way of life. In his interpretation, the environmental features of the Kazakh steppe heavily influenced the economic activities and cultural characteristics of the Kazakh people until the Soviet regime began to radically reshape this relationship. Masanov's interpretation of Kazakh identity on the eve of Soviet rule may place too much emphasis on the environment—as this book shows, culture and politics played a role in the shaping of Kazakh identities, too—but his rigorous analysis reveals the close relationship between the landscape of the Kazakh steppe and the strategies of the peoples who lived there.[41] Kazakhs' practice of pastoral nomadism was an adaption to the steppe's features, particularly the scarcity of good pastureland and water.

This region where Kazakh nomads could be found comprised several ecological zones, including steppe, semidesert (sometimes referred to as the "desert steppe"), desert, and mountains.[42] The steppe zone lay north of the Aral Sea and south of the forests of Western Siberia. It formed part of a larger steppe belt of grasslands stretching across the Eurasian continent. The semidesert and desert zones that Kazakh nomads frequented lay south of the steppe zone. They encompassed several major arid areas, including the Betpak-Dala, the Üst-Yurt Plateau, the Qara-qum at Aral Sands, and part of the Qïzïl-qum Desert. The Betpak-Dala, the largest of these territories, was an immense plateau located between the Sary-Su River in the west and Lake Balkhash in the east. Today, it lies at the heart of contemporary Kazakhstan, just south of the city of Karaganda. The Üst-Yurt, a smaller plateau, lay between the Caspian and Aral Seas.

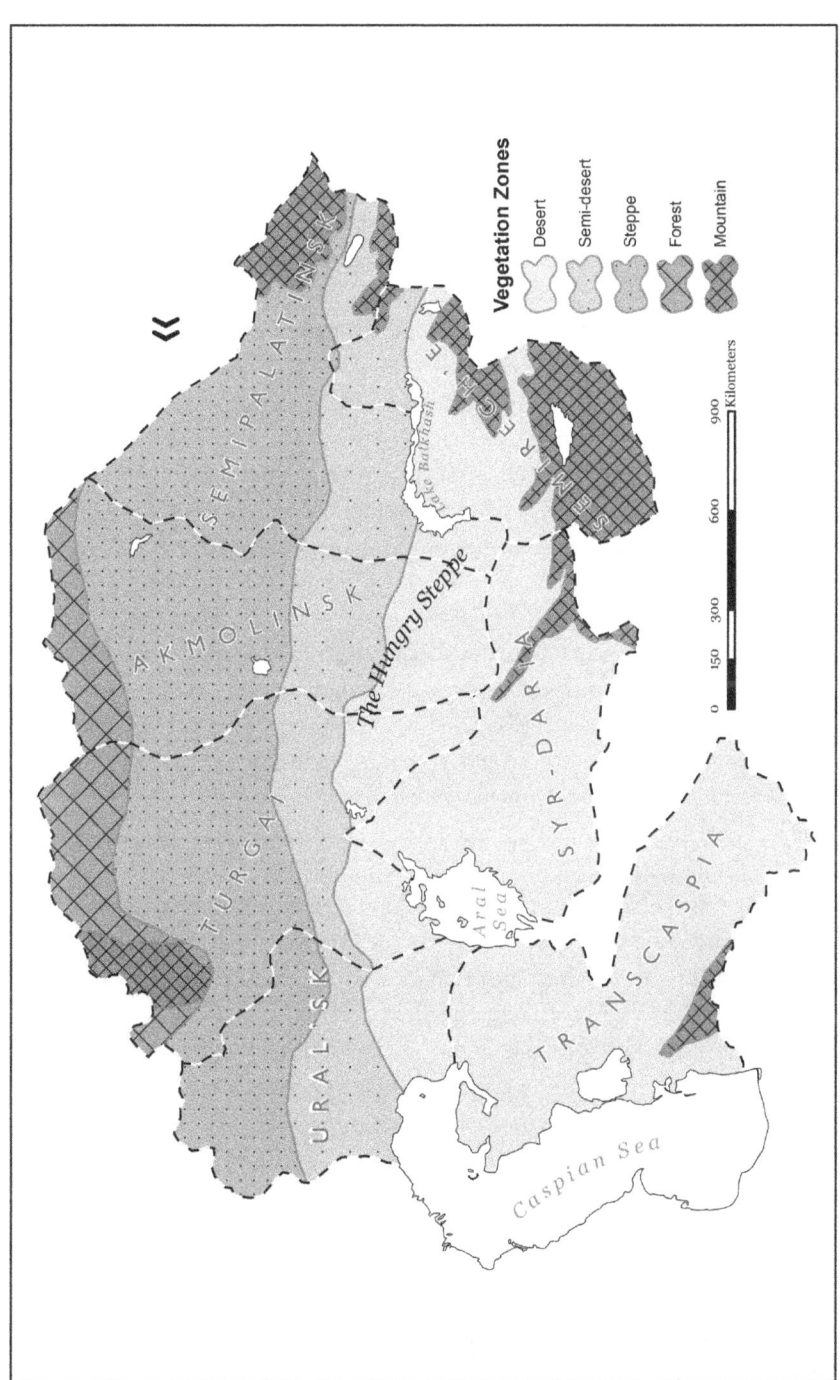

Vegetation Zones

Desert
Semi-desert
Steppe
Forest
Mountain

SEMIPALATINSK

AKMOLINSK

TURGAI

URALSK

The Hungry Steppe

Lake Balkhash

SYR-DARIA

Aral Sea

TRANSCASPIA

Caspian Sea

0 150 300 600 900
Kilometers

MAP 2. Vegetation zones of the Kazakh steppe and Transcaspia

The other two major arid areas where Kazakh nomads could be found, the Qara-qum at Aral Sands and the Qïzïl-qum, were classical deserts, with unsecured shifting sands.[43] Finally, there were two mountain ranges, the Tian Shan Mountains in the southeast and the Atai Mountains in the east, at the edges of the desert and semidesert zone. The area around these mountain ranges generally received more precipitation than the surrounding zones, and the Tian Shan overlooked a particularly fertile region, known as Zheti-su or Semirech'e (seven rivers). With the exception of the mountain ranges, the distinction among these zones was not precise: the climates of steppe, semidesert, and desert were closely related to one another. The borders of these ecological zones could also shift over time due to environmental change.[44]

All these zones had a sharp continental climate, with hot summers and very cold winters. Given the region's distance from oceans, its climate was much harsher than similar zones further west in European Russia. Winter temperatures could dip below −40°F, while summer temperatures could reach well over 100°F. Only the southern reaches of the steppe, such as the city of Vernyi (present-day Almaty), enjoyed average January temperatures above freezing.[45] The region's precipitation was shaped by winter westerlies from the Atlantic. Shifts of the North Atlantic Oscillation (NAO) determined the distribution of this rainfall over the centuries. A negative NAO mode might bring ample rainfall to the region, while a positive NAO mode brought little rainfall. During the Little Ice Age (roughly 1500–1850 AD), the steppe appears to have enjoyed plentiful rainfall. By the late nineteenth century, however, the climate of the steppe was entering a warm, dry phase.[46] Aridity had become one of the Kazakh steppe's defining features.

Not only was the amount of rainfall low, but rainfall patterns in the Kazakh steppe were more unstable than in the steppes in the European part of Russia. The amount of rain might fluctuate dramatically from year to year and season to season. For the desert and semidesert zones, the period of maximum precipitation was generally in the spring, with the hot, dry summers bringing little or no rainfall. By contrast, the wettest period for the steppe zone was usually the summer. Thus, seasonal vegetation, such as grasses, appeared first in the desert and steppe desert zones and only later, in June and July, in the steppe zones.[47] But the overall amount of yearly rainfall decreased markedly the farther south one traveled, from steppe to semidesert to desert. The steppe might receive between ten to twenty inches of rain, the semidesert six to ten inches, and the desert less than four inches. In each zone, the most important indicator of climate was not the amount of rainfall but rather the ratio of precipitation to evaporation, which was generally quite low. Due to long, sunny cloudless days and high temperatures, the rain that fell in these regions usually evaporated quickly.[48]

In the north, the region had *chernozem*, "black earth" soils. These contained a high percentage of humus and could produce good agricultural yields. Chestnut soils could be found further south, in the semidesert zone. Like the black earth soils, chestnut soils could be quite fertile. Yet they had far less humus than black earth soils, and repeated plowing could quickly exhaust their ability to support crops. Two other soils, *solonchak* and *solonetz*, were sprinkled throughout, occurring with greater frequency in the desert and semidesert regions. Solonchak soils were formed as groundwater rose to the surface. As this water evaporated, it left white, salty patches across the surface of the soil. Solonetz soils were solonchak soils that had been leached through irrigation or increased rainfall. As water passed through the soil, sodium carbonate formed, and the soil became highly alkaline. Neither of these two soils was fertile, but their distribution was uneven—chestnut soils could be interspersed with solonetz and solonchak soils—and changeable, as weather or irrigation patterns shifted.[49]

Hot, dry winds (*sukhovei*) swept across all these zones. These gusts could create enormous piles of sand or whip up violent dust storms.[50] Given the arid conditions of the region, fires started easily, and these winds could quickly transform a small fire into a fearsome blaze that could move more than ten kilometers in an hour.[51] These drying winds also contributed to evaporation from open water sources, such as lakes and rivers. Due to this evaporation and other factors, such as periods of little or no rainfall, the region's bodies of water, including the Aral Sea, exhibited a chameleon-like quality, rapidly changing their size and form. This desiccation was particularly pronounced in areas with a high salt content. The Russian zoologist Nikolai Zarudnyi, who traveled widely throughout Central Asia, reported that small lakes could dry up under the hot summer sun in the course of just one day, becoming marshes sprinkled with a white dusting of crystal salt.[52]

The climate in the Betpak-Dala—literally, The Ill-Fated Steppe—was particularly severe. It had hot summers, cold winters, and a very short spring. During the summer months, temperatures could fluctuate radically, with high temperatures during the day and a sharp drop in temperature at night. There was generally little cloud cover, and the sun in the plateau could be unrelenting. It had very few open water sources and little rainfall. When rain did fall, it was quickly absorbed deep into the plateau's coarse soil.[53] In the steppe and the semidesert zones, grasses and wormwood (*Artemisia*) were common. But due to the harsh conditions on the plateau, there was little vegetation, save low-growing, drought-resistant shrubs, such as saksaul and dzhuzgun (*Calligonum caput medusae*), which could send their roots deep into the soil to tap the plateau's groundwater reserves. These shrubs were sparsely distributed and light gray in color, giving the Hungry Steppe a uniform, single-toned appearance.[54] Due to these conditions and the plateau's immense size—approximately 75,000 square kilometers, about as big as Scotland—passage across the Betpak-Dala was difficult.[55] It was with good reason that the territory was known not only as The Ill-Fated Steppe but also by a Russian name, *golodnaia step'* (The Hungry Steppe).[56]

Both Russian imperial and Soviet officials regularly characterized the Kazakh steppe as a "natural" landscape, one largely untouched by human influence. They looked for markers of sedentary life, such as permanent dwellings, and finding none, assumed that the landscape of this region had never been altered by human activity.[57] But contrary to their impressions, Kazakh nomads, like other pastoralists, regularly sought to change it to suit their needs. To encourage the growth of fresh grasses that their livestock could eat, they burned areas of the steppe. These fires, as well as the trampling of the steppe by pastoralists' animal herds, helped prevent the spread of shrubs and trees.[58] In the Hungry Steppe and other areas where there was little surface water, Kazakhs built wells deep into the steppe to tap groundwater reserves.[59]

All the steppe's ecological zones suffered from periodic bouts of drought, as well as devastating late-spring frosts, a phenomenon known as *zhŭt* (Kazakh) or sometimes as *gololeditsa* (Russian). The former was a common feature of pastoral environments, particularly the drylands of Africa and the Middle East, while the latter was a hazard particular to Central Eurasia.[60] In a zhŭt, a cold snap would set in after the spring thaw, leading to the formation of an ice crust over the ground. With their fodder trapped below the ice, Kazakhs' animal herds would begin to starve. Due to the cyclical nature of large-scale zhŭts, which appeared every ten to twelve years, Kazakhs also referred to them by the name *qoyännïng zhŭtï* (zhŭt during the Year of the Hare), a reference to a particular year in the Zodiac cycle.[61] Zhŭts could be catastrophic for nomads, with more than 90 percent of the herds in a nomadic encampment perishing.[62]

To utilize this landscape, Kazakh nomads migrated along predetermined routes to pasture their animal herds. These migrations were not carried out by individual households but rather were conducted in small groups, a nomadic encampment known as an aul. Each aul was generally made up of two to eight households, and together all the members of the aul assumed responsibility for the care of their herd. The number of animals associated with a given aul varied widely (sheep, for instance, generally took less effort to tend than horses), and these numbers could fluctuate, depending on seasonal or environmental variations. New auls could form when animal numbers grew too large to be supported by the original aul's pastures.[63]

Most auls pastured mixed herds, rather than relying on a single type of animal. Animals that could travel great distances and easily paw at fodder trapped under the snow, such as sheep and horses, were of particular importance given

FIGURE 1.1. A Kazakh yurt in the Tekes valley, 1926. Morden and Clark Asiatic Expedition of 1926, American Museum of Natural History Library, Image #267740.

the steppe's climate. Horses were prized for their meat and fermented mare's milk (*qïmïz*), in addition to serving as a source of transport for people and goods, while sheep were raised for their mutton and wool. The camel, ill-suited to uncovering fodder trapped under snow, was much less common than sheep or horses in the Kazakh steppe. Camels, however, could be found in the west of the steppe, where Little Horde Kazakhs migrated. In this arid region, the camel was the sole animal capable of sustaining long journeys and, by extension, the only means of transporting goods.

Kazakhs' migrations were seasonal, and they followed the appearance of vegetation in the steppe, assuming a circular, south to north to south pattern. Each aul generally had separate spring (*kökteu*), summer (*zhaylau*), fall (*küseu*), and winter (*qïstau*) pasture. The summer pastures were particularly important, as they provided the thick grasses that were necessary for the fattening of nomads' livestock. In the winter months, it was critical to find a sheltered pasture, where the snow was not too deep and the animals might find some relief from the wind and the cold. Both the spring and the fall pastures were usually located close to the winter pasture: nomads would bring their herds to the spring pasture when the snow had melted, but before the summer pasture's grasses had begun to bloom. When the vegetation in the summer pasture began to fade, they would move their herds to the fall pasture, then migrating to the winter pasture with the first snowfall.[64]

Beyond seasonal change, the particular way that a given aul migrated—the length and speed of their migrations and the time spent in seasonal pastures—was influenced by factors such as the terrain of the landscape, the availability of water and fodder, the particular types of animals that the aul tended, and the presence and density of other people and livestock.[65] Some auls, for instance, might migrate fairly modest distances over the course of a year—traveling a total of fifty to one hundred kilometers—while other auls, such as those that inhabited the arid Mangyshlak Peninsula, where good pasture and water sources tended to be scarce, might travel one thousand to two thousand kilometers in a single year.[66] Indeed, the extraordinary length of some Kazakh nomads' migrations distinguished their practices from those of other pastoral nomadic peoples in Central Asia, such as the Turkmen or the Kirgiz.[67] Cataclysmic events, like the Zunghar invasion into the south of the steppe in the eighteenth century, might shift nomads' migration routes, thereby intensifying the competition for good grazing lands in other areas of the steppe.

Genealogy played a crucial role in Kazakh nomadic life. Originally, the term "qazaq" had denoted a political identity, those peoples who had broken away from Abu'l-Khayr, khan of the Uzbeks. But by the nineteenth century, members of the black bone (commoner) strata had increasingly come to define themselves by their ancestry, which they complied in oral or written registers. They understood their genealogical ties as approximating the shape of a tree. At the top of the tree was Alash, the mythical ancestor from whom they claimed descent. Alash then had three sons, Bekarys, Akarys, and Zhanarys, each of whom founded one of the three Kazakh hordes. The offspring of these sons then formed tribes within their particular horde. As time went on and these tribes grew larger, their descendants founded sections and subsections, as a way of identifying themselves and clarifying the exact way that they were related to their supposed founder, Alash.[68] The smallest unit of a given lineage was an aul, and members of this group considered themselves to be part of the same kinship group.

Kinship, however, was not just a source of identity. It also governed crucial economic aspects of pastoral nomadic life. In a practice known as *ata qonïs*, individual clans claimed grazing rights over particular pastures, and these privileges were then passed down along genealogical lines. When nomads' migration routes were disrupted or pressure on pastures increased, such as during the Zunghar invasion, the leaders of various clans would meet to reallocate the usage of pastures.[69] Pastoral nomads also relied upon practices of mutual aid as protection against the effects of environmental instability. In *saün berü*, a Kazakh with large numbers of cattle might loan a poorer kin member a milk cow for the winter. This poorer kin

FIGURE 1.2. Kazakh nomads in the Tekes valley, 1926. Morden and Clark Asiatic Expedition of 1926, American Museum of Natural History Library, Image #267742.

member would be responsible for pasturing and feeding the cow yet would gain the benefits of its milk and, potentially, its offspring. Such aid practices constituted a necessary survival strategy in a landscape where distinctions between "rich" and "poor" could shift rapidly over the course of a single season.

To varying extents, Kazakh nomads supplemented their practice of pastoralism with activities such as agriculture, hunting, fishing, or trade. In 1833, the General Staff officer Aleksei Levshin, perhaps the most famous Russian imperial chronicler of Kazakh life, published an account based on his experiences in Orenburg province. He noted that some Kazakhs, usually poorer Kazakhs who had lost their livestock, engaged in agriculture close to rivers and lakes. But he cautioned against equating the spread of agriculture with Kazakhs' adoption of settled life: "However, agriculture does not make them settled. They nomadize close to their fields only until the time when the grain is ripe. After threshing it, they take what they need with them, bury the remainder in the ground until the next sowing, and then leave for another place."[70] As Levshin's account illustrates, Kazakhs adapted their practice of agriculture to suit their nomadic way of life and the steppe's conditions. Nomads tended to cultivate grains that had a short growing season, such as millet, and store them in hollows in the ground (*ŭra*). Where irrigation was necessary, they constructed *aryk*s, canals that funneled water across the steppe.[71]

Settlement of the Kazakh Steppe

While the settlement of the Kazakh steppe was part of the larger migration of Slavic peoples to Siberia, the Russian Far East, and Central Asia during the late nineteenth century, it had several distinctive features. Unlike Siberia, the Kazakh steppe was used only infrequently as a place of exile during the period it was under Russian imperial rule. The writer Fyodor Dostoevsky, who spent time as a corporal at the Semipalatinsk garrison, is perhaps the most well-known figure to have been banished to the region. The steppe had a significant native population—by 1897, as much as three million—in contrast to the more dispersed and less numerous native populations of Siberia and the Far East.[72] The environment of the Kazakh steppe also presented particular challenges for the establishment of settled agriculture: when compared with lands farther north, the land received less annual rainfall and its soils were generally of poorer quality. Due to the steppe's dry climate, spring wheat, the favored crop of settlers, was generally of high quality. But the frequent occurrence of droughts meant that these spring wheat harvests were unpredictable, and that yields varied greatly from year to year.[73]

Generally, there was a close relationship between peasant settlement and the ecological conditions of the steppe. By 1898, the area where most Kazakhs migrated was split into several different administrative regions. The Governor-Generalship of the Steppe, which roughly corresponded to the northeast of the Kazakh steppe (the provinces of Akmolinsk and Semipalatinsk), the Governor-Generalship of Turkestan (which included, among other parts of southern Central Asia, the provinces of Semirech'e, Syr-Daria, and Transcaspia, all of which had large numbers of Kazakh nomads), and Turgai and Ural'sk provinces, which were not part of any administrative unit.[74] In the steppe provinces, peasant settlement came to resemble a belt, which corresponded to the amount of annual rainfall that the land received. With its fertile soils, Akmolinsk province quickly became the favored destination for peasant settlers. Over time, the northern reaches of Turgai, Semipalatinsk, and Ural'sk provinces also became important sites of settlement. But due to the lack of rainfall, few settlers could be found further south within these provinces, and the eight-inch annual precipitation line roughly marked the southern extent of peasant settlement.[75]

Farther south in Russian Turkestan, the pattern of settlement in Kazakh lands was a bit different, but it was also closely linked to the region's ecological conditions. Fearing the potentially disruptive effects of large-scale peasant settlement in this region, administrators had closed Turkestan to settlement in 1896, adding Semirech'e to this list when it was returned to the auspices of the Governor-Generalship of Turkestan in 1898. But unauthorized settlers continued to arrive and the pressure for new, fertile lands grew: In 1890–91, parts of European Russia experienced a devastating famine, and impoverished, starving peasants fled as far south as Turkestan in search of better lands. In 1910, as part of the far-reaching agrarian reforms spearheaded by Prime Minister Pyotr Stolypin, St. Petersburg permanently lifted the ban on settlement in Turkestan.[76] Settlers concentrated heavily in Semirech'e, with its abundant rainfall and good soils, and to a far lesser extent in the river valleys of Syr-Daria. Due to its aridity, extreme heat, and poor soils, few settlers colonized Transcaspia, and this province was largely untouched by the phenomenon of peasant settlement.[77]

The peasants who settled in Turkestan or the lands of the steppe provinces came primarily from the Middle Volga, as well as the left bank and steppe of Ukraine.[78] But within these peasant communities, there were differences: those who had settled the steppe at the beginning of this migration tended to be known as the *starozhily* (old-timers) while more recent arrivals were often referred to *novosely* (new settlers).[79] In Semipalatinsk province, a group of peasants, including many Old Believers, migrated to the Altai Mountains. They became known as the Altai peasants or the *kamenshchiki* (stone people), and over time they developed traditions distinct from other peasants in the region.[80] Kazakhs referred to all these settlers by a number of nicknames, including *qarashekpendïler* ("black coats," a reference to peasants' traditional dress) and, more snidely, *kelsïmsekter* (those who came without invitation).[81]

The particular way that peasants found the land that they occupied varied. Some contracted with land scouts who would arrange for the rental of suitable land from Kazakh or Cossack communities prior to their arrival. After the legalization of this practice, scouts could enroll migrants directly in government-surveyed areas.[82] As part of an effort to solidify the Kazakh steppe's new border with China, officials offered special subsidies to those who settled in the eastern parts of Semirech'e and Semipalatinsk provinces.[83] The most destitute arrivals simply poured into existing peasant settlements. Once there, they often appropriated "unused" pasturelands from nomads' seasonal migration routes, and frequent conflicts over land, water, and livestock rights broke out. Due to these tensions, as well as fears about the peasants themselves, particularly their poverty and supposedly uncivilized nature, regional officials pleaded, albeit unsuccessfully, with the Ministry of Internal Affairs to halt the flow of settlers.[84] The Kazakh saying *khalïq osedï, zher ospeidï*—"people arrive, but the land does not move"—hints at the overcrowding that occurred on particularly fertile lands.

On moving to the steppe, many new arrivals struggled to adapt to an unfamiliar climate. They bemoaned the insects, such as mosquitoes, gadflies, horseflies, and gnats, which appeared at the beginning of the summer, as well as the burrowing effects of rodents, such as the jerboa, which could destroy crops.[85] In the treeless landscape, they struggled to find enough wood to light fires or construct shelters.[86] But they also fought against more severe problems, such as droughts, severe frosts, and plagues of locusts. In 1907, settlers in Semirech'e suffered from droughts and destitution so severe that officials in the region began to organize food aid.[87] That same year, a detachment of the Russian Society of the Red Cross, after surveying the steppe region, observed that there were people in every village suffering from scurvy due to a poor diet.[88] In 1911, part of the Kazakh steppe experienced a severe drought: officials in Omsk uezd estimated that the harvest of wheat and other grains was 80 percent less than the previous year. Due to these harvest failures, peasants were not able to collect enough seeds for the following year's sowing or sufficient hay to feed their livestock. During the drought, the grass on the steppe perished, and peasants' livestock sickened from eating it.[89]

Due to these environmental challenges, as well as other factors, such as conflict with local officials and Kazakh nomads, large numbers of Slavic settlers—some 20 percent—ultimately returned back to European Russia prior to 1917. Many of those who remained sought to diversify their activities, moving away from an exclusive focus on grain farming as a way to manage hazards such as drought: some peasant settlements in Turgai and Semipalatinsk provinces were primarily or exclusively focused on livestock production rather than grain farming.[90] With the construction of the Trans-Siberian railroad and the introduction of ferry service along the Irtysh River in the 1880s, settlers began to import new technologies to the Kazakh steppe, including mechanized means of clearing hay (*senokosilka*) and heavy iron plows that could break up the sod more effectively than wooden plows.[91] Settlers' continuing ties with regions in European Russia, including the travel back and forth of family members, brought to the steppe new seeds, especially hardier varieties of wheat, the favored crop of settlers, as well as animal breeds, most notably the black sheep prized by Russians and Cossacks.[92]

As peasant settlement continued, Kazakhs began to adapt their practice of pastoral nomadism to the changing circumstances of life on the steppe. Due to the demarcation of borders and the physical presence of areas of Slavic settlement, Kazakh nomads could not use the land in the way that they had previously. In Akmolinsk and Semipalatinsk provinces, which roughly corresponded to the lands of the Middle Horde, nomads began to cultivate hay as a source of winter fodder, to compensate for the loss of some of their pasturelands. To protect these hay fields and their winter pastures from encroachment by peasants or other nomads, some Kazakhs began to spend nine months of the year on their winter pastures, migrating just a short distance to their summer pastures in the remaining three months.[93] Some Little Horde Kazakhs, by contrast, increased the length of their seasonal migrations, as peasant settlement forced them to travel farther in search of reliable water sources and good pasturelands.[94]

Due in part to this shift in land use practices, many pastoral nomads changed the composition of their herds. Those Kazakhs who had shortened their migrations began to include animals suited to minimal migrations, such as cattle, followed by sheep and then horses. Prior to the late eighteenth century, cattle had not formed a major part of Kazakhs' herds. They were difficult animals to herd across long distances, and in comparison to sheep or horses, their grazing habits could be fickle: cows tended to subsist entirely on the top layer of grass rather than grazing more intensively.[95] But in a significant shift, cattle now constituted an important part of many Kazakh nomads' herds.[96] By contrast, the numbers of camels in the steppe began to decline, as fewer nomads were able to carry out the long migrations needed to pasture them.[97] Though the steppe's overall animal population was growing rapidly, the number of animals that a particular aul pastured was going down, as few auls were able to sustain the long migrations needed to pasture large herds.[98]

In other cases, Kazakhs developed new strategies to cope with the challenge of Slavic colonization. In 1906, at a meeting of the Turgai provincial administration on the question of land apportionment, officials noted that Kazakh households in Kustanai and Aktiubinsk uezds had begun to plow up their pastures for grain, an outcome that seemed to confirm the predictions of those who had heralded the end of nomadism. On closer inspection, however, they discovered that the Kazakhs in these uezds had secretly rented these lands to Russian settlers, who were farming them. They concluded, "In spite of the growth of agriculture, the Kirgiz [Kazakhs] in these uezds are a long way from giving up nomadism."[99] Though the rental of pasturelands was technically illegal—St. Petersburg claimed to own nomads' pasturelands—nomads in areas of intense peasant settlement, such as the northern reaches of Turgai province, began to utilize it to supplement their practice of pastoralism.

In addition, Kazakhs increased their trade with Russia. This steppe trade was distinct from the caravan trade between Russia and Central Asia that passed through the Kazakh steppe, and it had grown in importance as the Russian empire advanced into the region. Kazakhs sold live animals, as well as animal products such as hides, butter, and wool, and they purchased items such as grain, tea, kerosene, matches, pottery, and Russian manufactured goods from traders, mostly Muslim merchants. These exchanges were conducted near areas of peasant or Cossack settlement, at seasonal trade fairs or deep within the steppe itself at so-called "mobile markets," where traders would travel with nomadic encampments. The biggest markets tended to take place at the end of the spring, just as the livestock was beginning to gain weight, and in the fall, so that Kazakhs did not have to pasture these animals over the winter.[100] By the late nineteenth century, Kazakhs became increasingly focused on raising animals for Russian markets They sold them directly to Slavic peasants or to traders, who, with the construction of the Trans-Siberian railroad, shipped them to consumers in European Russia. The railheads of Omsk and Petropavlovsk became centers for this trade. In 1908, the steppe provinces and parts of Semirech'e and Syr-Daria exported 400,000 head of livestock, 6 million hides and skins, and nearly 6,000 tons of meat by rail to European Russia.[101] This trade almost certainly played a role in shifting the composition of Kazakhs' herds, as cattle were more sought after by Russian consumers.[102]

St. Petersburg had promoted the steppe trade as early as the rule of Catherine the Great. It was profitable—Russian officials obtained livestock cheaply and offloaded grain that otherwise would have been difficult and expensive to transport back to Russia—and it was believed that the growth of the grain trade would help "civilize" Kazakhs, making them into loyal subjects of the empire.[103] During the period of intense peasant settlement (1896–1916), officials continued to link the consumption of grain with the adoption of sedentary life. In 1907, as part of a survey of Kazakh land use practices in Akmolinsk province, the statistician V. K. Kuznetsov proclaimed, "The mass of the population has gradually given up a purely nomadic way of life, relying on new means of existence and at the same time adopting the habits of a more cultured way of life, particularly the consumption of grain."[104] The "ancient Kazakh diet" (*starinnaia Kirgizskaia pishcha*) of meat and fermented mare's milk (*qïmïz*), he predicted, would soon give way to a diet based primarily on grain and cow's milk.[105]

Previously, Kazakhs' diet had been based on meat and milk products from sheep, horses, and, to a lesser degree, camels. Meat was the primary focus, and the consumption of meat depended on one's social position, with better-off nomads consuming more meat. During the late fall, Kazakhs would slaughter a portion of their herds. This meat would then be preserved for use during the winter, a process known as *soghïm*. During the warmer months (April to October), when their animals produced fresh milk, Kazakhs shifted their diet, relying to a greater extent on milk products. They consumed soured milks, such as qïmïz, *shŭbat* (fermented camel's milk), and *ayran* (fermented sheep's milk), as well as a variety of cheese and butter products. Kazakh nomads supplemented this meat- and milk-based diet in various ways: some hunted or fished, while others consumed limited amounts of grain.[106]

But there is evidence to suggest that Kazakhs' diet began to change as economic practices in the steppe shifted in the nineteenth and early twentieth centuries. After a series of food crises in the 1830s and then again after the disastrous 1891 famine, the Russian state became increasingly interested in managing the food supply in the Russian countryside. In an effort to halt further outbreaks of famine, imperial officials began to discuss the relationship between food and health. By the 1880s, local government (*zemstvo*) officials began to collect data on peasants' food consumption habits to understand exactly how much food peasants needed to survive. Armed with this data, these officials sought to develop a consumption model applicable to all of Russia, which would indicate what types of foods needed to be produced and how much of this food could be sold.[107]

By contrast, nomadic nutrition was far less well understood. The Kazakh steppe, like many other non-Russian parts of the empire, did not have zemstvos. However, the various statistical expeditions tasked with understanding how much land nomads needed to survive also collected limited data on nomads' consumption habits, which they sought to compare to those of "standard"—that is, settled—households. In 1907, Kuznetsov found that Kazakhs in Kokchetav uezd had begun to consume less food. Individual consumption of meat and milk had declined dramatically in comparison with 1896, while individual consumption of grain had remained fairly stable.[108] Though Kuznetsov tried to explain these declines in meat and milk consumption by pointing to various inaccuracies in the data, he concluded, "the nourishment of nearly half of the Kirgiz [Kazakh] population does not reach an average level."[109] Though Kuznetsov's data is taken from an area of intense peasant settlement, Akmolinsk province, during a year

FIGURE 1.3.   A Kazakh woman preparing *bauïrsaq*, a dish made with flour. Pavlodar province, before 1917. Republic of Kazakhstan Central State Archive of Film, Photo and Audio Documents, Image # 5-3511.

when parts of the Russian empire suffered from famine, it hints at the various ways that Kazakhs' diet had begun to change. Overall, Kazakhs consumed less meat and milk, and as a result, grain had come to constitute an increasingly important part of their diet. Though some Kazakhs grew this grain themselves, most acquired it through trade with settled populations. Given the shift in the composition of Kazakhs' diet (from meat to grain products), it also seems likely that Kazakhs had begun to consume fewer calories overall.

During the last decades of the Russian empire, the Kazakh steppe's human and animal population grew dramatically. Over the course of twenty years (1896–1916), the number of people living in the steppe increased by over two million, with three-quarters of these new arrivals Slavic settlers.[110] In one decade, 1906–16, the number of livestock in the northern oblasts of the Kazakh steppe grew by nearly three million, an increase of 79 percent. In Akmolinsk province, the situation was particularly pronounced: livestock numbers in the province increased 135 percent during that same ten-year period.[111] Several factors help explain this tremendous human and animal growth, including the influx of new peoples, Kazakhs' growing involvement in the livestock trade, and the relative absence of warfare on the steppe in comparison with the eighteenth century.[112]

This rapid human and animal growth placed greater stress on the steppe's environment. With more livestock, pastures were being used far more frequently. Moreover, many settlers did not practice crop rotation. Once the fertility of a piece of land was depleted, they moved on to plow other areas, and soil exhaustion became a problem in areas of heavy peasant settlement.[113] Kuznetsov argued that the steppe's population increase had worsened the overall conditions of the region's water supply: "Everywhere the woods are thinning out and with each year they are depleted more and more, threatening the deforestation of whole large areas and increasing the natural desiccation of bodies of water."[114] As the steppe's animal population grew and these herds came into close proximity to one another, epizootics, large-scale epidemic outbreaks of disease among animal populations, became more likely. In 1890, officials in Akmolinsk province reported that thousands of livestock had died from Siberian anthrax (*Sibirskaia iazva*) and the plague (*chuma*).[115] In 1911, a large epizootic led to the death of over a thousand head of cattle in Ust-Kamenogorsk, part of Semipalatinsk province.[116]

By the early twentieth century, the most striking phenomenon was a trend toward the settlement of the Kazakhs. Russian imperial officials noted the appearance of *dzhataki*, poor Kazakhs without livestock. These Kazakhs could be found near areas of Russian settlement, where they worked as hired laborers.[117] In other cases, nomads began to maintain just two types of pastures, summer and winter, instead of a pasture for each season. With this decrease in mobility, pastoralists began to rely less on their yurts during the colder months. They constructed semipermanent adobe dwellings (*zimovki*), as well as shelters for their animal herds on their winter pastures.[118]

In 1914, the Russian empire entered World War I, beginning a nearly ten-year period of economic and social crisis on the Kazakh steppe. During this period, two distinct famines afflicted areas where Kazakhs migrated. From 1917 to 1920 a famine raged in Russian Turkestan, and from 1920–21 a famine hit the Volga and Ural River regions.[119] The latter famine was concentrated in European Russia, but it also came to encompass two Russian provinces with seasonal Kazakh populations, Orenburg and Astrakhan. Both of these famines were closely intertwined with the political turmoil of the period. In 1916, a massive revolt, sparked by an order to conscript the Muslim peoples of Central Asia for military labor battalions, broke out, and violence spread throughout Russian Turkestan and the steppe.[120] In February 1917, the Russian empire fell, and by 1918, the steppe was plunged into civil war.

This turmoil upended economic relationships across the steppe. The beginning of World War I disrupted Kazakhs' livestock trade with European Russia, and the price for animals within the steppe began to fall. Brigades requisitioned Kazakhs' horses for the use of the Russian army. Due to fighting associated with the 1916 revolt, the grain harvest for Semirech'e province in 1916 plummeted to half what it was in 1914.[121] Across Russian Turkestan, the effects of the revolt were then intensified by a massive zhŭt in the winter of 1916–17, which led to a 20 percent reduction in Kazakhs' herds, and a drought in the summer of 1917.[122] During the last decades of the Russian empire, the cotton-growing areas of Russian Turkestan had become heavily dependent on shipments of grain from European Russia. But by 1918, the rail lines between Russian Turkestan and points north were blocked due to fighting, and much of the grain supply for Russian Turkestan was cut off. A newly formed Tashkent Soviet of Workers and Soldiers' Deputies assumed control over the food supply in Russian Turkestan, wielding food, particularly grain, as a means of control over the local population.

The primary cause of both famines appears to have been forced grain requisitions, which were carried out by armed detachments. In each case, the effects of this policy were intensified by environmental phenomena, the zhŭt and drought in Russian Turkestan, and a drought in the Volga region in 1920–21. And in both cases, patterns emerged that would repeat in some fashion during the Kazakh famine of 1930–33. Large numbers of refugees, both from the Volga and Ural famine and from the Turkestan famine, flooded the city of Tashkent, on the rumor that this city, which would become nicknamed "The City of Bread," had food. Encampments of starving people filled the city's streets.[123] Soon diseases, such as typhus and cholera, began to spread, and officials struggled to cope with this public health crisis. During the turmoil of the 1916 revolt, more than 300,000 nomads (Kazakhs and Kirgiz) fled to China, many perishing as they escaped.

Both crises exacted a particularly heavy toll on the region's economy. In 1931, Ĭzmŭkhan Kŭramïsov, then Kazakhstan's deputy party secretary, estimated that the republic's livestock numbers in 1923 were only 35 percent of their 1916 levels, with its sown field area for 1923 just 52 percent of its 1916 level.[124] Though Kŭramïsov's calculation is anachronistic—the borders of Soviet Central Asia were not drawn until 1924—it gives some sense of the devastation of these years. Due to famine, violence, and refugee flight, Russian Turkestan's population dropped by more than two million people from 1916 to 1920.[125] The effects of this crisis on Russian Turkestan's nomadic population, Kazakhs and Kirgiz, were particularly severe, as their herd numbers fell by 63 percent from 1917 to 1920.[126]

The crisis of 1914–24, particularly the disruption to Kazakhs' seasonal migration routes and the loss of their animal herds, caused some Kazakhs to settle and others to reduce their mobility.[127] More generally, it accelerated a process of Kazakh settlement first sparked during peasant colonization of the Kazakh steppe.[128] This reduction in mobility generally bore a close relationship to patterns of peasant settlement. By the 1920s, nomads who migrated year-round could be found only in areas that had few settlers, such as Transcaspia, populated by Little Horde Kazakhs. A minority of Kazakhs, perhaps less than 10 percent, had settled. The vast majority of Kazakhs continued to rely on the practice of pastoral nomadism. However, they had begun to shorten their migrations and supplement their practice of pastoralism to a greater degree than before with other activities, such as trade and agriculture.[129]

The last decades of Russian imperial rule led to important demographic, economic, and environmental changes in the Kazakh steppe. On the most basic level, the Kazakh steppe, dominated by Muslim, Turkic-speaking peoples since the fifteenth century, gained a significant Slavic minority population. Though Slavic settlers continued to arrive and depart throughout the early Soviet period, the first Soviet census, tabulated in 1926, gives some idea of the enormity of the demographic shifts that occurred under Russian imperial rule: Kazakhs held a slim majority in their new republic (57.1 percent), with Russian (19.6) and Ukrainian (13.2) settlers constituting the bulk of the remainder.[130] Due to the delimitation of international borders, there was now also a significant Kazakh minority in Xinjiang (Chinese Turkestan). As new lands were brought under cultivation during this period of intense peasant settlement, observers noted important ecological shifts, including the drying up of water sources and the exhaustion of soils. These new settlers also found that it was challenging to make the Kazakh steppe into an agrarian region. In a pattern that would continue into the Soviet era, periodic droughts, frosts, and changes in the soil made it difficult to ensure that there would be a stable harvest from year to year.

Many Russian imperial observers had predicted that Kazakhs' pastoral nomadic way of life would disappear due to their encounter with the Russian empire, but the vast majority of Kazakhs continued to practice some form of pastoral nomadism on the eve of Soviet rule. Historically, pastoral nomads in Central Eurasia had relied on various strategies to adapt to changing political or environmental conditions, and Kazakhs responded to the challenge of Slavic settlement by limiting their mobility, increasing the level of their trade with Russia, and renting out some of their pasturelands, among other shifts. Though this period marked a trend toward nomadic settlement, what Russian imperial officials referred to as "semi-nomadism," the disappearance of nomadic life under Soviet rule was by no means preordained or inevitable. As the broader history of Central Eurasia reveals, forms of "semi-nomadism" in the steppe could be long lasting and stable. Though some ecological, social, and political factors might cause groups to settle, others might cause groups to nomadize, with "semi-nomads" or settled groups taking up nomadic life.[131]

But in a crucial development, Kazakhs began to consume more grain, and they became increasingly tied to the networks of Russian traders that supplied this grain. It is also likely that they began to consume less food overall, making them more vulnerable to hunger. Many of these changes were magnified by the destruction of the period 1914–24, which saw Russia's entrance into World War I, the fall of the Russian empire, and the onset of civil war. When the boundaries of what would become known as Soviet Kazakhstan were set in 1924, the region's economy was in a state of crisis, with agricultural yields and livestock numbers well below their pre-World War I levels. It is clear that the Kazakh famine of 1930–33 would not have occurred without the Soviet regime's radical interventions. But, as this chapter has shown, the legacies of Russian imperial rule must be considered an important contributing factor. This period set in motion crucial changes that would magnify the scale of the Soviet famine of 1930–33. When Moscow imposed heavy grain procurement requirements on the republic as part of the First Five-Year Plan, these procurements severed the grain trade networks that had become so important to Kazakh nomads' existence under Russian imperial rule. By the fall of 1930, parts of the Kazakh steppe began to suffer from famine.

CAN YOU GET TO SOCIALISM BY CAMEL?

The Fate of Pastoral Nomadism
in Soviet Kazakhstan, 1921–28

The new Soviet republic of Kazakhstan seemed an unlikely place for socialism to take root. It had been created from disparate parts in 1924 as part of a process known as the "national delimitation," whereby Moscow sought to create national territorial units across the territory of the former Russian empire. The republic's central region, the so-called Hungry Steppe, was arid and subject to frequent droughts, and it bore little resemblance to the more fertile landscapes of European Russia. The predominant economic activity in the republic was not factory work or settled agriculture. Rather, it was pastoral nomadism, and with the national delimitation, the republic had the Soviet Union's largest group of pastoral nomads, far outweighing other neighboring republics with large nomadic populations, such as Turkmenistan and Kirgizia. In the last decades of Russian imperial rule, large numbers of Russian and Ukrainian peasant settlers had settled the republic's northern and southeastern regions, transforming parts of the steppe into an agrarian landscape. But communications and road systems in the Kazakh steppe remained very poorly developed. The best way to reach remote parts of the republic was often an arduous trek by camel. Kazakh culture was primarily an oral rather than a literary culture, and illiteracy rates in the Kazakh aul remained above 90 percent.

For some, the idea of bringing socialism to this territory, a place dotted with camels and nomads, was absurd. A prominent Kazakh cadre Sŭltanbek Qozhanov went so far as to circulate a joke: "You can't get to socialism by camel!" (*Tüyemen sotsializmge zhete almaysïn!*).[1] On one level, the joke was simply a humorous dig at Moscow's outsized ambitions or a sarcastic remark by a disgruntled cadre (in 1925, Qozhanov would be fired from his position as the republic's second secretary). But on a deeper level, Qozhanov's joke reveals that during 1921–28, a phase of Soviet rule generally known as the New Economic Policy (NEP), there were many unresolved questions about what the Communist Party's transformation of the Kazakh steppe would look like. Could you get to socialism by camel? Was nomadism compatible with socialist-style modernity? Or, by contrast, was a nomadic way of life incompatible with socialism?

In much of the Soviet countryside, the period of NEP marked the beginning of a period of relative peace. Moscow ended its previous economic policy, War Communism, in favor of a kind of market socialism. In addition to many other market-oriented changes, NEP replaced the brutal forced requisitioning of War Communism with a tax in kind. Peasants were now permitted to keep their grain surplus and sell it on the free market. But many within the party believed that the policy was only a temporary concession. Ideologically, they saw the appearance of markets and private traders as phenomena incompatible with socialism. Remembering the history of peasant rebellion during the Civil War, they continued to look with deep suspicion on the Soviet peasantry. If the Soviet Union were truly to become a workers' state and overtake the West, the "capitalist practices" of NEP would need to be eliminated, and the peasantry shunted into collective farms.

The scholarly literature on the NEP era has concentrated on the "peasant question," or the issue of how the regime might incorporate a recalcitrant peasantry into the framework of the state.[2] But the case of Kazakhstan reveals that the NEP era was not defined by the issue of the peasantry alone. In Kazakhstan, like other parts of the Soviet east, Moscow confronted alien social groups, ranging from pastoral nomads to hunters and gatherers to fisherman, who were clearly not peasant in their orientation.[3] If the Bolsheviks struggled to fit the peasantry into their Marxist-Leninist worldview, then it was even less apparent where these groups might be placed in the Marxist-Leninist timeline of history. If the primary resource to be extracted from the peasantry was grain, then it was less clear what these regions, parts of which were characterized by severe cold, poor soils, or arid conditions, might produce.

During the NEP era, the fate of Kazakh nomads, like that of the Soviet Union's peasantry more generally, lay undetermined, as experts and officials experimented with different policies and debated how best to integrate them into the state.[4] Initially, Moscow took a contradictory approach to "the nomad question" in Kazakhstan. Some programs, such as the 1921–22 land reforms, weakened the economic basis of nomadic life by altering land tenure systems.[5] By contrast, other initiatives worked with, rather than against, Kazakhs' mobile way of life. To improve their outreach to the republic's remote corners, Soviet activists migrated seasonally with nomadic encampments, and a series of rulings reaffirmed animal husbandry (*skotovodstvo*) as the major basis of Kazakhstan's economy.[6] Within the republic's Commissariat of Agriculture (Kaznarkomzem), experts, such as agronomists, ethnographers, and geographers, many of whom had non-Bolshevik backgrounds, maintained that pastoral nomadism was the most efficient use of the republic's landscape, and they warned that any attempt to settle the Kazakh nomads would result in catastrophe. Kazakh cadres also weighed in on the question of nomadism: Akhmet Baytŭrsïnov, a former member of Alash Orda, a Kazakh political party that had sided against the Bolsheviks during the Civil War, argued that Kazakhs already practiced communism in the aul.

By 1927–28, as economic policy across the Soviet Union began to harden, the idea that nomadism needed to be quickly eliminated throughout the republic began to gain the upper hand. Those specialists who had argued that nomadism was the most productive use of arid parts of the republic's landscape were thrown out of Kaznarkomzem and denounced as "bourgeois." Baytŭrsïnov, like several other former Alash Orda members, was arrested in 1929. Experts now framed pastoralism as a fundamentally unstable means of production, pointing to the fluctuation in pastoral nomads' herd numbers during droughts, zhŭts, or epizootics. Denouncing those who had predicted that arid portions of the steppe could not support settled life, officials proclaimed that a specifically socialist state could overcome the limits that the steppe's arid environment appeared to place on human activity.

In concert with this shift, experts began a rereading of Kazakh history through a Marxist-Leninist lens. They proclaimed the "backward" practice of nomadism to be at odds with the regime's avowedly anti-imperial nationality policy, which pledged to support Kazakhs' development as a national group. Nomadism, they argued, impeded Kazakhs' development into a modern, Soviet nation. Fracturing Kazakhs' "petty bourgeois" consciousness required their sedentarization as a group. Experts began to harness the language of Soviet nation making to reinforce the change in agricultural policy. Nomadism was denounced as both economically inefficient and culturally backward.

By showing that alternate ideas about the fate of pastoral nomadism existed and at certain levels of the party-state even predominated prior to the 1928 confiscation campaign, this chapter reveals that Moscow's assault on pastoral nomadic life was far from predetermined. The presence of this "pronomadism" strain within Soviet thought also stands in contrast to the policies of other states toward nomadic peoples during the same period: portraying nomadic life as unproductive, experts in these states argued that settling pastoralists would reduce environmental degradation.[7] Nonetheless, this chapter finds that there were aspects of Kazakhs' practice of pastoral nomadism, including its distance from markets and tendency for frequent fluctuations in animal numbers, that brought this way of life into clear tension with the proposals for more rapid industrialization that began to circulate during the NEP era. The crackdown on heterodoxy that accompanied the shift away from NEP, in turn, made the ideas of the non-Bolshevik experts and members of the Kazakh intelligentsia who had supported pastoral nomadism much more vulnerable. By 1928, Moscow had disregarded their warnings. The regime launched the "bai confiscation program," which targeted elites in several nomadic societies, including Kazakhstan, Kirgizia, and Buriat-Mongolia. This campaign marked the beginning of the party's assault on nomadism and the unraveling of the cultural and economic basis of nomadic life.

The chapter begins by examining the relationship between Kazakhs and the new Soviet state immediately after the end of the Civil War but prior to the creation of the republic in 1924. It then turns to an analysis of Soviet Kazakhstan after the national delimitation, examining the efforts of the republic's newly installed party secretary Filipp Goloshchekin to transform Kazakh society through a program known as the Sovietization of the Kazakh Aul. If the NEP era saw relative stability in much of the Soviet countryside, this period in the Kazakh steppe was marked by turmoil, as Moscow struggled largely unsuccessfully to establish a firmer foothold in the region.[8] Finally, it analyzes the various debates and programs that led the party to conclude that pastoral nomadism had to be eliminated.

Kazakhs and the New Soviet State, 1921–25

In 1921, Red Army forces assumed a shaky hold over the Kazakh steppe. Soon after assuming control, Moscow faced two pressing questions, the issue of Soviet agricultural policy and the issue of Soviet nationality policy. Due to the disruption of the Civil War, the region was in the throes of an economic crisis, with livestock levels and sown field area well below their prerevolutionary levels. Kazakhs, who had seen their lands undergo intense peasant settlement during the last decades of the Russian empire, were particularly affected by this turmoil, and their animal herd numbers had plummeted. Not only did Moscow have to repair this agricultural crisis, a product both of the Civil War and intense peasant settlement under Russian imperial rule, but it had to develop an agricultural policy suited for the steppe's mixture of animal husbandry, practiced by nomadic Kazakhs, and settled agriculture, practiced by the peasants who had settled the Kazakh steppe during the last decades of Russian imperial rule.

Moscow also faced the question of how to put its avowedly anti-imperial nationality policy, which aimed to support and promote certain non-Russian groups, into practice. Several considerations had led to the development of Moscow's nationality policy. World War I was a critical moment in the spread and development of nationalism, as empires broke apart and activists wielded the language of national rights. During the Civil War, the Bolsheviks had utilized the language of nationality to distinguish themselves from the Whites and win over non-Russian groups. Vladimir Lenin argued that the Bolsheviks would right the wrongs of their "colonial" predecessor, the Russian empire, placing non-Russian minorities on equal footing with Russians. Moreover, ideologically, Lenin and others believed that nationalism was a necessary stage, a phase that all groups had to pass through on their way to becoming socialist. If Kazakhs and other non-Russian groups were to become socialist, then it followed that Moscow had to "assist" these groups in first reaching and then passing through this historical stage.

With the national delimitation of Central Asia in 1924, Kazakhs and several other Central Asian "nations" would receive their own republics, and subsequent years would see efforts to develop national languages, cultures, and histories.[9] Members of these new nations were enlisted as active participants in this nation-making project. Under a program known as *korenizatsiia* (indigenization), Moscow sought to diversify the ranks of each republic's bureaucracy with large numbers of native cadres. But while Moscow sought to promote these new Soviet nations, it also sought to control them. Native elites deemed to be "bourgeois nationalists" could be attacked or expelled from the party. The "content" of national groups also had to fit within certain parameters. To advance on the Marxist-Leninist timeline of history, for instance, Soviet nations had to be economically "productive."[10] As part of this nation-making project, alternate forms of identity, such as clans or allegiances to a hereditary elite, would come under assault.

In 1920–21, Moscow began one of the first attempts to put its nationality policy into practice in the Kazakh steppe, initiating a series of reforms aimed at returning key land and water rights to Kazakhs and other native peoples who had seen their lands undergo intense Slavic settlement under Russian imperial rule.[11] In June 1920, the Politburo began the process of land reform, authorizing steps to address the "unequal relationship" between Slavic settlers and the native population in the Turkestan ASSR.[12] This reform would lead to the forced expulsion of more than thirty thousand Slavic settlers, the imposition of a ban on further Slavic settlement in the region, and efforts to redistribute these confiscated lands to Kazakh and Kyrgyz nomads.[13] In 1921, farther north in the steppe, separate decrees authorized the seizure of lands previously held by Ural and Siberian Cossacks in Semipalatinsk, Akmolinsk, Turgai, and Ural'sk provinces and awarded these lands to Kazakhs.

Through this program of *zemleustroistvo*, or land reorganization, planners sought to encourage Kazakhs to abandon nomadism for a settled way of life. As well, Moscow anticipated that a sweeping reorganization of land use patterns would eradicate the influence of "wealthy" clan leaders, giving the regime a further foothold in the region.[14] In practice, however, efforts at land reform did little to address these goals. A plenipotentiary assigned to oversee land apportionment work in Semipalatinsk province observed, "The specialists sitting in land apportionment bureaus thought about these decrees in their own ways; some even were determined not to carry them out."[15] Meanwhile, he noted, Kazakhs, peasants, and samovol'tsy (illegal settlers), hearing rumors of the coming reforms, quickly moved to seize good lands before the state could redistribute them. Despite a ban on further colonization of the Kazakh steppe, tens of thousands of samovol'tsy continued to arrive, and officials with Kaznarkomzem struggled to halt the flow of illegal settlers.

There were even more severe problems in Dzhetisu (Semirech'e) province in the Turkestan ASSR, a fertile region that had been the focus of intense peasant settlement and frequent outbreaks of ethnic conflict under Russian imperial rule, most notably during the 1916 revolt. In Dzhetisu, attempts to seize settlers' lands aggravated existing ethnic tensions, and violence between nomads and Slavic settlers erupted. In 1924, the All-Russian Central Executive Committee (VTsIK) in Moscow created a committee to regulate land reform in Russian Turkestan. Due to the severity of ethnic conflict in the region, the committee began to investigate the possibility of forming four Slavic *okrugi* composed of Russian and Ukrainian settlers within Kazakhstan and placing these Slavic okrugi under the direct control of Moscow, rather than subordinating them to Kazakhstan.[16]

Though the plan to create Slavic okrugi was later abandoned, Dzhetisu's economy was in ruins after the land reforms. From 1915 to 1920, the sown field area for Dzhetisu fell by more than 50 percent and livestock numbers declined by 70 percent. Both of these precipitous declines continued in 1921.[17] Mikhail Serafimov, the head of this Moscow-based committee, blamed these shortfalls on Kazakhs' failure to adopt settled life, rather than the reforms themselves: "Arable land, taken from the peasants and given to the native population, is empty, weeds are growing, as the native population is not used to agriculture and with their primitive methods they cannot farm a field of any significance."[18] A later report by Kazakhstan's Party Committee cited "immense mistakes" in the execution of the land reforms in Dzhetisu and noted that prices for grain in the region skyrocketed due to the reforms. Though Dzhetisu had previously been a grain surplus region, it now could not even feed its own population.[19]

These failed land reform efforts were an early indication of the difficulties that Moscow would encounter in transforming this multiethnic region. They exposed clear tensions between the objectives of Soviet nationality policy and Soviet agricultural policy. Efforts to return lands to Kazakhs and address the wrongs of Russian imperial rule had served to deepen the region's economic crisis and aggravate ethnic conflict between Kazakhs and Slavic settlers. Moreover, efforts at land reform had not transformed Kazakhs in the manner that Moscow had originally hoped. Rather than abandoning nomadism for settled life, many Kazakhs had rented out the lands that they had been given to Slavic settlers, a long-standing practice by nomads during the Russian imperial era. Far from eradicating clans, a key feature of nomadic life, the land reform had appeared to have strengthened them.[20]

"The Sovietization of the Kazakh Aul"

In 1925, Goloshchekin, the republic's party secretary and leader, arrived in the republic's capital, Kzyl-Orda (Red Horde), a small frontier town of about twenty thousand people located in the southwest of the steppe, on the Orenburg-Tashkent railway line.[21] The appointment of a figure of Goloshchekin's stature was a sign of Moscow's increasing focus on Kazakhstan given the potential role that this immense, sparsely populated republic could play in supplying an emerging Union-wide economic system. But it was also an indication of just how daunting Moscow considered this prospect to be: as the struggles over land reform had illustrated, there were challenges to implementing Soviet nationality policy in a republic with a recent history of intense Slavic peasant settlement, as efforts to promote Kazakhs invariably inflamed ethnic tensions. Moreover, the 1920–21 land reforms had highlighted that Moscow's hold over the region was tenuous at best.

Goloshchekin's arrival in Kzyl-Orda was an event for those who worked there. A Ukrainian, Mikhail Riadnin, who would work closely with Goloshchekin as his personal secretary, remembered, "We only knew a little bit about F. I. Goloshchekin then, but that which we knew instilled in us a special respect for him." They had heard, he continued, of Goloshchekin's participation in the 1905 revolution, his relationship with famous revolutionaries such as Yakov Sverdlov and Stalin, and his role in the death of Tsar Nicholas II and his family. Of Goloshchekin himself, Riadnin observed: "He was a rather strongly built gray-haired man of about fifty, lively and unusually active; his blue, expressive eyes seemed to follow everything and observe everything. While thinking, he would stroke his pointed beard with his left hand from time to time."[22]

When he arrived in Kzyl-Orda, Goloshchekin came with an impressive resume of revolutionary credentials. He had joined the Russian Social Democratic Labor

Party (RSDLP) in 1903. During the split of the RSDLP, he sided with the Bolsheviks, signing up when they were a tiny underground organization with pipe dreams of revolution. Following the Bolsheviks' dramatic seizure of power in October 1917, the party's rank and file grew dramatically, as opportunists and idealists alike joined up. Old Bolsheviks, or those with prerevolutionary ties such as Goloshchekin, became a tiny group within the party, but they were widely revered for their early commitment to the revolutionary cause.

Goloshchekin had completed a degree in dentistry but left this profession to join the Bolsheviks in 1903. He had a colorful early career as a revolutionary: he participated in the revolution of 1905, and in 1909, he was arrested and exiled to Narymsk krai (territory). Goloshchekin fled his place of exile, returning to Moscow. In January 1912, Goloshchekin traveled abroad to the Prague Party Conference, where he was named to the Central Committee of the Bolshevik Party. On his return to Russia, he was again arrested and exiled, this time to Tobol'sk guberniia. Again, in 1913, he managed to escape his imprisonment. He was then arrested and exiled a third time, this time to Turukhansk territory, whereupon good fortune smiled upon him: in February 1917, the Romanov dynasty fell, and Goloshchekin was released.

Goloshchekin's time in exile strengthened his connections to radical circles. He was exiled to Narymsk with several other Bolsheviks, including Sverdlov and Berta Perel'man. Goloshchekin fell in love with Perel'man, a seamstress who, like Goloshchekin, had joined the Bolsheviks in 1903. They married, remaining together until Perel'man's death in 1918.[23] Goloshchekin also became close friends with Sverdlov, who would become one of the leading architects of the Bolsheviks' surprising seizure of power in October 1917. But it was during the Civil War that Goloshchekin would cement his legacy within the party: in June 1918, Lenin ordered the killing of Tsar Nicholas II and his family. Goloshchekin, then commissar of the Urals military district, traveled to Moscow to collect their death warrants. Goloshchekin returned to Yekaterinburg, where he, Sverdlov and others are rumored to have been in the small circle of party cadres who carried out Lenin's orders to execute the tsar and his family.[24] After the end of the Civil War, Goloshchekin continued to serve in a number of important roles for the party, becoming a member of the party commission charged with overseeing Turkestan (1919–21) and chairman of the Samara regional soviet (1922–25).

Goloshchekin found his new posting a challenging one, and he highlighted these difficulties in a 1926 letter to Politburo member Vyacheslav Molotov in Moscow. He wrote that ethnic Kazakh "exploiters," known as *bai*, held the real power in the republic: "The soviets are fictitious. Real power is in the hands of the elders and the personal representatives of the soviet, who are the agents and protégés of the bai. The bai reigns and subjugates all down to the Communists in

FIGURE 2.1. Filipp Goloshchekin. Republic of Kazakhstan Central State Archive of Film, Photo, and Audio Documents, Image #2-91443.

the aul; by the way, the connections of the bai spread further to the regional-level party workers and even to the republic-level workers." Throughout the republic, there had been little attempt to enforce Soviet rule, Goloshchekin concluded, "Lawlessness, arbitrary rule (*proizvol*), bribery, theft, and concealment, especially in the southern regions, reign above all." The Russian sector of the population, except for its propensity for "chauvinism" toward the local Kazakh population, might be deemed no worse than in the Russian Soviet Federative Socialist Republic (RSFSR), he argued, although the situation was very different in the Kazakh nomadic encampment, the aul: "As a rule, there are no party workers. The aul Communist is technically and politically illiterate. Kazakhs are grouped by the clan principle and most of all listen to the bai and to the main group; no one educates them, no one organizes them."[25] In Goloshchekin's assessment, the party had barely penetrated nomadic life, and the socialist development of Kazakhs compared unfavorably with the republic's Russian minority.

At the republic's fifth party congress of republic officials, only months before this revealing confession to Molotov, Goloshchekin had unveiled new programs and slogans that aimed to transform Kazakhstan. Under a policy known as *ocherednost'*, Kazakhs, as the republic's titular nationality, would receive first priority in the distribution of land. Other nationalities would receive land according to when they had arrived in the steppe, with priority given to those who had arrived prior to 1918. In an effort to halt illegal colonization, settlers who arrived after 1925 would not be given land.[26] Famously declaring that "October passed by the aul" (*Oktiabr' minoval aul*), or that the republic's nomads had yet to even experience the October revolution Goloshchekin proclaimed "The Sovietization of the Aul!" (*Sovietizatsiia aula!*).[27] This campaign would focus on initiatives to insert the party into the very fabric of nomadic life. It provided for the creation of local-level institutions, such as soviets, police forces, and district courts, and the organization of auls into population points, which would be known as "administrative auls." It also authorized further ethnographic studies of the Kazakh aul, including investigations of land use patterns and clan relationships.

A major goal of the Sovietization of the Aul campaign was the elimination of "backwardness," which encompassed everything from the introduction of Western medical practices to efforts to reduce the influence of clans. At the republic's sixth party congress, Goloshchekin had argued that the party needed to bring spoons, knives, and forks to the aul, to which other party members added the need for pieces of soap, stools, and chairs.[28] Through measures such as land reform, the taxation of wealthy clan leaders and the introduction of laws punishing those who incited clan warfare, the party sought to weaken powerful clans. The campaign also called for efforts to assist the representatives of "weaker" clans.[29] Though the long-term goal remained the eradication of kinship, the

FIGURE 2.2.   Report of Goloshchekin at the Sixth All-Kazakh Congress of Soviets. The President's Archive of the Republic of Kazakhstan, f. 896, op. 1, d. 1609.

regime sought to regulate clans through this system of "tribal parity," bringing kinship allegiances more firmly under the party's control.[30]

Though some elements of the Sovietization of the Aul campaign, such as land reform, sought to weaken the social and economic basis of nomadic life, other facets of the campaign, paradoxically, worked with nomads' mobile way of life. Under Goloshchekin's leadership, the party developed so-called mobile schools (*shkoly-peredvizhki*), where teachers migrated seasonally with their pupils. The party also deployed Red Yurts and Red Caravans. While traveling with nomadic encampments, activists with these programs disseminated party propaganda and educated nomads in Western medical practices. They also worked with nomads to raise the productivity of livestock breeding. Statisticians, meanwhile, went to enormous efforts to count the republic's nomads and accurately represent their locations on a population map for the first time.

In its broad outlines, Kazakhstan's Sovietization of the Aul resembled the Face to the Village campaign that Moscow had launched among the peasantry in the RSFSR in 1924.[31] Through extending the watchful eye of the state into the countryside, Moscow sought to minimize the threat of rebellion and disorder that groups such as peasants or nomads posed. Through these intrusions, the regime also sought to gather information about the groups that it governed, and it sent ethnographers and agronomists out into the countryside to study them. A series of poor harvests had heightened anxieties about the food supply, and Moscow sought to assess how goods such as grain or meat might reliably be extracted from nomads or peasants.[32]

As part of the Sovietization of the Aul campaign, the 1920s saw a flurry of new studies of the Kazakh aul. Statisticians with the republic's central statistical department worked to develop a population map of the republic.[33] Ethnographers collected updated information on clan distributions and lineages.[34] During the winter of 1925–26, many of these same officials helped tally the first Soviet census. Some of the questions that these ethnographers sought to answer were not new—some of these experts, such as V. G. Sokolovskii, had worked on Russian imperial ethnographic studies of the Kazakh steppe—but officials now critiqued these studies as outdated. Nomadic life had changed dramatically during the revolutionary period, and the party now needed answers to a far broader array of questions.[35]

But these ethnographers confronted a problem: nomads did not readily adhere to the categories or units of analysis that these experts used when studying the sedentary world. They began to debate the utility of applying these categories to nomadic life, as well as how the various features of nomadic life might be fruitfully measured and translated into statistics in a way that would be intelligible to planners like Goloshchekin. To begin the redistribution of nomads' pasturelands, for instance, a key component of the Sovietization of the Aul, officials needed to understand how much land a nomad used. Similarly, ethnographers began to debate the issue of "optimum herd size," or exactly how many animals a given nomadic encampment needed to survive.

As these scholars discovered, none of these questions had clear answers. Nomads undertook migrations rather than settling on a specific tract of land that might be readily measured through conventional units, such as hectares. The size of nomads' herds might vary widely, depending on the type of land that they migrated across and the occurrence of disasters, such as drought or zhŭt. Finally, there was also wide variation in the composition of nomads' herds: some auls might pasture cattle and sheep, while others pastured camels. Scholars now sought to understand if auls should be given different allowances based on the types of animals that they pastured.[36] In most areas of the Soviet Union, scholars calculated, there was a roughly 1:1 ratio of cows to people. In Kazakhstan, however, that figure was 1.61 cows per person.[37] Did nomads really "need" all those animals? Could nomadic life be made more efficient?

V. G. Sokolovskii, the head of the republic's Central Statistical Department, began to critique the categories that his colleagues used to categorize Kazakhs, such as "nomadic," "semi-nomadic," or "settled." Nomadic life had changed dramatically during the preceding decades, he argued, and many Kazakhs' practices did not fit easily into one of these three categories. Though ethnographers relied on certain metrics to decide who was "settled" or who was "nomadic," such as the type of economic activity practiced (grain cultivation vs. animal herding) or the distance of seasonal migration, these metrics rarely reflected the intricacies of steppe lifestyles, he concluded. A "nomad" who raised cattle might migrate every summer to a pasture only five to ten versts away from his *zimovka*, or winter dwelling, whereas a "settled" farmer practicing grain cultivation might travel twenty-five to thirty versts each year to his summer pasture.[38]

Statisticians working to count the number of nomads in the republic for the first Soviet census also encountered methodological problems. In European Russia, statisticians had frequently relied on a technique known as "percent calculations," whereby census takers, rather than visiting every household, relied on local knowledge or the assertion by a regional official that, say, one hundred households lived within a given region. Statisticians working in Kazakhstan, however, alleged that this methodology—which they termed derisively a kind of "census by correspondence"—was too unreliable, given wide variation in the size of nomadic households and a propensity for clan leaders fearful of further taxation to understate the size of their communities. Instead, statisticians proposed the selection of a handful of representative regions in the republic, which would provide a basis for calculating the republic's overall population.[39]

These statisticians proposed to use this information to create the republic's first comprehensive population map. According to the head of Kazakhstan's statistical commission Sokolovskii, there were only two existing maps that encompassed the republic's territory and population: the first, a forty-verst army topographic map dated from the 1860s, while the second, a schematic forty-verst map had been drafted by the state planning agency (Gosplan). Neither took account of the tremendous population movement and settlement in the region during the revolutionary period.[40] More important, neither map gave any accounting of the location of the republic's nomads, an indictment that Sokolovskii leveled in dramatic fashion before a crowd of assembled top party officials in Kzyl-Orda. Displaying the most current map of the region of Kzyl-Orda to his audience, he noted that were it not for the railroad line and the capital city of Kzyl-Orda, onlookers would have the "full impression of a steppe without human life."[41]

In the map that Sokolovskii triumphantly displayed to his audience, some 80 percent of the region's population was missing. The region's population appeared to be exclusively settled and overwhelmingly from European Russia. But in reality, Sokolovskii interjected, some fifteen to twenty thousand Kazakh households resided in the province of Kzyl-Orda, far outnumbering the population of the town by the same name. The total and utter absence of the republic's Kazakh population from maps was compounded by the fact that officials had no names for auls or groupings of auls, as they did for traditionally recognized units of settlement, such as towns and villages. To remedy this situation, Sokolovskii and other statisticians detailed plans to research and assemble a new ten-verst map, which would include the republic's nomadic populations on a map for the very first time.

The difficulty in mapping nomadic populations, Sokolovskii charged, came from combining understandings of nomadism with Western ethnographic methods for defining a population point (*naselennyi punkt*).[42] Within the district of Kzyl-Orda, there were 158 "administrative auls," a category of administration that was neither a small town (*poselok*) nor what ethnographers might define as a true "population point." Rather, an "administrative aul" consisted of several different auls located apart from one another; the radius, as well as location, of a particular "administrative aul" was dependent on seasonal patterns of nomadic migration. In the absence of names, Soviet officials referred to administrative auls as well as auls numerically—for example, aul no. 1, located in administrative aul no. 2 of such-and-such district (*raion*). Eight, ten, or even fifty auls might make up an "administrative aul," while an individual aul might have, on average, five to fifteen households, each of which had a movable yurt or semi-permanent winter dwelling. Each aul (sometimes referred to by party planners as a *khozaul*) was deemed to constitute a population point, although even within an aul the distance between individual yurts might be as much as five to ten kilometers.

On the ground, the regime struggled mightily to implement elements of the Sovietization of the Aul campaign. Many of its components, such as the organization of aul soviets, or councils, were difficult to implement in a mobile, dispersed population. Among the peasantry, village soviets were supposed to serve as the crux of local-level party activism. In addition to fulfilling critical administrative functions for the party—the chairman of a village soviet frequently assisted in the collection of state grain or meat procurements, for instance—they also served to channel enthusiasm and educate new recruits about the party. But in an aul soviet, party members might pasture many kilometers apart across a howling expanse of wind and snow. Several kilometers might separate households even within a particular aul, and these auls might be located many more kilometers from the administrative aul center, where the soviet would be held. Thus, simply spreading information about the party, let alone assembling an aul soviet was a difficult prospect.[43]

Activists soon found that the geographic distances that separated communities within a given administrative aul were not the only barriers to the formation of aul soviets. Communication, both among far-flung aul soviet members and with regional and central-level officials, presented a challenge. Earnest republic-level activists studied how to improve party communication with aul soviets, yet central expectations for technical development in the aul often hovered on the absurd. Questionnaires sent out to aul soviets (How many radios do you have in the aul?), were returned in some cases with an entirely unexpected answer: "With regard to the question of radios, we don't have those sorts of people in the aul!"[44]

Activists with the Red Yurt program encountered many obstacles. Few of them spoke Kazakh, while only a handful of aul members spoke Russian. One female activist from Moscow wrote of her disillusionment with the Red Yurt program, citing the republic's vast distances: "In the severe cold of winter, during these winters, to go across the barren steppe on foot for twenty to thirty versts is completely impossible. And by the way, at five versts, not everyone will venture to come. Winter then ended, spring came, and we again advertised the day of the delegates' meeting and again no one came."[45] She concluded that the party was "largely without strength" among the Kazakh nomads.[46] Strategies for activism in the RSFSR proved largely useless in the steppe, she concluded, and work among the nomads called for very different tactics and knowledge: "All the Kazakhs are so backward and uneducated that in this entire valley you will find only two to three literate people. Almost no one among them reads a newspaper, they have a very weak impression of the real face of Soviet power—but there is this—they have heard of Lenin."[47]

In 1926, at a closed session of the republic's party committee, officials discussed the difficulties that they had encountered in their efforts to sovietize the aul. One speaker noted, "The pre-election campaign showed that there was no party influence at the moment of the elections in any aul or in any Kazakh canton." The attempt to organize elections to the Communist Party, he concluded, revealed that "bais and kulaks" were far better organized than the party's own workers.[48] Efforts to redistribute nomads' pasturelands had also been problematic: activists had debated how they should measure the parcels of land (using the steps of a person or a horse or a piece of string?) and how to account for variations in land quality. Frequently, activists returned the next spring only to find that nomadic land use patterns had reverted to what they were prior to the redistribution, and the same clans retained control of the land.[49]

The failures of the Sovietization of the Aul campaign highlighted the difficulties that the party faced in penetrating the fabric of nomadic life. The party had tried to encourage nomadic settlement by offering tax reductions to those Kazakhs who settled, but few adopted settled life. These categories, "settled" and "nomadic," were themselves ambiguous, and party members themselves could not agree on what settled Kazakh life should look like.[50] The land redistribution campaign had not eliminated the influence of clans. By contrast, it appeared to have strengthened them. At the 1926 meeting of the republic's party committee, Goloshchekin expressed frustration with the results of the campaign. He warned that the party needed to take further steps to undermine the economic basis of kinship: "Unless we get rid of the economic conditions of these clans, then these clans have their own interests . . . which will reveal themselves in some way."[51]

The Future of Nomadism

During the first few years of Soviet rule, most experts associated with Kaznar-komzem maintained that nomadism was the best way of making use of arid regions of Kazakhstan. Like its parent institution, the RSFSR Narkomzem, the members of Kaznarkomzem tended to have "suspicious" prerevolutionary ties. With the Bolshevik seizure of power in October 1917 and the development of a one-party state, state institutions such as RSFSR Narkomzem and Kazakhstan's Narkomzem became arenas where these specialists, now exiled from influential party posts, could influence agrarian policy. Faced with a severe shortage of edu-cated personnel in their first years after taking power, the Bolsheviks were forced to rely on the expertise of these specialists even though they tended to see them as untrustworthy and "bourgeois."[52]

Within Kaznarkomzem, the economist and ethnographer Sergei Shvetsov became one of the leading proponents of the preservation of nomadism. Shvetsov had a long revolutionary pedigree: a former populist and zemstvo worker, he had been arrested and exiled to Siberia in 1878 for his involvement in revolutionary movements. Sometime after his release, he joined the Socialist Revolutionaries (SRs). After the October revolution, Shvetsov, by then a member of the Right SRs, or anti-Bolshevik faction of the SRs, had tried to call the first meeting of the Constituent Assembly to order in 1918, but he was pushed away from the podium by Bolsheviks and Left SRs.[53] Shvetsov soon left politics for scientific work, and he became one of the leading experts on the Kazakh steppe, heading a major scientific expedition to study the Kazakh aul in 1926.

In his major work, *The Kazakh Economy in Its Natural-Historical and Everyday Conditions,* published by Kaznarkomzem in 1926, Shvetsov argued that nomad-ism was just as advanced as settled agriculture: "The contemporary Kazakh econ-omy should be seen as the most adaptable to the surrounding nature, as the most productive under the current conditions."[54] Rather than seeking to eliminate nomadism, the party should work to make it more productive, he contended. Offering an eerily prescient warning, he noted, "The destruction of the nomadic way of life in Kazakhstan would represent not only the death of steppe livestock raising and the Kazakh economy but the transformation of the dry steppe into an unpopulated desert."[55]

Shvetsov and other experts grouped around Kaznarkomzem critiqued the idea that the far-reaching changes to nomadic life that had occurred under Russian imperial rule were part of a "natural" historical process, as nomadism "evolved" into settled agriculture. The scholar Evgenii Shemiot-Polochanskii challenged those who saw these changes, including a trend toward settlement and the emergence of markets, as the beginning of "class differentiation" among Kazakh nomads. What these specialists observed, he charged, was not class differentiation but rather the "degradation" of Kazakh households, as destitute nomads were forced to settle after colonists had seized their lands: "In those places where sedentarization has taken place, the poor [*bedniaki*] have not improved their position and the productive power of the country has not grown from this."[56] The party, he argued, needed to focus its efforts on repairing the wrongs of Russian imperial rule by building up animal husbandry, a practice that he deemed to be the best use of the republic's landscape.[57]

These scholars offered several suggestions as to how the party might assist nomads. The huge herd losses that nomads regularly incurred during zhŭts and droughts were of particular concern, and some experts proposed that the party take preventive measures, such as the organization of regional feed reserves.[58] Others suggested attempts to encourage nomads to move their winter pasture areas to more fertile lands or the construction of better winter dwellings for nomads and their livestock.[59] V. I. Skorospeshkin proposed introducing breeding programs to improve the quality of nomads' animal herds and deploying mobile units of veterinarians and zoologists who would migrate seasonally with nomadic encampments.[60] He staunchly defended the importance of livestock raising to Kazakhstan, "One can talk about strengthening this branch [livestock raising], about creating a durable feed base, one can talk about the reorganization of agriculture in the aul, but it is incorrect to pose the question of reducing the proportion of livestock raising in the aul and in the economy of Kazakhstan."[61]

In a 1928 article on livestock production in central Kazakhstan, another leading figure within Kaznarkomzem, the economic geographer A. A. Rybnikov noted that the dry climate of several US states, including Idaho, Wyoming, and Montana, was similar to the climate of central Kazakhstan.[62] Rybnikov, who had been active in populist movements in the prerevolutionary period and had been briefly arrested for "anti-Soviet activities" in 1922, noted that Americans had developed large-scale livestock ranches in these Midwestern states, and he suggested that these US ranches offered a useful model for the development of livestock production in Kazakhstan.[63] Through innovations such as the development of large-scale ranches, the regulation of seasonal pasture and water usage, the procurement of winter fodder for livestock, as well as the construction of winter stables, he argued, Americans had increased and stabilized livestock production in a dry, cold climate. These techniques, he contended, made the practice of animal husbandry in the United States far less susceptible to the effects of droughts or cold snaps, phenomena that continued to provoke sharp fluctuations in livestock levels in Kazakhstan.[64]

Others, such as M. G. Sirius, in a 1928 article "On the Question of a More Rational Direction of Agriculture in Northern Kazakhstan," used the example of the United States to warn of the dangers of extending the agrarian frontier farther south into the steppe.[65] The climate of the American Midwest resembled that of Kazakhstan, he contended. But he noted that farmers in the United States had battled a devastating series of droughts in recent years, and efforts to develop farming in these drylands had been much more costly and far less successful than American planners had originally anticipated. Sirius critiqued those who claimed that there was an enormous amount of free land suitable for agriculture in Kazakhstan: "one cannot speak or dream of colossal reserves of free, virgin land which is ideally suited for growing wheat. This is a completely unrealistic dream. The natural-historical conditions of the economy of northern Kazakhstan are so severe, that without an intense fight, without detailed study of every dot of land, it is completely inadvisable to develop new land for farming households."[66]

Resuming a debate that had preoccupied members of the Kazakh intelligentsia during the last decades of Russian imperial rule, leading figures within Kazakh society also began to consider the future of nomadism.[67] In a 1919 article, "The Kirgiz [Kazakhs] and Revolution," Akhmet Baytŭrsïnov, who would become the head of the republic's Commissariat of Education, took an aggressive stance against those who would portray the Kazakh aul as backward. Kazakhs had no need to build communism, he argued. Due to the lack of class differentiation or private property in the Kazakh nomadic encampment, he maintained, Kazakhs already practiced their "own distinctive form of communism" within the aul.[68]

Other Kazakhs offered different perspectives. In a speech before the first congress of the republic's teachers, Smaghŭl Säduaqasov, a young Kazakh from Akmolinsk province with links to several former Alash Orda members including Baytŭrsïnov, argued that the sedentarization of the Kazakhs was ultimately the correct course. But he cautioned against carrying out nomadic settlement quickly, arguing that the process should take several decades. Settlement, he proposed, should begin in the republic's north, where conditions for settled agriculture were more favorable, before gradually proceeding to the republic's south. In these settlements, Kazakhs, he argued, could continue to practice animal husbandry, and Säduaqasov hastened to correct the idea that only agriculture could be linked to a cultured way of life.[69]

But by 1927, the tenor of the discussions surrounding pastoral nomadism began to shift. After a few years of initial success, NEP had begun to show signs of weakness. Livestock production had begun to decline, and grain production remained below its prewar levels, despite 2–3 percent annual growth in the Soviet Union's population.[70] Additionally, there were two developments specific to Kazakhstan that had renewed debates about nomadism's future. The first was the beginning of construction of the Turkestan-Siberia (Turksib) railroad in December 1926. Previously, the only direct rail linkage between Central Asia and Russia had been the Orenburg-Tashkent railway line, which cut through the western edge of the Kazakh steppe. Other cities within Kazakhstan were disconnected both from the RSFSR and from points farther south in Central Asia. Alternate methods of transportation were arduous: the 1,400-kilometer trip between Semipalatinsk, a city in Kazakhstan's northeastern corner, and Frunze in Kirgizia could take up to seventy days by camel caravan.[71] The republic had few dirt roads or cars, and, during the spring mud and winter snow, these roads could quickly become impassable, a condition known as *bezdorozh'e*.

Moscow heralded the construction of the Turksib railroad as a way of alleviating the regime's dependency on foreign cotton. Once completed, the railroad would link the cotton-growing regions of southern Central Asia to markets in Russia and abroad. It would also cheaply transport grain from agricultural regions in Siberia and northern Kazakhstan to the cotton-growing regions of southern Central Asia.[72] But the prospect of connecting this once-distant region to other markets raised the question of what goods other parts of the steppe should produce and how these products might be reliably extracted by rail. As Goloshchekin himself noted in a letter to Gleb Krzhizhanovskii, the head of Gosplan: "The republic's potential in the area of natural resources and agriculture has now captured the attention of all the [Soviet] Union's organs, as they decide the importance of agricultural tasks."[73]

The second major development, which was interconnected with the first, was a revival of the question of peasant settlement. In 1927, VTsIK formed another commission, with the backing of the Central Committee, to examine land politics in the Kazakh steppe. This committee was charged with investigating the question of peasant settlement, the setting of "land norms," or how much land particular households would receive, and the issue of ocherednost', or Kazakh priority in acquiring land. The All-Union Resettlement Committee had proposed reopening settlement in Kustanai okrug and four gubernii (Ural'sk, Aktiubinsk, Akmolinsk, and Semipalatinsk), as well as southern regions close to the Turksib, then already under construction. Through peasant settlement, the committee predicted that the sown field area would more than double in farming areas of the republic and increase sixteenfold in "semifarming" (*poluzemledel'cheskie*) regions.[74]

Increasingly, officials began to frame settled agriculture as more productive than pastoral nomadism. In a 1927 speech before Zemplan (the planning division of the RSFSR Commissariat of Agriculture), the agronomist and economist A. N. Chelintsev declared, "It must be said that there is a colossal underutilization of natural resources in Kazakhstan, which is the result of a deficit of human energy [*vsledstvie nedostatka chelovecheskoi energii*]." An influx of settlers to Kazakhstan, he concluded, would dramatically increase the republic's productivity.[75] Chelintsev allowed that nomadism was the most effective use of the landscape in those areas that received less than two hundred millimeters of annual rainfall, but he argued that free land for settlers could be found in other regions of the republic, such as Ural'sk province.[76] By 1928, under pressure from this VTsIK commission, Kazakhstan voted to repeal both ocherednost' and the previous ban on immigration.[77]

In an atmosphere of tightening ideological correctness, the non-Bolshevik background of many of the experts and members of the Kazakh intelligentsia who had supported pastoral nomadism made their ideas more vulnerable. At the republic's sixth party congress in 1927, those experts who had been in favor of developing nomadism, such as Shvetsov, Rybnikov, and Sirius, were thrown out of the republic's Commissariat of Agriculture and accused of allying with Kazakh "nationalists," such as Baytŭrsïnov, who had been expelled from the party in 1921.[78] When Sirius's article was published in the republic's main agricultural journal *Narodnoe khoziaistvo Kazakstana* in 1928, the editors included a note critiquing Sirius for "ignoring the clear and concrete directives of the party." They argued that future agricultural development in Kazakhstan should adhere to three principles: "(1) the progressive transition from a livestock-raising economy toward a more intensive form; (2) the vigorous development of the grain economy; [and] (3) the incorporation of technical culture [cotton]."[79] Though this note did not call explicitly for the elimination of pastoral nomadism, it hinted at it, and it signaled a shift away from a focus on livestock rearing toward a focus on grain production.

Rybnikov, Shvetsov, Sirius, and other specialists who had advocated for the preservation of nomadism were now denounced for their "capitalist" approach to agriculture, and they were linked to the "bourgeois" policies of leading RSFSR Narkomzem experts such as Alexander Chaianov and Nikolai Kondrat'ev.[80] Chelintsev was also arrested and linked to a fictitious counterrevolutionary party.[81] Though Shvetsov appears to have died of natural causes in 1930, Rybnikov and Chaianov became defendants in an elaborate show trial that took place in Moscow in the winter of 1930. After "confessing" to anti-Soviet activities, Rybnikov suffered a nervous collapse while in prison. He was eventually freed, but then was arrested again in 1937 and shot in 1938.[82] After being expelled from the party,

Baytŭrsïnov was tracked closely by the Soviet secret police—the authors of one secret police report described him as like a "mosquito," biting the consciousness of the Kazakh people—and identified as one of the "leaders" of the Kazakh bais.[83] In 1929, he was arrested along with several other Alash Orda members before eventually being released. In 1937, he was also shot during the purges.[84] We will return to the story of Säduaqasov in the next chapter, but he, too, would eventually be jettisoned for his non-Bolshevik connections and "antiparty" views.

By 1930, Kaznarkomzem had been transformed by the expulsion of many of its leading members. An all-Union Narkomzem commission devoted to the question of livestock raising in Kazakhstan now found it to be one of the most backward areas of Kazakhstan's economy. The committee critiqued nomadism for its "primitive methods," its vulnerability to disasters, such as droughts, zhŭts, and epidemics, as well as its "entirely unorganized feed base and feed supply." The committee concluded that "it [nomadism] is an unstable branch of the economy, which fluctuates dramatically in size and has a low quality of production."[85] Other scholars reached similar conclusions, declaring zhŭt to be a "fundamental attribute of the nomadic economy," and they critiqued nomads for their failure to prepare feed reserves for their livestock during the winter.[86]

As the tide began to turn against nomadism, experts scrambled to produce ideologically correct studies, which would provide the "scientific" backing necessary for the party's assault on nomadism. A 1930 study, "Reasons for the Organization of the Settlement of Kazakh Nomadic and Semi-Nomadic Households," developed for the republic's Central State Executive Committee, explicitly compared the profitability (*dokhodnost'*) of Russian and Kazakh households, finding that Kazakhs produced less profit from one hectare of land than Russians did.[87] Another study produced in 1930 for the republic's state executive committee divided Russian and Kazakh households into three groups, according to the cost of the materials that these groups used for their work (*sredstva proizvodstva*). In every category, the study found that a Kazakh household was less productive than a Russian household.[88] Neither of these studies indicated how the authors calculated the metrics, such as gross output (*valovaia produktsia*) and profitability, but they illustrate how nomadic life was increasingly becoming framed as economically unproductive.

Experts now belittled the assertion that the environment might place certain limits on human activity. They announced a battle to reclaim the desert. Declaring a "fight for the agricultural development of millions of hectares of desert and semiarid land," these scholars critiqued earlier assertions that regions with an annual rainfall under 250 millimeters would be incapable of supporting settled agriculture.[89] Under socialism, I. A. Zveriakov argued, swamps might be emptied, entire deserts irrigated, and even the lowest-quality soil brought under cultivation. The ability of a specifically socialist state to conquer the environment demonstrates what little regard "contemporary man has for the 'unconquerable' powers of nature," he concluded.[90]

Scholars now declared nomadism to be a culturally backward way of life, one incompatible with Kazakhs' transformation into a Soviet nation. The ethnographer Aleksandr Donich proclaimed, "The debate is not about whether the nomadic economy is backward or not backward according to natural-historical conditions, and it is also not about how long the nomadic economy will continue to exist, nor is it even about how the nomadic economy should evolve according to our wishes, rather it is that the adaptation of contemporary culture to nomadism cannot be done." Donich declared a mobile way of life to be incompatible with the development of various features of "contemporary culture," such as schools, libraries, museums, telephones, telegraphs, electrification, a postal service, and the development of industry. If the party wanted to modernize Kazakhstan, he concluded, the Kazakhs would need to be settled.[91]

Experts began a rereading of Kazakh history, analyzing how pastoral nomadism might fit into a Marxist-Leninist understanding of the world. For Soviet scholars, existing Marxist-Leninist theory provided little guidance on how revolution might occur among pastoral nomads. Karl Marx had originally proposed that revolution might occur in industrial societies, and Lenin, radically modifying many of Marx's ideas, had argued that revolution could occur among another more "backward" social group, Russia's peasantry. But neither Marx nor Lenin had given any indication about how and if a socialist-style revolution might proceed among an entirely different social group, pastoral nomads, and applying the tenets of Marxist-Leninist theory to pastoral nomads involved yet another radical modification of Marx's original ideas.

Now party experts scrutinized Kazakhs through the lens of Marxist-Leninist theory, and they debated where nomads might fit into an eschatological timeline (primitive communism, slave-owning society, feudalism, capitalism, socialism) developed for use with settled societies. In this atmosphere of increased ideological correctness, this categorization of Kazakhs, whether it be "capitalist," "feudal," or something else, was crucial information. Only once Soviet experts had "correctly" identified pastoral nomads' proper Marxist developmental state could they identify the types of programs needed to modernize them, as well as the speed at which these programs might be implemented.

While much earlier ethnographic work on the Kazakh steppe had seen nomadism as a kind of primitive social order, a society without classes, experts now began to claim that Kazakh nomads might be labeled as "patriarchal-feudal," a kind of intermediary state between a kin-based patriarchal society and a feudal society.[92] In an early stage of development, clan-based societies such as the

Kazakhs might well exist without distinction between rich or poor, but in the last phase of a clan system, clan-based conflict would increase and a society based on class distinctions would appear, these scholars maintained.

In "The Kazakh Colonial Aul" (Kazakhskii kolonial'nyi aul), Ghabbas Togh-zhanov argued that Kazakhs had entered feudalism during the fifteenth century, after the Mongol invasion and the domination of the Golden Horde had destroyed the foundations of a previous clan society without classes. Toghzhanov, a Kazakh philologist who had studied in Moscow at the Institute for the National Economy named after Georgii Plekhanov, noted that feudalism among nomads was quite different from feudalism in Europe.[93] Toghzhanov described the dominance of "feudal sultans," a largely hereditary group, and "feudal clan leaders" among the Kazakhs. Moreover, he concluded, feudalism among nomads was largely based on a monopoly of cattle rather than a monopoly of land. Toghzhanov's findings were a key conclusion, as they provided an ideologically acceptable explanation for why efforts at land reform had failed to break up the influence of various Kazakh clans. This was the type of "answer" that Goloshchekin had sought: to break up the influence of powerful clans, the party needed to strip "wealthy" nomads of their livestock rather than their land. This ideological justification would prove critical to the regime's campaign against rural elites in 1928.

Toghzhanov argued that the Russian conquest of the steppe in the nine-teenth century had substantially changed existing patterns of feudalism among the Kazakh nomads. Noting the growth of seasonal markets where nomads and settled populations traded and, particularly the arrival in the steppe of cattle, an animal previously foreign to nomadic existence, he suggested that capitalism had begun to penetrate feudal life and that Kazakhs had progressed to an intermedi-ate stage, which he deemed "patriarchal-feudal." Though Toghzhanov acknowl-edged that the advancement of the "patriarchal-feudal" stage varied regionally across the steppe, he cited evidence that even pastoralists that undertook long seasonal migrations, such as the Adai on the Mangyshlak Peninsula, engaged in practices that might classify them as capitalists, such as trading.[94]

Yet over the course of this intermediate stage of "patriarchal-feudalism," Toghzhanov concluded, "The Kazakh bai has for decades striven to represent his class interests as if they were the interests of his clan, lineage, or aul and through all methods and means convince the Kazakh working class that he is not an exploiter but a benefactor, a protector of the rights and interests of the entire clan."[95] Toghzhanov and others thus sought to identify the nomadic equivalent of processes deemed exploitative in settled societies: mutual aid practices among Kazakhs, for instance, were labeled as the nomadic parallel of *barshchina*, a system of coerced, unpaid labor among the peasantry.[96] Recalling Stalin's formulation of Soviet national cultures as "national in form, socialist in content," Toghzhanov declared Kazakh society to be "clan in form, class in content."[97] Kazakhs might evolve into a people who were "national in form" only through the destruction of clan-based forms of affiliation, he argued.

But if a class system had existed among the nomads since at least the fifteenth century, why had these populations not progressed farther along the Marxist trajectory of history? The answer, scholars concluded, was nomadism itself, which isolated Kazakhs and reinforced the exploitation of the bai.[98] Nomadic life inherently fostered clan-based relationships, which in turn, led to abusive figures such as the bai. The further socialist evolution of Kazakhs thus required a twofold process: first, the removal of the bai; and second, the settlement of the republic's entire nomadic population. Labeling sedentarization the "sharpest weapon in the class war in Kazakhstan," scholars pushed for an acceleration of party-sponsored efforts to settle the Kazakh nomads, predicting that settlement would help fracture the "petty bourgeois" consciousness of Kazakhs and result "in the death of bais as a class."[99]

Can you get to socialism by camel? This was the question that Goloshchekin, Kazakh cadres, ethnographers, and agronomists considered in the period 1921–28. They weighed how and whether nomadism might fit into socialist-style modernity. At issue were the region's particular environmental profile and the future direction of Soviet nationality and agricultural policies. The seeming foreignness of nomadic life came to invite and demand input and interpretation from a wide array of actors. This was a landscape and a population that did not have clear parallels in the Marxist-Leninist categories that the party imported from European Russia.

Initially, the party pursued a contradictory approach to nomadic life in Kazakhstan. Some programs, such as efforts at land reform, aimed to weaken the economic basis of nomadic life, while other initiatives, such as mobile veterinary programs, sought to engage pastoral nomads and strengthen their practice of animal husbandry. At the level of policy, most experts within Kaznarkomzem maintained that pastoral nomadism was the best use of the republic's landscape, while some Kazakh cadres, such as Baytŭrsïnov, critiqued the idea that nomadism was backwards, arguing that Kazakhs already practiced their own distinctive form of communism in the aul. Like its predecessor, the Russian empire, the new Soviet state struggled to transform nomadic life in the manner that it wished, and Kazakhs made various adaptations, including the rental of their pasturelands, to maintain their nomadic way of life.

But as NEP began to disintegrate across the Soviet Union, those experts who had argued for rapid, rather than gradual, industrialization, began to gain the upper hand. Various features of Kazakhs' practice of pastoralism, including its distance from markets and the inevitable fluctuation in animal numbers, were in tension with plans for rapid industrialization. The idea that pastoral nomadism should be supported and intensified under socialism began to lose favor. The non-Bolshevik background of many of the experts who had originally promoted pastoral nomadism made their ideas doubly vulnerable, and they were thrown out of Kaznarkomzem and denounced as bourgeois. Baytŭrsïnov was expelled from the party and later arrested. In a pattern that would continue during the coming confiscation campaign and through collectivization, policy makers and other experts appropriated the language of Soviet nation making to back up and reinforce the regime's economic objectives: nomadism was declared a backward way of life, something incompatible with Kazakhs' development into a socialist nation. In 1928, the regime launched a campaign against rural elites in Kazakhstan and several other nomadic regions, marking the beginning of the party's assault on nomadic life.

But this period of fluidity in the 1920s does reveal that Moscow received clear warnings about the environmental challenges of the steppe: before they were expelled from Kaznarkomzem, Shvetsov and others clearly articulated the risks of nomadic settlement in this drought-prone region. Contemporary Kazakhstani scholars have argued that the regime's failure to account for the environment was one of the primary reasons for the Kazakh famine.[100] But given Shvetsov's and others' warnings, as well as the broader history of the Russian empire's troubled efforts to make the steppe into an agrarian region, which saw agricultural settlers endure ruinous droughts, frosts, and hunger, it seems clear that Moscow's approach to developing the steppe was more than just a failure to account for environmental factors. As the chapters that follow will show, Stalin and others on the Central Committee accepted the risk of catastrophe, knowing that Kazakhs might pay the heaviest price.

KAZAKHSTAN'S "LITTLE OCTOBER"
The Campaign against Kazakh Elites, 1928

In 1928, a group of twenty-six Kazakhs living in Semipalatinsk province sent an urgent telegram to Stalin. They wrote that their district, once a major livestock-raising area, had become an empty desert devoid of animals: "the growth and further management of our [nomadic] economy has become impossible," they concluded, noting that the devastation of their herds was a "source of unending hardship and suffering."[1] As the sorrow of these families suggests, every aspect of Kazakhs' lives as pastoral nomads changed as animal numbers plummeted in 1928. For Kazakhs, animals were an important source of food and a crucial means of transportation, used to ferry goods and people across the steppe. They relied heavily on animal products in the course of their seasonal migrations, using sheep's wool to form the felt sides of yurts, sheepskin to make heavy winter coats to withstand the steppe's bitter winters, and animal dung to fuel cooking fires. The exchange of animals was crucial to numerous social customs in Kazakh society, such as the payment of fines to another clan, the formation of political alliances between clans, and the payment of a "bride price" (qalïm), made by the groom to the bride's family before marriage.[2]

In Kazakhstan, 1928 was known as the year of the Little October. That fall, the party launched the bai confiscation campaign, a program to appropriate livestock and property from "wealthy" Kazakh elites who were supposedly exploiting their kin members. The campaign targeted seven hundred of the richest and most influential bais. These individuals and their families would be sent to distant regions of the republic or exiled from Kazakhstan altogether. The republic's party secretary, Filipp Goloshchekin, argued that the Kazakh aul, in contrast to the Russian village, had yet to experience the October 1917 revolution. This campaign would finally bring about a Little October, or an October-style revolution, expediting the process of class differentiation in the Kazakh aul and inserting the party into the very fabric of Kazakh life.[3]

The bai confiscation campaign was part of the party's war on "cultural backwardness," a project that had intensified across the Soviet Union by the late 1920s. This effort to transform culture had particular resonance in Central Asia, where everyday life and practices were very different from those in European Russia. [4] In its very design, the bai confiscation campaign was an assault on the cultural and economic foundations of nomadic life. It impoverished not only bais, the ostensible targets, but the many kin members who depended on their patronage and protection. With less livestock, it became far more difficult for Kazakhs to carry out their seasonal migrations, eat, find shelter, light fires, or make warm clothing. Even events such as marriage were fundamentally altered: Mukhamet Shayakhmetov, a famine survivor, recalls his sister Zhamba's fear and shame as she and her fiancée were forced to get married under the cover of darkness without a proper marriage ceremony or the payment of bride price.[5] Many of those named as bais belonged to the hereditary elite, and their expulsion from Kazakh communities led to a profound rearrangement of social hierarchies.

In the preceding decades, Kazakh nomads had endured massive peasant colonization of the steppe, civil war, famine, and the imposition of Soviet rule. These events had made Kazakhs more vulnerable to hunger: In early 1928, a report by the republic's party committee concluded that while agriculture had recovered from the devastation of the Civil War, production among nomadic households still remained 10–15 percent below prewar levels.[6] However, in all these cases, Kazakhs had found a way to adapt their pastoral nomadic practices to altered political, ecological, and social circumstances. But the bai confiscation campaign delivered a far more damaging blow to nomadic life, devastating herd numbers and ripping Kazakh society apart. By the end of 1928, Kazakhs' descent into hunger and, eventually, famine had begun.

Many historians have implied that Moscow's assaults on particular ethnic groups were carried out largely by outsiders, such as "Russians" or "officials sent from Moscow."[7] But as this chapter shows, the peculiarly destructive nature of the confiscation campaign was due to the fact that it was primarily carried out by *insiders*, rather than by outsiders.[8] In a strategy purposely designed to shatter old allegiances and sow violent conflict in the aul, Moscow empowered Kazakhs themselves to make some of the most crucial choices, such as who should be considered a bai and how much property to take from him. This design, which invested local bureaucrats and communities with considerable decision-making authority, would closely resemble later campaigns against the "kulak," or peasant class exploiter, elsewhere in the Soviet Union. Ultimately, the program would bring more than a thousand new Kazakh recruits into the bureaucracy, and it marked a massive escalation of the party's intrusion into Kazakh life. According to the new Kazakh leadership, in nine provinces of the republic, 3,488 meetings about the campaign were carried out, with a total of 290,796 participants.[9]

The decision to rely heavily on Kazakh involvement was born of both practical and ideological necessity. On a practical level, the regime simply did not have the resources to transform this vast territory without considerable assistance from locals, a point that the failures of the earlier Sovietization of the Aul campaign had underscored. Moscow needed information that only Kazakhs could provide, such as who was a member of the hereditary elite and who was not. The assertion that Moscow relied primarily on "outsiders" to carry out attacks against Kazakhs rests in part on the assumption that the regime had a fully formed party-state apparatus in the republic, a claim that the archival record for Kazakhstan in the 1920s simply does not bear out.

On an ideological level, Soviet nation making, or Kazakhs' transformation into a "modern" Soviet nation, was supposed to be participatory. Not only was Kazakh participation crucial to such tasks as the standardization of a national language or the creation of a national culture, but it was essential to moments of profound socioeconomic "national" transformation, such as the bai confiscation campaign. Only by mobilizing Kazakhs, rather than making them into passive agents of their transformation, could Moscow move Kazakhs forward into socialist-style modernity. As the extreme brutality of the confiscation campaign illustrates, the use of terror against national groups did not necessarily signal a turn away from the regime's nation-making policy. Rather, terror could serve as a way of consolidating national groups: through the confiscation campaign, Moscow sought both to eliminate potential "enemies" in Kazakh society and to engage other Kazakhs more fully in the project of socialist construction.[10]

The bai confiscation campaign did fulfill elements of the regime's "nation-building" objectives. It brought large numbers of native cadres into the lower-level bureaucracy. The campaign forced Kazakhs to engage with the regime's terminology, and they began to wield class categories imported from European Russia, such as *bedniak* (a poor peasant) and *seredniak* (a peasant of modest means). But at the same time, the campaign did not succeed in transforming Kazakh society entirely in the manner that Moscow wished. Many native cadres used the considerable flexibility given to them by the regime to manipulate the campaign in accordance with their own interests. On hearing rumors of the impending confiscation campaign, some Kazakhs slaughtered their livestock herds or sold their animals to prevent them from being confiscated. Though the regime had developed a new system of borders (internal, republic-level, and international), the confiscation campaign highlighted what little ability the regime had to enforce them, as Kazakh nomads fled to neighboring provinces, other republics, and to China, for fear of expropriation.

This chapter begins by examining several questions: How did Moscow conceive of a bai? What kinds of characteristics did this figure have? And what resemblance, if any, did this portrait of the bai's system of exploitation bear to the actual cleavages in Kazakh society? It then turns to how the program of confiscation was developed, looking at how two leading Kazakh cadres, Smaghŭl Säduaqasov and Oraz Zhandosov, responded to this assault on their own society. It then examines early efforts to implement confiscation in Semipalatinsk province, an episode that became known as the Semipalatinsk affair, before turning to the confiscation campaign itself.

The Figure of the Bai

Soviet scholars argued that the exploitative practices of bais or *bai-polufeodaly* (literally, "bai-semifeudals"), as they were sometimes known, had prevented Kazakhs from adopting settled life. Examining the history of the Kazakhs under Russian imperial rule, they claimed that Kazakhs had suffered from a system of "double oppression." The "colonial" policies of the Russian empire had repressed the Kazakh "nation," while the exploitative actions of "bais," many of whom worked for the Russian imperial state, had served to perpetuate nomadic life and the "backward" influence of Kazakhs' clans.[11] Kazakh society, these scholars concluded, had reached a state of historical development that might be characterized as "patriarchal-feudal," midway between feudalism and capitalism. To "help" the Kazakh aul "catch up" to the Russian village, reach capitalism and eventually socialism, party activists needed to remove the most wealthy and powerful bais, thereby allowing the bedniak and the seredniak to assume the central roles in the aul.

The Russian term "bai" was derived from the Kazakh word for wealthy ("bay"), and this figure, as imagined by Soviet scholars, had certain general characteristics. A bai, like his counterpart in the Russian village, the kulak, was well-to-do. This wealth was primarily held in livestock: by one estimate, bais constituted 6 percent of the Kazakh population, but they controlled 50 percent of the republic's livestock.[12] To tend their herds, bais relied on unpaid labor from a vast network of relatives. These relatives performed chores necessary to the maintenance of nomadic life, such as pasturing the bai's animals or milking his horses and camels. They did not perform these chores willingly, scholars argued. Rather, these relatives were coerced into doing so by a system of kinship ties that facilitated and strengthened the bai's economic oppression. Many bais were believed to be the leaders of particular clans or members of the Kazakh aristocracy.[13] A bai might also associate with mullahs, or Islamic clerics, and read the Koran. However, a willingness to exploit others, both economically and through ties of kinship, and a firm opposition to Soviet power were seen as more crucial to a bai's identity than his religious beliefs.[14]

While the figure of the bai was associated with these general characteristics, the label of bai, like the label of kulak, was ambiguous, shifting, and frequently contested.[15] It meant different things to different people at different times. The question of who was a bai and who was not a bai depended on who was being asked to judge. Ultimately, the category of a bai could include almost anyone who was Kazakh, and over the course of the collectivization campaign, the list of those identified as bais would come to include clan leaders, former Russian imperial officials, members of the hereditary elite, poor Kazakhs who had lost their livestock, and a number of Soviet officials. The uncertainty surrounding the exact definition of the term was purposeful, and it contributed to the fraying of the fabric of Kazakh society.

However, the portrayal of Kazakh nomadic life as embodied in the figure of the bai grossly misrepresented Kazakhs' everyday existence. Kinship underlay social and political functions crucial to nomadic life. Typically, each Kazakh knew his or her ancestry back at least seven generations and, on meeting another Kazakh for the first time, would recite this genealogy. These exchanges offered a window onto a stranger's biography and history, and they served as a kind of passport that structured relations between individuals on the steppe.[16] Kazakhs practiced a form of exogamy, and genealogical ties also played a role in adjudicating marriage practices: if a man and a woman shared a common male ancestor within seven generations, they were not supposed to marry.[17] Kinship also served important economic functions: using kinship, various lineages claimed the right to graze certain pastures at particular times of the year. In other cases, members of a given descent group were obligated to help a kin member in need of assistance, such as providing animals after a particularly severe winter.

Within Kazakh society, distinctions in status were usually based on factors such as descent, age, or intellect rather than economic wealth.[18] Clan elders were generally selected due to their leadership ability, military skill, or legal acumen, and they played an important role in mediating disputes between clans and resolving differences within their own communities. A *biy* served as a kind of nomadic judge, the administrator of customary law, known as adat, while an *aqsaqal* (literally, "white beard") selected routes and dates for Kazakhs' seasonal migrations and oversaw the pasturelands. Both were chosen from the "black bone" (*qara süiek*), or commoner, strata of Kazakh society, and the positions that they held were not necessarily hereditary.[19] Kazakhs also had allegiances to a separate aristocratic stratum known as "white bone" (*aq süiek*).[20] Members of this noble estate included the khans, the leaders of the hordes; the sultans, sons of khans; and a group known as töre, the descendants of the sultans. By the nineteenth century, many töre had become the rulers of individual clans. All three of these groups were Chinggisids, or populations that claimed descent from Chinggis Khan. They had rules of descent and kinship distinct from commoners, and unlike the clan elders, membership in this noble estate was hereditary.[21] Finally, a separate caste of elites, known as *qozhas*, served as important religious figures and mediators in Kazakh society. Qozhas claimed descent from the family of the prophet Muhammad. Like the Chinggisids, the qozhas adopted laws of descent distinct from commoners. Within Kazakh communities, qozhas oversaw a number of religious functions, including conducting Islamic rituals and overseeing Islamic education.[22]

Russian imperial rule did provoke important changes in this system of social stratification. Under a form of indirect rule, many Chinggisids retained their privileged position, becoming intermediaries for the Russian empire. But their influence in Kazakh society began to wane. Traditionally, the khans had legitimated the elite status of other Chinggisids, but as the steppe came under Russian imperial rule, St. Petersburg eliminated the position of the khans. Chinggisid status in Kazakh society was also challenged by the emergence of commoners. Taking advantage of opportunities for trade with the Russian empire, they began to control large amounts of land and livestock. By the end of the nineteenth century, resources were becoming increasingly concentrated in the hands of these individuals, and the factors that determined social status in Kazakh communities began to shift, with economic position competing alongside background and social status.[23]

Soviet scholars pointed to these "wealthy" individuals as proof of the arrival of capitalism in nomadic society, but the position of these stock holders was not quite so straightforward. They did not own the livestock that they pastured, nor did they ordinarily seek to accumulate wealth. Rather, they held this livestock communally, serving as the patron and protector of their relatives. Their animals, which were marked with the brand of their clan (*tamgha*), were regularly redistributed and reallocated among kin members. During times of crisis, kin members would turn to each other for assistance, such as the loan of animals. Livestock numbers could be highly volatile—due to drought, disease, zhŭt, or raids by neighboring clans, herd numbers could fluctuate dramatically over the course of a single season, quickly transforming a "wealthy" Kazakh into a poor one—and these mutual aid practices represented an important adaptation to the challenges of life on the steppe.[24]

FIGURE 3.1.   A Kazakh nomad, Pavlodar province, 1920s. Republic of Kazakhstan Central State Archive of Film, Photo and Audio Documents, Image #5-3497.

Divisions within Kazakh Cadres on the Future of the Kazakhs

Perhaps no group within the top levels of the republic's bureaucracy understood the destruction that the confiscation campaign would wreak on Kazakh society better than Kazakh cadres themselves.[25] Although most Kazakhs remained nomadic on the eve of the confiscation campaign, a small number had settled and entered institutions of higher education. Most had graduated from what were known as "Russian-native" schools. First founded in the Kazakh steppe beginning in the 1840s, these institutions offered education in Russian, as well as instruction in Kazakh using a modified Cyrillic script. A far smaller number of Kazakhs attended Muslim schools, where they received a traditional Muslim confessional education. Most members of this educated Kazakh elite came from the Middle Horde, and a number of them had studied in Semipalatinsk, Kazakhstan's largest city, located in the northeastern corner of the steppe.[26]

To fill the ranks of the republic's bureaucracy, Moscow drew from this educated Kazakh elite. But due in part to the scarcity of literate cadres, the number of Kazakh cadres had remained small, particularly at the republic level. In 1926, the Communist Party in Kazakhstan had 31,910 members, with 11,634, or 36.5 percent, of these members being Kazakhs.[27] At the republic level, only 158, or roughly 16 percent, of the 1,036 nomenklatura, or high-ranking positions, were occupied by Kazakh speakers.[28] The dearth of native cadres, particularly at the republic level, meant that many of the officials making crucial decisions about the republic's future did not always have detailed knowledge of nomadic life. It also meant that the regime, at least initially, had to forge an uneasy alliance with some Kazakhs who had once held decidedly anti-Bolshevik views.

The partnership between the Bolsheviks and the members of a native political party, Alash Orda (Horde of Alash), which had sided against the Bolsheviks during the Civil War, was one of the most prominent examples of this pattern. Alash Orda had been formed after the October 1917 revolution when a group of secular, Russophone Kazakhs, many of whom had originally sympathized with the liberal Constitution Democratic (Kadet) Party, declared an autonomous Kazakh state. The party's political platform included greater Kazakh autonomy, the extension of universal voting rights and the separation of church and state. As civil war enveloped the steppe, members of Alash Orda initially partnered with the Whites against Bolshevik forces. But by 1919, they surrendered to the Bolsheviks, and many of their supporters, including Älikhan Bökeykhanov (a töre and the grandson of Bökey Khan) and Akhmet Baytürsïnov assumed important roles within the Bolshevik Party.[29] Though younger, more radical Kazakh cadres opposed to Alash Orda bitterly decried their incorporation into the party, Moscow initially tolerated the presence of many Alash Orda members.

Prerevolutionary allegiances, such as ties to Alash Orda, and kinship played a role in determining the particular fault lines among native cadres, but ideological differences, particularly the question of how to promote "national" goals within a socialist context, also divided the small group of Kazakhs in the upper circles of the republic's bureaucracy.[30] Smaghŭl Säduaqasov, a young Kazakh who was married to Bökeykhanov's daughter Elizabeta, became one of the most vocal and eloquent critics of the regime's approach to promoting Kazakhs. Though Säduaqasov maintained close ties to Alash Orda—he also worked closely with Baytürsïnov during Baytürsïnov's time at the Commissariat of Education—he engaged deeply with Marxist-Leninist theory. He wrote several articles on cooperatives, and he critiqued the regime for its continuing reliance on Kazakhstan as a source of raw materials and its failure to build factories in the republic. He rose quickly through the ranks of the party, becoming the republic's commissar of enlightenment, the editor of the republic's major Kazakh-language newspaper, *Enbekshï Qazaq* (The Kazakh Worker), and even meeting with Stalin in March 1926.[31]

In a strident 1922 article, "What the Kazakh People Need," Säduaqasov outlined his view of what Soviet nationality policy should mean. He argued for

FIGURE 3.2. Smaghŭl Säduaqasov (left) and Mŭkhtar Äuezov in Semipalatinsk in 1921. The President's Archive of the Republic of Kazakhstan, Image #2-122944.

further representation of Kazakhs in the Soviet bureaucracy: "Non-Kazakhs [*basqa zhŭrt*] can't do our work for us. This isn't because they wish us ill, but because they don't know our language and traditions."[32] He critiqued those who would see his ideas as insufficiently "Communist." Rather, Säduaqasov argued, his fight to secure equal rights for Kazakhs fit neatly within Communist ideals: "Striving for equality is not nationalism [*tendĭkke tĭrĭsu—ŭltshĭldĭq emes*]. . . . Rather, striving for equality is the natural characteristic of those who are destitute."[33] Becoming a Communist, Säduaqasov contended, should not mean forgetting one's national traditions, and he critiqued the appearance of Communists in "sheep's clothing."[34]

But Säduaqasov's vocal critique of the regime's failure to assist Kazakhs, as well as his connections to Alash Orda, made him vulnerable to attack. In a 1924 article, "I Am Forced to Respond" (Erĭksĭz zhaüap), Säduaqasov struck back at those Kazakh cadres who would label him a "nationalist" (*ŭltshĭl*). Calling him a nationalist, Säduaqasov concluded, was simply a way for these native cadres to prove themselves as more "Communist" than others.[35] Other Kazakh cadres, such as Älĭbi Zhankekdĭ, who in 1915 became the first Kazakh to join the Bolsheviks, chose other methods of ensuring their own survival. Zhankekdĭ regularly wrote to Stalin to update him on the activities of Säduaqasov and the intricacies of various divisions among Kazakh cadres, a method perhaps of ensuring that Zhankekdï himself remained above reproach.[36]

The exact fault lines among Kazakh cadres depended on who was being asked to define them. It was not exactly clear what labels such as "right" or "left," which were used to indicate differences in ideological approaches among cadres in the Soviet Union's west, would mean in the Kazakh context. Leon Trotsky, who spent time in exile in Alma-Ata in the 1920s, noted that the regime regularly sought to manipulate factions among native cadres, through cleavages that were both real and imagined.[37] The project of sowing these divisions, he concluded, was made easier by the relatively recent arrival of Communism to the steppe: "In general, it seems that because of the low level of social differentiation in the milieu itself, the ideological groupings among the Communists must be inevitably fluid and unstable in character. This makes it easier than ever to label someone a member of a 'right' or 'left' faction." Administrators who sought to shore up their leftist reputation, Trotsky noted, would discover "pro-kulak" deviations in backward regions.[38]

On his arrival in Kazakhstan in 1925, Goloshchekin identified three major factions of Kazakh cadres: the first was led by Seytqali Mendeshev, the chairman of Kazakhstan's Central Executive Committee, the second by Sŭltanbek Qozhanov, a former editor of Alash Orda's newspaper who had risen to become Kazakhstan's second secretary whom we met in the previous chapter, and the third by Säduaqasov.[39] Goloshchekin referred to these divisions as *gruppirovka*, or factionalism, which he defined in the following way: "In many places it means that there is not a committee that leads but a 'leader.' Affairs are conducted according to this leader, not according to the directives of the party committee."[40] The national delimitation of 1924 had played an important part in creating these factions, Goloshchekin argued, as the Kazakh regions in the former Turkestan ASSR, previously the base of support for Qozhanov, had been added to the steppe region. Qozhanov and Säduaqasov, "bourgeois nationalists" on the "right," were now engaged in a bitter power struggle, he concluded.[41]

At the republic's fifth party congress in December 1925, Goloshchekin accused a number of high-ranking Kazakh cadres of creating a bloc, what he termed the "August alliance," which supposedly opposed his leadership of the republic and sought to block his every move.[42] He began a radical rearrangement of the hierarchy, firing two influential Kazakh cadres, Qozhanov and Mendeshev. Qozhanov and Mendeshev were exiled to posts in Moscow. Several officials were brought in from the RSFSR, including Nikolai Ezhov, who took Qozhanov's place as the republic's second secretary. The addition of Ezhov to the republic's ruling circle brought crucial revolutionary experience: Ezhov, like Goloshchekin, had joined the Bolsheviks prior to 1917, and he had previously served as the party secretary of Semipalatinsk province in the republic's north. While his tenure in Kzyl-Orda would be brief—Ezhov moved to Moscow in February 1926—he would support Goloshchekin's efforts to bring the republic more firmly under Moscow's control.[43] Some years later, Ezhov would later rise to a position of great prominence, becoming the head of the secret police during the height of Stalin's Great Terror (1936–38).

Though tensions over the republic's course continued to erupt—most notably, at a November 1926 Moscow meeting of non-Russian delegates to the sessions of the Russian and All-Union Central Executive Committees, where Qozhanov and the chairman of the republic's Central Executive Committee, Zhalau Mïngbaev, critiqued the slow pace of indigenization and industrialization in the republic—Goloshchekin was able to push through a resolution condemning Qozhanov's and Mïngbaev's actions at the krai committee plenum.[44] In December 1926, Goloshchekin wrote to Stalin, Molotov, and Stanislav Kosior in the Central Committee to update them on the progress of integrating Kazakh cadres into the party. He noted that more than twenty Kazakh cadres had made speeches to condemn Qozhanov, Säduaqasov, and Mïngbaev at the plenum. These speeches, he suggested, were not simply the actions of one group fighting against another. Rather, they revealed the "growth" of Kazakh cadres, "their desire to move on from factionalism, their closeness to the party and assimilation [*assimilirovanie*] into it."[45]

Mikhail Riadnin, Goloshchekin's personal secretary, noted that Goloshchekin approached his duties in Kazakhstan with considerable intensity: "Goloshchekin was demanding, sufficiently stern, and brusque."[46] He was quick to lose his temper, Riadnin observed, and he might interrupt meetings with a shout. Goloshchekin worked long hours, and he expected the same from those he supervised. Riadnin recalled that he might just get home from work when the phone would ring: "This meant that F. I. Goloshchekin had gotten some sort of idea and I would be given a new task." Inevitably, Riadnin would have to return to the kraikom headquarters or Goloshchekin's apartment for further work that evening.[47] Occasionally, Goloshchekin would soften, encouraging Riadnin to go see a movie with his wife or take a vacation at the sanatorium. But even then the republic's party secretary was apt to forget his promises, leaving Riadnin's wife alone at the movie theater and Riadnin, with some resignation, to return to the office.[48]

But while Goloshchekin could be demanding, there is no evidence that he held a specific animus against Kazakh cadres, as some Kazakhstani scholars have claimed.[49] Goloshchekin sought to jettison those native cadres who appeared to challenge his authority, such as Qozhanov, Mendeshev, and, eventually, both Mïngbaev and Säduaqasov, but he also worked to cultivate close contacts with others who could assist him in enforcing the party's rule, such as Oraz Isaev, who would serve as the chairman of the republic's Council of People's Commissars from 1929 to 1938, and İzmŭkhan Kŭramïsov, who would serve as the republic's second secretary from 1929 to 1931. As Goloshchekin himself argued during a speech at the republic's fifth party congress, there was a danger in becoming too close to the Kazakh intelligentsia, but also a danger in dismissing them entirely: "To adopt a purely negative attitude to the Kazakh intelligentsia is incorrect. We need to attract them to professional work . . . but this does not rule out a fight with bourgeois-nationalist ideology."[50]

Though Säduaqasov remained in the party, his conflict with Goloshchekin and other Kazakh cadres would come to a head over the bai confiscation campaign. At the republic's sixth party congress, which took place in Kzyl-Orda in November 1927, Goloshchekin began a discussion of expropriation from wealthy Kazakh elites. After Goloshchekin had spoken for more than seven hours, Säduaqasov, a man more than two decades Goloshchekin's junior, came to the podium. "I personally am not in agreement with the opinion of Comrade Goloshchekin," Säduaqasov declared, noting that he objected to Goloshchekin's assertion that social relations in the aul had remained unchanged since the 1917 revolution. Goloshchekin, Säduaqasov argued, had unfairly singled out the Kazakh aul alone for expropriation: "In short, our class politics in the village and in the aul should be the same. It is incorrect to carry out one type of politics in the Kazakh aul and in the Russian village carry out another. We should try to dominate [osedlat'] not only the Kazakh bai but also the Russian kulak."[51] In January 1928, immediately following the republic's sixth party congress, Säduaqasov published a widely circulated article, "On Nationalities and Nations," in the Soviet Union's major party journal, Bolshevik, which openly criticized Goloshchekin and detailed the party's failures in dealing with the national question in Kazakhstan. In Säduaqasov's opinion, continued resistance within the party apparatus itself rather than the supposed backwardness of eastern republics such as Kazakhstan explained the slow pace of indigenization.[52]

Other Kazakh cadres, such as Oraz Zhandosov, offered an entirely different view of confiscation. Born in the Almaty region, Zhandosov was one of the few Elder Horde Kazakhs in the party during its early years. He had been opposed to Alash Orda, and he became a Bolshevik party member in 1918. Educated in Moscow at an agricultural academy, Zhandosov moved easily between Russian and Kazakh circles. He was perfectly bilingual in Russian and Kazakh, and he was renowned for his skills as an orator. He was married to a non-Kazakh, Fatima Zhandosova (Sutiusheva), a Tatar from Tashkent.[53] In a May 1928 article, "A New Stage in the Resolution of the National Question," in Sovetskaia step' (Soviet Steppe), the republic's major Russian-language newspaper, Zhandosov argued that major strides had been made in addressing national inequalities, or Kazakhs' position as an "oppressed" nation. Kazakhs, he concluded, now needed to turn their attention to a more urgent question of national transformation, that of the "fight for liberation from social oppression." The economic might of the bai was so strong, he concluded, that the aul poor (*bednota*) remained in a position of semislavery that preserved "patriarchal-clan" ties. He called for efforts to liquidate this "semifeudal" relationship.[54]

On the conclusion of the republic's sixth party congress in November 1927, Goloshchekin pushed through a resolution calling for a confiscation campaign against wealthy Kazakh elites over the objections of Säduaqasov and several other Kazakh cadres. In May 1928, the presidium of the republic's party committee passed a resolution that declared Säduaqasov, Qozhanov, and Mïngbaev to be part of an antiparty deviation. The resolution critiqued Säduaqasov and other members of the group for their opposition to confiscation, their "incorrect understanding and mechanical application of korenizatsiia," and for bringing aul leaders under their sway.[55] Party literature linked the theories of Säduaqasov to those of Baytŭrsïnov, who had been denounced for his contention that Kazakhs already practiced their own form of communism in the aul.[56]

A series of purges, first in 1928 and then again in 1930, removed dozens of prominent native cadres, many of them former Alash Orda members, from positions of authority. Though these purges did not target Kazakh cadres exclusively, they affected them disproportionately, particularly as the number of high-ranking Kazakh cadres was so small.[57] In this atmosphere of heightened suspicion, the criteria for the advancement of native cadres began to shift. Riadnin, Goloshchekin's personal secretary, recalled that Eltai Ernazarov, a Kazakh from Syr-Daria province who replaced Mïngbaev as the chairman of the republic's Central Executive Committee, obtained his new position as chairman not through any particular skill, but rather due to the fact that he appeared not to be allied with one group or another: "His qualification was that he was not part of one gruppirovka, that he didn't belong to any of the gruppirovkas. And at this time this was very rare among Kazakh workers."[58]

As for Zhandosov and Säduaqasov, their careers went in opposite directions after the republic's sixth party congress, a sign of how Soviet nationality policy was shifting by 1927–28. After Säduaqasov's censure, Zhandosov assumed Säduaqasov's position as the commissar of enlightenment. He took on a leading role in the confiscation campaign, publishing articles explaining expropriation in the Kazakh-language press.[59] Zhandosov served on the party committee that oversaw confiscation and acted as a plenipotentiary (*upolnomochennyi*) for confiscation in the Dzhetisu (Semirech'e) region.[60] Later, he would go on to help found some of the first Kazakh universities. He also became the first director of Kazakhstan's national library. In 1938, he was killed in the purges.

Säduaqasov, by contrast, lost his post both as the commissar of enlighten-ment and as the editor of the republic's main Kazakh-language newspaper. He was sent out of the republic in late 1927 to a posting as the rector of the Kazakh Pedagogical Institute in Tashkent, Uzbekistan. He was fired from this post in Tashkent after just a few months and sent to Moscow, where he became a student at the Moscow Institute of Railroad Engineers.[61] In the fall of 1933, while work-ing on the construction of the Moscow-Donbass railroad, Säduaqasov fell ill. He died in a Moscow hospital at the age of thirty-two or thirty-three in December of that same year.[62]

Both men sought to play a major role in the shaping of a specifically Soviet Kazakh identity, but they understood the means by which Kazakh society should be developed and the direction that this should take quite differently.[63] Zhan-dosov's view, which now gained favor, called on Kazakhs themselves, guided by Moscow, to initiate a radical socioeconomic restructuring of their own society. Only this type of intervention, Zhandosov concluded, would allow Kazakhs to "catch up" to the Russian village. Säduaqasov, by contrast, rejected such violent means of developing Kazakh society from within, particularly when the Russian village was not treated similarly. He pushed for further development of coop-eratives as a more gradual means of transforming economic relations in both the aul and the village. In his view, some of the greatest impediments to the promotion of Kazakhs as a group were institutional—lingering resistance within the bureaucracy to indigenization, as well as insufficient financial support from Moscow—rather than within Kazakh society itself.

The Semipalatinsk Affair

While Säduaqasov, Zhandosov, Goloshchekin, and others debated the regime's campaign against the bai, the economic crisis in the republic—and across the Soviet Union more generally—was deepening. Bad weather had resulted in a smaller than expected grain harvest, and economic planning magnified these initial crop failures. Through a misguided state pricing policy, peasants began to hoard relatively underpriced grain and sell more lucrative animal products and so-called "technical crops," such as sugar beets, cotton, and sunflowers, to the state, and the supply of grain available for state purchase began to fall short of the urban population's needs. Fears of war and "capitalist encirclement" added to the overall sense of emergency and appeared to give credence to Moscow's claims that enemies lurked within.

In January 1928, Stalin traveled to southern Siberia, one of the Soviet Union's major grain-producing regions, and called for coercive measures to resolve the grain crisis. On January 20, while in Novosibirsk, Stalin sent a telegram to Goloshchekin in which he angrily condemned the dramatic rise in grain prices in northern Kazakhstan and adjacent Siberian regions, arguing that it threatened to further undermine state procurements.[64] Within the republic, Goloshchekin and Nikolai Kubiak, who would shortly become the people's commissar of agriculture of the RSFSR, toured crucial northern grain regions and began to organize "troikas," which would oversee grain procurements.[65]

In the northern grain regions that Goloshchekin and Kubiak had toured, as well as in southern Kazakhstan, the situation was worsening due to a series of droughts and zhŭts in 1927–28. In January 1928, the secretary of the southern Dzhetisu province wrote to the Central Committee to detail the province's disastrous economic position. Information from just three districts indicated that more than 10,649 head of livestock had died that January, and he detailed efforts to pasture some of the region's livestock in neighboring Kirgizia, where the grasses had not suffered as much from drought. A number of districts in the Dzharkent region, he continued, had begun to "literally starve."[66] There were also reports of drought and zhŭt in Syr-Daria province. As Kazakhs in Syr-Daria flooded regional markets with livestock that they could no longer pasture, the prices for animals plummeted, while the price of grain skyrocketed.[67] In the northern province of Semipalatinsk, there were widespread instances of starvation and pillaging, as well a "massive" drop in livestock levels due to a zhŭt.[68]

Though he was aware of the drought and zhŭt, Stalin introduced "temporary measures," articles 107 and 62 of the Soviet legal code, to arrest those deemed to be hoarding grain, an approach that would later come to be known as the Ural-Siberian method.[69] These measures were applied with particular force in Siberia, Kazakhstan, and other "grain-surplus" regions in an attempt to resolve the grain crisis and funnel grain to cities and work sites. As Moscow began to privilege the city over the countryside, the pressure for grain intensified across Kazakhstan. In Akmolinsk province, many households saw their taxation rates rise several fold, as plenipotentiaries levied taxes without any regard for the means of the household to pay them.[70] In Dzhetisu province, where districts were already suffering from hunger due to drought and zhŭt, the grain procurement plan was raised from 200,000 to 300,000 poods, an increase of 50 percent; additional party cadres were deployed to strengthen grain procurements in the regions.[71]

The intense pressure for grain provoked other eruptions of violence. Though the confiscation campaign would not officially begin until August 1928, local officials in Semipalatinsk province, operating under the orders of the Politburo, anticipated its start and began to requisition livestock, grain, and other goods from Kazakhs using threats, beatings, and coercion. The choice of Semipalatinsk province for a violent assault on Kazakh society was not accidental. Located on the territory of the Middle Horde, Semipalatinsk province was an important region for Moscow, both strategically and economically. Under Russian imperial rule, Russian and Ukrainian peasants had flooded the province, transforming it into a major grain-producing region. The province also shared a long, porous border with Xinjiang, the region of China to the east. By the early Soviet period, Xinjiang had become an important trading partner, and Moscow introduced regular ferry service along the Irtysh River, which connected Semipalatinsk with Xinjiang.[72] The province's major city, also known as Semipalatinsk, played a significant role in Kazakh culture. Under Russian imperial rule, it became known as a major center of Islamic learning within the Russian empire, one that was rivaled in importance only by the cities of Kazan and Orenburg.[73] A number of leading Kazakh literary figures, including the poet and philosopher Abay Qŭnanbaev and the novelist and playwright Mŭkhtar Äuezov, had studied in the city.

By the Soviet period, the region had become known for rebellion, as well as outbreaks of lawlessness and disorder. During the Civil War, the province had been the primary power base of Alash Orda. In the 1920s, members of various guerilla networks, known as *basmachi*, set up encampments in Semipalatinsk province and other border regions, using their proximity to China to cultivate connections with Turkic-speaking groups in Xinjiang. The province also became one of the focal points for construction of the Turksib railroad. Thousands of unskilled laborers from Russia, many of whom came illegally, moved to the city of Semipalatinsk in search of work, and the arrival of this new, rootless population sparked tensions with the city's existing communities. As the region's economic position worsened, violence broke out: in May 1928, thousands of these workers gathered in the city square to loot cooperatives and state stores.[74] In another incident, Russian laborers engaged in a mass beating of thousands of Kazakhs employed as laborers on the Turksib railroad.[75]

In the spring of 1928, after receiving more than three thousand complaints from Kazakhs affected by grain and livestock requisitions, the Politburo initiated an investigation into the brutality, which had become known as the Semipalatinsk affair. This investigation, which was headed by Aleksei Kiselev, secretary of the Central Executive Committee of the RSFSR, found that this "outrage" had specifically affected the Kazakh aul, not the Russian village.[76] Bureaucrats deployed arbitrary methods of levying fines and deciding whose grain and livestock would be confiscated: "A plenipotentiary comes to the aul, assembles the village soviet, and decides who has what amount of livestock . . . they do not bother to count. We received complaints that Kazakhs living two hundred versts away had their livestock counted in this manner."[77] Among the lower levels of the party, there was "the impression that one could impose as many fines as one wished and not be punished for this."[78]

The population had been "terrorized," the commission found. Approximately 423 households with 22,000 head of livestock had fled across the province's borders to China.[79] Overall, the commission estimated that 8,592 households in the province had been affected by the violence.[80] The report concluded, "In a word, the province, as we observed it over the course of several months, has been destroyed from all points of view—economically, politically, all sorts of economic relationships between the countryside and the city [*smychka*] have been destroyed."[81] Though Kiselev chastised the republic's party committee, finding that some of its members had encouraged the early start of the confiscation campaign, the primary blame for the affair was placed on the province's party committee, particularly the province's party secretary Isaak Bekker, who was fired from his job.[82] Grievance committees began work to return property and livestock to those affected by the violence, but these efforts proceeded haltingly.[83]

The dynamics of violence in the Semipalatinsk affair eerily foreshadowed the official confiscation campaign. In Semipalatinsk province, the regime sent out ethnic Kazakh plenipotentiaries into various regions and districts to conduct confiscation. There these plenipotentiaries worked in coordination with aul soviets, or meetings of party members from a given aul, to determine who would be named a bai. These plenipotentiaries were under intense pressure from the province's party committee to collect grain and livestock. Kiselev concluded, "Plenipotentiaries in the localities were given directorial mandates, which could not help but create the impression among local cadres that confiscation needed to take place at all costs and under any conditions."[84] But while the province's party committee insisted that these plenipotentiaries collect large amounts of grain and livestock, the exact instructions for how to conduct confiscation were kept vague. A later report on confiscation in the Chingistaiskii district observed: "There are no exact figures for the year in which the district underwent confiscation. Reports on confiscation were not filed, were not examined because with regards to confiscation there were no limits."[85]

Thus, in its very design, this campaign in Semipalatinsk, like the coming official confiscation campaign, anticipated and implicitly sanctioned "excesses." It also allowed and encouraged Kazakhs themselves to make crucial determinations, such as who would be considered a bai and who would not, as well as how much property and livestock to confiscate from a given individual.[86] In some cases, this meant that plenipotentiaries banded together with the communities whose supplies they were supposed to confiscate against the incursions of the regime. In Karkaralinsk region, the region's party committee reported that both aul Communists and district workers had come under the influence of the Akaev clan, which organized efforts to hide livestock. In a telegram to the province's party committee, they wrote, "We ask that the Akaevs be sent out of the boundaries of the region as a socially dangerous element."[87] Semipalatinsk province officials responded by calling the region's measures "insufficient." They ordered the creation of a temporary *piaterka* (a five-person committee) to oversee confiscation, with several "strong" party workers from the regional level, and they instructed the region's party committee to redouble its efforts to bring members of the poor, preferably of the Akaev clan, into the party.[88]

In other cases, officials reported that communities eagerly embraced the campaign against the bai, as well as the categories provided to them. But while party experts had predicted that an attack on the bai would weaken clan ties, the campaigns often served to maintain or even strengthen the salience of kinship. A plenipotentiary reported on confiscation in Aiaguzsk district, which had two rival clans, the Baigubak, controlled by Nurakhmet Maldybaev, the son of an influential clan leader Berikbol Maldybaev, and the Barlybai, a clan that, although it was more populous than the Baigubak, lacked the resources of the Baigubak. Members of the Barlybai clan had voted unanimously for the exile of Maldybaev, the plenipotentiary noted. He observed:

> In this way, the poor are active when they can see a real gain from Soviet power. For example, when there is not an influential representative from a particular clan among the poor . . . , then these poor expropriate a member of that clan. The poor are not only against bais from another clan, but they are against bais of their own clan. For example, in a meeting . . . where the population comes from the Barlybai clan, they voted for the exile of their bai in the presence of this very bai.[89]

Though some Kazakhs eagerly adopted the regime's categories, it was a different matter to get them to forge new linkages, such as class bonds with members of the poor from different clans. The plenipotentiary continued: "The down side of all this activity is that the active poor do not want to get help from the poor of another clan. In this instance, clan pride takes first place."[90]

The confiscation campaign interacted with and at times strengthened existing relationships, such as kinship. But it also created new fissures within Kazakh society, as when some accused others of violating Kazakh customs, such as *bereke*, a tradition of harmony in the aul. The plenipotentiary for the Aiaguzsk district detailed such a case:

> The bedniak Khuzani from Malo-Aiaguzskoi aul said that the poor from Sredno-Aiagyzskoi aul are already not Muslim or they wouldn't have handed over such a person as Maldybaev. But the Malo-Aiguzskoi aul Kazakhs are still Kazakh. They didn't break the Kazakh bereke and they decided not to hand over one bai. Furthermore, the active members of

the poor cannot get on with the passive members of the poor and therefore, in the meeting, a passive bedniak, falling under the influence of a
bai, begins to defend one or another bai, but the activist bedniak begins
to prove that it is absolutely necessary that this or that bai be exiled. A
debate begins, the debate turns into a fight, and the fight begins to take
on a clan character.[91]

As the plenipotentiary's account reveals, the campaign itself had begun to drive a
wedge into the heart of Kazakh society, opening up a debate about what it meant
to be "Muslim" or "Kazakh."

The orders to start the campaign against the bai in Semipalatinsk early came
directly from the Politburo. As Stalin later noted in sly fashion, "In the Politburo
we decided to confiscate the bai just a little bit [malen'ko] for the sake of the
bedniak and seredniak herder."[92] An investigation into the violence was begun
only once the effects of the campaign, particularly the flight of large numbers of
people to China and the precipitous drop in the province's livestock numbers,
threatened to undermine the regime's long-term economic interests.[93] Indeed,
some of the very same tactics that drew the Kiselev committee's ire during the
Semipalatinsk affair, such as beatings, coercion, and excessive fines, would be
redeployed on a far larger scale during the official confiscation campaign later
that same year. This time, there would be no official investigation from Moscow
and little promise of restitution to those affected.[94]

Moscow sought to utilize the Semipalatinsk affair to achieve several goals: to
collect grain to resolve the grain crisis, to neutralize the resistance of grain grow-
ers, as in other grain-growing regions of the Soviet Union, and to strike a blow
against those members of the Kazakh intelligentsia who posed a political "threat."
Bekker, for instance, corresponded with party secretaries in the regions about the
progress of efforts to arrest particularly influential individuals.[95] Though members of the Kiselev commission protested the "outrages" that had taken place in
Semipalatinsk, the actual steps that the commission took to address the wrongs
of the campaign were half-hearted. Bekker, the affair's "villain," was fired from his
posting, but his supposed punishment was light. From 1928 to 1930, he enrolled
in the Communist Academy in Moscow, where he took courses in Marxism-
Leninism. In 1932, he returned to Kazakhstan, becoming party secretary of
Karaganda province during the height of the famine. He was then promoted to
important posts in Tajikistan and Uzbekistan, before he died of an unknown illness in a Moscow hospital in 1937.[96]

The Semipalatinsk affair foreshadowed many of the features of the famine itself. Due to the enormous pressure for grain, local cadres forced Kazakh
nomads, a population that consumed grain but did not ordinarily grow it, to

meet onerous grain requisition requirements.[97] To fulfill these requisitions, Kazakhs flooded markets with their livestock.[98] The effects of drought and zhŭt, which destroyed much of the province's feed base, further propelled the sale of livestock, as Kazakhs sought to offload animals that they could no longer feed. In a feature characteristic of pastoral famines, the terms of trade for livestock worsened: grain became very expensive, while animals were relatively cheap.[99] With the start of the official confiscation campaign later that same year, the crisis in Kazakh society would continue to deepen.

The Official Confiscation Campaign

In the fall of 1928, the official confiscation campaign began.[100] The confiscation decree targeted those stock holders from the native population whose "social or economic influence hindered the Sovietization of the aul" and who relied on a "semifeudal, patriarchal, or clan relationship to perpetuate their rule."[101] Limited areas of the republic were excluded from the confiscation campaign, including areas where land reforms were still ongoing (the cotton-raising districts of Kara-Kalpakia and Syr-Daria province), as well as the remote Adai province due to the "specific conditions of its household development."[102] Characterizing Semipala-tinsk province as "riddled with bais, who have considerable ties to party workers in Kazakhstan and in Moscow," Goloshchekin successfully argued for the prov-ince, which was still struggling to recover from the destruction of the Semipala-tinsk affair, to be included on the official confiscation list.[103] Thus, even as the Kiselev commission was investigating how to offer restitution to those affected, Moscow was preparing to hit the province with a second devastating blow.

The Central Committee in Moscow set the broad outlines of the campaign, authorizing an assault on no more than seven hundred of the republic's most "malicious" (zlostnyi) bais.[104] The secret police then calculated the number of bais that would be "found" in each province. Two different types of bai house-holds would be pursued during the campaign, "large livestock holders" (krupnye skotovody) and "semifeudals" (polufeodaly), with a target of six hundred house-holds set for the former category and a target of one hundred households for the latter category.[105] The category of "semifeudal" encompassed those individuals who had "belonged to previously privileged groups," such as the descendants of sultans and khans (Chinggisids), and former Russian imperial officials. The primary criterion for the other category, "large livestock holders," was "wealth," as measured by the number of livestock a bai household owned. Under a new classi-fication scheme, which was developed to facilitate and strengthen the party's hold over the steppe, all of the republic's majority Kazakh districts were categorized as either "nomadic," "semi-nomadic," or "settled."[106] The criteria for determining a "large livestock holder" differed by district type, with members of nomadic districts allowed to have the most animals before they were categorized as a bai household. A household in a sedentary district, for example, could have up to 150 animals before it was declared a "bai household"; a household in a semi-nomadic district 300; and a household in a nomadic district up to 400.[107]

The process of determining exactly who was a bai involved many different levels of the party-state apparatus and sectors of Kazakh society. Plenipotentiaries with the secret police assembled profiles of potential candidates for confiscation, listing their activities, affiliations, and economic assets. Using these materials, the republic's party committee compiled a list of individuals who would be targeted. This list was forwarded on to provincial party committees, who proposed additions or subtractions to the list to the republic's party committee.[108] Once the list was drawn up, more than one thousand plenipotentiaries, all of them Kazakhs, were sent out into the districts to oversee the confiscation campaign. There they worked closely with district-level confiscation committees, as well as committees composed of members of the "poor," to conduct expropriation. Once named as a bai, an individual and his family members would be stripped of the vast majority of their livestock and property, with these goods earmarked for distribution to members of the poor and collective farms. Seventy-five bais and their family members were slated to be exiled outside the republic, while the remaining bais and family members would be sent to provinces within Kazakhstan far from their place of origin, a strategy that ensured that these families would be cut off from the networks of kin members who could assist them.[109]

Though this classification scheme and chain of command gave the campaign an appearance of legality, the bai confiscation campaign, even in its very design, invited disagreement, discord, and "excesses." The republic's Council of People's Commissars reserved the right to confiscate particular households as "large livestock holders" even if they did not meet the threshold for their particular type of district.[110] At the district level, plenipotentiaries and committees operated with little oversight, and they regularly took property and livestock from households that were not on the official confiscation list.[111] Due to the sheer number of state and party agencies at every level of the bureaucracy involved in confiscation, many of them with differing agendas, disagreements frequently surfaced. It was not uncommon for the fate of a particular bai to be the subject of a lengthy tug of war among regional, provincial, and republic-level officials.[112]

The black lists for confiscation changed frequently, as various sectors of Kazakh society sought to influence the campaign.[113] After reviewing the list for Semipalatinsk province, the chairman of the Council of People's Commissars, Nïghmet Nŭrmaqov, insisted that two more names, Musatai Maldabaev, "known in all quarters," and Kabdii Beisekeev, "a prominent bai who has a large house-hold both in the steppe and in the city," be added.[114] A secret police report sent to Goloshchekin noted that a "whole group" of relatives of the "right wing" of the party had ended up on the list, including the relations of Ghabbas Toghzhanov, who had replaced Säduaqasov as the editor of *Enbekshï Qazaq,* and Bekaydar Aralbaev, the former secretary of the republic's Central Executive Committee. These party workers were working furiously to halt the exile of their relatives, at the same time as the "left" wing of the party, led by Säken Seyfullin, was maneu-vering to keep these names on the list in order to "pick up the political prestige of their opponents."[115]

It was also not exactly clear what some of the campaign's key terms, such as "household" (*khoziaistvo*), would mean when applied to Kazakh society. In their daily life, pastoral nomads relied on an extended network of relatives, one much larger than the nuclear family. Should all these relatives be considered part of the same "household"? Such designations were crucial, as the addition of several relatives and their livestock to a household could cause that house-hold to become classified as a "bai household." In a letter to a party commission, Ïzmŭkhan Kŭramïsov argued that bais utilized the labor and resources of a wide range of family members, such as "stepmothers," "grownup sons," "stepchildren," "nephews," "adopted children," and "stepbrothers." All these family members, he argued, needed to be considered part of the same "household."[116] Similarly, Zhanaydar Säduaqasov, the plenipotentiary for confiscation in Syr-Daria prov-ince, urged a party commission charged with reviewing petitions from individu-als who felt that they had been wrongly categorized as a bai to keep in mind that "the number of people in a [Kazakh] family exceeds standard norms."[117] In an effort to address the practice of "falsely" putting together people and calling them a household, the chairman of the republic's Council of People's Commissars, Nïghmet Nŭrmaqov, sent around a telegram to provincial committees. He wrote, "There have been instances, where due to this approach forty-five to sixty people have been combined into one family, even though they have never met in their lives."[118] But despite Nŭrmaqov's warning, exactly what constituted a "house-hold" was never clearly defined at either the republic, provincial, or district levels, a situation that gave local bureaucrats latitude to implement the campaign in the manner that they wished.

The question of how to define a household had significant implications not only for the individual accused of being a bai but also for the many family mem-bers who faced impoverishment and exile. In a telegram sent to the provinces, Ernazarov, the chairman of the republic's Central Executive Committee, ruled that women who sought a divorce from their bai husbands and the daughters of bais who wished to get married would not be exiled. Instead, they might remain where they lived, and these ex-wives would receive a portion of the bai's property.[119] This strategy was designed to tear Kazakh families apart, and indeed many families faced heartbreaking choices: in Syr-Daria province, Zhanaydar Säduaqasov found that the phenomenon of "fictive" divorces had taken on a "mass character" in Syr-Daria province, as these women (and in many cases the bais themselves) sought to find a way to ensure the safety of their family members.[120]

The confiscation campaign, as well as a military draft of Kazakhs that same year, served to reduce the number of men in the aul. Those accused of being bais were almost exclusively men, and in the absence of their husbands (or ex-husbands, as the case may be), many women assumed a leading role in efforts to defend bais.[121] Shayakhmetov, the famine survivor, remembers how the courtrooms were filled exclusively with female defendants, including his mother, who had been summoned to court to respond to charges that her husband was a bai. His mother, like the other defendants, was sentenced to two years' house arrest, with little semblance of a trial.[122] With many of the adult men in Kazakh society under arrest or in exile, women were also often the only people left to chronicle the sheer terror of life in the republic during the fall of 1928. In a petition sent to Moscow, Zeineb Mametova sought the release of her husband, a former Alash Orda member, Soviet official, and school classmate of Oraz Zhandosov. She also described the violent expropriation of another man, Sadyk Zherdektabkanov, who lived in the same district. "The members of the committee undressed him until he was nearly naked," she wrote. "They bound up his mouth and pressed a revolver to his chest, demanding that he tell them where he had livestock and whether it had been hidden willingly and so on." When it was clear that Zherdektabkanov had no more livestock than what had already been confiscated from him, she continued, they beat his naked back with a whip and he began to bleed. His pregnant wife, arriving on the scene and seeing the pools of blood, died of a heart attack.[123]

The archives are full of letters of protest to Stalin, members of the Central Executive Committee of the RSFSR, or republic-level officials from those individuals arrested as bais and their relatives. Though it is unclear if any of these protests were ever successful, these letters illustrate how Kazakhs had begun to use the categories that the regime had provided.[124] In her petition, Mametova is careful to highlight her husband's lower-class origins, proclaiming him to be the son of an "ordinary Kazakh-bedniak." She also noted her husband's ancestry, in an attempt to illustrate that her husband was not from a powerful clan: "My husband comes from an impoverished clan, 'Shue,' from the tribe 'Naiman.'"[125] In another case, an individual in Semipalatinsk province detailed his Tatar ancestry in an unsuccessful attempt to prove that he was not Kazakh and thus should not be subject to confiscation.[126] Turaghul Ibragimov, the son of the well-known

Kazakh writer Abay Qŭnanbaev, went to elaborate lengths to downplay his family's noble origins. Though Abay Qŭnanbaev was the son of a sultan, Qŭnanbai, Ibragimov argued that a sultan was simply an "ordinary official." The confiscation decree, he contended, applied only to the "descendants of khans" and "agasultans," a group he claimed functioned as the khan's officials.[127]

These letters also testify to the extreme hardship that these individuals and their families faced in exile: elderly relatives of those named as bais, including eighty-five-year-old grandparents, faced deportation.[128] In a petition, Ibragim Mamanov wrote that he and his family had no livestock or farm equipment in their place of exile. No one would employ them because they were known as "deportees." He predicted, "Here we, with our small children, are practically doomed to a hungry death."[129] Ibragimov detailed similar destitution, noting that he had been sent nearly six thousand kilometers from his home, Semipalatinsk province, to Syr-Daria province. In Syr-Daria, he had no means to support himself or his family. Ibragimov's case was never reviewed, and in 1934, he died in Chimkent, his place of exile.[130]

Party documents from the period detail a way of life that was unraveling as activists plundered families. In a series of telegrams, Nŭrmaqov and Ernazarov noted many instances where "everyday household items," such as "carpets," "dresses," and "linens," had been confiscated.[131] In an indication of the campaign's effect on members of the Kazakh hereditary elite, officials ruled that items such as "ancient Arabic or Persian manuscripts," "clan charts," and "gold and silver dishes," should be confiscated and given to the republic's Central State Museum.[132] Though much of the expropriated livestock was designated for collective farms, many activists simply appropriated the best animals for themselves. In other cases, Shayakhmetov recalled, activists rounded up livestock and herded them into pens. They were left there, largely forgotten, without any shelter or food. As winter began, these animals, the very basis of Kazakhs' way of existence as nomads, began to perish in massive numbers, and officials conscripted locals to bury the rotting carcasses before epidemics broke out.[133]

Seeking a way to evade confiscation, some Kazakhs fought back. They redistributed their livestock among their relatives or sold or slaughtered their animals. In some cases, the relatives or supporters of those who were confiscated exacted revenge, and those activists who had "discovered" bais paid for this action with their lives.[134] But the most common response to confiscation was flight, a strategy that pastoral nomads often used in case of unfavorable political or environmental conditions. Kazakhs fled to Kirgizia, Siberia, or across the border to China.[135] Moscow had set up a new system of internal borders in the republic in late 1927, creating village soviets, districts, and provinces (okrugi). But the regime had little ability to enforce these borders, and Kazakhs regularly fled from one province to another to evade confiscation.[136] Even after their arrest, many of those named as bais took flight, disappearing into the sands around Lake Balkhash as officials attempted to escort them through the steppe to their place of exile.[137]

In a letter to the Central Committee on conclusion of the confiscation campaign, Goloshchekin argued that the "seredniak has become the central figure in the aul."[138] The party heralded the confiscation campaign as a fundamental moment in the shaping of the Kazakh bureaucracy: "The weight of the work for confiscation fell primarily on the shoulders of the Kazakh part of the organization. Plenipotentiaries [and] commission agitators were recruited wholly from Kazakh Communists."[139] Goloshchekin, however, acknowledged that there were shortcomings to the campaign, particularly the failure to reach the confiscation targets for livestock: "The object of confiscation—livestock—is easy to move around, easily dispersed, and easily sold in bazaars and markets."[140] He detailed that the party had confiscated 144,474 head of livestock, fulfilling the plan of 225,972 animals by only 64 percent.[141]

Party documents offer some insight into the types of people who were arrested as bais. Of the 696 bais who were expropriated, 73 percent were classified as "semi-nomadic," while roughly 18 percent were "settled" and 8 percent "nomadic."[142] Of the twelve provinces that underwent confiscation, the largest number of bais were uncovered in Syr-Daria province (106), followed by Alma-Ata province (82) and Ural'sk province (66).[143] According to official statistics, the bais that were arrested fell into the following categories: Russian imperial officials and the descendants of khans (245), aqsaqals and biys (76), mullahs and religious officials (8), and former Alash Orda members and functionaries (44). The remaining bais (323) were classified as "large stock holders," who were "anti-Soviet elements in the aul."[144]

These statistics illustrate how the composition of Kazakh society began to change in the aftermath of the confiscation campaign. Though Alash Orda had drawn support from a number of Kazakh tribes, its position was the strongest among educated Kazakhs from the Arghïn tribe of the Middle Horde.[145] The attack on Alash Orda therefore dramatically reduced the number of Arghïns in the upper levels of the party. Most of the individuals in the category of "Russian imperial officials and the descendants of khans" likely belonged to the hereditary white bone elite, and the campaign struck a particularly devastating blow against this sector of Kazakh society. By contrast, very few people from the religious elite, only eight, appear to have been arrested in the course of this particular campaign. The single largest category was that of "large stock holder bai." That fact, as well as the sheer number of livestock confiscated (given as 144,474), hint at the broader repercussions of the campaign on Kazakhs' pastoral nomadic way of life. Given the number of bais identified during the confiscation campaign (696), the total number of those deported (which included bais and other members of their "household") may have exceeded 10,000.

But it is important to note that several people who belonged to the groups that the regime claimed to target were not arrested. Sanzhar Asfendiarov, a töre, continued in his work as the rector of Kazakh State University (KazGU) and the Kazakh Pedagogical Institute.[146] Mŭkhtar Äuezov, who would become Soviet Kazakhstan's most famous writer, was not imprisoned until 1930, despite the fact that he had been a participant in the Alash movement and was, by many accounts, a qozha.[147] In a letter to Goloshchekin written after Äuezov's arrest in 1930, secret police officials argued that Äuezov, who had once "clearly expressed bourgeois-nationalist positions," had begun to abandon them. Based on this shift, as well as the "lack of Kazakh literary cadres," Äuezov, they contended, should be released from prison and permitted to study at the V. I. Lenin Central Asian State University (SAGU) in Tashkent.[148] By 1932, Äuezov was released, and he would embark on a distinguished literary career.[149]

In other cases, those who carried out the campaign were themselves members of the groups that the campaign claimed to target. Though Kärïm Toqtabaev had been a part of the leadership committee for Alash Orda in Turgai province, he became a member of the kraikom commission for bai confiscation, which oversaw the parameters of the campaign and mediated disputes over the fate of particular individuals. He also served as the kraikom plenipotentiary for confiscation in Semipalatinsk province, where the party's major assault on Alash Orda took place. According to secret police reports, as a plenipotentiary in Semipalatinsk, Toqtabaev played a role in shielding a particular clan, the Tabuktinsy, from confiscation.[150] In subsequent years, Toqtabaev continued to serve in crucial roles in the republic's bureaucracy: From 1929 to 1931, he was the republic's commissar for agriculture and, from 1931 to 1933, he was the republic's representative before the All-Union Central Executive Committee in Moscow. In the fall of 1933, he was arrested, and he died in exile in the city of Voronezh in 1936.[151] As the cases of Toqtabaev, Äuezov, and Asfendiarov illustrate, the category of a bai might be broadened to suit the regime's needs, but it also could be narrowed when politically necessary.[152]

In his influential book, *Seeing Like a State*, the scholar James C. Scott examined the failures of several state-sponsored social engineering projects, including collectivization in the RSFSR. His work emphasized that local, practical skills, or *savoir faire*, could serve as a corrective to the failures of authoritarian state planning, what he calls "high modernism."[153] But the case of Kazakhstan's Little October would seem at odds with Scott's conclusions about authoritarian state planning. In its very design, this state-sponsored social engineering project invited and encouraged local involvement, instead of excluding it. The Central Committee and the secret police set the broad outlines of the program (the overall number of bai households to confiscate and their distribution in each province), but Kazakhs themselves were entrusted with carrying out its crucial features. As this chapter has shown, Kazakhs' involvement ultimately shaped both the character of the campaign (who was ultimately targeted and who was not) and the scale of the violence. In this case local knowhow did not serve as a corrective to the failures of authoritarian state planning. Rather, it made it worse, and the confiscation campaign began to unravel Kazakh society from within.

For Moscow, many elements of the Little October were a success. The campaign achieved a partial social revolution in Kazakh society, neutralizing the resistance of "enemies" such as Alash Orda and members of the white-bone aristocracy, such as khans, sultans and töre. The ranks of the Soviet bureaucracy began to fill with black-bone commoners, a marked shift from Russian imperial rule, when Kazakh interlocutors with the Russian imperial state generally belonged to the white-bone strata. The participation of Kazakh plenipotentiaries in the confiscation campaign gave them a role and a stake in the regime's programs. Through the confiscation campaign, Moscow began the first steps to assemble the local-level party and state bureaucracy that would be needed to carry out collectivization.

But there were several unanticipated consequences of the bai confiscation campaign that would foreshadow some of the problems of collectivization itself. In many areas of the republic, there was almost no local-level bureaucracy, and Alma-Ata struggled to direct the campaign or even obtain accurate information about the course of events. To evade confiscation, large numbers of Kazakhs entered into flight. Rather than serving as the first step in sedentarizing Kazakh society, the confiscation campaign actually served to increase, rather than decrease, population movement throughout the republic. Due to the disruption of the campaign, livestock levels began to plummet, beginning a decline that would only accelerate during the collectivization campaign that would begin in the winter of 1929–30.

NOMADS UNDER SIEGE

Kazakhstan and the Launch of
Forced Collectivization

In late 1929, the Central Committee authorized the launch of a pivotal element of the First Five-Year Plan, forced collectivization. In 1927–28, a severe shortage of grain on state markets had highlighted long-standing tensions within the regime's economic policy, the New Economic Policy (NEP), which relied on individual peasants to market their grain to the state. By the close of 1929, a confluence of other factors, including economic choices, international developments, domestic politics, and ideological considerations, had finally tipped the scales in favor of forced collectivization.[1] Stalin abandoned NEP and introduced the First Five-Year Plan, a far-reaching program to transform the Soviet state. Industry would be built on the back of agriculture. Through collectivization, the Soviet state sought to assume control of the food supply and boost its production: grain would be sold abroad for hard currency, which would finance the massive industrial projects considered to be a hallmark of socialism. Both meat and grain would be funneled from the countryside to feed the growing ranks of hungry urban workers.

The transformation proposed for Kazakhstan was to be one of the most dramatic: the settlement of the Kazakhs, the Soviet Union's largest group of pastoral nomads and the republic's titular nationality. Continuing and accelerating the assault on nomadic life begun with the campaign against Kazakh elites in 1928, Moscow proposed to settle and collectivize Kazakh nomads simultaneously, what the republic's party committee referred as "sedentarization on the basis of full collectivization" (*osedanie na baze sploshnoi kollektivizatsii*).[2] Kazakhstan was to

become a "pioneer," the first area of the Soviet Union with a large nomadic population to undergo widespread sedentarization.[3] Nomadic settlement, it was believed,
would "free up" additional lands for grain cultivation, enabling a dramatic expansion of the republic's sown field area, and Moscow began to send thousands of
additional agricultural settlers to the republic.[4] Paralleling a global shift toward
producing meat for the "market," Moscow proposed to "collectivize" (i.e., confiscate) Kazakhs' animal herds and shunt them into immense state farms, which
would cover a total area of more than forty-five million hectares.[5] Giant combines
located near Kazakh railheads would process the livestock that these state farms
produced, enabling goods such as meat, hides, wool, and dairy products to shipped
easily by rail to other parts of the Soviet Union.[6] Kazakhstan, party experts maintained, would become a meat-packing center to rival Chicago.

Officials argued that the settlement of the Kazakhs would have immense economic benefits. Grigorii Grin′ko, the deputy people's commissar for agriculture,
claimed, "The transition of the Kazakh population to a settled way of life will
automatically free up large land surpluses [izlishki], which could be used partially for resettlement [pereselenie] but mainly for state farm [sovkhoz] construction."[7] The republic's party committee predicted that the republic's sown field
area would jump from four million to sixteen million hectares over the course of
the First Five-Year Plan.[8] The language of Soviet nationality policy, which sought
to consolidate groups such as the Kazakhs into modern, socialist "nations,"
served to further legitimize and reinforce the importance of this economic shift.
Izmŭkhan Kŭramïsov, a Kazakh who served as Goloshchekin's deputy, argued
that the settlement of the Kazakhs—what he euphemistically referred to as "the
reconstruction of the Kazakh aul"—was not in opposition to the republic's economic development. Rather, he urged party members to remember that "one
flows from the other."[9]

But as the First Five-Year Plan began, the orderly, enlightened sedentarization
promised under the auspices of the republic's newly formed Committee for the
Sedentarization of the Nomadic and Semi-Nomadic Kazakh Population (Osedkom) quickly foundered. Instead, Moscow pursued Kazakhs' impoverishment,
the loss of their animal herds and status as nomads, and their incorporation into
the state. Activists began to collectivize nomadic regions, levying dizzying grain
and meat procurements on these areas. At the same time, the republic's party
committee began to pursue denomadization through other routes, criminalizing
a range of practices essential to the maintenance of nomadic life, such as Kazakhs'
slaughter of animals during the wintertime or their ability to migrate across borders to seasonal pastures.

In the winter of 1931–32, areas of the Soviet Union with large peasant
populations, most notably Ukraine and the Volga, Don, and Kuban regions,

experienced terrifying famines due to collectivization. But in Kazakhstan, famine assumed a different pattern, striking several parts of the republic by the summer of 1930. This chapter traces the steps that provoked the outbreak of famine and then its escalation into a regional crisis by the end of 1931. As this chapter shows, there was not one single cause of the outbreak of famine in Kazakhstan. Though collectivization was the most important factor, this assault hit a society weakened, first, by massive peasant settlement of the Kazakh steppe under Russian imperial rule and, second, by the seizure of livestock from rural elites during the 1928 confiscation campaign. In the summer of 1931, a drought in the steppe worsened the disastrous effects of collectivization, deepening Kazakhs' descent into hunger.

There is no evidence to indicate that Stalin sought to deliberately starve the Kazakhs. But in Kazakhstan, as elsewhere, Stalin anticipated that some loss of life during collectivization would further the regime's larger political and economic goals. Disregarding the history of the Russian empire's troubled efforts to make the steppe into an agrarian region, as well as the repeated warnings of experts about the risks of agriculture in the drought-prone environment, the Central Committee pushed forward with nomadic settlement in the hopes of achieving fantastical grain yields. As disaster began, the production of grain, not the preservation of the republic's livestock herds, became the clear priority, and Central Committee members accepted the idea that Kazakhs might suffer the most from this choice. The Central Committee received news of Kazakh suffering at several key points throughout 1930 and 1931, but several factors, including the stereotype that Kazakhs, as nomads, had an abundance of livestock, meant that the pressure on the republic for grain and meat remained largely unabated throughout 1930 and 1931. In an act of extreme cruelty, Moscow began to send additional groups, including "special settlers" (internally exiled peasants) and Gulag prisoners, into the republic as famine broke out. Kazakhs were expelled from their land to make room for these new arrivals, and the presence of these additional groups increased the overall pressure on the republic's food supply.

Though Moscow anticipated that nomadic settlement would provoke hunger, the regime did not foresee the sweeping scope of the crisis. The Central Committee launched the project of collectivization in the republic with a bureaucracy insufficiently developed to supervise the process. Rather than serving to consolidate the party's hold over the steppe, collectivization exposed and, in some cases, exacerbated the fragility of the party's hold over parts of the steppe.[10] Though bent on eradicating nomads' practice of long-distance animal herding, Moscow struggled to develop a system of animal husbandry that could take pastoral nomadism's place, and massive herd losses, which imperiled the republic's status as the Soviet Union's major livestock base, quickly mounted throughout

1930 and 1931. By the winter of 1931–32, with their livestock numbers in ruins, Kazakh nomads entered into desperate flight, and the famine began a new phase, as Moscow sought to halt the exodus of the republic's population.

The Outlines of the Campaign

Kazakhstan's status as a mixed economic zone, a region where both peasants and pastoral nomads lived, was reflected in its position in the Soviet Union's overall collectivization drive. A large section of the republic, primarily northern grain-growing areas that had significant populations of Russian and Ukrainian peasants, was part of the first group of regions in the Soviet Union to undergo "full," or complete, collectivization.[11] This initial group, the Soviet Union's declared "grain-surplus" regions, was slated to complete collectivization by the spring of 1931.[12] The remainder of the republic, which included most of its nomadic regions, was scheduled to be collectivized at a slower pace, and this area would complete the transition to collective farming only at the end of 1933.

Officially, the project of sedentarization, like collectivization, was to unfold in stages. The first Kazakh nomads to be settled would be those who lived in the "grain-surplus" regions at the forefront of the republic's collectivization drive. In 1930, 84,340 households in these areas, approximately 20 percent of the republic's nomadic population, were scheduled to be settled and collectivized.[13] Following the principle of "sedentarization on the basis of full collectivization," Kazakh nomads in other regions of the republic would be sedentarized as the collectivization drive advanced in subsequent years.[14] Once settled, Kazakhs would be employed on collective farms or redistributed to work on various industrial projects.

But these elaborate plans for the republic's transformation were hastily developed. Under pressure from Moscow to proceed quickly with collectivization, the republic's party committee placed certain districts in the first wave of collectivization despite the fact that members of this committee openly admitted that they knew nothing about the conditions for agriculture in these districts. Only *after* the completion of the first collectivization drive did Oraz Isaev, the chairman of the republic's Council of People's Commissars, raise the question of studying the environmental profile of the republic's constituent districts.[15] Similarly, though there was a general sense that grain, alongside with meat and dairy products, constituted an important part of many Kazakh herders' diets, there was no concerted effort to understand this shift or to ensure that it was reflected in state planning for the First Five-Year Plan.[16] In 1928, an official in Petropavlovsk okrug had sounded an alarm. He wrote that the republic's state statistical commission was underestimating the amount of grain that Kazakhs now consumed:

> To say the least, we have gone blindfolded past the socioeconomic processes that have taken place in the aul in recent years. Out of seven Kazakh districts in Petropavlovsk okrug, there are no longer any purely nomadic districts; only one district remains semi-nomadic. From this we can determine that the [grain consumption] norms for the Kazakh population should, on an annual basis, begin to coincide more closely with that of the settled population.[17]

But there is no evidence to indicate that this official's calls for change were ever heeded. Under pressure from the Central Committee to move forward quickly, the republic plunged headlong into collectivization.

Finally, the Central Committee itself received yet another warning about the risks of developing the republic's drought-prone environment just before collectivization began. In 1928, Moisei Frumkin, then the deputy director of the Soviet Union's Commissariat of Finance (Narkomfin SSSR), alerted the Central Committee to the dangers of constructing state farms in areas such as Kazakhstan that had variable rainfall patterns and periodic hot, dry winds: "The production of grain in these conditions can give excellent results, but in individual years one should expect the ruin of a significant portion of the harvest."[18] But the Central Committee paid no heed to Frumkin's prediction, accepting that the rewards of a few years of good harvests in these lands were worth the risk of a disastrous year. When drought struck, as it did in the summer of 1931, Kazakhs would have to make up the grain shortfall, a development that would accelerate their descent into hunger.

The First Collectivization Drive

In theory, the massive collectivization drive launched in Kazakhstan in the winter of 1929–30 would draw and build on the republic's limited network of existing collective farms while dramatically intensifying the battle to "liquidate" the bai and the kulak. Prior to the 1929–30 drive, the most common type of collective farm in the republic was a TOZ (Association for the Joint Cultivation of the Land). In a TOZ, the simplest type of collective farm, members carried out agricultural labor jointly, while retaining the ownership of farm animals and most tools. But many of these "collective farms" existed only on paper, and previous efforts at collectivization had proceeded almost exclusively among the Slavic peasantry rather than among the republic's Kazakh population.[19]

In some respects, the 1929–30 collectivization campaign in Kazakhstan followed the pattern of collectivization common to most of European Russia, as
massive numbers of peasants, often far above the targets set, were violently forced
into collective farms in the winter of 1929, only to rapidly exit them by the spring
of 1930. As elsewhere in the Soviet Union, activists in Kazakhstan had been given
almost no instructions on how collectivization should proceed, and work proceeded chaotically. Some peasants were thrust into massive, unsustainable collective farms (*kolkhoz-gigant*), while others found themselves in an *artel*, a type
of collective farm where work animals and tools were confiscated and owned
"collectively."[20] Some twenty thousand kulak households in regions of full collectivization were targeted for deportation to remote regions of the republic.[21] By
March 7, 1930, officials with RSFSR Narkomzem claimed that 40 percent of all
households in Kazakhstan had been collectivized, a dramatic overfulfillment of
plans for collectivization in the republic by more than 150 percent.[22]

Meanwhile, the project of sedentarization, which the republic's party committee heralded as the "main project of socialist construction in Kazakhstan,"
quickly foundered.[23] The major committee entrusted with carrying out the work,
Osedkom, which had been created in January 1930, had a complicated structure:
It coordinated the work of a dizzying array of republic-level state agencies, from
the People's Commissariat of Agriculture to the People's Commissariat of Health
to the People's Commissariat of Enlightenment, which were to carry out the
elements of a planned sedentarization, including identifying suitable land and
building roads, wells, housing, schools, and hospitals for newly settled groups.
Though officials had estimated that this work would cost a princely sum—more
than 318 million rubles—organizers allotted less than 12 million rubles in state
budget funds to the project of sedentarization. Instead, they declared that sedentarization would be financed largely through the resources of the population
itself (*sredstva naseleniia*), a particularly ironic turn of events given that many
party experts had emphasized the poverty and indigence of nomadic life as a
reason for settlement.[24]

Without financial or organizational muscle, the project of planned sedentarization languished. As of May 1931, Osedkom still did not have any data on the
progress of sedentarization from thirty out of the sixty-five districts where it
was supposed to take place. Nïghmet Sïrghabekov, the vice chairman of Osedkom, concluded, "Partial investigations have shown that almost no work goes on
there."[25] In Gur'ev district, the district sedentarization committee failed to complete any work in 1930. When work was finally begun in April 1931, most of the
nomads slated to be sedentarized had fled, and out of five hundred households
only sixty-nine could be found to be settled.[26] In a 1931 letter to Isaev, Sïrghabekov
complained bitterly about the lack of progress. "Questions of sedentarization are

not given serious attention," he wrote. "Not one of these organizations actually knows how work for sedentarization in the regions is going."[27]

When efforts at nomadic settlement began, they quickly exposed the challenges of extending the agrarian frontier into remote regions of the republic. Previously, many nomads had drunk from streams or wells as they migrated. But settled life demanded that a supply of fresh water be located nearby. To settle the Kazakh nomads, Moscow needed to construct a vast network of wells in the republic's arid regions. Yet irrigation projects were woefully underfinanced: Kärïm Toqtabaev, the head of the republic's Commissariat of Agriculture, estimated that it would cost 4.48 million rubles just to construct the wells needed to supply newly settled groups, while the all-Union Narkomzem had allocated only 1.17 million rubles for irrigation projects in Kazakhstan in 1931 more generally.[28] In other cases, district sedentarization committees, under pressure from Alma-Ata to move forward quickly, did not even survey the lands that they had designated as settlement points, a practice that Sïrghabekov lambasted as "the 'drafting' of socialist 'cities' in the sand."[29] Frequently, Kazakhs found that their new homes were located in swamps, in ravines, or on solonchak soils unsuitable for cultivation.

The meager financing allotted to the project of sedentarization and Osedkom's complicated structure encouraged interinstitutional spats. In the republic's newspapers, authors denounced various commissariats for their self-interested behavior (*vedomstvennost'*) and failure to move forward with the project of settlement.[30] Officials with Osedkom critiqued commissariats for understanding nomadic settlement only in its most "simplified form," as the construction of a home or the apportionment of land: "as a result they don't understand the stakes in order of priority, that sedentarization is a complex of socioeconomic events for the fundamental reconstruction of nomadic households."[31] Furthermore, Osedkom officials found, no one seemed to understand what they should do with these households once they were settled: "Not one commissariat, krai, or provincial organization has a clear impression of what they will do in connection with the transfer to settled life of nearly ninety thousand Kazakh households."[32]

But while Osedkom was struggling to begin work, a different type of sedentarization was taking place, the rapid collectivization of nomadic regions and the plundering of nomads' animal herds. Despite the directive to collectivize in stages, many of the republic's nomadic regions were collectivized just as quickly as settled areas. Though this was not the planned sedentarization that that the party had touted, it served the same purposes: the creation of "surplus" land and the funneling of resources, such as labor and animals, to the state. The slogan, "sedentarization on the basis of full collectivization," which emphasized speed at all costs, underpinned and legitimized this assault on nomadic life. In Chelkarsk district, a majority Kazakh region that did not have a single collective farm as of February 1930, the provincial party committee decided to collectivize 55 percent of the district and create seven large state farms. An official in Chelkarsk detailed a chaotic scene, as nomads' animal herds were rounded up:

> It should be noted that on the question of collectivization in nomadic regions workers do not have any instructions. District and even provincial workers do not know how to approach collectivization in livestock-raising districts on a practical level. The plenipotentiaries working in the auls, who, by the way, are very poorly instructed, know only that everything needs to be collectivized, that they should collect the livestock, but as to what else to do—no one can answer this question."[33]

In Syr-Daria province, the orders given to district activists were so staggering—the creation of four state farms with eighty thousand head of sheep each in Sary-Suisk district and four state farms with a hundred thousand head of sheep each in Talass district—that a later investigation led by the secretary of the republic's Central Executive Committee Abdolla Asïlbekov found that "these plans, these numbers, were constructed without any consideration of whether they could be fulfilled." Noting the total absence of any housing for the collective farm members or any shelter for the sheep, Asïlbekov remarked dryly, "It is difficult even to say that these numbers were taken from the air [*vziaty s potolka*], because when you take numbers from the air you at least think about it and wonder whether the numbers fit."[34]

In Ukraine, the RSFSR, and other grain-growing regions, experienced party members and workers from Moscow and other industrial centers, known as 25,000ers (*dvadtsatipiatitysiachniki*) after a Central Committee decree calling for twenty-five thousand workers to be sent out to supervise collectivization, assumed a leading role in the process, working to train local cadres.[35] Kazakhstan received twelve hundred of these urban activists, but few, if any of them, appear to have conducted collectivization in the republic's nomadic regions.[36] Instead, collectivization in nomadic districts was overseen by plenipotentiaries selected by provincial party committees. In his investigation, Asïlbekov signaled out Comrade Safonov, a plenipotentiary sent to organize collectivization in Talass district, as a fairly typical example of this group. He was "a poor Kazakh [*batrak*], who had only just been promoted prior to his departure for Talass; he was semi-literate and on his arrival in the district he warned that he was a new recruit [*vydvizhenets*] who understood very little about the question of collectivization."[37]

Service as a plenipotentiary became a path to advancement for many young, upwardly mobile Kazakhs of modest means. One of the most famous Kazakhs to serve as a plenipotentiary was Shapïq Shokin, who later became president of Kazakhstan's Academy of Sciences. During much of his childhood, Shokin's family lived in poverty, surviving off the income from just one dairy cow. His father died from pneumonia when Shokin was just six years old.[38] In 1930, when Shokin was still a teenager, a provincial party committee selected him to become a plenipotentiary in the confiscation campaign that accompanied collectivization. Shokin recalled, "Like many others, I reacted with delight to 'the sign of the party's trust,' when I was chosen for the brigade of plenipotentiaries."[39] Shokin was assigned to conduct confiscation in Chubartausk district, an area far from his birthplace of Baianaul'sk district. This disorientation was purposeful, Shokin remembers: "They sent us that far away, apparently, because in these places, which were unknown to many of us, we did not have relatives, friends, or even acquaintances."[40] Shokin's service as a plenipotentiary earned him high praise from his superiors: he was offered a post as the party secretary of Chubartausk district but declined it, enrolling instead in the V. I. Lenin Central Asian State University in Tashkent, Uzbekistan.[41]

Plenipotentiaries and other local officials were encouraged to conduct collectivization as rapidly as possible, a strategy that encouraged lawlessness and excesses. Ghalym Akhmedov, a famine survivor, recalled that the behavior of many activists (*belsendĭler*) followed the principle of a Kazakh proverb, "If you give someone your hair to cut, then they will take off your head instead" (*shash alsa dese, bas aladĭ*). Activists overfulfilled procurement plans, whipping and beating populations into submission.[42] In Aksuisk district, a provincial official found, local cadres ruled arbitrarily. "[They] chatter, they ride around from aul to aul, it seems to me, occupied mostly with shady dealings (they steal meat, help others slaughter livestock)." The situation with the district's activists was not better: "In their words, they are for the kolkhoz, but in their deeds they corrupt it. None of these 150 activists carry out any work."[43] In Karkaralinsk district, an official with a state inspectorate commission observed, "On entering the kolkhoz, an ordinary collective farm member gives over everything, and he is only left the right to work steadily and starve." The activists in the collective farm distributed livestock and grain without any supervision, and they might beat or shoot a collective farm member simply "because they didn't like the looks of him." In one aul, kolkhoz activists threw dozens of people out of the collective farm. Half-dressed (the activists had taken their shoes) and left without shelter in the middle of winter, those expelled from the farm lost their toes due to frostbite.[44] The trauma of collectivization was particularly hard on elderly Kazakhs. Mukhamet Shayakhmetov, a famine survivor, remembered that activists lifted his sick grandmother out of bed, seizing her mattress, bed coverings and shawl. Two days later, she died from the shock.[45]

Very often, plenipotentiaries found that there was no party bureaucracy in the nomadic regions that they had been instructed to collectivize. The problem was particularly acute at the aul level, and some plenipotentiaries improvised, making the bureaucracy up themselves: "In the worst case, [the plenipotentiary] himself gathers together several people, calls them "activists' and during the meeting these activists put together a plan of action."[46] In other cases, an aul bureaucracy existed, but it bore little resemblance to a "workers' state." Speaking of the fifteenth aul in Iliisk district, the chairman of the republic's Central Executive Committee E. Ernazarov found that the wife of a mullah had been brought into the party and made chairman of the collective farm. The chairman of the aul soviet operated on the basis of "arbitrary administrative rule," bringing to justice anyone who dared file complaints about his leadership. "The party cells exist officially," Ernazarov concluded, "but for all practical purposes they don't carry out any work."[47]

When new Kazakh collective farms were formed, some looked quite different from what Moscow might have envisaged. Officials had urged the creation of "international," or multiethnic, collective farms, arguing that new settlers from

FIGURE 4.1.   Threshing on a Kazakh collective farm, Pavlodar province, 1930s. Republic of Kazakhstan Central State Archive of Film, Photo, and Audio Documents, Image #5-3660.

European Russia could help Kazakhs adapt to settled life and Kazakhs could teach settlers the local language and customs. They had also pushed for the creation of collective farms composed of several different clans, claiming that this would reduce the salience of kinship to Kazakh life.[48] But activists ignored these directives. In some cases, farms were formed according to clan ties, irrespective of whether that clan was the only one in the district or not.[49] In these so-called "clan collective farms" (*rodovye kolkhozy*), collective farm members appropriated state resources, including machinery and other agricultural equipment, rather than using them to produce grain and other goods to return to the state.[50] In this sense, some Kazakh collective farms served to maintain some of the very features of Kazakh culture that Moscow sought to eliminate.[51]

The party had touted the collective farm as a site for communal work and socialization, but many Kazakh collective farms challenged the understanding of what a collective farm was supposed to be. Some consisted of no more than ten to twenty Kazakh households, all residing in yurts. These households could be as much as two to three kilometers away from one another, and the overall radius of some Kazakh collective farms approached ninety kilometers. In some cases, collectivization did not lead to Kazakhs' sedentarization. On so-called "nomadic collective farms," Kazakhs continued to carry out their nomadic way of life, albeit in the form of a collective farm. In Sary-Suisk district, "the district center and all its party-soviet organizations nomadized together with the population, in the winter and in the spring, living in tents."[52] Members of the republic's collective farm union urged the party to renew its efforts to assemble mixed, rather than single-clan, collective farms, and they decried the existence of these "false collective farms" (*lzhekolkhozy*).[53]

But the most important consequence of the first collectivization drive was the Kazakhs' impoverishment. Kazakhs lost their herds because they were forced to deliver them to the collective farm, but they also lost their animals because they sold them to meet onerous grain procurement quotas. Though the environmental conditions in most nomadic regions were not conducive to growing grain, these districts and the collective farms were nonetheless given fantastical sowing plans. Karmakchinsk district had "no farm equipment, no water, and no suitable land," yet it was given a sowing plan of nine thousand hectares.[54] In Balkhash district, a nomadic region that had no settled agriculture, district officials had taken on a procurement plan of ten thousand poods of grain and fifteen thousand poods of seeds. Without means to grow this grain, Kazakhs were forced to purchase it. Ernazarov wrote: "A sheep was exchanged for fifteen funts of grain, a cow for one and a half poods, a mare for two poods, a camel for three poods, and a good horse for four poods. In this way, the Kazakh stock herder [*zhivotnovod*] in the district was forced to exchange his last cow for grain to fulfill the orders of the local organs."[55] The district overfulfilled its procurement plan, but at a terrifying price, the destruction of Kazakhs' animal herds.

Not all livestock were requisitioned or sold: some Kazakhs drove their herds across district or provincial borders to elude the grasp of the state. Zeitïn Aqï-shev, a famine survivor from Baianaul in Pavlodar province, remembers that his father urged the family to slaughter their livestock, believing that it was better to "eat it ourselves than give it to the dogs." Once a wealthy household, the family retained only one gray mare, which they hid in the mountains, fearing further waves of repression.[56] Animal slaughter was a method of evading state confiscation, but it was also a means of survival. Previously, many Kazakhs had obtained grain through trade with Russian and Ukrainian peasants in the republic's north. Collectivization severed these networks, eliminating an important element of the Kazakh diet. Without grain, Kazakhs were reliant on the meat from their dwindling herds to survive. Eventually, Aqïshev's family was forced to slaughter this mare, their sole remaining animal, to endure the winter. As the threat of hunger and theft intensified, Aqïshev's father held guard over the meat from the mare with an axe.[57]

Even when animals made it to the collective farm, herd numbers plummeted quickly. For nomads, mobility was a strategy, a way of finding sufficient grass and water for their herds in the arid conditions of the steppe. During the steppe's bitter winters, they sought out sheltered pastures for their animals. Bringing their herds—in 1928, the total number of livestock in the republic was estimated at 37.5 million, the most of any Soviet republic—into the collective farm system was a massive undertaking, requiring the construction of winter stables, the provisioning of water and fodder (a particularly challenging prospect in arid regions, where few water sources and little suitable land for growing hay or other fodder could be found), and the inoculation of animals unaccustomed to living in close quarters against various diseases.[58]

Pointing to the herd losses that nomads sustained during droughts or zhŭts, a range of party experts had declared pastoral nomadism to be a fundamentally unstable (neustoichivyi) means of production. Yet in the environmental conditions of the steppe the party struggled mightily to develop a stable form of animal husbandry that could take pastoral nomadism's place. In the state farm Ovtsevod in Kzyl-Orda district, 3,852 animals perished in just one month. Of these animals, 560 were sheep that died during one particularly frigid night, while another 176 sheep died from smallpox. In Samarsk district, the state farm could not account for the location of nine thousand cows. Due to the lack of winter stables and the failure to prepare fodder for the remaining animals, there were instances of massive livestock deaths.[59] Faced with the threat of disease and without means to feed the animals that they had confiscated, activists began to slaughter Kazakh herds

TABLE 4.1 Livestock Numbers in Kazakhstan, 1929–31 (in thousands)[1]

YEAR	HORSES	COWS	CAMELS	SHEEP AND GOATS	PIGS	TOTAL
1929	4,192	7,442	1,393	27,223	286	40,508 [sic]
1930	2,844	3,302	678	15,561	130	22,560 [sic]
1931	1,900	2,800	450	6,500	130	11,780

1. The figures in the table come from GARF f. R-1235, op. 141, d. 1007, l. 5 (Report on the condition of animal husbandry in the Kazakh ASSR, November 28 1931).

en masse. This butchery often took place in remote locations distant from railway lines. Without transport or storage facilities for the meat, animal carcasses rotted under the open air, becoming breeding grounds for disease.[60] Livestock numbers began a precipitous decline in 1930. In 1931, an investigation by VTsIK secretary Aleksei Kiselev found that the republic had lost more than 70 percent of the livestock it had in 1929 (see Table 4.1).

As herd numbers plunged, the entire rhythm of life in the Kazakh aul began to change. Shayakhmetov recalled, "an eerie silence hung over the aul: there was no mooing, bleating or neighing."[61] A similar silence reigned in the collective farms of Aksuisk district, an official from Alma-Atinsk province found: "The kolkhoz Zholaman of the sixteenth aul soviet has 140 households, but it does not have even one cow. Not only are there no horses, but there are no sheep or goats. In the entire kolkhoz, there is not even a watchdog. The kolkhoz Berlik of the fifteenth aul soviet has five half-living horses; the kolkhoz Orken has 210 households, but it has only three work animals and no other livestock." He continued: "If you take any collective farm—the work animals have been lost, stolen, or destroyed. Out of five hundred horses that the province gave the district, all of them have been eaten."[62]

Though Kazakhstan's livestock drop was perhaps the most dramatic, herd numbers in other areas of the Soviet Union with significant nomadic populations, such as Buriat-Mongolia and Kirgizia, also plummeted as a result of the first collectivization drive. Far from improving the efficiency of animal husbandry, collectivization was destroying a crucial economic resource, livestock. On February 20, 1930, in an effort to halt this decline, the Politburo issued a ruling, "On Collectivization and the Battle with Kulaks in Economically Backward National Districts." The ruling urged local officials to proceed cautiously in livestock regions, carrying out further preparatory work before beginning collectivization. But it offered few concrete policy changes save those focused on "correcting" the behavior of nomadic peoples, an approach that implied that nomads themselves rather than the party's own directives were to blame for the herd losses.[63]

Cross-border migration and animal slaughter were strategies, responses to the threat of collectivization. But they were also part of the nomads' everyday repertoire of economic practices. Many Kazakhs traversed the Sino-Kazakh border during their seasonal migrations. During the late fall, Kazakhs slaughtered a portion of their herds, preserving this meat for use during the winter, a practice known as *soghïm*. This practice ensured that Kazakhs would have food during the winter when their animals produced little milk, and it saved them from pasturing additional animals during the lean winter months. But with this ruling, the Central Committee began to blur the distinction between the everyday and the extraordinary, criminalizing a wide range of practices essential to the functioning of nomadic life: Officials were authorized to carry out raids, including the confiscation of livestock and property, from nomads "trying to emigrate across the border with the goal of driving across livestock," while the secret police (OGPU) was ordered to strengthen border patrols in nomadic regions.[64] Local authorities were authorized to take "decisive measures" against the slaughter of livestock in nomadic regions.[65] Officials in Kazakhstan now portrayed soghïm as a criminal act, effectively eliminating the Kazakhs' primary source of food during the wintertime.[66]

This assault on nomadic life deepened levels of popular unrest. During the first six months of 1930, more than eighty thousand people in the republic took part in uprisings, with some individual rebellions reaching three thousand participants or more.[67] Throughout the Soviet Union, unrest and chaos connected with the first collectivization drive spread. In a March 2, 1930, *Pravda* article, Stalin issued a retreat, suspending forced collectivization throughout the Soviet Union. Rather than critiquing the brutal methods that he chose, Stalin blamed the destruction of collectivization on local cadres who, he claimed, had become "dizzy with success" in their eagerness to overfulfill targets and collectivize large swaths of the countryside. Though it was Moscow that had encouraged the rapid collectivization of "backward" national regions, Stalin now chided local officials for "mechanically" transplanting collectivization to these areas, writing, "In determining the speed and methods of collective farm development, careful consideration must be given to the diversity of conditions in the various regions of the USSR."[68]

In much of the countryside, forced collectivization was temporarily halted, and peasants rapidly exited collective farms. In Kazakhstan, by contrast, collectivization rates continued to climb even after the release of "Dizzy with Success," exceeding 51 percent by April 1930.[69] A meeting of the republic's party committee meeting on March 21, 1930, determined that "the directives on distortions in the collective farm movements have still not penetrated the party mass." The committee concluded that the party lacked strength in the regions: "even several provincial workers cannot in fact ensure that the directives of the party are carried out."[70] When republic-level officials ventured out to investigate why collective farms in some nomadic regions had not yet disbanded, they brought along armed detachments of the OGPU.[71] By May 1930, collectivization rates finally began to plunge, yet this prolonged period of collectivization accelerated the decline of the republic's livestock numbers and deepened the Kazakhs' suffering.[72]

At the republic's seventh party congress, held May 30–June 6, 1930, in Alma-Ata, party cadres acknowledged that the first collectivization drive had exacted a particularly heavy toll on nomadic regions. Following Stalin's call for a differentiated approach to collectivization, cadres at the congress now eagerly criticized those who had rapidly collectivized nomadic districts. But as Goloshchekin noted, many of those present at the congress were guilty of the very crime that they now accused others of committing: "Look at yourselves, comrade leaders. You wrote that collectivization is going very well in nomadic and semi-nomadic districts." The Kazakhs' impoverishment, Goloshchekin argued, was a direct result of the particularly brutal manner with which collectivization had been implemented in nomadic regions: "When you collected grain from nonsowing households, what were they to do? How did they exchange livestock for grain? When in several places they collected wool, when they forced them to shear the sheep in the wintertime, didn't the sheep die from this?"[73]

By the summer of 1930, parts of the republic had begun to starve. A secret police report noted that in areas of the republic "food difficulties" had taken on "the character of a mass famine." In three northern provinces (Semipalatinsk, Pavlodar, and Aktiubinsk), 109,809 people were starving, while in twenty-four districts in other provinces unknown numbers of people were suffering.[74] In a letter circulated among several Central Committee members, Goloshchekin warned of an "extremely difficult situation with regards to the consumption of grain in rural regions," and he noted instances of death, severe illness, and swelling due to hunger.[75] In a sign of the republic's distress, more than a hundred thousand Kazakhs fled to the Middle Volga region. Arguing that these new arrivals had disrupted grain procurements and created conflicts with the local population, Molotov urged Goloshchekin to take measures to halt their flight from the republic.[76]

The First Five-Year Plan and the Adai

But within this immense republic, which was roughly the size of continental Europe, patterns of hunger differed. In the remote Mangyshlak Peninsula of western Kazakhstan, collectivization was not the most important trigger of

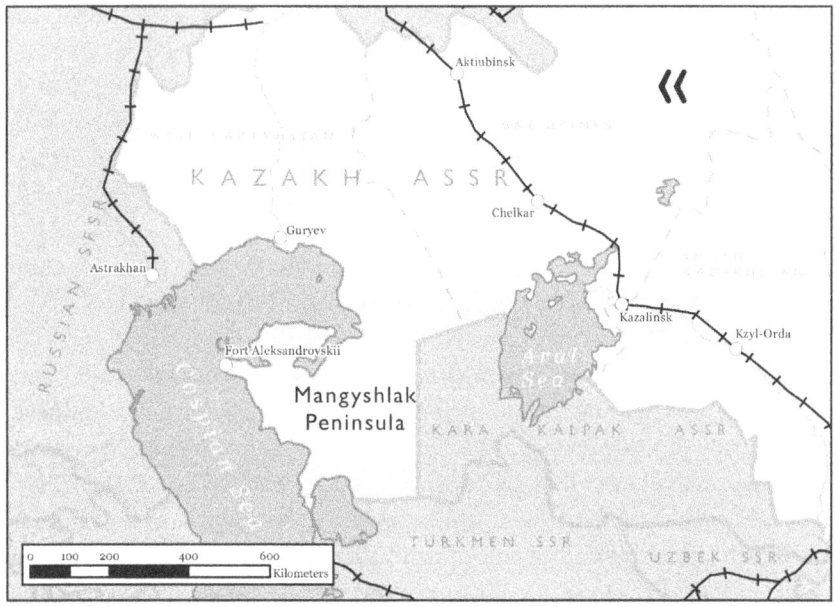

MAP 3. Western Kazakhstan in 1933

hunger. Rather, the Adai, the primary clan in the region, began to starve in 1929, prior to the first collectivization drive, due to a combination of drought, zhŭt, and various party interventions.[77] This region, which was known as the Adai okrug from 1928 to 1929, was regularly referred to as "the most backward of all of Kazakhstan's provinces."[78] It illustrated many of the challenges that the party faced elsewhere in the republic, such as the struggle to develop a reliable lower-level bureaucracy, communicate with far-flung regions and understand and develop the arid landscape, albeit in their most extreme form. For much of the 1920s, the Mangyshlak Peninsula was under only nominal Soviet control, and the party's initial attempt to integrate the region under the First Five-Year Plan would lead to the eruption of massive rebellions.

When it was assembled in 1928, the Adai okrug occupied some 345,000 square kilometers, significantly more than the state of France, yet it had a population of only 190,000 people.[79] It included the Mangyshlak Peninsula, which jutted out into the Caspian Sea, as well as the massive, rocky uplands of the Üst-Yurt Plateau. Travel to the region was arduous. Due to the lack of roads, a trip from the neighboring province of Aktiubinsk could take more than twenty days by camel. The area had a particularly harsh climate: winters were bitter, and soils in the region were poor. Neither the peninsula nor the plateau had running water on their surfaces, and the Adai utilized a far-flung system of wells. A party report concluded, "Fresh water is found so infrequently in the province that the Adai are accustomed to drinking fresh water with salt, as the natural taste of fresh water has the same effect on them that we would have from tasting a bowl of unsalted soup."[80] Due to these environmental features, as well as its overall isolation, the Mangyshlak Peninsula was largely unaffected by the waves of peasant settlement that had transformed other areas of the steppe under Russian imperial rule, and Adai province was almost exclusively Kazakh (97.7 percent).[81]

In a 1928 study of the Adai okrug by the Kazakhstan's Central Executive Committee concluded that the Adai's nomadic practices were distinct, finding that "the term 'nomadic' should not be understood here in the same manner in which it is understood in other provinces of Kazakhstan where there is a nomadic population."[82] In contrast to other nomads in the Kazakh steppe, the Adai migrated year-round rather than setting up seasonal encampments, a strategy designed to maximize their use of the region's scarce water supply. Over the course of a single year, a migratory encampment could cover a distance of more than two thousand kilometers.[83] The Adai pastured sheep, as well as a special breed of one-humped camels, which were particularly prized for their endurance. They traded these animals with the Russian empire and the Khivan khanate, exchanging them for grain.[84] But herd numbers in the Mangyshlak region were particularly volatile. During a zhŭt, or a late spring frost, the Adai regularly lost 35–40 percent of their herds. During a particularly severe zhŭt, their herd losses could approach 80 percent.[85]

FIGURE 4.2.   An aul, with a herdsman on the right. Kumdoil', the River Uil. Adai. Photo by S.I. Rudenko in *Kazaki: Antropologicheskie ocherki. Sbornik II*, 91

FIGURE 4.3.   Young camels on a tether. Zhangil'dy-Mola. Adai. Photo by S.I. Rudenko in *Kazaki: Antropologicheskie ocherki. Sbornik II*, 89.

The severity of the Adai's herd losses had made them an object of particular fascination for Soviet agronomists and scholars, who saw the Adai as emblematic of the "instability" and "low productivity" of nomadic life.[86] But the harshness of the region's climate, particularly the scarcity of water, raised questions about the limits of Soviet power to overcome environmental constraints. By the eve of the First Five-Year Plan, officials had begun to refer to the republic's most arid regions (which included the Hungry Steppe in the republic's center) as "Central Kazakhstan."[87] The territory of Adai province, the agronomist V. N. Semevskii concluded, was "Central Kazakhstan in Central Kazakhstan," or the most arid part of a very arid region.[88] Though Semevskii's depiction took some liberties with geography (Adai province was in the republic's west), it conveyed the challenges that the party faced. In 1929, a party report found that there was "literally nowhere to settle" in Adai province, with the exception of a small number of oases which were already overpopulated. The region's limited water supply made the cultivation of hay, key to the stabling of animals, impossible. The report concluded that the entire territory of the province was "not suited for sedentarization due to the features of its soil, climate, and hydrology."[89]

Both the Russian empire and the new Soviet state had struggled to gain a foothold in the Mangyshlak Peninsula. In 1928, state officials conceded that the 1917 revolution had barely touched the region.[90] For most of the 1920s, the Mangyshlak region was synonymous with the name of one man: Tobaniyäz Älniyäzŭlï.

Älniyäzülï had a noble lineage: he was the descendant of Konai batyr, a member of the Adai clan who had fought against the Khivan khanate. Under Russian imperial rule, Älniyäzülï had served as a biy (a judge and clan elder), as well as a canton administrator. Later, he sided with Bolshevik forces, becoming the chairman of the Adai uezd revolutionary committee.[91] But his ancestry and pre-revolutionary ties, as well as the overall authority that Älniyäzülï enjoyed among the Adai soon brought him under suspicion: the OGPU reported that the Adai referred to Älniyäzülï as their "khan" and that "under [Älniyäzülï's] rule, not one party or soviet measure was carried in the former Adai uezd without the permission of Älniyäzülï."[92] In 1924, Älniyäzülï was brought to court in Orenburg and removed from his position as chairman of the uezd revolutionary committee.[93] While no longer a Soviet official, Älniyäzülï still exerted an outsized influence over Mangyshlak's affairs: a number of officials sent from Alma-Ata lasted no more than ten days in the region before returning home.[94] In one particularly notorious incident, Shabden Eraliev, the vice-chairman of the province's central executive committee, fell off a boat and drowned in the Caspian Sea under mysterious circumstances, and Älniyäzülï was later linked to his death.[95] Due to the weakness of the party's hold over the province, Adai province was excluded from the 1928 bai confiscation campaign targeting rural elites. In 1928, a party report on the early Soviet period in the Mangyshlak Peninsula concluded, "During this time, the party was utterly unable to manage the work of the Soviet organs of power."[96]

But by 1929–30, as the First Five-Year Plan accelerated, Alma-Ata redoubled its efforts to strengthen its hold over the region. In June 1929, Alma-Ata dissolved the Adai okrug, distributing its constituent parts to Aktiubinsk province and Gur'evsk province, in an attempt to break up the power of the Adai clan.[97] That same year, the Migration Bureau (*Pereselencheskoe upravlenie*), a kind of small-scale precursor to Osedkom, determined that several thousand Adai—along with other households in "Central Kazakhstan"—would need to be resettled and sedentarized due to the "crisis state" of their households.[98] The economic position of the Adai had worsened, but this was in part due to the party's own interventions: in 1927, the province had endured a drought, which was then followed by a zhŭt in 1928. Due to the 1928 bai confiscation campaign as well as intensified grain procurements in the republic's northern provinces, the Adai had been unable to trade their livestock for grain, an important part of their diet. By the spring of 1929, some 60,491 Adai, roughly a third of the province's population, were starving.[99] In search of relief, thousands of Adai fled to Turkmenistan, a territory that many of them regularly traversed during their yearly migrations.

The Migration Bureau's interventions were an assault on the Adai's way of life, an attempt to incorporate a troublesome group that had largely eluded the grasp of both the Russian empire and the new Soviet state. Under the auspices of the Migration Bureau, those Adai who had fled to Turkmenistan would be returned to Kazakhstan. The border between the two republics would now be closed, cutting off the Adai's access to southern seasonal markets and pasturelands. Those Adai brought back from Turkmenistan as well as other groups of Adai targeted in the initial wave of sedentarization would be sent to "labor deficit" regions, including Syr-Daria province (where officials planned to expand a giant state farm devoted to cotton production, Pakhta-Aral), the shores of the Aral Sea (to work on fish production), and parts of Aktiubinsk province.[100] Officials concluded that the Adai had a particularly high number of bais, and bai households were scheduled for removal and deportation as part of the sedentarization process.[101] Eventually, in one of the most dramatic population rearrangements planned for any region of the republic, the entire population of the province was slated to be resettled and sedentarized, with those Adai remaining in the province to be moved near sites of irrigation.[102]

But the Migration Bureau's efforts only increased the chaos in the Mangyshlak region and furthered the Adai's impoverishment. Though two thousand Adai who had fled to Turkmenistan were scheduled to be settled in Syr-Daria province, only 240 households were sedentarized. The rest fled back to Turkmenistan. No housing and little food had been prepared for those who remained, and thirty-five of them died.[103] Those Adai slated for resettlement in Aktiubinsk province refused to move and threatened plenipotentiaries with violence.[104] By December 1929, an OGPU report detailed the emergence of "counterrevolutionary" bands in the Mangyshlak Peninsula, armed with weapons left by White forces during the Civil War. According to the report, bais, former tsarist officials, and even several party members were part of the bands, and the participants demanded the restoration of the Adai okrug.[105] Älniyäzülï was reported to have led 350 Adai households across the border to Turkmenistan, where he had gathered together a group of sixty armed men.[106] In the fall of 1930, Älniyäzülï and several of his followers were captured and shot to death by a troika of the OGPU.[107] By early 1931, the Mangyshlak Peninsula had erupted into a state of open rebellion. The party's initial attempt at integrating the region had failed.

Repression Continues in 1931

Across the rest of the republic, repression continued. In March 1930, Golosh-chekin had pleaded with Stalin for a reduction in the republic's meat procure-ments. He argued that fulfilling these procurements would mean the slaugh-ter of some 30–35 percent of the republic's herds, endangering future sowings (without livestock the fields could not be plowed) as well as the growth of the herd.[108] But by July 1930, the secretary of the Central Committee, Pavel Posty-shev, warned that the supply of meat to Moscow had nearly collapsed. He ordered that the pressure on Kazakhstan and other regions that supplied the city with meat be intensified.[109] Kazakhstan soon became the major meat supplier to both Moscow and Leningrad.[110] In the last three months of 1931, as the republic's herds dwindled to just 30 percent of their 1929 levels, the republic was slated to deliver 59,500 tons of meat to Moscow and Leningrad, more than twice that of any other region or republic.[111] The persistent yet erroneous belief on the part of many Central Committee members that Kazakh nomads continued to harbor enormous amounts of livestock contributed to this pressure. After touring two majority nomadic regions, Kazakhstan and Kirgizia, in January 1931, Anastas Mikoian, the people's commissar for external and internal trade, concluded in a cable to the Central Committee, "In reality, there is a tremendous quantity of unaccounted livestock."[112]

While officials in Moscow and Leningrad dined in comfort on Kazakhs' animal herds, the republic's party committee, under pressure from Moscow, instructed district secretaries to redouble their efforts to uncover even more livestock. They authorized mass campaigns to find livestock that had been "hidden" or "driven into the mountains and deserts," and they promised rewards to collective farm members who found any animals.[113] Though Kazakhstan's economic position was far worse than Leningrad's, Goloshchekin, under pressure from the Central Committee, promised to send an additional fifteen thousand head of cattle to Leningrad due to the city's "difficulties." Noting that this livestock would have to be rounded up from the republic's remote regions, he asked for additional materials and experienced cadres from the RSFSR to reinforce efforts to confis-cate cattle and drive them toward the railway lines.[114] The Mangyshlak Penin-sula endured particularly brutal livestock procurement campaigns.[115] After the temporary retreat of "Dizzy with Success" in the spring of 1930, collectivization rates accelerated again in 1931, skyrocketing from 32 percent in January to 68.9 percent in December.[116] The republic's party committee encouraged activists to push Kazakhs from a looser form of collective farm, the TOZ, into a more restrictive one, the artel.[117] The purpose of this assault was twofold: it produced more meat for city dwellers' dinners at the same time as it impoverished the Kazakhs, facilitating the loss of their status as nomads and their incorporation into the state. Stripped of their herds, the Kazakhs could no longer carry out their seasonal migrations.

In theory, Kazakhs were supposed to be supplied with additional grain to compensate for the loss of their previous food base, their animal herds. But the republic's third secretary, Lev Roshal', admitted that this project was going "very badly," as various agencies squabbled about who had failed to supply Kazakhs with adequate amounts of grain.[118] Moreover, many nomadic regions were still being asked to deliver grain: in the fall of 1930, during a heated exchange with Molotov at a Central Committee meeting on grain procurements, Roshal' had cautioned that the pressure for grain on nomadic regions could not be the same as on "European regions." Any increase in the republic's share, he argued, would come "at the expense of the sedentarized Kazakh population."[119] Nonetheless, in March 1931, Nikolai Shvernik, an emissary of the Politburo, toured Kazakhstan, concluding that there was "considerable amount of grain" to be found in "remote regions" of the republic.[120] On July 1, 1931, Stalin sent Goloshchekin an angry telegram, informing him that he would hold him personally responsible for the delivery of sixty-four thousand tons of grain from the republic's remote regions.[121]

Faced with Stalin's wrath, Roshal' quickly began to demand more grain from the regions. In a telegram to Aksuisk district, a majority Kazakh region, he ordered the delivery of two hundred tons of grain within five days, warning, "The kraikom will consider the slightest delay in the fulfillment of the plan as your personal deliberate desire not to fulfill the task of the party."[122] But by mid-July 1931, much of Kazakhstan, particularly its northern grain-growing regions, was suffering through a terrible drought. The northern city of Semipalatinsk, for instance, received just 4.2 millimeters of rain in June 1931 and 3.4 millimeters of rain in July 1931, when on average the city tended to receive somewhere between 30 and 40 millimeters of rain in each of these months.[123] Writing from Aktiubinsk, where he had been sent by the kraikom to survey the state of grain procurements, Roshal' detailed: "In the steppe, there is a truly unbearable heat, the ground is literally groaning for moisture. Later sowings like wheat, oats, and millet as a rule have not developed."[124] By the close of July 1931, several leading members of the kraikom (Goloshchekin was in Moscow) wrote to Stalin and other Central Committee members to tell them of the impossibility of fulfilling the republic's grain procurement plans due to drought.[125] Frumkin's prediction that the republic's variable weather patterns would result in intermittent poor harvests had come to pass. In the logic of Stalinist planning, neither Moscow nor the weather could be to blame: the republic would have to make up the grain shortfall.

But even as the harvest failed, Moscow sent more people into Kazakhstan, increasing the competition for food. By 1931, Kazakhstan had become one of the major destinations for "special settlers" (*spetspereselentsy*), kulaks who had been forcibly exiled from their home communities during the preceding months' collectivization drive. From 1930 to 1931, a total of 261,227 special settlers were deported to Kazakhstan under the auspices of the OGPU.[126] Most of these deportees came from outside the republic, primarily from European Russia, although internal deportees, or those kulaks and bais resettled within the republic itself, constituted a small group (6,765 households) within the special settler category.[127] In 1930, the first wave of special settlers were sent to work in fish production on the banks of the Aral Sea, while subsequent arrivals in 1931 were slated to work in wheat, cotton, or coal production at various sites within the republic.[128]

The vast majority of special settlers (253,637) arrived in 1931, even as it was clear that the republic's economic position was worsening. Nikolai Boldyrev, sent with his family to Kazakhstan, recalls, "They dumped us out of wagons, without any water or food, into the dry solonchak steppe ten kilometers from the mining city of Karaganda, which was just beginning to be built." He continued, "With the exception of feather grass and thorns, there was nothing."[129] Special settlers sent to the Aral Sea suffered grievously for lack of potable water. Zoia Alekseeva, who was sent there with her family, remembers the onset of famine in 1930: "They fed us badly, and many died."[130] Compounding the chaos and desperate struggle for survival ongoing inside the republic, some 150,000 people, escaping dekulakization in Siberia, had fled across the border into Kazakhstan in 1930.[131]

But even in the midst of this human misery, Moscow continued its relentless focus on industrial development. In August 1931, the Central Committee declared that the Karaganda coal basin in Kazakhstan would become one of the Soviet Union's most important producers of coal.[132] Previously, a number of special settlers (such as Boldyrev's family) had toiled in Karaganda's mines, but this announcement promised a dramatic escalation in Karaganda's size and scope. To feed the growing number of workers at Karaganda, Moscow needed to ensure that a ready supply of food was located nearby. In 1931, the Moscow founded the Karaganda Corrective Labor Camp (KarLag), stationed near the Karaganda mines, and prisoners began to be sent to KarLag from all over the Soviet Union. Once at KarLag, prisoners focused primarily on agricultural labor, growing crops and tending livestock to feed those who worked in the mines. While Kazakhs could starve, coal mine workers could not, and the arrangement highlighted the regime's prioritization of industry at all costs. By December 1932, KarLag had 10,400 prisoners.[133] In the intervening years, KarLag would grow, becoming one of the Soviet Union's largest and longest-lasting corrective labor camps.[134]

To expand Kazakhstan's corrective labor camp system and the special settler program, Moscow began to seize Kazakh pasturelands and "resettle" (i.e., deport and forcibly sedentarize) Kazakhs in other areas of the republic. In May 1930, the republic's Council of People's Commissars transferred 110,000 hectares in Karkaralinsk province, a majority Kazakh region, to the jurisdiction of the OGPU.[135] As hunger increased throughout the republic in 1931, starving Kazakhs sought to return to Karaganda: Dämesh Ermekova, the wife of Temïrbek

Zhurgenov, who would serve as the republic's commissar of enlightenment from 1933 to 1937, recalled that "starving people dragged themselves with their last strength to Karaganda." She continued, "It was several tens of kilometers to Karaganda, and many did not survive the rigors of the trip; they fell and died right along the road."[136] As Ermekova's anecdote illustrates, Kazakhs had descended into a state of extreme suffering. Even Karaganda, a center of forced labor, appeared to offer a greater possibility of finding food than the arid regions of the steppe into which starving Kazakhs had been cast.

With the onset of the First Five-Year Plan, Moscow laid siege to nomadic life. Collectivization, as well as debilitating grain and meat procurements, facilitated the Kazakhs' impoverishment and the loss of their animal herds, the basis of their nomadic way of life. To destroy nomadic life at its roots, officials began to criminalize a range of nomadic practices. Though officials heralded the benefits of planned sedentarization—the "freeing up" of land, resources, and labor and a dramatic increase in the republic's agricultural productivity—efforts to carry out this initiative quickly fell apart. As famine took hold in the winter of 1930–31, Moscow took steps that deepened the level of human suffering in the republic. The regime sent more people into the republic (special settlers, free agricultural colonists, and prisoners) and seized the nomads' lands for these new arrivals, even though elaborate plans to "resettle" the nomads living on these lands had yet to be implemented. Proceeding in part on the basis of a stereotype of nomadic abundance, the Central Committee prioritized the interests of industry (feeding workers in Leningrad, Moscow, or Karaganda) over providing any relief to starving Kazakhs.

In trying to categorize the regime's intentions with regards to collectivization, scholars have typically separated out the weather as an independent variable, something that the regime could not control.[137] Others, focusing on collectivization prior to the outbreak of famine in the Soviet Union's west, have argued that the regime's failures in the period 1929–32 can be attributed to the Soviet regime's inability to understand, anticipate and respond to the natural environment.[138] But this chapter, by contrast, puts the question of environmental factors in a different light. It stresses that the Central Committee had clear information about the risks of nomadic settlement and the possibility of a drought. Focused on increasing the production of grain, the Central Committee accepted the possibility that some Kazakhs might suffer as a result.

But while Moscow had anticipated hunger, the disaster also had many unexpected consequences for the regime: the republic's local and district-level bureaucracy proved to be insufficiently developed to supervise the process of collectivization. Parts of the republic were only nominally under Soviet control. Livestock levels began a precipitous drop, as the regime struggled to develop a system of animal husbandry to take the place of nomadism. Relying on a classic pastoral nomadic strategy, flight, Kazakhs began to escape to neighboring republics and to China. By the end of 1931, the famine had entered a new stage, becoming a widening regional crisis that Moscow would struggle mightily to manage.

5

VIOLENCE, FLIGHT, AND HUNGER
The Sino-Kazakh Border and the Kazakh Famine

In October 1930, just before the winter's snow would make long distance travel impossible, forty families, composed of Kazakhs and Dungans (Chinese Muslims), as well as an individual from European Russia, gathered together from different border districts in an attempt to flee Soviet Kazakhstan.[1] Their journey would take them to the east, into barren, uninhabited stretches of steppe, and finally into the Ili Valley, in the Chinese province of Xinjiang. In preparation for the arduous trek—and perhaps in anticipation of the fact that they might never again return to their homes in the Soviet Union—these families would have taken along their most valuable possessions, including horses and camels (the former primarily for transport of people, the latter for transport of goods). Smaller livestock—sheep, goats, and perhaps cattle, which could not move quickly across the rugged terrain—would either have been sold or slaughtered prior to departure.[2] Their journey would end, it was hoped, in a part of China closely linked to eastern Kazakhstan by geography, culture, and kinship. Though difficult, the route chosen was well traveled: it had been used for centuries by pastoral nomads engaged in regular, seasonal migration.

However, this particular trek was to end quite differently than planned: as the group approached the Chinese border, a band of pursuers, who had been following them since they left the border town of Tekeli, opened fire. Nine families managed to flee, while the others were either killed or captured. A summary of the incident by a state oversight agency, the republic's People's Commissariat of the Worker-Peasant Inspectorate (NK RKI), noted that secret police (OGPU)

122

officials stationed in the region offered conflicting reports on the incident. Most OGPU officials identified the pursuers who had opened fire on the nomads as state border guards. One official noted that eighteen people, including three children and some women, were killed, while another noted that nineteen people, including three children and four women, were shot.[3] Although one of these officials maintained that weapons, specifically, three rifles and one saber, had been confiscated from the families, all of the OGPU officials interviewed pointed out that the families had failed to put up any resistance to their assailants.[4] Summarizing the reports of OPGU officials that detailed the pursuit of those who fled and the accompanying violence, the NK RKI report continued: "According to the materials that we have in Karatal District, [the OGPU] notes that, first of all, there was no resistance on the part of those fleeing; second, that among those killed, there were many members of the poor; and third, among the living, several women and children were raped. And fourth, there was looting of those killed and those who remained alive, so it is necessary that we examine this affair more closely."[5] Subsequent inquiries by additional local OGPU officials served to corroborate that those killed included poor people and those of modest means; a doctor, after examining the women and children, confirmed that many had been raped.[6]

This incident, which became known as the Karatal affair, was only one instance of a much broader pattern of harrowing violence along the Sino-Kazakh border in the early 1930s. Newly opened archival collections in Kazakhstan, many holding secret police reports, correspondence between regime officials, and dispatches by members of the Soviet consulate in Xinjiang, bring to light a largely unknown fact: thousands of people seeking to escape increasingly desperate economic conditions in Kazakhstan were shot and killed in 1930–31 while trying to flee to China.[7] Between 1928 and 1933, a far greater number of people, perhaps as many as two hundred thousand, successfully crossed into Xinjiang.[8]

The flight of these families was prompted by the particularly disastrous repercussions in Kazakhstan of Stalin's First Five-Year Plan, which sought to settle and collectivize the pastoral nomadic Kazakhs simultaneously. By late 1930, large numbers of people in the republic had begun to starve, parts of the republic had erupted into open rebellion, and Kazakh nomads had entered into desperate flight. Relying on their knowledge of seasonal migration routes, as well as historic connections between the Kazakh steppe and western China, starving Kazakhs thronged passages across the republic's border into Xinjiang.

As efforts to halt this exodus, as well as lure Kazakhs back from Xinjiang, failed, the regime responded with violence, using terror as a method of policing this remote borderland. This violence was a reflection of both the region's general lawlessness and the regime's desperation in its struggle to transform the embattled republic into a modernized state. Through a particularly violent enforcement of border controls, authorities in Moscow hoped to halt the republic's economic losses, particularly the massive outflow of labor and work animals to China. This brutality also reflected the regime's struggle to implement its nationality policy or consolidate selected groups into cohesive, defined nationalities in this complex borderland. Seeking to eliminate existing markers of identity, officials used border controls to sever "problematic" cross-border linkages, such as ties of kinship or religion. The language of nationality policy, which stressed that nationality was linked to territory, reinforced the idea that cross-border migrations should be seen as threatening.

Rather than conceding that the policies of the First Five-Year Plan, including collectivization and high grain procurements, were to blame for this exodus, authorities in Moscow invented enemies. Though networks of rebellion did exist alongside the peaceful cross-border migrations of pastoral nomads, officials now recast all cross-border traffic as the machinations of foreign spies and rebels. These brutal measures led to the deaths of thousands, ruptured many longstanding connections between the two regions, and increased tensions with the Republic of China.

Popular Rebellion

The conflict on the Sino-Kazakh border was part of a broader pattern of unrest throughout the republic, which began in 1929. That year, the OGPU, with assistance from Red Army detachments, put down three major uprisings in the republic, each involving several hundred participants.[9] By early 1930, as collectivization began, unrest in Kazakhstan, like other parts of the Soviet Union undergoing rapid collectivization, spread: the OGPU recorded eight major rebellions in the republic that year, many involving thousands of insurgents.[10] Rebels, relying in part on stockpiles of weapons left by White forces during the Civil War, successfully seized control of a city in the republic's south, Suzak, and a city in central Kazakhstan, Irgiz. On assuming control, the rebels returned confiscated property, released prisoners from local jails, and destroyed grain depots. Others fought to reopen mosques closed during the regime's campaign against Islam or to free religious authorities. The Mangyshlak Peninsula in western Kazakhstan, where the regime had struggled to gain a foothold for much of the 1920s, saw some of the fiercest fighting. There were fifteen separate armed conflicts in the peninsula from 1929 to 1931, involving a total of fifteen thousand rebel participants.[11] As fighting continued, the peninsula began to empty out, as thousands of Kazakhs fled to Turkmenistan. Across the republic, the spread of unrest was marked by a dramatic escalation in the use of violence, which both sides appear to have employed to frighten or demonstrate strength over their opponents. Upon seizing control of Suzak, rebels reportedly cut off the heads, hands, and ears of local party workers.[12] In other cases, OGPU officers and district officials were reputed to have drunk the blood of those that they shot.[13]

Most of the uprisings in the republic originated in nomadic areas, which endured some of the harshest grain and livestock requisitions during the first wave of collectivization. But grain and livestock procurements do not appear to have been the only cause of unrest. In the republic's south, which was closer to the holy sites of Central Asia, religious factors appear to have played an important role. Protestors demanded the reopening of mosques closed as part of the regime's campaign against Islam.[14] The party's own district or aul bureaucrats were frequently themselves participants in the unrest, joining forces with the rebels to fight against Red Army forces. Due to the total dissolution of the regime's local-level bureaucracy in these areas, the OGPU was often the party's sole informant on the course of events in rebel-held regions.

Many rebel leaders had a similar profile to Tobaniyäz Älniyäzŭlï, the outlaw who ruled the Mangyshlak Peninsula as his own patrimony for much of the 1920s. They claimed noble lineages and had served as volost' (canton) administrators under Russian imperial rule.[15] In other cases, the leaders of uprisings were religious figures who had a history of conflict with the Soviet regime: Il'ias-Ishan, who claimed descent from the prophet Muhammad, organized uprisings in the Karakalpak Autonomous Oblast, and incited disturbances among the Adai. Ili'as-Ishan's father, Idris-dzhan Kutlykhodzhaev, known as the Kara-Kum Ishan, had led a massive uprising against Soviet power in Ural'sk in 1919. According to OGPU reports, during the 1920s the Kara-Kum Ishan enjoyed "immense popularity and authority" in religious circles stretching from the KAO to Kazakhstan proper to the territory of the former republic of Khorezm.[16] With his death in 1927, Ili'as-Ishan assumed his father's legacy and religious influence.

Numerous environmental factors favored the rebels: V. Popov, an OGPU officer who assisted efforts to put down unrest on the Mangyshlak Peninsula in 1930–31, recalled the difficulty of neutralizing rebellions in remote areas. Though some OGPU officers had cars, the motors of their cars filled with sand when traveling through dusty regions. When they tried to pursue the rebels on horseback, their horses did not have sufficient strength to keep pace with the hardier breed of horses kept by the rebels.[17] Many insurgents had a detailed knowledge of the region's water supply, crucial information given the scarcity of water in arid outposts. On leaving an encampment, Popov recalled, rebels would poison the wells to prevent Red Army forces from following them deeper into the steppe.[18] Due to the difficulties of travel across the steppe, the OGPU occasionally relied on a tactic adopted by other states with nomadic populations. They used planes to gather intelligence, scouting the size and location of rebel bands from the air.[19] The planes then bombarded insurgents with machine gun fire.[20]

Ethnic tensions do not appear to have been the primary cause of the revolts, but the unrest sharpened ethnic conflict in the republic. Most of the participants in the uprisings were Kazakhs, while the OGPU or Red Army forces deployed to end revolts were overwhelmingly from European Russia. Warning that such conflicts drawn along ethnic lines were "politically disadvantageous" to the party's work in the region, OGPU officers urged wider use of the Red Army's sole Kazakh cavalry division to makes such assaults on rebel bands more "effective."[21] In Mangyshlak, where most of the participants in the unrest belonged to the Adai clan, Alma-Ata tried a different tactic. The leaders sent party members from the Adai clan to the peninsula to resolve the conflict. Seytqali Mendeshev, the republic's people's commissar of enlightenment, attempted to negotiate with the rebels and halt the flow of people to Turkmenistan, while Tölesın Äliev headed the Kazakh cavalry division that fought against the insurgents.[22] Ultimately, their efforts would come to fruition: the Mangyshlak uprising was finally put down in late 1931, becoming one of the last major revolts in the republic to be subdued.[23]

The conflict in the republic intensified the mass migration of people first put into motion by hunger: starving people fled advancing Red Army forces, as well as attempts by rebel leaders to levy taxes on them or conscript them for service in rebel armies.[24] Rebels sought refuge in remote areas of the steppe or fled to neighboring republics. This vast sea of people on the move was a mixed group, encompassing nomads carrying out their normal seasonal migrations, refugees seeking relief from hunger, and rebels searching for hiding places from Red Army attacks. But by 1930, Moscow had to come to frame all mobility in the republic from any of these groups as threatening. And in Kazakhstan and elsewhere in the Soviet Union perhaps no form of flight was perceived as more threatening than flight abroad. It raised the specter that borders might be penetrated from the other side, by foreign agents and spies seeking to incite rebellion in the Soviet Union and encourage greater numbers of people to leave.

Scholars of the western Soviet Union in particular have shown how the Bolshevik regime adopted a "carrot and stick" policy in the borderlands during the First Five-Year Plan.[25] Officials in Moscow offered special dispensations and benefits to border districts while threatening tougher measures, including intensified efforts to identify and expel class enemies.[26] As collectivization shifted into high gear in late 1929 and early 1930, security concerns mounted, and the Soviet Union's western borderlands, including those with ethnic groups belonging to the titular nationality of a bordering country such as Poles and Latvians, came under additional scrutiny. In March 1930, Moscow ordered the removal of thousands of Poles from the western borderlands to the Soviet interior.[27]

But in Kazakhstan by late 1930, the situation along the border was both more desperate and more volatile.[28] Massive uprisings had broken out in both Kazakhstan and Ukraine by this period, but in Kazakhstan, rebels used the political instability in Xinjiang to seek cover, regroup, and plan additional attacks. Simultaneously, hundreds of thousands of starving people began to seek relief in Xinjiang, and containing these peaceful refugees, an itinerant population accustomed to seasonal migrations with their herds, in the Soviet Union presented an entirely different challenge from controlling sedentary populations in Ukraine and Belarus. Moreover, when nomads fled Kazakhstan, they took their livestock with them. The departure of large numbers of people was itself a very worrisome political and economic development, but the loss of increasing numbers of animals needed for plowing and transportation dramatically impeded Soviet efforts to transform agriculture.

Interconnected Lands

Although the Sino-Kazakh border was to become one of the Soviet Union's more violent outposts during the First Five-Year Plan, the extent of the bloodshed in this part of Central Asia during the early 1930s marked a departure in the region's history. The lands of eastern Kazakhstan and the territory that would become known as Xinjiang (New Frontier) had long been linked by geography, bonds of kinship, religion, and trade. Distance and enormous natural barriers in the form of deserts and mountains served to isolate Xinjiang, particularly its border with Kazakhstan, from the Chinese heartland. Several valleys in Zungharia, Xinjiang's semidesert northern region, provided unimpeded access to the Kazakh steppe. The Emin Valley led on to central Kazakhstan, including the city of Karaganda, while the Irtysh Valley opened up the direct route to one of Kazakhstan's few cities, Semipalatinsk. The fertile Ili Valley was also easily accessible from Kazakhstan and the west, while largely isolated from the rest of the Chinese province by the Tian Shan and the Borohoro Shen Mountains.

Xinjiang was located in a particularly important geographic position. Throughout the nineteenth and early twentieth centuries, it became a prominent theater in the "Great Game," or the strategic rivalry between the British empire and the Russian empire for supremacy in Central Asia. By the early twentieth century, Xinjiang bordered seven different states or Soviet republics: Russia in the north; Mongolia in the east; Kazakhstan, Kirgizia, and Tajikistan in the west; and

MAP 4. The Sino-Kazakh border in 1930

Afghanistan and India in the south. The geographer Owen Lattimore famously dubbed Xinjiang the "pivot of Asia" for its strategic position.[29]

The Sino-Kazakh borderlands were a complicated intermixture of ethnicities and lifestyles, Muslim and non-Muslim, nomadic and sedentary.[30]

Turkic-speaking Muslim groups, recognized by both regimes as Uyghurs and Kazakhs, populated the Kazakh-Xinjiang borderlands in large numbers.[31] These parts of Central Asia, including Xinjiang, were historically considered part of "Turkestan," a term used to distinguish the territories of the Turkic-speaking nomads from those of Persian speakers farther south. Later, a distinction arose between "Russian Turkestan," the territories controlled by the tsar to the west, and "Chinese Turkestan," the lands held by the Qing dynasty to the east.[32] Xinjiang was a majority Muslim province, where Muslim groups, such as the Uyghurs, greatly outnumbered Han Chinese settlers.

Under tsarist and Qing rule, inhabitants on each side of the border had remained intimately connected with people of the same religion on the other side by means of various networks. The sufis and scholars of Semipalatinsk, an important center of Islamic education in the eastern Kazakh steppe, were linked with the communities of Chinese Turkestan.[33] Jadidism, an Islamic modernist reform movement that arose in the Russian empire, flourished in Xinjiang due to the influence of Muslim Tatars.[34] With the rise of the Republic of China and the Soviet Union, networks of pan-Turkic nationalism helped create a sense of unity that defied national borders. Members of the guerrilla Basmachi movement of Soviet Central Asia also cultivated ties in Xinjiang and often sought refuge there.

The various cross-border groups might be mapped as follows: Kazakhs made up a national majority on the Soviet side and an important national minority in Xinjiang; Uyghurs were the majority population in Xinjiang (although only a small group within greater China) and a national minority in small parts of Kazakhstan. Various other groups, including Kirgiz and Dungans (also known as Hui), populated both sides of the border in lesser numbers. Slavic settlers (Russians and Ukrainians) and small numbers of Siberian Cossacks also inhabited these regions. Additionally, several Kazakh clans also had a significant cross-border presence.[35]

Throughout the early period of Soviet and Republican Chinese rule, numerous counterrevolutionary movements spilled over into Xinjiang and eastern Kazakhstan. Throughout the 1920s, bandits from the Basmachi, a pan-Central Asian guerrilla group, fled across the border into Xinjiang, as well as to Iran and Afghanistan, where they continued to cultivate contacts with groups in Soviet Central Asia.[36] Xinjiang itself was ruled by a succession of warlords, who often chose to align the province more closely with the Soviet Union than with the Chinese government. One of Xinjiang's more colorful warlords, Sheng Shicai (who ruled from 1933 to 1944), welcomed Soviet advisers into his government and granted the Soviets economic concessions to Zungharia's mineral wealth. In the 1930s, movements of pan-Turkic nationalism began to emerge in Xinjiang, and by 1933, separatists declared a short-lived "East Turkestan Islamic Republic."

During 1932–34, much of Xinjiang was in open rebellion. Soviet military intervention on behalf of Sheng Shicai, however, helped crush these rebellions and restore warlord rule.[37]

Cross-Border Flight Begins

The 1881 Treaty of St. Petersburg formally demarcated the border between Russian Turkestan and Chinese Turkestan.[38] Groups that had freely crisscrossed the boundary between the two states were forced to declare loyalties and curtail their migration. Nonetheless, communities living on one side of the new division or the other continued to steal across the border to flee repression or unfavorable economic conditions. The guards who policed the borders might have on occasion overlooked such activity, especially when the arrival or departure of a particular group was considered desirable. However, both Russia and China sought to assert control over border traffic, at times seeking the extradition of certain groups deemed to be living on the Russian or Chinese side.

The first major cross-border flow during this era began with the closure of the border in 1881, when some fifty thousand Dungans and Uyghurs fled Chinese Turkestan and Qing rule and settled in Semirech'e.[39] From 1912 to 1914, as Russian and Ukrainian settlers from European Russia poured into the Kazakh steppe, thousands of nomadic Kazakhs fled to the Ili Valley in search of pasture.[40] St. Petersburg sought the repatriation of many of those who fled, but Beijing insisted that the number of repatriates could not exceed six thousand. Beginning with the revolt of 1916 in Central Asia and continuing into the revolutionary and Civil War eras, large numbers of communities living in Central Asia fled one revolutionary regime—what was to become the Soviet Union—for another—the nascent Republic of China.[41] Hundreds of thousands of Kazakhs, Kirgiz, Dungans, and Slavic settlers took flight from Russian Turkestan, while White Army officers set up camp in Kuldja (present-day Yining), just over the border in the Ili Valley, where they plotted reprisals against the Soviet government.[42]

During 1925–28, pastoral nomadic groups continued limited cross-border migrations. By early 1928, however, large numbers of people began to flee Kazakhstan once again due to the rumors of the coming confiscation campaign against Kazakh elites. According to party statistics, 423 households, with 22,000 head of cattle, from Semipalatinsk province fled to China, most well before violence began.[43] OGPU officials stationed in the border districts kept detailed lists of those arrested while trying to cross into Xinjiang and the amount of livestock confiscated in the process.[44] Officials expressed surprise that the majority of those who fled could not be considered bais but rather were members of the poor. They maintained that cross-border kinship networks, as well as the exploitative influence of bais, had contributed to these departures. In the version of events presented by Goloshchekin and other Soviet officials, bais coerced fellow kin members to flee, while foreign agents engaged in smuggling.[45]

While relatively small in number, there were nonetheless enough refugees from Semipalatinsk to worry party members. Although the loss of resources (workers and cattle) was bad enough, top party members (including Stalin and Georgii Chicherin, the people's commissar of foreign affairs) expressed concern about the broader political impression of flight, especially that of Kazakhs from their own autonomous republic to China.[46] At a time when the Soviet state was promoting formerly "oppressed" nationalities, such as the Kazakhs, the readiness of so many people from these ethnic groups to flee across the border to their brethren and put themselves at the "service of Asian China" was an unintended and frustrating outcome.[47] In response, party members discussed, but never implemented, the creation of a buffer zone along the Kazakh border to Xinjiang.[48] As in the case of the 1916–20 wave of flight from revolutionary Russia, officials tried to lure these groups back to Kazakhstan. Under an amnesty program, Kazakhs and Slavic settlers were allowed to return from Xinjiang, with their cattle, through February 19, 1929.[49]

But despite the considerable attention given the Sino-Kazakh border during the investigation into the flight from Semipalatinsk, by 1930, as attempts to accelerate the First Five-Year Plan within Kazakhstan intensified, flight from the autonomous republic reached a critical stage. Borderland populations began to disappear. A steady flow of people from the border districts into China continued, as entire auls vanished overnight. In the Zaisan district (a majority Kazakh district), some 1,238 households left for China in 1930, nearly one-third of the population.[50] According to "incomplete" party data for the three border districts of Semipalatinsk province, in 1930 alone, border guards halted some 2,481 households trying to flee with "enormous collections of livestock."[51] In Kegen district, worried officials noted that six hundred households had relocated in mountains near the border, where they waited for the arrival of spring to cross into China.[52] According to incomplete OGPU figures, 15,302 people fled in 1930 and 36,985 in 1931.[53]

This new wave of cross-border flight, Soviet bureaucrats noted, was primarily a problem among ethnic Kazakh and Uyghur communities.[54] The predominantly Kazakh border districts were losing people with increasing rapidity—"Here, we have many instances of even the flight of collective farm workers, even the collective farm as a whole under the leadership of its chairman"—while in neighboring Russian border districts "no movements of out-migration" were reported.[55] Even aul Soviet leaders and Komsomol members were fleeing to China, especially the Kazakhs, followed by Uyghurs.[56] Astonished state officials found themselves always one step behind the next surge of flight. A secret police report recorded that before fleeing across the border, collective farm members had scrawled a parting message across the walls of the collective farm: "We fulfilled the Five-Year Plan in one day. Take an example from us!"[57]

These tales of a better life in Xinjiang were lent further credence by a severe shortage of household goods along the Kazakh-Xinjiang border. Basic items, such as matches, kerosene, salt, and iron, were extremely difficult to find. Observers reported that Kazakh communities clothed themselves in sheepskin for want of anything else to wear.[58] In October 1931, OGPU reports continued to detail a severe shortage of essential products. The distribution of goods reached the absurd: while many living near the border lacked sugar or even shoes, provincial officials had delivered large shipments of perfume to several border districts.[59]

But more than any other good, it was a severe shortage of tea, a crucial element of Central Asian cuisine, that contributed to smuggling, as well as the continuing exodus of people, party officials noted:

> To buy, for instance, a sheep for money is not easy, and you will have to pay fifty rubles for the sheep. But it is enough to have 1/4 [of a brick] of tea, and you can get any sheep. Horses (the most convenient form of property during a flight) are more expensive, but two bricks of tea, it is said, can be exchanged for a horse. Wealthy and famous is he who has the most tea. It is no wonder that a bai, if one were to judge his possessions by the amount of livestock, appears to be a bedniak. It is no wonder that after this, in one of the Dungan or [Uyghur] kishlaks,[60] one might say that due to tea the sowing campaign was wrecked. It is no wonder that tea is the main contraband good. It is no wonder that livestock, a mobile and simple property, which can be found only among the Kazakhs, is sent with great difficulty and risk to China, so that they [Kazakhs] can trade it there for tea.[61]

In the eyes of the regime, the overwhelming desire for tea among border communities (especially Kazakhs, Uyghurs, and Dungans) was a worrying development, especially given the mobile nature of Kazakh "wealth" (livestock). By engaging in the lucrative tea trade (rather than collecting livestock), a bai might easily disguise himself and wreak havoc in border communities more interested in trading their last animal for tea than in joining party-sponsored drives to sow the fields. And through an illegal trade network that favored tea above all else, a bai might covertly stockpile tea, rapidly exchange it for horses, assemble a group of fellow kin members, and vanish across the border overnight. Imagined networks, such as those of tea-hoarding, border-crossing bais, came to preoccupy Soviet authorities determined to stop the refugees.

As flight to Xinjiang intensified, officials in Alma-Ata worked to develop strategies to halt the flow of population and livestock. An April 1930 ruling of the Kazakh Council of People's Commissars provided that a wide assortment of groups seen as disruptive to the republic's security would be sent one hundred kilometers away from the districts bordering on China into the Kazakh interior. These included bais and kulaks caught attempting or planning to flee, bais and kulaks whose families or property had already crossed the border, and all the members of a bai or kulak family, if the head of the family had already crossed the border.[62] Since many officials believed cross-border ties of kinship abetted flight, plans to deport bais with family members abroad were a logical preventive measure.

Yet as widespread flight began to paralyze border regions and reports of bai intervention continued to emerge, desperate local officials began to take increasingly creative measures to check flight. Significantly, district officials, in cooperation with border guards and the OGPU, used the April 1930 ruling to collect detailed biographical sketches of suspicious community members, including the amount of time they had spent abroad and the existence of familial ties in Xinjiang. At the initiative of district officials, persons or families seen as particularly troublesome were exiled from the borderlands.[63] Local OGPU officials anxiously tried to develop indicators of flight to thwart the exodus of groups before they left for the border. Most flight, officials noted, occurred in the springtime; an increase in the sale or slaughter of small livestock, such as sheep, in border regions was yet another indicator that a group might be preparing to flee to China.[64] On occasion, local officials, acting on their initiative, engaged in preventive raids, confiscating items essential for flight, such as horses.[65] Although some district officials proposed population transfers, such as moving groups residing near the border farther west, officials with the OGPU in Alma-Ata rejected such suggestions, proposing instead a renewed focus on party work.[66]

But while officials in Alma-Ata framed energetic work among collective farm workers and the poor and renewed attention to the distribution of state grain collections as the antidote to flight, border district officials protested that directives from Alma-Ata, specifically onerous state-mandated grain procurements, were precisely what was driving people to flee. After repeated requests to lower his district's oat and livestock quota were turned down by officials in Alma-Ata, an exasperated local official questioned, "Is strengthening flight to China, for the most part bedniaks, really in the interest of the party?"[67]

By March 1931, in a letter to Molotov and Stalin, Goloshchekin and Shalva Eliava proposed a number of changes, including supplying border districts with additional bread and goods. They also suggested that the party pay closer atten-tion to the composition of state collective farms in border districts. Single-clan collective farms, or those collective farms where members were closely organized along kinship lines, were seen as particularly susceptible to cross-border flight, and Goloshchekin and Eliava recommended that they be disbanded entirely. Activists would now work to replace these types of farms with "real collective farms" (*deistvitel'nye kolkhozy*), those organized from a multitude of different kinship lineages, while bais and clan leaders would be exiled from them altogether.

Spies and Rebels: The Search for Scapegoats

Officials in Alma-Ata portrayed flight to Xinjiang as a "class problem. They saw its increase in 1930 and 1931 as the harbinger of an intensifying "class war," as migrants, described as "wealthy bais and kulaks," fought to keep their privileges.[68] The 1928 confiscations were done poorly in border districts, wrote officials, hence the inordinate influence of the exploiting social classes.[69] But as bureau-crats tallied data on the social composition of would-be migrants, they came to a disquieting conclusion: the majority of those fleeing to Xinjiang could not be classified as bais, but as people of much more modest means.[70] Republic-level officials tried to rationalize this flight, arguing that bais had manipulated the "excesses" or "mistakes" of the lower-party bureaucracy to convince other social classes to flee with them. Yet Soviet officials also concluded that bais relied heav-ily on the bonds of kinship as well, a particular problem in a vast territory where state boundaries rarely coincided with familial connections.

Bais, officials maintained, helped spread fantastical rumors about collectiviza-tion, chief among them the widespread suspicion that children would be collec-tivized (much like livestock) and sent away from their families. As official after official in the districts reported this misconception,[71] policy makers in Alma-Ata suggested a rethinking of the party's approach toward the Kazakh population: "At first glance, it seems absurd that such a nonsensical rumor could be taken for the truth. But if we are to take into consideration the complete unenlightened darkness and the almost full illiteracy of the population, which does not have any impression of newspapers and books nor the Soviet message, then it becomes clear how the most foolish rumors are understood by the population, strongly worrying them and directing them toward fear."[72] While the rumor that the state would appropriate children was perhaps one of the most pervasive, other rumors, including one to the effect that the state would confiscate all household goods, continued to spur migration.[73] Much like the Semipalatinsk affair, during which entire communities fled across the border based on rumors of a looming confiscation campaign, large numbers of Kazakhs departed in 1930 based on rumors about collectivization.

But rather than addressing the root causes of these departures, including violent, forced collectivization and hunger, the dissemination of rumors by "foreign agents'" became one of the party's official explanations for flight. Officials argued that foreign agents peddled border populations a story of a new life in China free from the burdens that a continued existence in Soviet Kazakhstan seemed to offer: "Through these persons, rumors about a free life in China, where there are no poor, but all are rich, where there is much bread [and] manufactured goods, and taxes are negligible, and that the Chinese government gives emigrants assistance, including giving them land, all the way to setting aside refugees in their own independent region, assist flight."[74] Many of these purported foreign agents worked in conjunction with bais, who due to historical traditions of migration, continued to freely cross the Sino-Kazakh frontier, officials held.[75]

Soviet border guards stationed in the districts bordering China, among whom numbered Konstantin Chernenko, later to become general secretary of the Communist Party, played an important role in halting flight.[76] They compiled lists of influential bais believed to be fomenting opposition or conducting armed raids into Soviet territory from the other side of the border.[77] They also tracked the names of clans seen as particularly troublesome, such as the Kerey, a lineage with significant cross-border presence, and qozhas, members of a religious elite in Kazakh society.[78] On occasion, individuals considered particularly influential, such as Alen' Chzhinsakhanovich Kugedaev, a Kerey leader who had been living in Xinjiang since the 1916 revolt, were kept under surveillance. Erroneously labeled a "Kazakh prince" by the Soviet border guards who shadowed his activities in Xinjiang, Kugedaev was said to have refused "categorically" Soviet and Chinese requests for the extradition of particular Kazakh migrants, asserting that "these were his brothers."[79] For the Soviets, Kugedaev's invocation of kinship in conjunction with his refusal was a worrisome development. The seeming influence of this "Kazakh prince" raised the possibility that the Soviets were falling behind in their battle to subordinate kinship ties to class interests.

OGPU reports were particularly preoccupied with a group they called *Kitkazakhi*, or Kazakhs with Chinese citizenship. The Kitkazakhi, according to the police, exploited cross-border familial ties, regularly penetrating Kazakhstan's border districts to guide their relatives back into Xinjiang: "Often, there is direct assistance from Kazakhs with Chinese citizenship to those fleeing, such as sending armed gangs from abroad for assistance in crossing."[80] Tales of "armed gangs of Kitkazakhi" alarmed officials for several reasons: Kitkazakhi, officials believed, operated in the murky world of clan-based ties, using bai influence to coerce their kin to flee across the border with them. These backward, clan-based forms of affiliation, in turn, hampered the Kazakhs in developing their own class interests in Soviet Kazakhstan, the theory went. Moreover, in the eyes of the Soviet authorities, the Kitkazakhi were "Chinese," and they were "armed." For the Soviets, Kitkazakhi embodied two persistent yet interconnected official fears: the threat of popular rebellion and an obsession with Chinese influence in Kazakhstan.

Official fears of banditry and uprisings on the border were further magnified by a steady stream of illegal immigrants, some 150,000, from Siberia into eastern Kazakhstan in the spring of 1930. As Goloshchekin detailed in a telegram to Molotov and Kaganovich many of these illegal immigrants (*samovol'tsy*) should be classified as "kulaks" or "kulak hirelings." Even more troubling, many of these new arrivals had begun to settle near the Sino-Kazakh border, where they established cross-border ties via a number of activities, including the laundering of money (as much as "2,000 rubles in gold and 10,000 rubles in currency" in the case of one individual) for White Army officers in western China. Goloshchekin reported that provincial officials had begun to ban samovol'tsy from Kazakhstan's border districts, yet the presence of these settlers continued to cause "serious complications" for party work.[81]

Throughout 1930 and 1931, the regime struggled to maintain control over the republic's eastern border. Rebels, many armed with weapons left by White forces during the Civil War, crossed into Xinjiang to regroup before reentering Kazakhstan. Desperate officials in the border districts reported that efforts to stop cross-border flight were futile. Open combat had erupted as border guards and party activists chased down and shot armed rebels and helpless refugees alike. OGPU reports recorded an almost daily toll of violence as border guards shadowed groups of migrants of four hundred or more. In the bloody clashes that almost inevitably followed, some emigrants were shot while others were taken prisoner; scores more fled into the depths of the mountains to hide. Party officials seized hundreds of horses as well as numerous rifles, munitions, and sabers.[82]

Blocked in their efforts to cross into Xinjiang, migrants from Kazakhstan frequently swung south into Kirgizia in the hope of making the crossing there. The arrival of thousands of migrants alarmed Kirgiz officials, who viewed these people as disruptive to the political balance in their own republic. Top Kirgiz officials began to pen angry missives to Goloshchekin, charging that the migrants from Kazakhstan spread "counterrevolutionary rumors among the Kirgiz population about famine . . . and strengthened the mood for emigration into China."[83] In the eyes of Kirgiz authorities, Kazakhstan's disastrous economic situation and the resultant failure of Kazakh officials to secure their own border with China had become a threat to stability and security throughout Soviet Central Asia.

Though Goloshchekin, as well as other top republic-level officials, were aware that tens of thousands of people in Kazakhstan were starving by 1930, they continued to depict the violence directed at migrants as a means of defending the revolution, a tactic necessary to halt rebels and restore order.[84] However, members of the OGPU deployed just across the Chinese side of the border in Kuldja recounted in 1931 that even the "most merciless measures" had failed to curtail flight along the border:

> No severe measures by the border guards in fighting the flow across the border gave any real results in halting the tide of flight. The measures were of the most merciless kind. Over the course of the year [1930] more than 1,000 people who were trying to flee illegally to Chinese territory were killed on the border with the Illi region. . . . This year, in connection with massive flight, movements of banditry strengthened. They were formed for the most part on Chinese territory from refugees from the Kazakh ASSR who were well acquainted with the border territory. These refugees carry on a strengthened agitation for flight and on the other hand carry on an invasion of the peaceful inhabitants of the border zone.[85]

As these intelligence operatives portrayed the problem, flight and revolt were intimately connected; the eradication of flight was a critical step in combating insurgency in border districts. Insurgents, it was believed, cultivated "nationalist" aims, including connections with the since-disgraced Alash Orda, a provisional Kazakh government that had ruled parts of the Kazakh steppe during the Civil War era. One of Alash Orda's strongholds had been Semipalatinsk, and its former members were now believed to be staking out counterrevolutionary cells just across the border.[86]

The accounts of individual border incidents, to return to the Karatal affair described at the outset, provide insight into how violence was used to discourage migration. Though officials in Alma-Ata launched an inquiry into the Karatal affair, the question of who ordered and carried out the attack on the forty families—border guards, overzealous collective farm members, or perhaps someone else altogether—remained unclear throughout the investigation. While it is perhaps unsurprising that the perpetrators in the Karatal affair did not immediately come to light, the conduct of the NK RKI investigation, particularly its tardiness and lackluster nature, is instructive. While ostensibly an investigation into identifying those responsible for the shootings, the party also sought to use the inquiry to monitor the cross-border activities of influential individuals and their family members. In his report, the head of the NK RKI investigation carefully noted that several relatives of a powerful clan leader, Seid-Akhmet Mukhamed, had fled across the border into China during the shootings of the other families.[87]

NK RKI launched an investigation into the affair on January 24, 1931, well over three months after the October 1930 shooting.[88] The NK RKI representative, who signed his name simply as Panchekhin, collected conflicting accounts of the affair from district officials and charged that some OGPU officials in Karatal district (Taldy-Kurgan district after the redrawing of district borders in late 1930) had taken charge of the investigation and had deliberately scuttled any serious inquiry. Many local officials interviewed by Panchekhin charged that bai and clan-based connections had hampered a full examination of the affair, as party activists who were from the same clan as the perpetrators sought to protect them. Moreover, as Panchekhin discovered, the bodies of those killed still lay near the border, rotting in the winter snow; district officials rejected as "meaningless" suggestions that the bodies be examined. It was better, they concluded, to continue the party's work with the poor. The affair was also discussed in a separate report on district redistricting, which was sent to the kraikom, yet this report was equally inconclusive.[89]

Some Karatal District officials interviewed during the NK RKI investigation insisted that the families had been armed and had therefore had been shot "correctly." Others, however, questioned whether the families had been armed at all. They believed instead that an unrealistic grain procurement campaign, implemented by overly aggressive district officials, had left destitute families of various ethnicities no other choice than to flee. The difference was one between depicting the victims as "armed rebels" or as "starving refugees." As the Karatal affair illustrates, Soviet officials were willing to turn a blind eye to indiscriminate violence, ignoring, when expedient, real distinctions between "rebel" and "refugee," but the dispute over defining the victims in the Karatal affair concerned more than domestic issues.

A Diplomatic Row Ensues

At the same time, the level of frustration among Soviet officials was driven to new heights by events in China. During the period of high migration to Xinjiang, 1928–33, China was itself in considerable turmoil, and the Soviet Union broke off and resumed diplomatic relations with China several times during this period.[90] In September 1931, imperial Japan occupied Manchuria, while Xinjiang continued to be ruled by a series of warlords. If the Soviets were engaged in a struggle to control their side of the border, then the same had to be said of the Chinese in monitoring border traffic from within Xinjiang. Soviet fears of a Chinese state too weak to patrol its borders in turn served to bolster concerns among officials in Moscow, thus helping make the Soviets more willing to resort to violence to stop the flow of migrants to the east.

Other powers, such as the British and the Japanese, cultivated contacts in Xinjiang, and the possibility of interference by either power helped magnify Soviet fears over the porous 1,700-kilometer border that separated Xinjiang and Kazakhstan. Under Sheng Shicai's rule, Xinjiang gained a reputation for "murder, intrigue, espionage and counter-espionage," as these powers worked to bring Xinjiang under their sphere of influence.[91] Turkic rebels in Xinjiang sought military support from Japan, and in 1933, several Japanese generals were linked to a plot to install a puppet regime in Inner Asia, including Xinjiang.[92] The possibility of British influence in Xinjiang was also a source of concern. In the late nineteenth century the British used the vantage point of British India to station agents in Kashgar, and throughout the early period of Soviet rule, the British continued to collect surveillance on Xinjiang and Soviet Central Asia from India.

The Soviet regime's ever-increasing paranoia over the disorder in Xinjiang helped bolster the suspicion that those who fled were "rebels" and not "refugees." In January 1931, OGPU reports sent to Lev Karakhan, the Soviet Union's ambassador to China and a deputy people's commissar for foreign affairs, detailed the seeming persistence of rebel networks near the border: "These gangs were carefully organized. They had their own organizers, connecting with separate individuals from the lower apparatus of the Chinese administration . . . [the Chinese contacts] conducted agitation for the departure to China of parts of the population in the Soviet border zones, offering cooperation in fleeing and assistance in getting set up on the Chinese border."[93]

By March 1931, several months prior to the Japanese invasion of Manchuria, official fears of foreign interference in Kazakhstan had reached the highest levels of the party bureaucracy. Goloshchekin and Eliava, the deputy people's commissar of foreign trade and deputy people's commissar of light industry, warned Stalin and Molotov that the Soviet diplomatic and trade missions in Xinjiang were "contaminated with foreign elements," including "Russian white army officers" who assisted the Chinese government in sponsoring flight from Kazakhstan. Soviet border officials posted along the Sino-Kazakh frontier, Eliava and Goloshchekin concluded, were similarly contaminated. Yet foreign interference in Kazakhstan's affairs, they warned, could not be attributed solely to the Chinese. "We have reports that Nanking is increasing its pressure on Xinjiang province and even more strongly tying it under their influence, and, behind the back of Nanking, the English are developing a big political and trade interest in Xinjiang."[94] As Eliava and Goloshchekin's report suggests, the Soviets were closely following developments in Xinjiang. Attempts by the authorities in Beijing to tie the warlord-ruled province more closely to the Chinese central government and, by extension, to the British, were seen as interference in the Soviets' own affairs.

Confronted by many of the themes from the Great Game, the Soviets began to envision double agents and foreign spies at every turn. After one scare involving "agents" allegedly engaged in clandestine talks with the Chinese consulate in Alma-Ata, it was ordered that all official correspondence be carried out only through OGPU channels.[95] Reports in *Kazakstanskaia pravda,* the republic's main Russian-language newspaper, speculated that the British, perhaps even the Japanese, were plotting to invade the Soviet Union via Xinjiang.[96] The permeable nature of the Sino-Kazakh border alarmed Soviet authorities, who recast every incident on the border as the work of foreign emissaries.

Diplomatic correspondence between Chinese officials in the Ili Valley and the Soviet consulate in Kuldja from 1930 to 1931 shows that the Soviets' twin fears of rebellion and foreign interference on the Sino-Kazakh border had laid the foundations for an international dispute. By 1930, as the flood of refugees from Kazakhstan began to tax China's resources, the fate of the refugees and the security of the Sino-Kazakh border became the subject of heated talks between representatives of the Soviet consulate and Chinese diplomats. As wave after wave of migrants arrived, Chinese officials reported that Kazakhstan's disastrous economic situation was creating a refugee problem of such enormity that it was impossible to police Xinjiang's border effectively. Migrants from Kazakhstan, in their efforts to elude Soviet border guards, were resorting to "tiny, little paths" that were difficult to monitor or staking out high-altitude base camps, where they waited for weeks for border patrols to pass before crossing into Xinjiang.[97]

In a series of angry letters to the Soviet consulate in Kuldja, Chinese diplomats alleged that Soviet officials had disrupted order and security in the region. In Kazakhstan, Soviet border guards—unable to check the flow of refugees or staunch the threat of counterrevolution from abroad—had begun to conduct armed raids into Chinese territory, where, according to Chinese reports, they carried out the "harshest measures" of reprisal, including the shooting of refugees, the confiscation of cattle, and the looting of the dead. In one particular case, Soviet border guards followed a group of two hundred to three hundred people into Xinjiang; once both parties had crossed the border, a bloody melee ensued.[98] In another incident, a wandering shepherd informed Chinese border guards of a mass grave in a desert region near the Soviet border. On inspection, the bodies of over fifty Kazakh refugees, including adults and children, as well as eight dead horses, were found. Investigators determined that all had died from injuries sustained from firearms or sabers.[99]

The Chinese protested Soviet raids into Xinjiang, describing them as a violation of "international law" and "Chinese sovereignty" and warned that they posted a threat to the "friendly relations" of neighboring countries: "If our border guards had heard the gunshots and had returned fire, a great border conflict would have emerged and the responsibility for that conflict, which would be clear to everyone, would have been on the Soviet side."[100] Soviet attacks on Chinese territory terrorized Xinjiang's own people, who, Chinese officials reported, had fled areas near the border in fright, even leaving their yurts and possessions behind. Soviet diplomats, Chinese officials charged, were recalcitrant, demanding the extradition of refugees and livestock, while unwilling to return to Xinjiang and collect the bodies of those they had killed.[101] Xinjiang officials, however, did cooperate in the Soviets' requests for repatriation: During the spring of 1930, over two thousand people were extradited from Xinjiang.[102]

With Kazakhstan's crisis spilling over the border, Soviet and Chinese officials sparred over the border instability created by the refugee problem. Increasingly, the inflammatory Sino-Kazakh border involved the highest levels of the party. On February 13, 1931, Stalin and Molotov cabled Eliava on the issue of the border, instructing him to take "immediate actions together with Goloshchekin at the local level."[103] Responding to Stalin and Molotov on March 8, 1931, Goloshchekin and Eliava warned that the "political situation of the regions that border Kazakhstan is an emergency situation, notwithstanding the measures that have been taken by the kraikom." They proposed a purge of all Soviet representatives in Xinjiang, including the trade mission and consulate. Despite the armed attacks on migrants, in Kazakhstan and in Xinjiang, in the spring of 1931 flight was "beginning once again to gather strength," they warned.[104]

Securing the Sino-Kazakh border presented particular challenges for Soviet officials. Along this remote and porous boundary, even concerted efforts to check cross-border flight were defeated by the impenetrability of the steppe, a landscape where migrants might always find yet another hiding place. While the physical environment of this borderland afforded refugees cover, the mobility of certain key resources—people and cattle—further exasperated officials intent on rooting populations in one place. The border that separated Kazakhstan and Xinjiang divided relatives and families. The Soviet regime's attempts to police this border with violence began to tear apart those ties.

In their attempts to secure the Sino-Kazakh border, Soviet bureaucrats confronted problems very different from those in the western borderlands of the Soviet Union, namely a highly mobile group accustomed to seasonal migration (Kazakhs), as well an economy based on an easily transportable commodity (livestock). The twin challenges of geography and lifestyle were further compounded by the emergence of a famine of staggering scale, proportionately the Soviet Union's worst collectivization disaster. As widespread hunger set in, thousands of people, some searching for food, others cultivating rebel networks, began to cross into Xinjiang.

Rather than deporting troublesome groups, an approach the regime had pursued in the western borderlands, officials responded with violence, slaughtering several thousand people who attempted to cross the border. Though it is difficult to determine whether Moscow ordered these killings, it tacitly endorsed them. Violence, chaos, and armed incursions across the border continued, even when they undermined Soviet relations with China. The Soviet regime's response was in part due to paranoia among officials about the weakness of the Chinese state and the extent of foreign influence, especially Japanese and British, within China. It also represented an attempt to neutralize popular rebellion, and during the famine Kazakhstan saw some of the Soviet Union's largest revolts. A key principle of Soviet nationality policy, the idea that nationality was linked to territory, served to underpin and justify this violent assault on Kazakh life.

6

KAZAKHSTAN AND THE POLITICS OF HUNGER, 1931–34

"Suffering was not leaving our heads; our eyes were full of tears." With these words, Duysen Asanbaev, a famine survivor, recalled the desperation of the Kazakh famine's final phase, as more than a million starving Kazakhs fled, seeking refuge elsewhere in the republic and beyond its borders.[1] Moscow's policy of collectivization, launched in the winter of 1929–30, had provoked immense human suffering throughout the republic in the preceding two years, including famine and population flight, particularly across the border to China. But by the winter of 1930–31, the food crisis inside the republic had deepened to the extent that almost every Kazakh was in flight. For Kazakhs, the decision to leave was not an easy one, as it meant abandoning their ancestral pasturelands and belongings. After seeing his father and several of his younger brothers die of hunger, Sëden Mëlïmŭlï, then an eleven-year-old boy, remembers that he and his mother made the difficult choice to flee their aul for the district of Ulken-Naryn. Russians worked in the district's mines, and Sëden and his mother believed that it would be a more likely place to find food.[2] With their herds in ruins, those who remained behind faced an almost certain death: Zeitïn Aqïshev, who worked as a teacher in the city of Semipalatinsk, remembers touring abandoned settlements on the city's outskirts. Most huts were empty, but in one he found two skeletons intertwined, lovers trapped in an embrace.[3]

Moscow had anticipated that the party's assault on Kazakh nomadic life would provoke hunger, but this massive migration, the region's most far-reaching population displacement since the Zungar invasion of the Kazakh steppe in the early eighteenth century, was an unanticipated consequence. Those who fled were almost exclusively Kazakh, a reflection of the famine's particularly disastrous effects on the Kazakh aul, as well as Kazakhs' status as pastoral nomads, a group that regularly used flight as a means of seeking relief from unfavorable political or environmental conditions. In its scale and scope—refugees flooded cities and industrial worksites within Kazakhstan, as well as neighboring Soviet territories, including Western Siberia and the Middle Volga of the RSFSR, Uzbekistan, Kirgizia, and Turkmenistan, and international destinations (China and, to a much lesser degree, Iran and Afghanistan)—the Kazakh refugee crisis far exceeded population flight due to hunger in the Soviet Union's west. In the space of just eight months (the period June 1931–February 1932), the number of registered households in the republic dropped by 22.8 percent, as more than three hundred thousand households, over a million people, entered into flight.[4] Reflecting on 1931, the year this immense population movement began, a district-level official later commented: "The entire population of the Kazakh auls was, one might say, on wheels."[5] Some Kazakhs found relief where they fled, but for most this mass exodus from the countryside did not ease their misery. By the famine's end in 1934, some 1.5 million people, a quarter of the republic's population, had perished in a cataclysm of unprecedented proportions.

Moscow framed this tide of suffering people on the move as a sign of success and progress. Kazakh refugees were not referred to *bezhentsy* (refugees) but rather as *otkochevniki* (literally, nomads who are moving away). For Filipp Goloshchekin, the republic's leader and party secretary, the appearance of otkochevniki was part of a necessary *perekhod*, or transition, in Kazakhs' development into a socialist nation, as Kazakhs began to shed the backward practice of nomadism. He concluded, "The old aul is now breaking apart, it is moving toward settled life, toward the use of hay fields, toward land cultivation; it is moving from worse land to better land, to state farms, to industry, to collective farm construction." Those who were "panicking" or "predicting destruction," he argued, simply longed for the past and did not understand the socialist future.[6] This transitional stage demanded extra vigilance, officials warned, and the party intensified its assault on nomadism, declaring fantastical plans to settle the Kazakhs even more quickly than before. As happened elsewhere in the Soviet Union during collectivization, Moscow introduced a range of brutal tactics in response to this social cataclysm: the closure of borders so that the starving could not flee, the processing and surveillance of refugees, the expulsion of famine-stricken people as "undesirable elements" from the cities, and the "blacklisting" of certain districts within the republic, a severe penalty that included a total ban on trade and deliveries of food.[7]

But Moscow could not control the crisis: focused on implementing a breakneck program of state-driven modernization, officials had ignored warnings from medical experts who, noting the republic's relative lack of modern medical services, had urged the party to devote more resources to the development of public health services and vaccination programs in the republic.[8] As famine enveloped the steppe, diseases such as typhus, smallpox, cholera, and tuberculosis began to spread, and the steppe's relative underdevelopment served to magnify the effects of the disaster. As hungry people slaughtered their last surviving animals for food, the republic's livestock numbers spiraled downward, imperiling Kazakhstan's status as Moscow and Leningrad's major meat supplier. Due to the lack of work animals, collective farmers began to sow the fields by hand, and officials increased the purchase of livestock from China to build up the republic's herds. Ultimately, Goloshchekin became the scapegoat for these meat and grain shortfalls, and in the midst of the catastrophe he was fired and replaced by an Armenian, Levon Mirzoian.

Initially, the language of Soviet nationality policy had reinforced the regime's war on nomadic life, as Moscow presented the eradication of nomadism as beneficial both to Kazakhs' growth as a Soviet nation and to the republic's economic development. But the flood of Kazakhs into neighboring Soviet republics brought the tensions between Soviet nationality policy and Soviet agricultural policy into sharp relief. Waves of violence broke out as locals sought to expel "foreign Kazakhs" from their republics, while officials in these republics protested that proposals to settle Kazakhs where they fled represented a violation of their republic's "national" rights. Tŭrar Rïsqŭlov (Turar Ryskulov), the deputy chairman of the RSFSR Council of People's Commissars in Moscow (RSFSR Sovnarkom), declared the "internal question of Kazakhstan" to be a "general question" for the Soviet Union as a whole.[9] If the national delimitation of 1924 had first institutionalized the linkage between nationality and territory, then the refugee crisis served to embed this concept at the local level.[10] But it also illustrated that the language of nationality was a powerful tool, one that Moscow could not always control. In 1934, the famine finally came to an end, as republic-level officials renewed their attention to building up the republic's livestock herds, halting the spread of disease and resolving the refugee question. For those who survived, the reverberations from this calamity would be painful and long lasting.

The Refugee Crisis

By the fall of 1931, Kazakhstan's economy was a disaster. Livestock numbers had continued to plummet. In a belated acknowledgment of the scale of the devastation, the Central Committee created a commission headed by Aleksei

Kiselev, the secretary of the Central Executive Committee of the RSFSR who previously had led the investigation into the Semipalatinsk affair in the republic in 1928, to study the problem of the republic's livestock losses. The commission found that the republic had lost an astonishing 28.7 million head of livestock in the first two years of the First Five-Year Plan, nearly 70 percent of its livestock herds. In an attempt to absolve Moscow of any responsibility, the commission concluded that many of these losses could be attributed to Kazakhs' sale and slaughter of their livestock (*razbazarivanie,* literally, squandering), as well as the mistakes of local officials.[11] In a limp response that belied the urgency of the situation, the Kiselev commission suggested no concrete policy changes. Instead, it proposed the creation of yet another commission, which would tour Kazakhstan and offer recommendations on the problem to the Central Committee.[12]

Inside the republic, officials were contending with a problem closely linked to the republic's dramatic livestock drop: population flight. As the previous chapter has shown, the first wave of flight, which began with the 1928 confiscation campaign, was largely across the border to China. By the end of 1931, as hunger deepened, the flight of starving Kazakhs within the Soviet Union had intensified, taking on an increasingly desperate character as people spilled out across the steppe. Initially, most refugees fled north to the RSFSR, particularly Western Siberia and the Middle Volga, regions that were an important part of some Middle Horde Kazakhs' seasonal migration routes. As the famine wore on, increasing numbers of refugees began to travel south, to Kazakhstan's southern provinces as well as to Uzbekistan, Kirgizia, and Turkmenistan. Duysen Asanbaev, a famine survivor, remembers waves of *arqa qazaqtar,* or Kazakhs from the Hungry Steppe, crowding the southern provinces of Kazakhstan where he and his family lived.[13] Some resumed pathways that they had taken in previous times of hunger, streaming towards Tashkent, which had been an important destination for refugees seeking relief from famine during the civil war. Dĕmetken Shotbaev, a famine survivor, recalled that the roads leading into Tashkent became lined with the dead, Kazakhs who perished before reaching their goal.[14] Still others continued to flee to China and, to a far lesser extent, to more distant destinations, such as Iran and Afghanistan.

Initially, some refugees took their livestock and family possessions with them as they fled. But by the winter of 1931–32, most of those who fled had nothing, and sources emphasize their indigence and total destitution. In Western Siberia krai, an official wrote, "As a general rule, Kazakhs go about in large groups, poorly dressed by our standards, without any supplies of food."[15] Elsewhere in the krai, a manager of a district women's department observed: "These Kazakhs wander for entire days from house to house, asking for alms, but they are not given anything and they are driven away and they are not even allowed to warm themselves because they all are frozen, infested with lice, half-naked, and just barely alive."[16] The total impoverishment of the refugees who migrated south began later, but by the winter of 1932–33 they too were described in similar terms. In a report on Kazakh refugees in Kara-Kalpakia, Seytqali Mendeshev, who had returned from his exile in Moscow to become the head of the republic's Commissariat for Enlightenment, wrote: "They became a disorganized impoverished, starving, destitute mass, in the literal sense of the word. They moved spontaneously throughout all the districts of Kara-Kalpakia, covering their tracks with fresh graves and often with corpses."[17]

Refugees fled toward cities, railway stations, and industrial worksites in the hopes of finding food. In a letter to the Presidium of the Central Executive Committee, five deportees living in city of Pavlodar wrote: "Still more and more starving people are coming to Pavlodar from districts where there is famine. Along all the roads, people drag themselves with their last strength to Pavlodar and die along the way."[18] At the Balkhash copper mine in central Kazakhstan, hundreds of refugees tussled with speculators and dealers outside the workers' cafeteria in an effort to obtain a ration card for food, the manager of the Department for Nonferrous Metals reported.[19] Along the republic's railway lines, travelers encountered scenes of horror: Kamil Ikramov, the son of Akmal Ikramov, Uzbekistan's leader and party secretary from 1929 to 1937, traveled by train through the Kazakh steppe in the 1930s with his father. At the Kazalinsk train station, Kamil Ikramov remembered seeing "living skeletons with tiny child skeletons in their hands," begging for food.[20]

Refugees sought shelter in railway stations, abandoned buildings, or churches. When these could not be found, they lived under the open sky. In his memoirs, the revolutionary Victor Serge, who spent part of the 1930s in exile in Orenburg, a city in the Middle Volga, recalled: "Among the ruins of churches, in abandoned porches, on the edge of the steppe, or under the crags by the Ural, we could see Khirghiz [Kazakh] families lying heaped together, dying of hunger."[21] Due to the lack of clean water and sanitation, these refugee encampments became breeding grounds for disease. Typhus, smallpox, tuberculosis, and cholera began to spread. As winter set in, refugees began to succumb to the cold. In Western Siberia, a local official wrote: "I report that in our Kliuchevsk district, the situation is getting worse every day, it is turning into an utter nightmarish horror . . . Kazakh women wander with young children in their arms, and they, these children, are already frozen to death, and the women themselves are swollen with hunger."[22]

FIGURE 6.1.   Famine refugees. Pavlodar province, 1930s. As these refugees have some warm clothing, they are likely first-wave refugees. Republic of Kazakhstan Central State Archive of Film, Photo, and Audio Documents, Image #5-3621.

As the refugee crisis escalated, so did the party's rhetoric on the importance of quickly settling the Kazakhs. In a secret resolution in December 1931, the kraikom and the republic's Council of People's Commissars set the goal of settling all the Kazakh nomads by the end of 1932, a dramatic acceleration of previous plans for sedentarization.[23] Similarly, the slogan "sedentarization on the basis of full collectivization," which stressed that extraordinary speed was necessary to "help" the Kazakhs "catch up" to more advanced peoples, returned to widespread use, a reversal of a February 1930 Politburo ruling that had urged "caution" in carrying out collectivization in "economically backward national districts." The idea of completing planned sedentarization, which planners promised would bring "European-style" homes and cultural institutions to newly settled groups, by the end of 1932 was a fiction.[24] The project of planned sedentarization had languished since its inception in 1930, stymied by bureaucratic infighting and a lack of finances. Instead, otkochevniki, a population that was by definition on the move, became the scapegoats for the party's own failure to implement sedentarization, and the hardening of the party's line on nomadic settlement became an invitation to use violence against anyone who appeared in violation of it.

Officials framed the appearance of otkochevniki as a sign of the intensifying class war. Newspaper articles advised "a careful purge of the ranks of otkochevniki from foreign class elements and their agents," and they warned officials to keep their eye "on the bai and kulak who with all their strength will try 'on the sly' to place the otkochevnik once again on the camel."[25] In Kirgizia, groups of otko-chevniki from Kazakhstan were reported to have spread "counterrevolution-ary rumors among the Kirgiz population about famine . . . and strengthened the mood for emigration into China."[26] In their reports, OGPU officers used more menacing terms, such as *bandotkochevka* (rebel bands of otkochevniki) and *vooruzhennaia otkochevka* (the movement of armed otkochevniki), thereby implying that there was little difference between starving people and the rebel bands that the Red Army was fighting against.[27]

Rather than provoking sympathy, the figure of the otkochevnik was seen as threatening. He was associated with disease, disorder, and counterrevolution-ary behavior. The actions of many refugees seemed to confirm these depictions: increases in crime and antisocial behavior are hallmarks of famine, as starv-ing people take increasingly desperate actions to secure food.[28] In the city of Slavgorod in Western Siberia krai, where starving Kazakhs congregated, otko-chevniki engaged in horse theft and looting, the krai party secretary wrote in an angry letter to Goloshchekin. They stole bread "from citizens not only in the streets but in their own homes, to which Kazakhs arrived in groups of five to eight people, demanding to be given bread." In the city's cafeterias, starving Kazakhs "pick crumbs of bread off the floor, lick clean the plates, and even take food directly from those who are dining."[29] Inside the republic, bands of otkochevniki streamed north toward Siberia, an official in Maksim Gor'kii district detailed. As they crossed through various districts, they stole horses and livestock, he wrote, and there were instances of highway robberies "not only at night but during the day."[30] Instead of blaming the root cause of this behavior, Moscow's breakneck pursuit of collectivization, officials held otkochevniki responsible for the disor-der, creating a cycle that only encouraged further waves of repression against the starving.[31]

In neighboring Soviet republics, where hundreds of thousands of Kazakhs fled, the category of "Kazakh" and the category of "otkochevnik" began to blur. Everyone who was Kazakh began to appear threatening, including those Kazakhs who were not refugees but had long migrated through these regions, now demar-cated by new "national" borders. In effect, otkochevniki began to be seen as dou-bly transgressive. Not only did they represent a backward social category that the regime had pledged to eliminate, nomads, but they were "foreigners"—a nation-ality, "Kazakh," displaced from their titular republic, Kazakhstan. Their presence in neighboring republics posed a direct challenge to the principle, established by Moscow with the national delimitation of 1924, that held that nationality should coincide with territory. Now, faced with a crisis—their own survival in hungry times—locals appropriated this understanding of nationality, one first delineated by the regime, for their own purposes, using it to justify and underpin assaults on "foreign" Kazakhs.

In Western Siberia, where many first-wave refugees fled, these assaults were intensified by long-standing tensions over land use rights between the region's peasant population, who farmed the land, and Kazakh nomads, who crossed through these farmlands during their regular, seasonal migrations. In a letter to Robert Eikhe, the party secretary of Western Siberia krai, a local official detailed outbreaks of "great power chauvinism," or discriminatory behavior by Russians toward Kazakhs. In Aleisk district, a group of drunk Russians out celebrating a religious holiday collided with a group of Kazakhs, breaking the shaft of the Russian group's wagon. "Using this as a pretext, the Russians leapt out of their wagon and began to beat the Kazakhs," he wrote. In the district's train station, he continued, "the manager beat and insulted a Kazakh and threw him out on his ear from the buffet." He concluded, "The beatings, for the most part, are without reason—they beat them because they are Kazakhs."[32] In a revival of the peasant practice of *samosud*, or improvised judgment, hundreds of Kazakhs were lynched in the mining areas of the Kuzbass.[33] Locals put forward proposals to prevent Kazakhs from going out after sundown and demanded that all Kazakhs be sent out of the region.[34]

In the winter of 1931–32, as the flow of starving Kazakhs increased and the threat of disease in factories and cities intensified, Western Siberia began to forcibly expel Kazakhs. In Aleisk and Shipunovsk districts, a member of the party committee of Eastern Kazakhstan province wrote: "The police and members of the village soviet rounded up Kazakhs without any agitation work, without any regard for social position and without the participation of the party-Komsomol society. These 'organizers' gave themselves a task: in the course of twenty-four hours clear the district of Kazakhs."[35] As they collected Kazakhs, they smashed in the doors and windows of their huts, the author detailed. They then stuffed Kazakhs into crowded train cars that had no water, food, or heat and sent them to Kazakhstan.[36] In Eastern Kazakhstan province, officials reported that starving Kazakhs were dumped across the border without any regard for their districts of origin.[37] In an effort to control their border, the Western Siberia krai executive committee ordered the creation of "isolation-admission" points at train stations near the Kazakh border, which would check passengers for disease before allowing them to travel farther north.[38]

As the movement of Kazakhs back and forth across the border continued, Goloshchekin and Eikhe—a figure who, like Goloshchekin, had been active in the revolution's early days, beginning as a member of the Latvian Social Democratic Party before becoming the commissar for supplies in the Urals and later the head of the Siberian Revolutionary Committee—entered into a bitter dispute, one that reflected the different meanings that each sought to attach to this cross-border flight.[39] For Goloshchekin, the vast majority of those who fled were "bais" who had a "significant amount of livestock." Offering an explanation that would be used repeatedly by officials in Kazakhstan as the conflict with neighboring republics over Kazakh refugees escalated, he accused officials in Western Siberia krai of appropriating the livestock of those who fled for their own purposes. Only then, Goloshchekin argued, did officials in Western Siberia declare these Kazakhs, who now had no livestock, to be "famine refugees" and "border violators" and attempt to send them back to Kazakhstan. In fact, Goloshchekin alleged, Western Siberian officials had begun to send back anyone who was Kazakh, including those who had long worked in the area on collective farms. He asked that Western Siberia provide assistance to impoverished Kazakh households, weed out any "bais" among them, and then begin returning otkochevniki to Kazakhstan in stages, focusing first on those who had livestock and could be included in the spring sowing campaign.[40]

There was some truth to Goloshchekin's accounting. Prior to the winter of 1931–32, some Kazakhs had fled to neighboring republics with their livestock. Sparing no detail in his accounting, the author of an OGPU report itemized the livestock lost by Kazakhstan to Uzbekistan in 1931 as "9,399 camels, 2,253 horses, 99,243 sheep and goats, and 1,125 donkeys."[41] In 1930, OGPU reports found that Turkmen authorities had sought to lure Kazakhs and their livestock across the border, even going so far as offering Kazakhs free ferry rides to Turkmenistan (the quickest route to Turkmenistan from parts of western Kazakhstan was across the Caspian Sea) and then forbidding these ferry captains from transporting any Kazakhs back.[42] In one particularly notorious dispute, known as "The Affair of the Andizhan Camel Drivers," Kazakh officials accused Uzbek officials of trying to integrate thousands of Kazakhs (and their camels) into Uzbekistan's economy.[43] But it was not just republic level officials who sought to appropriate the language of nationality. Those who fled also sought to use the idea of nationality to their advantage: to prevent their forcible return to Kazakhstan, some first-wave refugees in Turkmenistan argued that they should be considered "Karakalpaks" rather than "Kazakhs."[44]

But by the spring of 1932, when Eikhe and Goloshchekin began their dispute, any attempt to characterize the impoverished Kazakhs who fled as "wealthy" or to demand the return of those who had "livestock" rang hollow. In his response, Eikhe ridiculed Goloshchekin's claim that the majority of those who had crossed into Western Siberia were bais: "The real question is why the counterrevolutionary work of the bai-kulak was so successful this year that he was able to lead thousands of bedniak-seredniak households astray." Eikhe argued that the organization of assistance to otkochevniki could be done only in Kazakhstan: "Organizing any sort of base for supplying Kazakhs in need in Western Siberia krai will only strengthen the ongoing flight." He rejected Goloshchekin's proposal that Western Siberian authorities cull out "bais," arguing instead that this work "can be done only in Kazakhstan."[45] In a report, a plenipotentiary from Eastern Kazakhstan province cited a Western Siberian OGPU plenipotentiary who framed the issue in even stronger terms: "You wish to turn our krai into an experimental camp, so that we count your citizens according to the district that they came from and their social position—produce statistics, after this gather them together and feed them, and, finally, send them back only on your orders— we do not agree to this!"[46]

In a subsequent letter, which highlighted just how charged the issue of border control had become, Goloshchekin criticized Eikhe for failing to control Western Siberia's border, arguing that nearly one thousand people, mostly "kulaks" and "peasant manual laborers" arrived in Kazakhstan from Western Siberia every day. Goloshchekin reluctantly conceded that Kazakhstan would take back those that Western Siberia sent, although he stressed, repeatedly, that the republic was in no position to accept any more people, given the extreme economic difficulties it already faced.[47] Later that month, the kraikom ordered the creation of a committee headed by Oraz Isaev, the chairman of the republic's council of people's commissars, which would oversee the return of those of modest means ("bedniak and seredniak households") and send them on to factories and worksites throughout the republic.[48] In an effort to prevent further cross-border flows, light cavalry units began to patrol the boundaries between Kazakhstan and other Soviet republics.[49]

By 1932, the republic also faced the increasing threat of disease. The kraikom declared the existence of a typhus epidemic in three northern provinces (Eastern Kazakhstan, Karaganda, and Aktiubinsk) and the existence of an epidemic of black smallpox (*chernaia ospa*) in one of these provinces, Aktiubinsk. The kraikom warned that by the fall there could be "mass illness among the population of cities and villages."[50] Industrial worksites, such as the Karaganda coal basin, where refugees would intermingle with workers, were of particular concern.[51] In an acknowledgment of the intertwined "threat" of otkochevniki, who were seen both as carriers of disease and as harboring "socially harmful elements," all refugees were to be processed at so-called filtration points before being sent on to worksites, an approach that closely resembled the party's treatment of "special settlers," internally exiled peasants.[52] At these filtration points, doctors would conduct full medical inspections (including bathing refugees, delousing them, and inoculating them against smallpox), while officials would conduct interviews to ascertain that only refugees of the appropriate social background were sent on to worksites.[53] The increasing "medicalization" of the discourse surrounding otkochevniki—all otkochevniki were to be quarantined initially in isolation wards—further reinforced the idea that they were a group to be regarded with suspicion.[54]

The processing of refugees proceeded disastrously. No one seemed to have any idea of how many refugees had returned. Speaking of Karaganda province, a plenipotentiary wrote, "On the number of returning households there are several figures (7,000, 6,000, 9,000)—all of them inexact and sometimes even made up."[55] In April 1932, as part of a series of small-scale food loans to Kazakhstan and other regions throughout the Soviet Union, the Politburo authorized the release of one million poods of food (sixteen thousand tons) to "Kazakhs returning from other districts."[56] Yet little of this food reached starving refugees. In Eastern Kazakhstan province, the head of the provincial health department found that the daily rations had been set at three hundred grams of bread, despite the fact that six hundred grams per day had been authorized. Moreover, he discovered that there were "no ration cards, no accounting. Everything is done by eyeballing." He continued, "The weak, who are not in a condition to go get the food themselves, remain without food, while the strong, including Semipalatinsk thieves and speculators, receive several portions and sell them in the bazaar."[57] Without adequate shelter at filtration points, many refugees continued to live under the open sky. The death rate among otkochevniki soared: out of 11,000 refugees in the city of Semipalatinsk, 4,107 of them died.[58]

The integration of refugees into worksites and collective farms proceeded poorly. Many were so weakened by hunger and disease that they could not work. In the city of Semipalatinsk, a factory that received four hundred otkochevniki fired half of them within three days and denied the other half their food rations.[59] Most refugees were impoverished nomads who did not speak Russian, and their skills did not translate easily into factory or collective farm work. In Aktiubinsk province, factory managers were reported to have said, "Otkochevniki are unsuited for work, they are loafers." In other cases, managers refused to accept otkochevniki, demanding, "Give us workers from the Russians."[60] Many factory managers preferred to take special settlers as workers over refugee Kazakhs, so much so that the kraikom sought to forbid the practice due to the "large number of Kazakhs without work."[61] Thrown out of factories and collective farms, many refugees returned back to neighboring republics, a phenomenon that officials referred to as *obratnaia perekochevka*. Others, hearing rumors of assistance, fled to other districts within the republic, and the republic's party committee urged districts to intensify their battle against such flight, portraying it as "led by bais."[62]

Efforts to stop population flight were hampered by a rapidly deteriorating economic situation. In a secret resolution in June 1932, the republic's party committee declared the existence of a massive famine inside the republic.[63] In July 1932, a report by the republic's Commissariat of Agriculture found that Kazakhstan had "fully lost" its significance as the Soviet Union's main livestock base. The small amount of livestock that still remained in the hands of nomads, the report estimated, could not even meet the "minimal needs of the population for milk." The republic's nomadic population, the report concluded, was "now in a very critical condition, demanding the most immediate practical measures."[64]

It is difficult to explain Moscow's failure to intervene at this point. Stalin and other members of the Central Committee had little concern for the needs of starving Kazakhs, but the republic's precipitous drop in livestock numbers, which was apparent to everyone on the Central Committee by 1932, directly affected the regime's economic interests. The republic was Moscow and Leningrad's major meat supplier. Given the scarcity of tractors and cars in the republic, Moscow was heavily reliant on animals to plow the republic's grain fields or transport officials across the republic's vast distances. Some blame for Moscow's failure to respond must be attributed to Stalin, who seems to have paid little attention to matters relating to livestock, in contrast to his obsessive preoccupation with grain procurements.[65] But Moscow's delay might also be attributed to the persistence of a stereotype about nomadic life, the idea that nomads had immense numbers of animals. In a letter to Stalin and the Central Committee about the republic's livestock drop, Goloshchekin complained: "Several of the party workers in the center imagine Kazakhstan as in olden times. They imagine nomadic and semi-nomadic districts with an uncountable number of livestock and this gives rise to a series of negative occurrences."[66] Proceeding from this fantasy of Kazakhstan as a land of unimaginable riches, Stalin and other Central Committee made no major adjustments to the republic's livestock policies, and herd numbers continued to plummet.

Survival

By 1932, the horror of famine was everywhere in the republic. Whether in the countryside, the factory, or even in the republic's capital, Alma-Ata, where corpses littered the city streets, residents could not escape the catastrophe. Though the heart of the crisis was located in the Kazakh aul, by 1932 almost everyone, whether Russian collective farm member, local party bureaucrat, or factory worker, was hungry. Survival demanded ingenuity, good fortune, and, on occasion, ruthlessness and cruelty. In his examination of human behavior during famine, based in part on his observations of the Civil War famine in Russia, the Russian-American sociologist Pitirim Sorokin found that starvation could override the strongest taboos and inhibitions, even compelling some to commit the "supremely antisocial act of cannibalism."[67] The Kazakh famine was no exception in this regard: as hunger set in, incidents of crime and theft rose, and communal bonds started to break down.

Those who survived the famine remember that life became dominated by the struggle to find food. In his memoirs, Mukhamet Shayakhmetov recalled that old family friends turned him out into the cold, refusing even to give him a place to stay for the night: "Everyone was now preoccupied by getting something to eat for the following day—or that same day, or that very moment, to relieve their hunger pangs. Even the kindest-hearted people and closest friends and relatives could no longer help one another out."[68] In the village of Burlo-Tube, a band of hungry people engaged in crime and theft. A plenipotentiary wrote: "The members of this band did not hesitate to kill an otkochevnik for his bread. Right in front of us, one member of a band knocked an otkochevnik to the ground with one blow, where he lay unconscious for a long time."[69] Due to the danger of assault or the possibility of contracting disease, anyone who traveled through the steppe during the famine put his or her life at risk. Köken Belgïbaev, a famine survivor, recalled that his friend Moldaqash hoped to return to his aul to save several starving relatives but ultimately determined that the trip across the steppe was too dangerous to undertake.[70]

Some tried to help the starving as best as they could: Zeitïn Aqïshev, a famine survivor whom we met in a previous chapter, recalled that some party officials ventured out into the steppe at great personal risk to collect abandoned children and bring them to orphanages.[71] In her diary, the seventeen-year old Tat'iana Nevadovskaya, the daughter of Gavril Nevadovsky, a professor exiled to Kazakhstan, recorded her efforts to bring food and water to the starving.[72] But as the dead and the dying overwhelmed cities, a certain callousness began to set in among many witnesses to the famine. The indigence of starving Kazakhs began to seem ordinary, and their deaths in squalid shelters or along city streets commonplace. In Western Siberia, an official wrote: "The groups of Kazakhs present a horrifying picture. To give one example, I relay the following fact: at the train station in Slavgorod the body of a dead Kazakh lay on the ground for three days, and no one paid any attention to it."[73] In Orenburg, Victor Serge remembered: "There were Khirgiz [Kazakhs] lying under the sun on waste ground, and it was hard to tell if some of them were alive or dead. People passed by without looking their way: poor people, hurrying and shabby;

functionaries, military men, their bourgeois-looking womenfolk; in brief all those we termed 'the satisfied 8%.'"[74]

Fear transformed everyday life. Vera Rikhter traveled through the steppe with her father, Vladimir Rikhter, an exiled Socialist Revolutionary (SR), as a young girl. When they stopped for the night, Vera wandered out of their lodgings to look at the camels tended by some nearby Kazakhs. Unable to find Vera inside the house, Vera's mother came rushing out of the house to find her daughter. "Her hands were shaking when she took me by the shoulders and brought me into the house," Vera recalled. "Sometime later I understood her terror: they thought that the starving would snatch me up."[75] Her mother was not the only one to be frightened, Vera remembered. The emotion was widely felt: "The population of the village in which we stopped was not starving (or at least in those houses in which our convoy was lodged) but they were afraid of hunger and of the starving. . . . They carefully locked their doors and locked themselves in. They were taciturn, sullen, unfriendly."[76]

Rumors of "murder cannibalism," or the murder of people for human meat, were a constant source of anxiety during the Kazakh famine, particularly for parents who feared that their children might be kidnapped by the starving. Such rumors were especially prevalent in Western Siberia and the Middle Volga, where tales that otkochevniki ate Russian children quickly spread.[77] During the famine, witnesses recorded instances of "murder cannibalism": In Chu district, at a feeding point for the starving, an official named Daneman recalled seeing a refugee cut into the stomach of a dying refugee, remove his liver, and give it to a starving person who ate it raw.[78] Other sources offer accounts of what appears to be "survivor cannibalism," or the consumption of the corpses of those who were already dead.[79] In February 1933, OGPU officials detained a woman in Aulie-Ata for the sale of human meat. On examination, a medical expert estimated that the meat came from a child who was six to seven years old.[80] Ghalym Akhmedov, a famine survivor, remembers coming across starving people boiling human meat.[81]

Many turned to surrogate foods to survive. Famine survivors remember eating rodents and wild grasses or combing through fields to collect the rotting remains of the harvest, known as *masaq*.[82] Others recall refusing to eat rodents, believing their consumption to be an affront to their Muslim faith.[83] In Chu district, Daneman detailed, starving people collected the thorns of a local plant, *dzhigim*. It could take up to a day to collect enough thorns to make a single loaf of bread, he noted, and it gave those who ate it terrible stomach pains.[84] Others, "mainly children and the truly starving," resorted to eating their bedding, he observed. They cooked the wool from their bedding over a fire and then chewed it, while they soaked the leather from their beds in a little dish full of water and then ate it. "These things had little food in them," he remarked, "but all of them had something."[85]

The number of abandoned children, or *besprizornye*, a category that included both orphaned children and homeless children, swelled: according to party statistics, there were 20,700 abandoned children in the republic by 1932, and nearly triple that amount, 71,000 abandoned children, by early 1933.[86] Most conceded that these figures grossly underrepresented the actual totals. In 1932, officials with the republic's children's commission reported that there were more than 1,700 starving children gathered outside the coal mines of Karaganda alone.[87] In Pavlodar, the five deportees wrote, the city's orphanages were overflowing, and they had stopped accepting any new children: "In the city every day one comes across tens of abandoned, frozen, emaciated children of all ages who are swollen from hunger. Their typical response is: 'My father died, my mother died, I have no home, I have no bread.'"[88]

In some cases, these abandoned children were indeed orphans. Sëden Mëlïmülï, whom we met in the chapter's opening pages, was placed in an orphanage during the famine due to the death of his mother.[89] But for many families, abandoning a child was a gut-wrenching survival strategy.[90] Those families had more mouths than they could feed, and parents faced excruciating choices about which child to take and which child to leave behind.[91] Others may have believed that abandoning their child at an orphanage offered the child a better chance of survival than life with its parents. It is unclear, however, whether being placed in an orphanage actually did improve a child's odds of survival: in Pavlodar, the deportees wrote, the shelters where some starving children had been put "should more precisely be called a morgue." No one had bothered to pick up the bodies of the children who had died, and their corpses were strewn across the floors.[92] In Kzyl-Orda district in the republic's south, the death rate for children who entered orphanages during the first few months of 1933 was 60 percent.[93] In Orenburg, Serge recalled trying to give a starving child to some soldiers to take to an orphanage. The soldiers declined, explaining, "But they're running away from there [the orphanage], because they're starving to death!"[94]

One of the most pressing problems became the burial of the dead. In his trip to the village of Guliaevka, Daneman described seeing corpses "scattered about" on the roads or tossed into the saksaul, the shrubs that lined the sides of the roads.[95] In the village of Ush-Tobe, an official from the republic's transport division reported, corpses littered the roads and filled the ditches that ran along the side of the railroad tracks. The inhabitants of the village had exhausted their strength to dig new graves, and every possible pit in the village was already jammed full of corpses and covered with snow.[96] In cities and other settlements, the timely removal of the dead was of the utmost importance. The stench of unburied bodies began to spread quickly, bringing with it the specter of diseases, such as cholera and typhus. In their recollections of the famine, survivors frequently refer to the *arba,* or horse-drawn cart that collected corpses from city streets.[97] These corpses were then dumped in mass grave sites on the outskirts of cities. For those who survived the famine, seeing loved ones buried in this fashion was deeply traumatic: these mass burials violated Muslim tradition, which called for the faces of the dead to be wrapped in cloth and their bodies turned toward Mecca before burial.[98]

What factors determined who lived and who died? Simply being a party member did not mean that you were going to survive the famine. Detailing the horrifying situation at a refugee feeding point in Guliaevka, where the "feet of the dead were on the faces of the living," Daneman wrote: "Among the returnees there were party members and Komsomol members. The chairman of the village soviet Belousov told me that they even showed him their party cards. But they also died along with everyone else."[99] But a connection to state structures did help many survive: Zeitïn Aqïshev took a position as a schoolteacher in Semipalatinsk during the famine. As a teacher, he remembers, he was able to get a steady supply of millet through the state.[100] Those who labored in industrial worksites, such as the Karaganda coal mines or the copper mines at Balkhash, appear to have had a far better chance of survival. Party documents reaffirm this: as the crisis in the republic escalated in the summer of 1932, officials with the Soviet Union's Commissariat for Heavy Industry urged that the supply of grain, meat, and other goods to the republic's "remote regions" be cut off and redirected to industrial sites within the republic, such as Balkhash.[101] Expelled from these worksites in favor of special settlers and other groups capable of performing labor, Kazakh refugees had little hope of finding food.

There was a sharp contrast between the predicament of Kazakh refugees and the lives of the party elite, who glimpsed the horrors of the famine through the windows of well-appointed railway cars. In her memoir, Agnessa Mironova, the wife of Sergei Mironov, the OGPU plenipotentiary representative for Kazakhstan, recalled a train trip through the Kazakh steppe during the famine: "So it was in the winter of 1931 I passed through Karaganda with Mirosha. We traveled in a Pullman car that dated to the time of Nicholas II. The salon was all in gold velvet, the bedroom in red velvet. The conductors (they were also cooks) fed us gloriously."[102] Though Mironova saw starving people outside, she remembered: "But at the same time, in the midst of this dying hamlet, we had plenty of provisions in our velvet train car. We carried with us frozen ham, chickens, mutton, cheeses, just about everything you could want."[103] As Mironova's memoir reveals, the years of the famine produced extreme inequities, impoverishing Kazakh nomads but propelling members of the party elite into lives of extreme privilege.

"People Died When We Had the Possibility to Save Them"

In the fall of 1932, Moscow announced a number of policy changes for the republic, the centerpiece of which was a ruling by the Central Committee on September 17, 1932.[104] The ruling, which was known as the September 17th decision, freed all nomadic households in the republic from centralized meat and grain procurements for two years. As well, it authorized additional grain and seed assistance to these households by the center. Under the policy change, Kazakh households in livestock districts could now keep up to one hundred sheep, eight to ten cattle, three to five camels, and eight to ten horses for their personal use. Similar, although less generous, livestock allowances were made for districts classified as settled. The ruling also changed the type of collective farms decreed as appropriate for livestock regions, moving away from the more restrictive artel to the far simpler TOZ.[105] In combination with this ruling, the party revoked the slogan, "sedentarization on the basis of full collectivization," and sought to promote a more gradual approach to collectivization among newly settled groups.[106]

But the September 17th decision did little to alleviate Kazakhs' suffering. In the opening lines of the ruling, the Central Committee reiterated that the settlement of nomadic Kazakhs was the correct policy, giving license to further repressions against starving refugees. Republic-level officials complained that many of the grain shipments that Moscow had promised never arrived or were heavily delayed. Though the September 17th decision promised household livestock allowances for nomads, this policy modification meant little when there were almost no livestock left in the republic to possess. Officials at the republic, regional, and district levels relegated the distribution of aid and the execution of the changes promised by the September 17th decision to a policy of low priority, entrusting bureaucrats with little or no oversight to carry out their implementation.

While officials in Moscow touted the new policies of the September 17th decision as setting the republic on the path of economic recovery, Molotov and Stalin continued to pressure the republic's officials to procure more grain. On November 8, Molotov and Stalin wrote leading officials within the republic's party and state bureaucracy to demand an "immediate turnaround" in Kazakhstan's grain collections.[107] On November 10, the kraikom approved the blacklisting of districts within the republic, explicitly modeling this campaign of terror on techniques deployed a few days earlier against starving Ukrainians and others in the Kuban.[108] On November 21, a telegram from Stalin charged that grain procurements in the republic had "undergone sharp declines" and were "headed toward an actual cessation in collections." Stalin urged the kraikom and KazSovnarkom to switch over to a "repressive track."[109] Ultimately, some thirty-one districts in the republic would be blacklisted.[110] In December 1932, a Politburo decree ordered the deportation of thousands of Kuban Cossacks: approximately ten thousand were sent to Kazakhstan, increasing pressure on the food supply and deepening the republic's misery.[111]

Ultimately, Goloshchekin became the scapegoat for these grain shortfalls. Through an order from the Central Committee in Moscow, Goloshchekin was removed as the republic's party secretary in early 1933. Officially, Goloshchekin took on a new role as the main state arbitrator before the Soviet Council of People's Commissars in Moscow. Yet his career would soon suffer a rapid decline. In February 1933, Goloshchekin's departure from Kazakhstan was quietly marked with a small article buried on page three of the republic's newspaper.[112] By August 1933, Goloshchekin was publicly critiqued in the same newspaper for "errors" in his leadership and for "flagrantly violating the Leninist-Stalinist line."[113] In Moscow, Goloshchekin suffered from depression due to his fall from official favor and contemplated suicide[114] In 1941, he was shot as part of the purges, meeting a fate shared by many others who had joined the party in its early years.

While the order to remove Goloshchekin from his position as party secretary came from the Central Committee in Moscow, little is known about the details of Goloshchekin's fall into disfavor among Stalin and other top party officials. On the republic level, some of the support that Goloshchekin had received from his colleagues eroded in the months before his ouster, although it is not clear if this discontent was sparked by an impetus from the center. In July 1932 in a letter to Stalin, Isaev linked the republic's disastrous economic position partially to Goloshchekin's leadership. He confided that he did not think that "Comrade Goloshchekin has the necessary strength for a decisive turnaround."[115]

In a series of angry letters to Stalin and Kaganovich some months after his removal, in August and September 1933, Goloshchekin protested the "unceremonious public criticism and fanatical disparagement of me that is taking place in Kazakhstan under the leadership of the republic's party committee." He called on the Central Committee to intervene in the dispute with his former colleagues in Kazakhstan and provide a clear accounting of his supposed mistakes.[116] Goloshchekin categorically rejected his successor Levon Mirzoian's attempts to characterize his entire seven-year tenure in Kazakhstan as "anti-party and anti-Leninist" and, by way of explanation, reasoned that the Central Committee had regularly endorsed and supported his actions over the course of his time in Kazakhstan.[117]

Despite a letter to Stalin in September 1932 critiquing the "mistakes and shortcomings" of the collectivization campaign in Kazakhstan, Goloshchekin became the scapegoat for the republic's shortfall in grain procurements. Like many of his peers in neighboring republics, Goloshchekin was a brutal leader, one who had worked ruthlessly to effect the republic's transformation. Yet Goloshchekin was also a pragmatic administrator, one who sought to manage the consequences of the party's actions in Kazakhstan, and he petitioned the party to soften their policies for the republic when they appeared counterproductive to the regime's own economic interests. Goloshchekin may have also operated under different constraints than his successor, and Mirzoian assumed leadership of the republic as central policies for Kazakhstan began to shift. Although repressions continued under Mirzoian's leadership, other policy changes would signal Moscow's interest in repairing the economic damage.

Mirzoian arrived in Kazakhstan in early 1933 to replace Goloshchekin. Born to an Armenian peasant family in a village in Nagorno-Karabakh, Mirzoian completed only an eighth-grade education before abandoning his studies to move to Baku, a major port on the Caspian Sea and a political hub for the Caucasus region. There he joined the Bolshevik Party, working under the leadership of Sergei Kirov, a prominent and well-connected revolutionary who would later assume leadership of the Leningrad party organization. With the beginning of the First Five-Year Plan, Mirzoian relocated to the RSFSR, first assuming a position as the party secretary for Perm, followed by a similar posting in the Urals region, before moving to take on his new position as party secretary of Kazakhstan.

Mirzoian and his predecessor shared some characteristics in common. Both joined the Bolsheviks early, prior to the October 1917 revolution, and ultimately they would share the same fate, executed as part of party purges (Mirzoian in 1939, Goloshchekin in 1941). But there were also important differences between the two men, who hailed from different generations. Goloshchekin, approximately twenty years Mirzoian's senior, came of age in the 1890s, in an era when Marxist movements in Russia began to grow. Mirzoian, by contrast, was born in 1897, and had a very different upbringing, entering public life after a serious challenge to autocracy, the 1905 revolution, sparked the mobilization of groups across the political spectrum. Mirzoian's wife, Iuliia Tevosian, linked Mirzoian closely to the top ranks of the Moscow party bureaucracy (Iuliia's brother, Ivan Tevosian, was the Soviet commissar for heavy industry, and he would later become ambassador to Japan), and she assumed an active role in public life in Almaty during Mirzoian's tenure, becoming director of the city's Institute for Marxism-Leninism.[118]

For Mirzoian, his new life in the unfamiliar surroundings of Kazakhstan presented something of a shock. The contrast between life in Kazakhstan and Mirzoian's previous postings in the Soviet Union's west or in the Caucasus was enormous. Though the republic had completed the First Five-Year Plan, which officials had boasted would usher Kazakhstan into socialist-style modernity, Mirzoian viewed the republic as mired in backwardness. Alma-Ata, the republic's capital and his new home, he wrote in a letter to Kaganovich in Moscow posted soon after his arrival, remained nothing more than a "backward village," which was "several times worse than any station in the North Caucasus." Workers fled the city because the dormitories reserved for them were in such a dilapidated state, he continued. Due to disputes among city agencies, Alma-Ata had no electricity, and kerosene lamps remained the only source of light after dark.[119]

Most striking of all to Mirzoian was the republic's terrible plight. Detailing the bodies of the dead that filled the city streets, he wrote to Kaganovich, "I left the city of Moscow confident that the situation in Kazakhstan was difficult, but what I saw here exceeded all my expectations."[120] Not only had the party failed in its efforts to modernize agricultural work—local officials, for instance, regularly complained that promised deliveries of tractors never arrived—but party cadres had resorted to farming methods that were more primitive than those used before the First Five-Year Plan. In Kazakhstan's southern districts, where the fields had once been plowed using oxen and cattle, collective farm workers, for want of livestock, now resorted to plowing the fields by hand. This method was grossly inefficient: eighteen to twenty people might labor for a day to sow just one hectare. But due to the utter decimation of the republic's animal herds, Mirzoian calculated that thousands of hectares in the republic might need to be sown in this manner.[121]

Though Mirzoian would oversee Kazakhstan's recovery, his record is more mixed than the largely uncritical evaluation he has received from Kazakhstani historians would indicate.[122] Like his predecessor, Mirzoian employed ruthless tactics in pursuit of the party's goals. Soon after his arrival, in a letter to Kaganovich, he announced that the republic would take severe measures against organizers of flight (*otkochevka*), as well as those who stole grain or livestock. Though Mirzoian's description of these so-called "enemies" might apply to almost every starving refugee within the republic, he pushed for the party to increase its use of the most brutal forms of punishment, including shootings.[123] Mirzoian roundly criticized those party cadres who sent him "teary telegrams" to ask for more food aid for their regions, and in response to their desperate pleas, he denied their regions further assistance and fired many of them instead.[124]

Some of the disaster's most appalling cruelty occurred under Mirzoian's leadership. Republic-level agencies made little effort to ensure that food aid actually reached starving refugees: in one notorious incident, a plenipotentiary stuffed documents that ordered the release of food aid to nearby refugees into his pocket. While hundreds starved nearby, he organized a large wedding for himself, finally producing the documents that would have saved dozens from a horrible death only after a month of drinking, celebrating, and feasting.[125] In another instance, in eastern Kazakhstan, collective farm workers murdered a refugee by throwing him into a ditch of two meters in depth and pouring cold water on top.[126] In this, the famine's final stage, an opportunity to mitigate the disaster's terrifying death toll was lost. In 1933, a local official reflected on the continuing crisis in his own district; his shrewd observation also speaks to the debacle of relief efforts in the republic more broadly: "People died from hunger when the district had the possibility to save them."[127]

In November 1932, officials had dissolved Kazakhstan's sedentarization commission, a decision that implicitly acknowledged the scale of the refugee crisis, as well as the impossibility of implementing the regime's previous plans to settle the Kazakh nomads. As interrepublic disputes continued to erupt and Kazakhstan's neighbors, overwhelmed by the number of new arrivals, petitioned Gosplan in Moscow for food aid, the center intervened. Rïsqŭlov, who was the most prominent Kazakh in Moscow, was charged with heading a new Union-level commission that would oversee the question of how to manage those otkochevniki who had fled the republic. In Kazakhstan, officials created a separate committee that assumed the duties of the now defunct sedentarization committee; this new agency, however, was charged with handling the affairs of Kazakh otkochevniki and returnees (*vozvrashchentsy*) rather than settling the Kazakh nomads.

FIGURE 6.2. Kazakhs returning to Pavlodar province from Western Siberia, 1932. Republic of Kazakhstan Central State Archive of Film, Photo and Audio Documents, Image #5–3568.

On February 22, 1933, at a meeting of the Union-level commission, Rïsqŭlov ruled that the agency's first task would be to determine an accurate tally of the numbers of Kazakh refugees, particularly their distribution among neighboring republics. Second, it would oversee the return of refugees to work, including incorporating them in the spring sowing campaign.[128] Overruling the many protests of representatives gathered from Western Siberia, the Middle Volga, Kirgizia, and other areas, Rïsqŭlov held that the party would now work to settle most Kazakh refugees where they had fled, rather than returning the majority of them to Kazakhstan, as had been the policy previously. He charged each region with appointing officials who would supervise the process of placing Kazakh refugees in worksites in their respective regions. A very limited number of Kazakh refugees, those for whom suitable work could not be found, would become the responsibility of the Soviet Union's Department of Labor, and Rïsqŭlov proposed a plan to create large collective farms where these refugees would be put back to work.[129]

Mirzoian soon began to travel around Kazakhstan and started an active correspondence with colleagues in neighboring republics, in a campaign to support the party's shift in policy. Writing to colleagues in Kirgizia on March 12, 1933, he noted that the death toll in Kazakhstan was "considerable" and urged them not to send more otkochevniki back to the republic.[130] In a letter to party officials in Ural'sk and Petropavlovsk in northern Kazakhstan, also on March 12, 1933, Mirzoian informed them that the return of otkochevniki had been brought to a "temporary halt" and instructed them to take in no more refugees.[131] On March 29, 1933, Mirzoian wrote to Stalin and Molotov in Moscow. Calling on the Central Committee to increase its work with neighboring republics to halt the return of refugees back to Kazakhstan, he reported that the situation with otkochevniki inside the republic remained "very difficult."[132]

Relations between Kazakhstan and its neighbors continued to deteriorate as Kazakh officials alleged that refugees suffered mistreatment and discrimination at the hands of officials in neighboring republics.[133] In late April 1933, Isaev penned an angry letter to his counterpart in Kirgizia in which he criticized the "soulless, indifferent relationship of the Soviet organs of your republic to Kazakh-otkochevniki." In Isaev's recounting, a crowd of eight hundred starving Kazakh refugees had gathered at the Frunze train station from April 19 to 23, 1933, in the hopes of receiving food or assistance. "The condition of these otkochevniki was nightmarish," Isaev reported. "Every day among them appeared six to seven corpses, dead from hunger." In Isaev's assessment, "The Kirgiz government took no measures, except for asking to send these otkochevniki back to Kazakhstan," and he condemned the Kirgiz for their callous attitude toward Kazakhs' suffering.[134]

As waves of starving Kazakh refugees arrived throughout the broader region, local officials reported continuing outbursts of violence and disorder. These outbreaks provoked a response from Rïsqŭlov. In July 1933, he sent a warning to the leaders of regions flooded with otkochevniki and ordered them to strengthen their attention to the project of integrating refugee Kazakhs into worksites.[135] Later that same month in the Middle Volga, the chairman of the party's regional committee issued circulars to local officials with instructions on how they might include refugee Kazakhs in the region's collective farms. He cautioned that many otkochevniki might not be able to fulfill "complicated work" at first, particularly the use of agricultural machinery, yet he noted that the party specially prohibited "violence or illegal actions against Kazakh nomads."[136]

Recovery

In 1934, party observers marked the first growth in the republic's livestock numbers since 1928 and, though limited parts of the republic continued to suffer from hunger throughout 1934, the scale of the suffering had diminished.[137] In part, this shift in the republic's fortunes was brought about by a policy change, the belated decision to reallocate all the resources once devoted to sedentarization to the resolution of the refugee question. Mirzoian may also have been a more effective administrator than Goloshchekin, one more attuned to the party's problems in implementing programs on the ground in Kazakhstan, and his correspondence with authorities in Moscow, especially on the question of Kazakh cadres, reveals a willingness to frankly assess some of the party's failings. Ultimately, however, Mirzoian's tenure also benefited from a certain amount of good luck, including excellent weather and a good harvest in 1934, as well as renewed attention, initiated by a variety of state agencies in Moscow, to problems stemming from the famine, including the rise of disease and large numbers of homeless children.

As the movement of vast numbers of people throughout the republic continued, officials began efforts to halt the spread of disease. By early 1933, more than 450,000 people, approximately 10 percent of the republic's total population, were gathered in encampments near railway stations. In April 1933, as part of an effort throughout the Soviet Union to cleanse cities of "undesirable elements," republic-level officials ordered regional officials to clear hundreds of thousands of refugees from the vicinity of Kazakhstan's railway stations and relocate efforts at processing and returning refugees to work further into the steppe.[138] In southern Kazakhstan, where smallpox and typhus had broken out, officials ordered school teachers to vaccinate students in remote regions. With the teachers' assistance, the party conducted over two hundred thousand smallpox inoculations throughout southern Kazakhstan in 1933.[139]

More so than his predecessor, Mirzoian appears to have been attuned to the precarious state of Kazakh refugees and the need for immediate action. In a June 1933 letter to Stalin and Kaganovich, Mirzoian outlined a major shift in policy:

> The question of sedentarization in the old sense of the word practically does not exist, for essentially in Kazakhstan today there are no nomadic or semi-nomadic groups that are not in flight (*otkochevka*). . . . If earlier it was the grave mistake of the Kazakh party to force the sedentarization of the nomadic population, then now it has become an absolutely necessary task to force the sedentarization of otkochevniki, as this population, which has no equipment and no livestock, has become a burden on the state [*nakhoditsia fakticheski na shee gosudarstva*].[140]

Others, such as Kiselev, viewed the republic's refugee problem in even blunter terms, framing the renewal of settlement efforts as a matter of "life and death" for the encampments of refugees with no method of subsistence.[141] Thus, if the program of sedentarization had once legitimized violent assaults on Kazakh life, sparking the famine itself, it had now been reintroduced with another goal, saving destitute Kazakhs and resolving the republic's economic crisis. By the middle of 1933, republic officials, renewing their efforts at sedentarization, forcibly relocated and settled over half a million refugees. The vast majority (402,627) were sent to work in collective farms, with the remainder distributed in cotton, beet, or tobacco production (33,000) or state farms (73,806) in the republic.[142]

At a meeting of the Rïsqŭlov commission, Rïsqŭlov announced that the party would provide additional aid to homeless Kazakh children, both within Kazakhstan and in neighboring regions, as well as double the number of social workers (*vospitateli*) working in the republic's orphanages.[143] In combination with this effort, officials in the republic were charged with forming "children's brigades," which would walk the republic's city streets in an effort to bring abandoned, starving Kazakh children into orphanages. By the late fall of 1933, the crisis of homeless children in the republic appeared to ease slightly, and an official with the children's commission, discussing the problem of abandoned children, noted, "The insufficiencies are still many, but they are already less than before."[144]

There were also indications of shifts in the party's approach to livestock raising. In June 1933, the Soviet Union's Council of People's Commissars authorized additional purchases of livestock from Xinjiang to replenish the republic's herds, a striking admission of how much Kazakhstan's livestock numbers had plummeted. The republic, previously the Soviet Union's major livestock supplier, was now dependent on animals from China. Some fifty thousand animals, including horses, cows, sheep and goats, would be purchased in Xinjiang, while another seventy thousand animals would be bought from Chinese traders at seasonal markets set up inside the republic in Alma-Ata province and Eastern Kazakhstan province.[145]

By late 1933, the policy of settling refugee Kazakhs where they fled eased, and by 1934, officials declared the massive outflow of Kazakhs beyond the republic's borders to be "liquidated."[146] Officials once again renewed their efforts to bring limited numbers of refugees back to Kazakhstan; the project, which focused on settling Kazakh refugees in "labor deficit regions," particularly the republic's beet- and cotton-growing regions, would continue for much of the decade. Despite party officials' earlier warnings, these return efforts were again plagued by accusations of discrimination and "national antagonisms." On the local level, officials in neighboring republics reported that many of their efforts to integrate Kazakh refugees into local communities were an abject failure, as locals forcibly expelled new waves of otkochevniki. On the republic level, Kazakhstan's officials continued to accuse neighboring republics of neglecting Kazakh refugees or, alternately, profiting from refugees' labor or livestock.

But the arduous, state-sponsored relocation of refugees would far outlast the famine itself, continuing for much of the 1930s. In Uzbekistan in 1935, thousands of the most destitute Kazakh refugees remained on the margins of society. Living under the open sky and traveling from collective farm to collective farm in search of food, they were shadowed by taunts from locals that they were "cannibals" or "non-Muslims." Some Kazakh refugees able to work had been incorporated into factories and farms, and Kazakhstan's officials angrily accused the Uzbek government of refusing to return the best refugee workers (*udarniki*) back to Kazakhstan.[147] Even when Kazakhstan and its neighbors could agree on how the return of refugees should proceed, many return efforts only served to increase the death toll. In late 1933 in Kara-Kalpakia, officials gathered together a group of Kazakh refugees, with the intention of sending them back to Kazakhstan by ferry across the Aral Sea. Many refugees waited so long for the arrival of the ferry that they perished for want of food; others, realizing that transport might never arrive, set off by foot across the desert. Once the ferry finally docked, many more Kazakh refugees perished during the long boat trip across the sea back to Kazakhstan due to inadequate supplies of food and water.[148]

The Kazakh famine's final phase was marked by both a social crisis—the emergence of over a million starving Kazakh refugees, who moved both within the republic and beyond its boundaries—as well as the total collapse of the republic's economy. In this phase, the causes and responses to famine became intertwined: The refugee crisis provoked further waves of repression by Moscow, which only intensified the suffering of the starving. At the same time, Moscow took no measures to resolve the republic's dramatic livestock decline, and herd numbers continued to plummet during the period 1931–33. Due to the death of more than a quarter of the republic's population during the famine, the disaster provoked a labor crisis, as the lands of the Hungry Steppe emptied out and collective farms stood empty for lack of workers. Far from increasing the productivity of animal husbandry through nomadic settlement and collectivization, Moscow had sparked the republic's total economic collapse.

Only in 1934 did Moscow successfully reverse this trend. The program of sedentarization, reimagined in another guise, became a means of reversing the republic's economic crisis, and the end of the famine marked a far-reaching rearrangement of the republic's population. The Kazakhs were now collectivized, although most remained in the simplest form of collective farm, a TOZ, not the enormous state farms that Moscow had once envisaged. The refugee crisis served to entrench the language of nationality at the local level, and Kazakhs now began to think of "Kazakhstan" as territorially defined. But for Kazakhs themselves, the long and agonizing process of healing from the trauma of the famine was just beginning, a process that the conclusion and epilogue will explore.

Conclusion

For Kazakhstan, the postfamine years saw a prolonged and agonizing period of recovery. Many of those who survived described a feeling of trauma: Ibragim Khisamutdinov, who lived through the famine as a young boy, saw starving Kazakhs dying in the streets on his way to school. More than fifty years later, he noted, "To this day, I can hear the desperate cries of the dying and their calls for help."[1] For others, the end of the famine marked the beginning of a long struggle to find family members who had been separated from them during the disaster. Sëden Mëlïmülï, a famine survivor whom we met in a previous chapter, ended up in an orphanage due to the death of his parents during the disaster. Several years later, his older brother, who had been imprisoned during the famine, was finally released. In 1937, four years after the famine's end, the two brothers finally reconnected, and Sëden's older brother brought him home from the orphanage.[2] Others were not as fortunate: as a young boy, Däwitbek Nŭrtazin, the future husband of the memoirist Nŭrziya Qajïbaeva saw all his relatives die of hunger during the famine, and Däwitbek grew up in an orphanage.[3] Many young Kazakhs shared his fate, and the population of the republic's orphanages swelled in the famine's aftermath. As most orphanages were primarily Russian-speaking environments, this shift had important implications for the Kazakh children who grew up in them.

In important respects, the project of Soviet modernization had fallen desperately short of its goals. Collectivization was an economic and humanitarian catastrophe across the Soviet Union, but nowhere were its effects more disastrous than in Soviet Kazakhstan. The republic lost one-quarter of its population, some 1.5 million people, due to famine, and officials struggled to cope with labor shortages on the republic's collective farms and factories in the disaster's aftermath. Though Kazakhstan had been the Soviet Union's most important livestock base prior to the crisis, by its end the republic had lost 90 percent of its animal herds.[4] Only in the 1960s did the republic's sheep and cattle numbers finally reach their prefamine levels.[5] The republic's camel population never recovered to its former numbers. In 1933, after the First Five-Year Plan had been declared complete, the republic still lacked basic elements of infrastructure: Moscow did not have a direct telegraph connection with the republic's capital, and there were also no direct telegraph communications between Alma-Ata and many of the republic's provincial centers.[6] Alma-Ata itself had no electricity and was lit by kerosene lamps.[7] But in other respects, Moscow achieved its goals: pastoral nomadism was destroyed as an economic system. Collectivization sparked a dramatic increase in Kazakhs' integration into the institutions of the party-state. Nationality became a key element of Kazakh identity. Nonetheless, the nature of Kazakhstan's transformation should make us think differently about the "leap" in state capacity and mobilization that the Soviet Union achieved during the interwar period, as it transformed itself from a predominately rural society into a power that would eventually defeat Nazi Germany and rival the United States for global supremacy.[8] The contours of this leap were uneven, and they looked quite different in Kazakhstan than they did in parts of the Soviet Union's west.

In one reflection of the problems the regime had encountered in its attempt to transform the Kazakh steppe's arid landscape, by October 1932 leading officials in Moscow began to reconsider whether seasonal migrations might be the best method of pasturing the republic's animal herds, reversing the previous emphasis on creating giant livestock farms fixed in one place. In a letter to Stalin, Rïsqŭlov questioned the previous focus on providing fodder for stabled livestock, as opposed to using the republic's "immense natural pastures" to feed the animals. Provided the party was willing to consider "the climactic and natural particularities of Kazakhstan," he argued, the latter could serve as means for building up the republic's livestock levels. He cited seasonal shifts in the republic's south as an example: during the winter months, livestock could prosper in the lowlands, but in the summer months these same pastures became unbearably hot. The grasses that the animals ate died off in the heat, while the animals themselves suffered from ferocious biting insects. To use the republic's environmental features effectively, Rïsqŭlov argued, it was necessary to drive the animals to mountain pastures during the summer months and return them to lowland pastures during the winter months.[9]

The postfamine years would see a shift toward the use of seasonal migrations as a method of pasturing livestock. During World War II, Moscow evacuated large numbers of cattle to the steppe from the front lines of the war, and collective farmers used Kazakhs' old migration routes to pasture them.[10] In the 1950s, the party promoted the practice of *otgonnoe khoziaistvo*, or "roving animal husbandry," in parts of the republic to build up livestock herds. Abandoning the previous emphasis on the construction of permanent "European-style" dwellings, yurts were now praised as the style of home best suited for certain regions of the steppe.[11] Herders still conducted seasonal migrations on horseback, but they now enjoyed technical support from the regime, including tractors to transport heavier goods and trucks to resupply remote areas with food. To make optimum use of the terrain, herders occasionally crossed boundaries, utilizing pastures in Kirgizia or Uzbekistan.[12]

But this was not the revival of pastoral nomadism. Rather, it represented its final desecration, as the former institutions of Kazakhs' nomadic way of life were given new, ideologically appropriate names: the leaders of Kazakhs' seasonal migrations (the former aqsaqals) were now called "specialists," while the migratory encampments (the former auls) were referred to as "brigades."[13] Ultimately, the number of Kazakhs who would engage in seasonal migrations was small, perhaps no more than a hundred thousand people.[14] Most Kazakhs who survived the famine found their previous way of life destroyed. After fleeing his aul during the famine and watching his father and grandmother die of hunger, Töken Bekmaghambetov returned home to find the aul deserted. Human bones littered the banks of the river, and abandoned yurts had begun to rot.[15] With the countryside in ruins, some Kazakhs fled to the city, and in the disaster's aftermath the republic became more urbanized.[16]

The lands of central Kazakhstan, which included the Hungry Steppe region, were hit particularly hard by the famine. "Once central Kazakhstan was the major place for Kazakh cattle breeding," Mirzoian confessed to Stalin in December 1933, "but now this region has fallen into decline and its resources are not being utilized due to the small number of people and the lack of livestock."[17] Though the death toll in the Kazakh famine awaits a full-scale demographic study (unlike the case of the Ukrainian famine, there has been no comprehensive attempt to break down the death toll in the Kazakh famine at the provincial or district levels), it is likely that this region—the traditional grazing grounds of Middle Horde Kazakhs—was particularly affected.[18] Famine survivors elsewhere in the republic remember the waves of refugees who arrived from central Kazakhstan. Due to their total impoverishment, some of these refugees were mocked as "cannibals."[19] In the disaster's aftermath, the population of the republic's southern regions grew, fueled by the arrival of refugees, as well as the regime's efforts to relocate people to the south to develop the cotton industry there.[20]

But for Moscow, the emptying out of the lands of central Kazakhstan also presented an opportunity.[21] In the postfamine years, the republic would become a vast canvas for Moscow to pursue radical population politics. KarLag, the forced labor camp system located in central Kazakhstan, grew dramatically, becoming one of the largest and longest-lasting camps in the Gulag system. It came to occupy an immense slice of the republic larger than many European countries, and hundreds of thousands of prisoners, most from the Soviet Union's west, passed through its doors.[22] The republic also became one of the primary dumping grounds for various exiled groups: during World War II, close to a million people, including Germans, Chechens, and Crimean Tatars, were brutally uprooted from their homes elsewhere in the Soviet Union and deported to the republic.[23] In important ways, the famine precipitated and enabled a far-reaching demographic transformation of Kazakhstan during the Soviet era. Plunged into the minority after the famine, Kazakhs would not constitute more than 50 percent of the population in their own republic again until after the Soviet Union's collapse.

Collectivization fundamentally altered Kazakhs' relationship to the party-state. Nŭrziya Qajïbaeva recalled that on the eve of collectivization, "The people of our auls just had a vague idea about Lenin and Stalin; only a few Kazakhs had heard these names."[24] But in the famine's aftermath, participation in the regime structured her everyday life. Having fled to China during the famine, her family returned to Kazakhstan, and her father Qajïbay joined a collective farm. There he won awards from the regime for his work, and he became head of a sheep farm. Nŭrziya attended a Soviet Kazakh school, and she became an active participant in several Communist youth organizations, including the Young Octobrists and the Young Pioneers.[25] Mukhamet Shayakhmetov remembers that the Soviet regime had little impact on his family's nomadic way of life prior to 1929. But after suffering grievously during collectivization (his father was labeled a kulak and died during the famine), Shayakhmetov abandoned nomadism, settled in a Russian village, and became a leader for the Young Pioneers.[26] In subsequent years, the regime's efforts to mobilize Kazakhs for World War II would play an important role in further consolidating Kazakhs' integration into Soviet institutions.[27] But by stripping Kazakhs of their livelihood and destabilizing existing social structures, collectivization dramatically increased their reliance on the party-state.

In the aftermath of the famine, nationality became the most important marker of Kazakh identity.[28] In his short story, "An Ethnographic Tale," first published in 1956, the prominent Kazakh journalist and fiction writer Ghabit Müsïrepov (Gabit Musrepov) relayed the adventures of a young activist who sought to understand why the people of Zhanbyrsi aul refused to join a collective farm. On traveling out to the aul, he discovered that its residents were töre, members of the Kazakh hereditary elite, and he contrasted the decay and stagnation that he found in this aul, "a living graveyard," with the collective farms he knew near his home. "How many centuries, how many fruitless centuries had we lost—we, the Kazakh people—while these töre ruled over us?" the activist exclaimed.[29]

Müsïrepov's recounting of collectivization, which suggests that Soviet rule allowed Kazakhs to cast off the vestiges of the past and come together as a nationality, might be read as a depiction of his own life as a Kazakh under Soviet rule: Müsïrepov writes the story in the first person, and like the activist depicted in the story, he worked as lecturer at the Borovoe Forestry School as collectivization began. Müsïrepov witnessed the horrors of the famine—he was one of the signatories to the "Letter of Five," a June 1932 letter to Goloshchekin from five members of the Kazakh intelligentsia that critiqued the party's approach to developing animal husbandry in the republic—but he later rose to great prominence as a Kazakh writer, becoming chairman of the Union of Kazakh Writers and secretary of the Union of Soviet Writers.[30] Müsïrepov's career embodies some of the paradoxes of Soviet rule in Kazakhstan: even as the famine devastated Kazakh society, the regime created opportunities for other Kazakhs to pursue education and upward mobility.

Müsïrepov's short story ends with the young activist's hurried departure from the moribund aul, and it does not indicate whether "the Kazakh people" continued to relate to the forms of identity that Müsïrepov criticizes in his short story, such as kinship, Islam, or allegiances to a hereditary elite, in the postfamine era. But evidence indicates that the famine did not eradicate these existing linkages. Rather, it transformed them. Kinship allegiances changed as Kazakhs moved away from their families or extended families in the disaster's aftermath—some half of all Kazakh households fled their district of residence during the famine, and many never returned home—and they lost the economic functions that they had performed previously when Kazakhs had been nomads.[31] But they continued to have an impact on Kazakh life: in 1950, an ethnographic expedition to the Kegen' district in Alma-Ata province found that most collective farms in the region were composed of a single tribal subdivision (rü). When they married, collective farm members practiced what the study's author termed "collective farm exogamy" (kolkhoznaia ekzogamiia). Adhering to a Kazakh tradition that prohibited marriage within a given tribal subdivision, Kazakhs took a spouse from another collective farm.[32] Likewise, Nürziya Qajïbaeva remembers that in the years after the famine a töre who lived in the village became her "spiritual adviser." Members of the village would get together to recite Islamic poetry, and the Koran remained her father's most treasured possession.[33]

In Kazakhstan today, nomadism has not disappeared. Rather, it functions as a kind of usable past, an element that the Nazarbayev regime uses in the service of its nation-building project. To stress the deep and ancient roots of Kazakh culture, some Kazakhstani scholars claim that the origins of the Kazakh people can be traced to the Scythians, who became the steppe's first known nomadic empire in the first millennium BCE.[34] Various state-sponsored projects stress the innovative and sophisticated nature of the nomadic societies that ruled the steppe prior to the Russian conquest. In the late 1960s, Soviet archeologists found the remains of a Scythian warrior in a burial mound in the republic. In Kazakhstan today, this warrior, known as "The Golden Man" (*Altïn adam*) for his gold-plated dress, has become an important state symbol. A monument to "The Golden Man" can be found in the heart of Almaty and outside the Kazakh embassy in Washington, DC.[35]

What light might the Kazakh case shed on collectivization and famine elsewhere in the Soviet Union? In February 1932, Iusup Abdrakhmanov, the chairman of Kirgizia's Council of People's Commissars, noted the encampments of Kazakh refugees that had sprung up on the outskirts of Kirgizia's capital, Frunze, in his diary. Detailing their utter destitution, he wrote: "Doesn't the fate of the Kazakhs show the future of the Kirgiz? It seems so."[36] Abdrakhmanov's prediction never came to pass: Kirgizia did not endure widespread famine during collectivization. But his observation raises the question of why famine did not afflict the other pastoral nomadic peoples of the Soviet Union with nearly the same intensity as it did the Kazakhs. Though Kazakhstan and Kirgizia shared common features— each had a large native pastoral nomadic population and a significant population of Russian and Ukrainian settlers—famine in Kirgizia was far less severe. In Kirgizia, some thirty-nine thousand people are estimated to have perished due to famine.[37]

The history of Moscow's efforts to collectivize mobile groups is still being written, but a general picture has begun to emerge.[38] Many mobile peoples were sedentarized and collectivized simultaneously, and collectivization marked a violent rupture from their previous way of life. Border making, an important adjunct to collectivization, was by its very nature particularly destructive to nomadic peoples: the policing of district, provincial, republican, and international borders cut pastoralists off from key resources, such as wild animals and pasturelands, and it rendered their previous way of life unsustainable. Despite a plan to collectivize the Soviet Union in stages, with the "more advanced" (i.e., agricultural) regions proceeding first, some nomadic districts were collectivized even more rapidly than settled areas.[39] Animal numbers declined across the Soviet Union due to collectivization, but pastoral regions sustained especially devastating herd losses.

In Buriat-Mongolia, herd numbers declined by 62 percent.[40] In the Soviet satellite of Mongolia, close to a third of the livestock was lost.[41] In Kirgizia, 78 percent of the herd was destroyed.[42] As conditions worsened, pastoral nomads turned to a strategy, flight, on which they had long relied to seek relief from unfavorable political or environmental conditions, and flight in pastoral regions was particularly extensive.[43]

Of these pastoral regions, however, only Kazakhstan saw severe famine. Why might this be so? Mongolia avoided an even greater catastrophe because Stalin, after having received reports on the devastation and uprisings that had engulfed the republic, ordered the Mongolian People's Party to retreat from collectivization in 1932, before it was complete. The Mongolian People's Party was forced to denounce its policies as a "leftist deviation" and commence a policy of socioeconomic gradualism, which would become known as "The New Turn."[44] Collectivization became voluntary, and many pastoralists continued a nomadic lifestyle. Ultimately, the process of collectivizing Mongolia would take decades; only in 1959 was collectivization considered complete.[45]

Inside the Soviet Union, however, the forced collectivization of pastoral regions continued. More detailed data, including a comparison of weather patterns in pastoral regions and a study of famine mortality in pastoral regions at the provincial and district levels, is necessary to conclusively answer the question of why Kazakhstan's death toll was so extreme. Nonetheless, it is possible to make a few hypotheses. The historian Niccolò Pianciola has highlighted differences in policy as a possible explanation: the Communist Parties of Turkmenistan and Kirgizia, the two other Central Asian republics with large pastoral nomadic populations, were under the auspices of the Central Asian Bureau, which steered much of the region under its purview toward cotton production. Kazakhstan, by contrast, was in a different economic zone. It was subject to different policies and developed as a net grain and meat producer to supply places like Moscow, Leningrad, and the cotton-growing regions of Central Asia. When the pressure for procurements increased, the republic, as a food-producing region, suffered disproportionately.[46] Other factors may also help explain the scale of the Kazakh famine, including Moscow's decision to send two hundred thousand special settlers to the republic and clear Kazakhs from their land to set up KarLag. This decision undoubtedly intensified the competition for food inside the republic.

The Kazakh and Ukrainian famines were the two big collectivization famines of the Stalin era. In Ukraine, somewhere between 2.6 to 3.9 million people (out of a population of 33 million) are believed to have died due to hunger and related diseases, while in Kazakhstan, available evidence indicates that 1.5 million people (out of a population of 6.5 million) perished. The question of how these losses break down by ethnicity is more complex, but numerous studies have singled out the Kazakh famine for its particularly devastating effects. In 1998, a US Commission charged with investigating the Ukrainian famine concluded that the Kazakhs lost a greater percentage of their population due to famine than the Ukrainians.[47] In 2010, the Parliamentary Assembly of Europe passed a resolution commemorating the victims of the Soviet collectivization famines. With respect to the Kazakh famine, the resolution noted that "the ration of the dead to the whole population is believed to be the highest among all peoples of the former Soviet Union."[48]

It is difficult to compare the Kazakh and Ukrainian famines, as there is a clear information imbalance. The Ukrainian famine has been the subject of extensive scholarly investigation. Many of those who have researched the topic have examined it through a particular lens, seeking evidence to convict Russia of crimes against Ukrainians as an ethnic group. By contrast, the Kazakh famine has been the subject of far less study, and Kazakhstani authors have focused less on the question of ethnic targeting. Moreover, many of the Kazakh Presidential Archives' most important holdings on the Kazakh famine, such as *fond* (collection) 719, have become available only in the last fifteen years and hence were not available to the first wave of Kazakhstani scholars of the famine. With the Nazarbayev government's current turn away from the subject of the famine, these materials have remained underexplored. In Ukraine, in contrast to most of the former Soviet states, the former secret police archives are open, permitting a greater understanding of how repression was deployed during the famine. In Kazakhstan, the former secret police archives remain closed except to a handful of local scholars.

Nonetheless, a few conclusions are possible. First, the case of the Kazakh famine shows that the regime's treatment of starving Ukrainians was not uniquely brutal, as many scholars of the Ukrainian famine claim. Many tactics held to be distinctive features of the regime's response to the Ukrainian famine, such as the closure of borders so that the starving could not flee, the expulsion of famine refugees from cities, and the blacklisting of famine-stricken districts, were also deployed against starving Kazakhs.[49] In Kazakhstan, Moscow also committed acts of extreme cruelty, such as the slaughter of thousands of starving Kazakhs along the Sino-Kazakh border and the expulsion of Kazakhs from their pasturelands at the height of the famine to construct KarLag, that had no clear parallel in Ukraine. Indeed, it might be argued that in many respects the Kazakh famine was more destructive than the Ukrainian famine, as the Kazakh famine brought about a cultural transformation, the loss of Kazakhs' nomadic way of life, which was even more far-reaching than that endured by the Ukrainians.

Second, the case of the Kazakh famine reveals that several existing explanations of the Ukrainian famine no longer hold. Collectivization was not just an assault on the peasantry but an attack on alien social categories throughout the Soviet Union more broadly. The Kazakh crisis began prior to the Ukrainian crisis (widespread famine struck Kazakhstan in the winter of 1930–31 and Ukraine in the winter of 1931–32), and Moscow's deployment of several violent techniques in Kazakhstan, such as border closures, preceded their use in Ukraine. This finding challenges the contention that the regime's use of similar tactics against starving Ukrainians marked a new and distinctive phase in its treatment of national groups.[50] Other brutal strategies deployed in Kazakhstan were explicitly modeled on those used against starving Ukrainians. On November 10, 1932, Kazakhstan's party committee authorized a wave of terror similar to a grain requisitions terror deployed against starving Ukrainians in Kuban just a few days earlier. As these examples make clear, Moscow did not think of these famines in isolation from one another. Rather, the regime's responses to these crises informed one another.

Finally, the inclusion of the Kazakh case in the narrative of collectivization points to the need to rethink the relationship between state-sponsored violence against particular ethnic groups and assumptions and attitudes in the Soviet state. Ukrainians had a historically troubled relationship with the regime, while the Kazakhs did not. But on the level of policy, there is little to distinguish the regime's brutal response to the Ukrainian case from that of the Kazakh case. In Kazakhstan, like Ukraine, there were several crackdowns on native cadres over the course of the famine, including the assault on members of Alash Orda. As in Ukraine, agricultural failures in Kazakhstan were explicitly linked to questions of national culture. As famine intensified, party members relied upon stereotypes about nomadic life, particularly the idea that nomads held an immense number of animals, to intensify their attacks on Kazakh nomadic life.

In December 1932 in two separate decrees, the Politburo critiqued the policy of Ukrainianization, which had provided support for the promotion of Ukrainian cadres and the Ukrainian language. Scholars have seen these rulings as exceptional, marking a decisive turning point in the evolution of Soviet nationality policy and a shift toward punishing Ukrainians as a national group.[51] But as the Kazakh case shows, the fate of native cadres was marked by constant tension. Moscow sought to promote Kazakh and Ukrainian cadres but also to control them. These Politburo decrees were part of this broader pattern.

Should the Kazakh famine be termed a genocide? That depends on the definition of genocide used. The term "genocide" was first coined by Raphael Lemkin, a Polish Jewish lawyer, who explained his understanding of the term in his book, *Axis Rule in Occupied Europe* (1944).[52] Lemkin's term then acquired another meaning when the United Nations General Assembly adopted the Convention on the Prevention and Punishment of the Crime of Genocide (known as the "Genocide Convention") in 1948. The Genocide Convention defines genocide as:

> any of the following acts committed with intent to destroy, in whole or in part, a national, ethnical, racial or religious group as such: (a) killing members of the group; (b) causing serious bodily or mental harm to members of the group; (c) deliberately inflicting on the group conditions of life calculated to bring about its physical destruction in whole or in part; (d) imposing measures intended to prevent births within the group; (e) forcibly transferring children of the group to another group.[53]

Thus, for an action to fit the legal definition of genocide, it must have both the act itself [a–e], as well as the intent "to destroy, in whole or in part, a national, ethnical, racial or religious group." Notably, the legal definition excludes "political groups," limiting targets of genocide to national, ethnic, racial, or religious groups. During the negotiations for the convention, the Soviet Union, among other states, lobbied successfully to prevent the inclusion of "political groups" as targets of genocide.[54]

The regime sought to carry out a sweeping transformation of Kazakh society, with little regard for the tremendous human suffering that this would provoke. But there is no evidence to indicate that these plans for violent modernization ever turned into a desire to eliminate Kazakhs as a group. Though Moscow instituted brutal crackdowns at the height of the famine, such as the expulsion of hungry refugees from cities and the blacklisting of villages, these tactics were directed at resolving issues the regime perceived as political problems, such as the spread of disease and disorder in cities and the lack of grain on state markets, rather than being an assault on Kazakhs as such. Thus, under the Genocide Convention definition, which is the legal definition of genocide, the Kazakh famine would probably not be considered a genocide, as available evidence does not indicate that the regime's intent was to destroy Kazakhs as an ethnic group. However, if we rely on Lemkin's original formulation of genocide, which included nonphysical methods of destruction, such as political, social, cultural, and social destruction, then the Kazakh famine probably would be considered a genocide. Through collectivization, Moscow sought to destroy nomadic life, a key feature of Kazakh culture and identity.

But a fixation with the question of genocide obscures the bigger picture. The Kazakh famine was a crime against humanity, one that resulted in the deaths of more than a million civilians and terrible anguish for those who survived. Though genocide has taken root as the ultimate "crime of crimes" in the popular imagination, that the Kazakh famine does not appear to fit the legal definition of genocide does not make this atrocity any less worthy of attention nor lessen the scale of Kazakhs' suffering. Rather, the fact that the Kazakh famine, though one of the most heinous crimes of the Stalinist regime, does not fit readily into the legal definition of genocide should challenge historians to rethink the ways that we categorize and study mass atrocities and their perpetration. In placing so much emphasis on those cases that fit a particular definition of genocide, we may conceal other cases of mass violence, such as the Kazakh famine, that also stemmed from a political process and that were no less destructive to human life.

Epilogue

In 2011, Nŭrziya Qajïbaeva, a survivor of the Kazakh famine of 1930–33, remarked that some Kazakhs appeared to have turned away from the subject of the famine. She related an anecdote about a relative, Khamit, a "Soviet Kazakh" who was a Komsomol member and a student of a medical institute. Though Khamit's grandfather had perished in the famine, Khamit chastised his parents for speaking to him about the matter, asking: "Why do you keep harping on about that famine? Why didn't you eat at least some bread?" Critiquing Khamit's approach, Qajïbaeva exclaimed: "How elusive the memory is! Or have our descendants become *mankurts*?"[1] The legend of the "mankurt," or a people who had lost their memory, was popularized by the Kirgiz writer Chingiz Aitmatov in his seminal work, *I dol'she veka dlitsia den'* (subsequently translated into English as *The Day Lasts Longer than a Thousand Years*).[2] First published in 1980, Aitmatov's novel offered a subtle critique of the Soviet regime, and, over time, the word "mankurt" became a derogatory term, used to refer to members of non-Russian nationalities who had lost their cultural and linguistic identity under Soviet dominance.[3]

In Kazakhstan, the term "mankurt" and several close synonyms, such as "shala-Kazakh" (half-Kazakh) and "asfal'tnyi Kazakh" ("asphalt Kazakh," used specifically to refer to urban Kazakhs), gained resonance due to the dramatic transformations that Kazakhs endured during the Soviet era. By 1989, 62 percent of Kazakhs claimed fluency in Russian, while other Central Asian nationalities had far lower rates of Russian proficiency.[4] Many Kazakhs, particularly those in urban areas, had difficulty speaking Kazakh, a phenomenon due in part to unofficial practices that accorded the Russian language a privileged status. Transformed by the regime's policies of migration and deportation, which brought not only Russians but Ukrainians, Germans, Koreans, Poles, and other ethnic groups to the republic, Kazakhstan had one of the highest rates of interethnic marriage of any republic in the Soviet Union by the late 1980s.[5] Though many arrivals left Kazakhstan after the Soviet collapse, others remained. Today, Kazakhstan is a multiethnic society, with a large Russian minority (23.7 percent).[6]

Qajïbaeva's question raises several broad issues: How have Kazakhs remembered the famine? Why, in stark contrast to Ukraine, where the Ukrainian famine has served as a crucial event in the creation of a national memory, is there relatively little public discussion of the famine in Kazakhstan today? This epilogue cannot provide definitive answers to these questions—the issue of how the Kazakh famine has been remembered in Kazakhstan deserves a full-fledged study in its own right—but it aims to be suggestive, pointing out areas for further research.[7] It shows that the question of the famine has become entangled with broader questions about how Kazakhs should remember the Soviet past, as well as Kazakhstan's present-day relationship with Russia. The Ukrainian famine has, in turn, come to serve as both model and antimodel for Kazakh activists seeking to remember their own famine. Recent efforts by the Nazarbayev regime to reopen discussion of the Kazakh famine have exposed tensions between the regime's simultaneous attempt to promote a multiethnic civic identity and appeal to an explicitly ethnic vision of Kazakh nationalism.[8] But crucial questions of individual agency and responsibility for the crisis have continued to receive relatively little attention.

After an explosion of interest in the late 1980s and 1990s that focused heavily on vilifying Goloshchekin as the main architect of the famine and lionizing Kazakh opposition to Soviet rule, public discussion of the famine in Kazakhstan slowed by the late 1990s. Calls by Kazakh activists for a public trial of the perpetrators of the famine disappeared from public life.[9] There were far fewer popular or scholarly studies of the famine produced. When I spoke to Kazakhstani doctoral students as I was conducting research in 2007, they told me that their supervisors had encouraged them to work on topics other than the famine. In what was perhaps the most visible symbol of a turn away from public discussion, a memorial to the victims of the Kazakh famine in Almaty (the former Alma-Ata), planned since 1990, remained unbuilt, marked only by a simple stone placard. When I visited the monument site in 2007, the path to the placard was choked with weeds, and empty beer bottles littered the pavement beside it.

In 2012, public discourse on the famine resumed, albeit in a more limited fashion than before. President Nazarbayev authorized a major international conference, "Famine in Kazakhstan: The Tragedy of the People and the Lessons

FIGURE 7.1.   An Unfinished Monument to the Famine's Victims in Almaty. The inscription, which is written first in Kazakh and then in Russian, reads: "A monument to the victims of the famine of 1931–1933 will be established in this place." Photograph by the author, July 2007.

of History," to commemorate the famine's eightieth anniversary in May 2012, and the proceedings of this conference were widely discussed and broadcast on state media.[10] The conference was accompanied by the dedication of a famine memorial in Astana, which had become independent Kazakhstan's capital. The memorial was composed of a "Wall of Grief" overlaid with a latticework design (which recalled the interior wood structure, or *kerege*, of a Kazakh yurt), with a sculpture depicting starving Kazakhs in the foreground. Since 1997, Kazakhstan had observed May 31 as "The Day of Remembrance of the Victims of Political Repression." But after 2012, this day of remembrance began to include explicit reference to the victims of the famine as well. In 2017, twenty-five years after the spot in Almaty was first marked by a placard, a memorial to the famine victims in Almaty was finally built. Made of bronze and granite, the sculpture portrayed a Kazakh woman carrying an emaciated child, with an empty *qazan*, or cooking vessel used in Kazakh cuisine, at her feet.

But this renewed public discussion of was different in tone from the first: in a speech at the dedication of the famine memorial in Astana, Nazarbayev not

FIGURE 7.2.   President Nursultan Nazarbayev speaks at the dedication of a memorial to the victims of the Kazakh famine in Astana. Photograph by the author, May 2012.

only refrained from calling the famine a genocide, a term that had once been a staple of his regime's discourse on the famine, but also said relatively little about the responsibility of the Soviet regime for this mass atrocity. Instead, Nazarbayev cautioned Kazakhs against the dangers of "politicizing" the disaster, a reference that evoked Ukrainian efforts to seek reparations for their famine from Russia.[11] Since this reopening of public discussion, scholarly investigations into the famine have resumed but are different in focus from the first wave of interest in the 1990s. Rather than producing new interpretations, scholars have focused on the important (but perhaps less controversial) work of publishing document collections related to the famine, identifying the names of the dead, and locating the mass graves sites where many victims are buried.[12]

What might explain this period of silence followed by a limited public discussion of the disaster? Identifying the reasons for these shifts will require further study, although it is possible to offer some hypotheses. Kazakhstan has a close relationship with Russia, and Nazarbayev may fear that a full discussion of the famine will incite diplomatic tensions or anger Kazakhstan's large Russian minority. Indeed, Nazarbayev's current approach to the Kazakh famine resembles the line that some scholars in Russia, with the backing of the Russian government, have taken. Pointing to the existence of famine in several areas of the Soviet Union, these scholars have dismissed Ukrainian claims of genocide, arguing that the Soviet collectivization famines were a "common tragedy of the Soviet peoples," one that should "unite" rather than divide the peoples of Russia and Ukraine. But they have not said much about the culpability of the Soviet regime for these disasters.[13] In turn, it is no coincidence that an outsider, Tat'iana Nevadovskaya, the daughter of Gavril Nevadovsky, a professor exiled to Kazakhstan during the famine, has become the most celebrated memoirist of the famine in Kazakhstan. Nevadovskaya's moving depictions of the hungry years of the famine and her efforts to help starving Kazakhs, which she recorded in her diary and wove into her poems, would seem to fit an official interpretation of the famine focused more on interethnic cooperation and shared suffering than Kazakh victimhood and blame.[14]

Public pressure appears to have played a role in Nazarbayev's decision to begin official commemoration of the disaster in 2012. In 2008, the Organization for Security and Cooperation in Europe (OSCE) Parliamentary Assembly was held in Astana. The OSCE Parliamentary Assembly adopted a resolution that paid tribute to the victims of the Ukrainian famine. The resolution recognized that the famine was brought about by "the cruel, deliberate actions and policies of the totalitarian Stalinist regime" but, to the disappointment of some Ukrainians, it stopped short of calling it a genocide.[15] Some Kazakh commentators then questioned why the Nazarbayev regime appeared to support the Russian government's position on the Ukrainian famine during the Astana meeting. The Kazakhs, they argued, should support Ukrainian claims of genocide and put forward a request to the OSCE to recognize the Kazakh famine as a genocide too.[16] In 2010, the Parliamentary Assembly of Europe (PACE) passed a resolution commemorating the victims of the Soviet collectivization famines. This resolution noted that the Kazakhs are believed to have the highest death ratio due to famine of any people in the Soviet Union, a statement that provided further impetus to Kazakhstani activists seeking to end the Nazarbayev regime's silence on the Kazakh famine.[17] A number of deputies to the Kazakh parliament then petitioned Kazakhstan's prime minister for greater official recognition of the Kazakh disaster, including the construction of a memorial complex to the victims.[18]

These events contributed to the Nazarbayev regime's decision to begin commemorating the famine in 2012, but other factors may explain the relative lack of discussion in Kazakhstan more generally. The question of victimhood in famines is complicated, and a full excavation of the disaster would likely force Kazakhs to confront difficult parts of their own history, including the role that many Kazakhs themselves played in the making of the catastrophe. Another thorny question is who to blame. Some Kazakhstani authors have pointed squarely at Russia, using the example of the famine to proclaim the evils of Russian influence in Kazakh society.[19] But others have argued that that Russia cannot be accused of creating the famine. As Aldan Smayïl, a deputy to Kazakhstan's parliament, argued, "One should not ask for an apology [for the famine] because there is no one to ask for an apology from—this country no longer exists."[20] In this version of events, the Soviet Union, not Russia, should be held responsible for the disaster.

For other Kazakhs, a reluctance to discuss the famine is also connected to the larger question of how to evaluate the Soviet past. As a Kazakh colleague explained the issue to me, many Kazakhs acknowledge that the Soviet experience led to enormous loss of life, yet they contend that Soviet modernization, including Kazakhs' transformation from a "backward" nomadic society into a modern settled one, had positive effects as well.[21] After independence, Kazakhstan's Shoqan Uälikhanov Institute of History and Ethnography, one of the country's leading academic institutions, produced a five-volume study, *The History of Kazakhstan from Ancient Times to the Present Day*.[22] But in a sign of the difficulties that Kazakhs have encountered in crafting a usable narrative of the Soviet past, the volume that pertained to the Soviet period was issued only after multiple delays.

Reflecting the lack of consensus on how to view the famine, there is no generally accepted name for the Kazakh famine in Kazakhstan, as there is for the Ukrainian famine in Ukraine. (The Ukrainian famine is often known by a shorthand, "Holodomor" (an amalgamation of the Ukrainian words *holod* [famine] and *moryty* [kill].) Instead, the Kazakh famine is known by variety of different names, including *aqtaban shŭbïrïndï* (The Barefooted Flight), *ŭlï asharshïlïq* (The Great Famine), *velikii dzhut* (The Great Zhŭt), "Goloshchekin's genocide," and "Kazakhstan's Holodomor." Each of these names would seem to suggest a slightly different emphasis. The phrase *aqtaban shŭbïrïndï*, for instance, was first used to refer to the devastating Zungar invasion of the Kazakh steppe in 1723, and the use of this phrase situates the Kazakh famine within a larger narrative of Kazakh history and suffering. The term *velikii dzhut* recalls Kazakhs' nomadic past, when massive herd die-offs, or zhŭts, hit the steppe with some regularity, but it leaves open the question of human agency in the making of the famine. Finally, the term "Kazakhstan's Holodomor," hints at the ways that the memory of the Kazakh famine has developed in the shadow of the Ukrainian famine.

There are also tensions within the Nazarbayev regime's current discourse on the famine. Official calls to avoid politicizing the disaster are frequently intertwined with subtle appeals to an aggrieved sense of ethnic Kazakh nationalism. At the May 31, 2017, dedication of the Almaty famine memorial, the mayor of

Almaty, Bauïrzhan Baybek, noted, "According to scholarly figures, the [Kazakh] famine set the growth of the country's population a hundred years back." He noted that the statue of a Kazakh woman carrying her emaciated child was appropriate, given that "the mother is the source of everything pure, the foundation of the nation, the guarantee of the future."[23] For many Kazakhs, the issue of the famine is intertwined with the tendentious issue of the country's ethnic balance, an issue that Baybek's comment and arguably the statue's very design clearly evokes. Some Kazakhstani scholars claim that if the famine had not happened, the worldwide population of Kazakhs would be twenty-five million or more rather than the eighteen million that it is now.[24]

Since independence, the Nazarbayev government has attempted to boost the number of Kazakhs in Kazakhstan. Through promises of land and citizenship, it has wooed back almost a million Kazakhs from abroad.[25] Many of these returnees, who are known as *oralmandar,* are descendants of Kazakhs who fled Kazakhstan during the famine's course. But reintegrating oralmandar back into a country profoundly altered by the Soviet experience has proved difficult. Some do not speak Russian, now the predominant language in many Kazakh cities, while others learned to read and write in Kazakh using a modified Arabic script, rather than the Cyrillic script that was used for much of the Soviet period and remains in use today.[26] Some Kazakhstani Kazakhs approach oralmandar with suspicion, believing that Kazakhs who fled Kazakhstan during the famine abandoned Kazakhstan during a time of great need.[27]

There is still much to be explored about how Kazakhs have remembered their famine, including the important question of how Kazakhs discussed and passed down memories of the disaster over the generations. Meanwhile, Kazakhs' own investigation into the famine, which simultaneously created a new Kazakh national identity even as it devastated Kazakh society and transformed Kazakh culture, remains an unfinished project.

Acknowledgments

It is a pleasure to acknowledge the institutions whose financial support made this project possible. Though they bear no responsibility for my findings, this project could not have been completed without their generous assistance. The research and writing of this project began at Yale University. There I benefited from a Yale Graduate Fellowship, an Enders Fellowship from Yale, a Smith Richardson Fellowship from Yale's International Security Studies Center (ISS), a MacMillan Center for International and Area Studies Dissertation Research Grant from Yale, a Fulbright Student Fellowship for Kazakhstan, and an American Council of Learned Societies (ACLS)/Mellon Dissertation Completion Fellowship. I also received financial support for German, Russian, and Kazakh-language studies, and I thank the US Department of State Foreign Language and Area Studies Program, the US Department of State Title VIII program, the Social Science Research Council (SSRC), ISS, and Yale's Graduate School of Arts and Sciences for their assistance. Other funds allowed me to conduct additional archival research to expand the scope of the project and provided me with the uninterrupted writing time necessary to transform this project into a book. For this opportunity, I am indebted to a Mellon/ACLS Postdoctoral Fellowship at Yale's MacMillan Center, a Title VII Post-Doctoral Fellowship at the Woodrow Wilson International Center for Scholars, a research grant from the International Research and Exchanges Board, a Carson Fellowship at the Rachel Carson Center for the Environment and Society, a Summer Research and Scholarship Award from the Graduate School at the University of Maryland-College Park, a Harry Frank Guggenheim Foundation Research Grant, and a Kluge Fellowship at the Library of Congress.

At Yale and beyond, Laura Engelstein has been an outstanding mentor. She helped nurture this project from the beginning, impressing on me the need for clarity, rigor, and empiricism in my writing. She willingly fielded countless questions and last-minute crises. Long after I was no longer formally her student, she continued to give generously of her time, writing letters of recommendation on my behalf, commenting on grant applications and reading (and rereading) draft chapters of this book. She offered incisive critiques that helped shape this book's pages, but also encouragement when I needed it the most. In a profession where we all have so many demands on our time, Laura's extraordinary commitment to mentorship is unusual. But it is precisely this work, which is all too often unrecognized and underappreciated, that allows the field of history to grow and develop, permitting projects such as mine to come to fruition.

At Yale, I would also like to thank Tim Snyder. He has been supportive of this project from the very start, and this encouragement has meant a great deal to me over the years. Tim played a crucial early role in fishing out ideas from messy chapter drafts, and his thoughtful suggestions for improvement made this project into a much better book. Ben Kiernan offered helpful feedback and consistently read drafts with great care. I am also grateful to Abbas Amanat, Paul Bushkovitch, Ute Frevert, John Merriman, Peter Perdue, Steve Pincus and Marci Shore. At Yale, I was fortunate to be part of a collegial and friendly cohort of graduate students, including Laia Balcells, Haydon Cherry, Faith Hillis, Charles Keith, Anja Manthey, Kathleen Minahan, Philipp Nielsen, Helen Veit, Iryna Vushko, and Charlotte Walker-Said. Jessica Csoma became a good friend. I am indebted to those friends who patiently read early drafts of this project as part of a graduate student reading group: Daniel Brückenhaus, Lisa Pinley Covert, Catherine Dunlop, Yedida Kanfer, Carmen Kordick, Eden Knudsen McLean, Laura Robson, and Nick Rutter. They provided much needed encouragement during the long days of writing, and their suggestions helped shape the book.

My research trips to Kazakhstan brought many adventures, and I am grateful to have stumbled on such a wonderful spot to be a foreign researcher. I benefited from numerous conversations with Kazakhstani historians, as well as the materials that they kindly shared with me. I thank Zhuldusbek Abylkhozhin, Talas Omarbekov, Säbit Shïldebay, and Maqash Tätimov (who sadly passed away before the publication of this book) for giving generously of their time. I hope this project attests to the vibrancy of Kazakhstani scholarship. Archivists at the Presidential Archives, the Central State Archives, the Almaty Oblast Archives, the Center for the Documentation of New History in Semey, and the State Photo Archives were helpful and supportive. I would like to express my appreciation to Saule Satayeva for her assistance in tracking down some of the photographs in this book. I met the Aubakirova family on my very first trip to Kazakhstan, and Almaty was always brightened by their kindness and good humor. Asel Shayahmet became a loyal friend, and her family always provided a welcoming home for me on my trips to Kazakhstan. Over the years, Asel has also patiently answered many of my questions about Kazakh culture. In Almaty, thanks are also due to Brian Carlson, Stanley Currier, Meg Driscoll, Anna Genina, Janet Kilian, Albert Lang, Megan Rancier, Del Schwab, Asiyat Suleimenova, and Mira Tuleup. In Moscow, I am grateful to Jennifer Foort, Irina Plevako, and Jeanette Leeney Saraiva.

I am fortunate to be part of a welcoming and intellectually stimulating group of scholars who study Central Asia. Adrienne Edgar first encouraged my interest in the region, read early drafts of the project, and in the intervening years continued to be a source of indispensable advice. For guidance and assistance with queries relating to Central Asia, I thank Marysia Blackwood, Ian Campbell, Virginia Martin, Gabriel McGuire, Jeff Sahadeo, and Ed Schatz. The study of the Kazakh famine has blossomed in recent years in the West, and I am grateful to the other scholars who work on the Kazakh famine—Robert Kindler, Isabelle Ohayon, Matt Payne, and Niccolò Pianciola—for their collegiality and generosity. My understanding of the Kazakh famine has benefited greatly from exchange with their ideas and research.

In different ways, many others also contributed to this project's transformation into a book. Without the initial encouragement of Amir Weiner, I might never have become a historian, and I am indebted to him for his early support. As an undergraduate, I had the good fortune to work closely with Lou Roberts, and she has continued to be a model for me in the intervening years. I would also like to express my appreciation to those scholars who provided me with the opportunity to share chapter drafts and present preliminary research findings from this project at their institutions over the years. Though they are too numerous to name individually, I am grateful to them and their audiences for engaging so thoughtfully and productively with my work. Jeremy Friedman reviewed the book manuscript in its initial stages and provided helpful suggestions for revision. Others also offered critiques or ideas that proved influential, including Nicholas Breyfogle, Kate Brown, David Brophy, Krista Goff, Andrea Graziosi, Philippa Hetherington, Faith Hillis, Paul Josephson, Viktor Kondrashin, Christof Mauch, Timothy Nunan, Cormac Ó Gráda, and Stephen Wheatcroft.

At the University of Maryland-College Park, where I teach, I have found a lively intellectual home. I am indebted to the chair of my department, Phil Soergel, for his support and for permitting me to take the research leaves that allowed me to complete revisions to this book. I am grateful to have two exceptional colleagues in Russian and East European history, Mikhail Dolbilov and Piotr Kosicki. Kate Keane has become a wonderful friend. At Maryland, I also thank Ala Creciun, Ahmet Karamustafa, John Lampe, Elizabeth Papazian, Richard Price, Marsha Rozenblit, Liuda Sharaya, and Tom Zeller. The Washington, DC, area is a terrific place to be a Soviet historian, and my thinking about this project has also benefited from exchanges with colleagues at the Russian History Workshop held at Georgetown University.

This project would not have been possible without the assistance of many archivists and librarians. Tanja Lorkovic and the entire staff of the Slavic Reading Room at Yale's Sterling Library helped hunt down hard-to-find materials from Central Asia. At the Library of Congress, Harry Leich and Joan Weeks provided important support. At McKeldin Library at the University of Maryland-College Park, I thank Eric Lindquist. For help with tricky Kazakh-language translations and other research assistance, I am indebted to Serik Beisembaev, Ulan Bigozhin, Talgat Kadirov, Olga Litvin, and Arystan Moldabekov. Nathan Burtch designed the beautiful maps that are in this book.

A version of chapter 5 appeared as "Violence, Flight, and Hunger: The Sino-Kazakh Border and the Kazakh Famine, 1930–31," in *Stalin and Europe: Imitation and Domination, 1928–1953*, ed. Raymond Brandon and Timothy D. Snyder (Oxford, 2014), 44–73; and a version of chapter 1 is forthcoming as "'People Arrive but the Land Does Not Move': Nomads, Settlers, and the Ecology of the Kazakh Steppe, 1870–1916," in *Eurasian Environments: Nature and Ecology in Eurasian History* (Pittsburgh), edited by Nicholas B. Breyfogle. I am grateful to both publishers for the opportunity to republish versions of these chapters here.

It has been a pleasure to work with Cornell University Press on the production of this book. I thank Roger Haydon for taking an initial interest in the project. Along the way, he has fielded my questions with good humor and patience, and he has provided many sensible editorial suggestions that have improved this book. Roger should also be credited with identifying two wonderful reviewers, David Brandenberger and Rebecca Manley. I thank David and Rebecca for the considerable care and attention they put into reviewing the book. Their challenging critiques helped hone my argument and saved me from several errors. Carolyn Pouncy was a terrific copyeditor. I am grateful to Karen Laun and Ellen Murphy for their assistance with the production process and to Carmen Adriana Torrado Gonzalez for her help with the marketing of the book.

I am indebted to the family and friends who have supported me in the end stages of this project. Yedida Kanfer commented on several chapters, offering valuable feedback. Isabelle Kaplan supplied last-minute assistance. Jean Galbraith has been a superb friend for over thirty years. She read the entire book manuscript and provided helpful suggestions. Kate Galbraith also commented on the entire book, and her keen editorial eye improved the book's readability. My parents, my sister, Anne, and my brother-in-law, Aly, have been a constant source of love and encouragement. My daughter Isabel arrived as this project was near completion, and she has brought so much happiness to my life ever since. But thanks are due above all to my husband, Arnd. He has lived with this project for too many years, but he has never faltered in his support. His joy for life has been an inspiration, and his gentle sense of humor a source of comfort during even the most difficult days. It is to him with love and gratitude that I dedicate this book.

Appendix

Precipitation Levels for the Kazakh Steppe, 1921–33

a. Monthly measured precipitation levels in select Kazakh locations by month, 1931 (in mm)

LOCATION	JAN	FEB	MAR	APR	MAY	JUN	JUL	AUG	SEP	OCT	NOV	DEC	SUM
Alma-Ata	31.8	7.3	33.5	94.6	125.8	77.2	21.9	17.8	1.1	22.5	45.4	29.4	508.3
Fort Aleksandrovskii	2.7	0.0	7.0	14.0	8.4	73.4	2.2	6.5	0.3	13.1	5.4	21.3	154.3
Kzyl-Orda	10.7	0.0	10.2	3.1	18.1	17.4	0.0	16.5	0.0	1.1	12.8	46.0	135.9
Semipalatinsk	13.2	6.2	54.8	11.4	13.4	4.2	3.4	19.2	39.9	24.6	32.8	31.3	254.4
Turgai	8.9	0.0	52.6	8.5	6.3	25.3	0.9	37.2	7.6	24.4	11.0	36.2	218.9

b. Average measured monthly precipitation levels in select Kazakh locations by month, 1921–30 (in mm)

LOCATION	JAN	FEB	MAR	APR	MAY	JUN	JUL	AUG	SEP	OCT	NOV	DEC	SUM
Alma-Ata	24.7	32.9	55.9	94.9	94.4	43.4	47.4	28.3	27.1	54.6	44.7	30.9	579.2
Fort Aleksandrovskii	6.2	9.7	10.8	23.2	11.4	11.6	17.8	30.6	16.3	16.8	12.6	8.2	178.8
Kzyl-Orda	12.2	17.4	14.7	15.3	6.7	6.8	5.4	0.4	2.6	9.3	11.6	13.1	115.6
Semipalatinsk	18.6	13.5	21.4	19.3	28.6	32.3	38.3	23.5	25.3	23.4	37.0	19.5	297.5
Turgai	8.4	10.1	9.7	25.3	25.2	18.9	10.4	12.3	10.8	20.3	9.4	6.0	183.9

c. Year with lowest measured precipitation level in select Kazakh locations by month, 1921–33 (in mm)

LOCATION	JAN	FEB	MAR	APR	MAY	JUN	JUL	AUG	SEP	OCT	NOV	DEC	SUM
Alma-Ata	1923	1925	1930	1927	1926	1927	1927	1932	1922	1931	1922	1923	1927
	(8.6)	(2.0)	(12.5)	(17.6)	(47.7)	(3.3)	(7.6)	(3.0)	(0.0)	(22.5)	(17.9)	(17.9)	(453.5)
Fort Aleksandrovskii	1922/28	1931	1925/29	1932	1921/24	1922	1922/27	1924/29	1927	1928	1928	1922/23	1924
	(1.4)	(0.0)	(2.3)	(4.3)	(0.0)	(0.0)	(1.0)	(1.1)	(0.0)	(4.4)	(0.3)	(1.5)	(107.5)
Kzyl-Orda	1923	1931	1925	1927	1921/ 23/29	1922/23/ 30/32	1921–23/ 25/29/ 31	1922–25/ 29/30	1927/30/ 31/33	1928	1921	1929	1929
	(5.9)	(0.0)	(2.2)	(0.0)	(0.0)	(0.0)	(0.0)	(0.0)	(0.0)	(0.0)	(0.0)	(1.3)	(75.6)
Semipalatinsk	1930	1927	1932	1921/27	1923	1931	1931	1923	1927	1933	1929	1928	1923
	(9.0)	(0.7)	(6.0)	(0.0)	(8.9)	(4.2)	(3.4)	(0.0)	(8.1)	(4.9)	(12.5)	(5.3)	(212.6)
Turgai	1928	1931	1926	1930	1927	1930	1927/31	1927	1925	1928	1928	1928	1926
	(1.5)	(0.0)	(1.4)	(1.1)	(5.4)	(2.0)	(0.9)	(0.0)	(0.0)	(1.0)	(1.3)	(1.6)	(145.5)

Source: Compiled from the data contained in M. W. Williams and V. G. Konovalov, Central Asia Temperature and Precipitation Data, 1879–2003 (Boulder, 2008). If data in the original source were missing, then the calculations of the averages were adjusted accordingly.

Glossary

adat customary law in Kazakh society

AO Autonomous oblast, a national territory below the level of an ASSR

aqsaqal clan elder in Kazakh society who selected routes and dates for seasonal migrations and oversaw the pasturelands

artel intermediate type of collective farm where work animals and tools were owned collectively. Higher degree of socialization than in a TOZ

ASSR Autonomous Soviet Socialist Republic, a national territory included within a union republic

aul nomadic encampment, generally made up two to eight households. Also used by the Soviet regime as an administrative term to indicate a Kazakh area below the level of a district

bai term used by the Soviet regime to refer to an exploitative or wealthy Kazakh

bedniak poor peasant. Also used to refer to a poor Kazakh

biy clan elder in Kazakh society who served as the administrator of customary law, known as adat

black bone commoner strata of Kazakh society

Gosplan State Planning Commission

horde supra-tribal confederation in Kazakh society

kraikom krai party committee. Here, used to refer to the Communist Party body in charge of the Kazakh ASSR

khan leader of a horde, part of the white bone elite in Kazakh society

kolkhoz collective farm

korenizatsiia indigenization, a policy of supporting non-Russian languages and promoting non-Russian elites in non-Russian territories

Narkomzem People's Commissariat for Agriculture

NEP New Economic Policy

Osedkom Committee for the Sedentarization of the Nomadic and Semi-Nomadic Kazakh Population

OGPU Unified State Political Administration, the secret police from 1922 to 1934

ocherednost' policy that gave Kazakhs priority in acquiring land

otkochevniki literally, "nomads who are moving away." A term used to refer to Kazakh refugees during the famine

pood Russian weight, equivalent to thirty-six pounds

qozha religious figure in Kazakh society who claimed descent from the prophet Muhammad

RSFSR Russian Union of Federated Socialist Republics

samovol'tsy literally, "self-settlers." Peasants who settled illegally

seredniak middle-income peasant. Also used to refer to a middle-income Kazakh

solonchak type of soil formed as groundwater rose to the surface, leaving white, salty patches

soghïm Kazakhs' annual fall slaughter of animals to serve as winter food

sovkhoz state farm

Sovnarkom Council of People's Commissars

SSR Soviet Socialist Republic, a union republic
sukhovei hot, dry winds that regularly swept over the steppe
sultan a son of a khan, part of the white bone elite in Kazakh society
töre descendants of the sultans, part of the white bone elite in Kazakh society
TOZ Association for Joint Cultivation of the Land, the loosest form of collective farm. All animals and most tools are privately owned.
TsIK Central Executive Committee
verst unit of measurement equivalent to 3,500 feet
white bone aristocratic strata of Kazakh society. Includes khans, sultans and töre
zhŭt a late spring frost that could lead to massive herd losses for pastoral nomads

List of Abbreviations Used in the Notes

Archival terms
d. delo (file)
f. fond (collection)
l. ll. list, listy (page, pages)
ob. oborot (verso)
op. opis' (register)

Archives

APRF	President's Archive of the Russian Federation
APRK	The President's Archive of the Republic of Kazakhstan
GAAO	State Archive, Almaty Oblast
GANO	State Archive, Novosibirsk Oblast
GARF	State Archive of the Russian Federation
RGAE	Russian State Archive of the Economy
RGASPI	Russian State Archive of Sociopolitical History
RGIA	Russian State Historical Archive
RGVA	Russian State Military Archive
RTsKhIDNI	Russian Center for the Preservation and Study of Contemporary Documents, now part of RGASPI
TsA FSB RF	Central Archive of the Federal Security Service, Russian Federation
TsDNIVKO	The Center for the Documentation of New History, Eastern Kazakhstan Oblast
TsGAKFFDRK	Republic of Kazakhstan Central State Archive of Film, Photograph, and Audio Documents
TsGANKh	Central State Archive of the National Economy, (now known as RGAE)
TsGARK	Central State Archive of the Republic of Kazakhstan

Publications

GVS	*Golod v SSSR 1929–1934*, ed. V. V. Kondrashin
IIDK	*Iz istorii deportatsii Kazakhstana 1930–1935 gg.: Sbornik dokumentov*
IIVTK	*Iz istorii velichaishei tragedii kazakhskogo naroda 1932–1933 gg.: Sbornik dokumentov*

KKhAO   *Kirgizskoe khoziaistvo v Akmolinskoi oblasti, KKhAO*

KSKK   *Kollektivizatsiia sel'skogo khoziaistva Kazakhstana (1926–iiun' 1941 g.)*

LMK   *Levon Mirzoian v Kazakhstane: Sbornik dokumentov i materialov (1933–1938 gg.)*

NKG   *Nasil'stvennaia kollektivizatsiia i golod v Kazakhstane 1931–1933 gg: Sbornik dokumetov i materialov*

SDA   Stalin Digital Archive https://www.stalindigitalarchive.com

SDG   *Sovetskaia derevnia glazami VChK-OGPU-NKVD: Dokumenty i materialy*

TKA   *Tragediia kazakhskogo aula, 1928–1934*

TKN   *Tragediia kazakhskogo naroda: Sbornik dokumentov i materialov: (golod 20-kh, 30-kh godov XX veka v Kazakhstane)*

TSD   *Tragediia Sovetskoi derevni: Kollektivizatsiia i raskulachivanie. Dokumenty i materialy*

Notes

INTRODUCTION

1. Zh. Äbïshülï, "Ötkennïng öksïgï," in *Qïzïldar qïrghïnï*, ed. B. Khabdina (Almaty, 1993), 57.

2. Nürsültan Äbdïghanülï, "Qïzïl qïrghïn qasïretï," in *Qïzïldar qïrghïnï*, 37–39.

3. The death toll in the Kazakh famine awaits a comprehensive study, but it is clear that the famine claimed a staggering number of lives. Relying on a population reconstruction method, which subtracts the deaths that would have occurred had there not been a famine from the overall number of deaths, the authors of a recent demographic study estimate Kazakhstan's excess deaths (what they term "direct losses") at 1.3 million and lost births (what they term "indirect losses") at 228,000 for the period 1932–34. The authors caution, however, that this is only a partial estimate of the Kazakh famine's overall toll as severe famine in Kazakhstan began prior to 1932. See Omelian Rudnytskyi et al., "Famine Losses in Ukraine in 1932 and 1933 within the Context of the Soviet Union," in *Famines in European Economic History*, ed. Declan Curran et al. (New York, 2015), 208, 210. Relying in part on the number of officially registered deaths in Kazakhstan during the famine period, Stephen G. Wheatcroft and R. W. Davies conclude that 1.3 to 1.5 million people died in the Kazakh famine (*The Years of Hunger* [New York, 2009], 412).

4. Based on data from the Presidential Archives in Kazakhstan, the editor of one document collection argues that 1,130,000 people fled the republic from 1929 to 1933. See L. D. Degitaeva, ed., *Levon Mirzoian v Kazakhstane* (Almaty, 2001), 292. Zhetpïs Taldïbaev offers a similar figure based on research in the secret police archives ("Ashtïqtan kelgen demografiialïq apat," *Abai*, no. 1 [2000], 28–33).

5. On the Kazakh diaspora, see Gul'nara Mendikulova, *Kazakhskaia diaspora* (Almaty, 2006).

6. As this book explains, the label "nomad" is contested, and different observers define it in various ways. Nonetheless, Soviet statistics give some idea of Kazakhs' economic practices on the eve of collectivization. According to data from 1929, 26.9 percent of Kazakhs were settled, while the rest practiced some form of nomadism. See B. Rodnevich, *Ot kolonial'nogo vyrozhdeniia k sotsialisticheskomu rastsvetu* (Moscow, 1931), 15.

7. On the long history of pastoral nomadism in the steppe region, see Michael D. Frachetti, *Pastoralist Landscapes and Social Interaction in Bronze Age Eurasia* (Berkeley, 2008).

8. Nurbulat Masanov, *Kochevaia tsivilizatsiia kazakhov* (Almaty, 1995, repr. 2011), 548. On the history of the term "Kazak" as a social category, see A. Samoilovich, "O slove 'kazak,'" in *Kazaki*, ed. S. I. Rudenko (Leningrad, 1927), 16.

9. D. Äuelbekov, "Tïshqan etïn zhegïzgen," in *Qïzïldar qïrghïnï*, 73–75.

10. These programs included the deportation of so-called "special settlers," the deportation of various nationalities, the evacuation of factories and other industrial centers to Central Asia during World War II, and Nikita Khrushchev's Virgin Lands program, which brought hundreds of thousands of agricultural settlers to the Kazakh steppe in the 1950s. See Sebastian Peyrouse, *The Russian Minority in Central Asia* (Washington, DC, 2008), 2.

11. According to the 1999 census, Kazakhs constituted 53 percent of Kazakhstan's population (ibid., 1).

12. On the comparison between Kazakhstan and Chicago, see Niccolò Pianciola, "Sacrificing the Kazakhs: The Stalinist Hierarchy of Consumption and the Great

Famine in Kazakhstan of 1931–33," in *Thirty Years of Crisis: Empire, Violence, and Ideology in Eurasia from the First to the Second World War,* ed. Uyama Tomohiko (Sapporo, forthcoming).

13. A secret police report in October 1933 calculated that animal numbers in the republic had dropped by 90.8 percent in comparison with 1929. The losses in nomadic districts were even more severe, estimated at 99.5 percent. See TsA FSB RF f. 2, op. 11, d. 1050, ll. 53–56 (Spetssoobshchenie PP OGPU po Kazakhstanu o sostoianii zhivotnovodstva v respublike, 25 October 1933), in TSD, vol. 3, ed. V. Danilov, R. Manning, and L. Viola (Moscow, 2001), 811.

14. On the decline in the republic's livestock numbers, see Roy H. Behnke, Jr., "Reconfiguring Property Rights and Land Use," in *Prospects for Pastoralism in Kazakstan and Turkmenistan,* ed. Carol Kerven (New York, 2003), 76.

15. R. W. Davies, *The Socialist Offensive* (London, 1980); Sheila Fitzpatrick, *Stalin's Peasants* (Oxford, 1994); Andrea Graziosi, *The Great Soviet Peasant War* (Cambridge, MA, 1996); Moshe Lewin, *Russian Peasants and Soviet Power* (New York, 1968); Stephan Merl, *Bauern unter Stalin* (Berlin, 1990); Lynne Viola, *The Best Sons of the Fatherland* (New York, 1987); Viola, *Peasant Rebels under Stalin* (New York, 1996).

16. Viola, *Peasant Rebels under Stalin,* 15.

17. In the Soviet Union's west, there were also mobile groups, such as the Roma people, who were not peasants. On the Roma, see Brigid O'Keefe, *New Soviet Gypsies* (Toronto, 2013).

18. On the global shift toward producing meat for the "market" rather than individual household consumption, see Paula Young Lee, ed., *Meat, Modernity, and the Rise of the Slaughterhouse* (Durham, NH, 2008) and Chris Otter, "Planet of Meat," in *Challenging (the) Humanities,* ed. Tony Bennett (Melbourne, 2013), 33–49.

19. On Reza Shah's state-building efforts in Iran, see Stephanie Cronin, *Tribal Politics in Iran* (London, 2007). On British imperial efforts to manage the Bedouin, see Robert S. J. Fletcher, *British Imperialism and 'The Tribal Question'* (Oxford, 2015).

20. For an exception, see Wheatcroft and Davies, *Years of Hunger.*

21. Omelian Rudnytskyi et al. estimate "direct losses" for the period 1932–34 at 8.7 million ("Famine Losses in Ukraine in 1932 and 1933," 208). Wheatcroft and Davies estimate excess deaths for the period 1930–33 at 5.7 million (*Years of Hunger,* 415).

22. Focusing on the period 1932–34, Rudnytskyi et al. estimate Ukraine's "direct losses" at 3.9 million and "indirect losses" at 600,000 ("Famine Losses in Ukraine in 1932 and 1933," 208, 210). Jacques Vallin et al. also rely on a population reconstruction method, estimating Ukraine's direct losses due to famine at 2.6 million ("A New Estimate of Ukrainian Population Losses during the Crises of the 1930s and 1940s," *Population Studies* 56, no. 3 [2002, 249–64]). Some scholars of the Ukrainian famine give higher numbers: Robert Conquest claims that five million ethnic Ukrainians died in Ukraine and another one million ethnic Ukrainians died in the North Caucasus (*The Harvest of Sorrow* [New York, 1986], 303).

23. For an overview of the memory politics of the Ukrainian famine, see John-Paul Himka, "Encumbered Memory," *Kritika* 14, no. 2 (2013): 411–36.

24. Most Russian scholars, with the backing of the Russian government, dismiss these claims of genocide. See O. Antipova, ed., *Golod v SSSR: 1930–1934 gg.* (Moscow, 2009); Viktor Kondrashin, *Golod 1932–1933 godov* (Moscow, 2008); and Kondrashin, ed., *Golod v SSSR, 1929–1934,* vols. 1–3 (Moscow, 2011).

25. See, for instance, the introductory essay to *The Holodomor Reader,* ed. Bohdan Klid and Alexander J. Motyl (Edmonton, 2012), xxxiv–xxxvii, which claims to set the Ukrainian famine against the broader backdrop of collectivization but makes no mention of the famines in the Volga and Don regions or in Kazakhstan.

26. We still know too little about both these cases. An important exception is D'Ann R. Penner, "Stalin and the Ital'ianka of 1932–1933 in the Don Region," *Cahiers du monde russe* 39, no. 1–2 (1998): 27–67.

27. According to the 1926 Soviet census, the last measure of the republic's population before the famine, Kazakhs held a slim demographic majority in their republic (57.1 percent), while Russian (19.6 percent) and Ukrainian settlers (13.2 percent) constituted significant ethnic minority groups. See *Vsesoiuznaia perepis' naseleniia 17 dekabria 1926 g.* (Moscow, 1927), 82.

28. Rudnytski et al. do not break down the deaths in Kazakhstan by ethnicity. Wheatcroft and Davies conclude: "The number of Kazakhs who died from famine in 1931–1933 was probably more than one million, and together with the deaths of Russians and other nationalities inhabiting Kazakhstan, the total probably amounted to 1.3 to 1.5 million" (*Years of Hunger,* 412). Martha Brill Olcott estimates that 1.5 million ethnic Kazakhs died in the famine ("The Collectivization Drive in Kazakhstan," *Russian Review* 40, no. 2 [1981]: 122–42). Some Kazakh scholars have concluded that the total was much higher: In 1992, Nursultan Nazarbayev, Kazakhstan's president, authorized an investigation into the famine, and this commission estimated that 2.2 million ethnic Kazakhs perished in the famine. On the findings of this presidential commission, see M. K. Kozybaev, ed., *Nasil'stvennaia kollektivizatsiia i golod v Kazakhstane 1931–33 gg.* (Almaty, 1998), 15. Maqash Tätimov and Zh. Aliev estimate that 2.5 million ethnic Kazakhs perished in the famine (*Derbestïmïz-demografiiada* [Almaty, 1999], 216).

29. US Commission on the Ukrainian Famine, *Investigation of the Ukrainian Famine, 1932–1933* (Washington, DC, 1998), 136; Conquest, *Harvest of Sorrow,* 198.

30. Yuri Slezkine, *The Jewish Century* (Princeton, 2006), 178–80.

31. An anecdote related by Maksut Dzhelisbaev in his autobiography. For the autobiography, see *Krasnyi terror,* ed. M. K. Koigeldiev et al. (Almaty, 2008), 113.

32. Daniiar Ashimbaev, ed. *Kto est' kto v Kazakhstane* (Almaty, 2010), 287.

33. Soviet historians did not mention the existence of a famine, though they acknowledged "mistakes" and "excesses" during collectivization that they blamed largely on Goloshchekin's wrong-headed leadership. See A. B. Tursunbaev, *Kazakhskii aul v trekh revoliutsiiakh* (Almaty, 1967); Tursunbaev, *Kollektivizatsiia sel'skogo khoziaistva Kazakhstana 1926–1941 gg.* (Almaty, 1967); Tursunbaev, *Pobeda kolkhoznogo stroia v Kazakhstane* (Almaty, 1957); and G. F. Dakhshleiger and K. Nurpeisov, *Istoriia krest'ianstva Sovetskogo Kazakhstana* (Almaty, 1985).

34. On the discussions surrounding the 1937 census, see Francine Hirsch, *Empire of Nations* (Ithaca, 2005), 282.

35. Nazira Nurtazina, ed. "Great Famine of 1931–1933 in Kazakhstan: A Contemporary's Reminiscences," *Acta Slavica Iaponica* 32 (2012): 127.

36. See, for instance, Smaghŭl Elübaev, *Aqboz üy* (Alma-Ata, 1989); Adam Mekebaev, *Küpiyä koima* (Alma-Ata, 1979); and Balghabek Qïdïrbekŭlï, *Alataü* (Alma-Ata, 1986).

37. See, for instance, S. Abdairaeiymov, ed., *Golod v Kazakhskoi stepi* (Almaty, 1991); Zh. B. Abylkhozhin, M. Kozybaev, and M. B. Tatimov, "Kazakhstanskaia tragediia," *Voprosy istorii*, no. 7 (1989): 53–71; Abylkhozhin, *Traditsionnaia struktura Kazakhstana* (Almaty, 1991); Talas Omarbekov, *Zobalang (küshtep üzhumdastïrugha karsïlïq)* (Almaty, 1994); and Omarbekov, *20–30 zhïldardaghï Qasaqstan qasïretï* (Almaty, 1997).

38. The commission concluded: "The scale of the tragedy was so monstrous that we can with full moral authority designate it as a manifestation of the politics of genocide." See Kozybaev, *Nasil'stvennaia kollektivizatsiia i golod,* 6.

39. See, for instance, Abdairaeiymov, *Golod v kazakhskoi stepi*; and Abylkhozhin, Kozybaev, and Tatimov, "Kazakhstanskaia tragediia."

40. It is likely that "Filipp Isaevich" was not his original name. By several accounts, Goloshchekin's original first name and patronymic were "Shaia Itsovich-Isakovich."

See Iu. V. Goriachev, ed. *Tsentral'nyi komitet KPSS, VKP(b), RKP(b), RSDRP(b) 1917–1991: Istoriko-biograficheskii spravochnik* (Moscow, 2005), 178; and Ashimbaev, *Kto est' kto v Kazakhstane,* 287. Like other fellow revolutionaries who were ethnic minorities, Goloshchekin may have chosen to adopt a more Russian-sounding name. It is unclear whether his last name, "Goloshchekin" (which sounds like the Russian for "shaved cheek" [*golaia shcheka*]), was his last name from birth.

41. See Valerii Mikhailov, *Khronika velikogo dzhuta* (Almaty, 1990, repr. 1996) and Esenghazï Quandïqov, *Süreng salghan sürqiyä sayäsat* (Almaty, 1999). Mikhailov, a journalist descended from special settlers, first published his account of the famine in 1990 in Russian. It was subsequently translated into Kazakh and went through several Russian editions, and it became one of the most widely read works on the famine. The book has now been translated into English. Some of the most virulently anti-Semitic references in the Russian original have been expunged, but several have been retained. (Goloshchekin is referred to as the "tsar-slaying Bolshevik" and likened to a "vampire" with a thirst for "blood"). Nevertheless, it is praised by its editors as a "groundbreaking work," and they make no note of its clear anti-Semitic overtones. See Mikhailov, *The Great Disaster,* trans. Katherine Judelson (London, 2014), 100, 113–14. Anti-Semitism has also played a role in the memory of the Ukrainian famine. See Himka, "Encumbered Memory."

42. An important exception is Olcott, "Collectivization Drive in Kazakhstan." Olcott, who did not have access to the Kazakh or Russian archives, frames the catastrophe largely as a miscalculation on the part of Stalin and other authorities in Moscow, who, she argues, poorly understood the complexities of the pastoral nomadic economy. In a small section on the Kazakh famine, Robert Conquest relies heavily on Olcott's work and reaches similar conclusions (*Harvest of Sorrow,* 189–98).

43. Teresa Cherfas, "Reporting Stalin's Famine: Jones and Muggeridge. A Case Study in Forgetting and Rediscovery," *Kritika* 14, no. 4 (2013): 775–804.

44. In 1988, this commission ruled, among other findings, that "Joseph Stalin and those around him committed genocide against Ukrainians in 1932–1933." See US Commission on the Ukrainian Famine, *Investigation of the Ukrainian Famine, 1932–1933,* vii.

45. In a brief discussion of the Kazakh famine, Norman M. Naimark writes: "Here, Moscow's shameful neglect of the negative effects of having destroyed the Kazakhs' nomadic economy with its compulsory policy of 'sedentarization' was the primary cause of starvation, rather than any purposefully murderous action on the part of the government" (*Stalin's Genocides* [Princeton, 2010]), 76. Robert Conquest argues that the Kazakh disaster was due to economic and political miscalculation, yet even more profoundly "a misunderstanding of cultures in the widest meaning of the term" (*Harvest of Sorrow,* 194).

46. The American scholar Matthew Payne is also at work on a book-length study of the famine.

47. Isabelle Ohayon, *La sédentarisation des Kazakhs dans l'URSS de Staline* (Paris, 2006).

48. Niccolò Pianciola, *Stalinismo di frontiera* (Rome, 2009).

49. Robert Kindler, *Stalins Nomaden* (Hamburg, 2014), 16. An English translation of Kindler's book is forthcoming with the University of Pittsburgh Press.

50. Pianciola labels this process "etatization," which he defines as "incorporating the Kazaks within the state governed from Moscow." See Niccolò Pianciola, "Famine in the Steppe: The Collectivization of Agriculture and the Kazak Herdsmen, 1928–1934," *Cahiers du monde russe* 45, no. 1–2 (2004): 147. Kindler calls this process "Sovietization through hunger," which he defines as "the Bolsheviks' program of forcing people to become subjects of their rule by provoking a crisis" (*Stalins Nomaden,* backcover).

51. Contrast my approach with that of Robert Kindler, who has argued that those scholars who focus on Soviet nationality policy "orientalize" Central Asia, artificially

separating it out from the broader Soviet story. Nation making, he argues, never trumped broader socialist policies (*Stalins Nomaden*, 25–26).

52. The literature on Soviet modernization has largely concentrated on the Soviet Union's west, to the exclusion of the Soviet east. An exception is Yuri Slezkine, *Arctic Mirrors* (Ithaca, 1994).

53. On the role of World War I in politicizing the Russian peasantry, see Stephen Kotkin, "Modern Times," *Kritika* 2, no. 1 (2001), 127. Kazakh men, like other Central Asian men, were specifically excluded from active combat until the summer of 1916, when an order to draft Central Asian men to serve in labor battalions behind the front lines resulted in a massive anticonscription revolt. On the 1916 revolt, see Daniel R. Brower, *Turkestan and the Fate of the Russian Empire* (New York, 2003), chaps. 1 and 6; Jörn Happel, *Nomadische Lebenswelten und zarische Politik* (Stuttgart, 2010); and Edward D. Sokol, *The Revolt of 1916 in Central Asia* (Baltimore, 1953).

54. According to party statistical data from the 1920s, 93 percent of Kazakh men and 98 percent of Kazakh women were illiterate (APRK f. 141, op. 1, d. 1643, l. 104, "Stenograficheskii otchet zasedania biuro kraikoma VKP(b).").

55. In 1926, Kazakhstan had a population of 6.5 million people (*Vsesoiuznaia perepis' naseleniia 17 dekabria 1926 g.* [Moscow, 1927], 82).

56. This post system was not particularly efficient: auls, for instance, might receive a circular advertising a March 8 International Women's Day celebration in July. See A. P. Kuchkin, *Sovetizatsiia kazakhskogo aula* (Moscow, 1962), 112.

57. For the use of similar rhetoric toward the hunters and gathers of the Russian Far North, see Slezkine, *Arctic Mirrors*, 220.

58. US Department of Agriculture (USDA), Foreign Agricultural Service, "Commodity Intelligence Report: Kazakhstan Agricultural Overview," https://www.pecad.fas.usda.gov/highlights/2010/01/kaz_19jan2010/.

59. As of 2002, eighty thousand "private family farmers" were engaged in livestock production in Kazakhstan. See Frauke Jungbluth and Tjaart Schillhorn Van-Veen, *Kazakhstan's Livestock Sector* (Washington, DC, 2004). On the contemporary practice of mobile pastoralism in southern Kazakhstan, see Gabriel McGuire, "By Coin or By Kine? Barter and Pastoral Production in Kazakhstan," *Ethnos* 81, no. 1 (2016): 53–74.

60. On the idea of nature as an obstacle to be "conquered," see Douglas R. Weiner, *Models of Nature* (Bloomington, 1988), 168–71. On the struggles of colonial powers to transform arid regions, see Diana K. Davis, *The Arid Lands* (Cambridge, MA, 2016).

61. Michaela Pohl, "The Virgin Lands between Memory and Forgetting: People and Transformation in the Soviet Union, 1954–1960" (PhD diss., Indiana University, 1999).

62. Marc Elie, "Desiccated Steppes," in *Eurasian Environmental History*, ed. Nicholas B. Breyfogle (Pittsburgh, forthcoming); and Ihor Stebelsky, "Wheat Yields and Weather Hazards in the Soviet Union," in *Interpretations of Calamity from the Viewpoint of Human Ecology*, ed. K. Hewitt (Winchester, MA, 1983), 202–18. Independent Kazakhstan's wheat production continues to be affected by frequent droughts, and the USDA has declared the Kazakh steppe to be a "zone of risky agriculture" (USDA Foreign Agricultural Service, "Commodity Intelligence Report: Kazakhstan Agricultural Overview," https://www.pecad.fas.usda.gov/highlights/2010/01/kaz_19jan2010).

63. Other studies of the Soviet periphery have also stressed the ways that environmental relations fundamentally shaped the Soviet experience. For the argument that nature itself was a participant in the Communist project, see Andy Bruno, *The Nature of Soviet Power* (Cambridge, 2016).

64. On Soviet nationality policy from a central perspective see, among others, Hirsch, *Empire of Nations*; Terry Martin, *The Affirmative Action Empire* (Ithaca, 2001); Ronald

Grigor Suny, *The Revenge of the Past* (Stanford, 1993) and Yuri Slezkine, "The USSR as a Communal Apartment, or How a Socialist State Promoted Ethnic Particularism," *Slavic Review* 53, no. 2 (1994): 414–52.

65. Martin, *Affirmative Action Empire*, 9, 12.

66. On the Soviet Union as a work in progress, see Francine Hirsch, "The Soviet Union as a Work-In-Progress: Ethnographers and the Category Nationality in the 1926, 1937, and 1939 Censuses," *Slavic Review* 56, no. 2 (1997): 251–78.

67. D. A. Amanzholova, *Na izlome: Alash v etnopoliticheskoi istorii Kazakhstana* (Almaty, 2009); Gulnar Kendirbaeva, "'We Are Children of Alash . . . ,'" *Central Asian Survey* 18, no. 1 (1999): 5–36. On the roots of Alash Orda, see Pete Rottier, "Creating the Kazak Nation: The Intelligentsia's Quest for Acceptance in the Russian Empire, 1905–1920" (PhD diss., University of Wisconsin, 2005); and Steven Sabol, *Russian Colonization and the Genesis of Kazakh National Consciousness* (New York, 2003).

68. Nurtazina, "Great Famine of 1931–1933," 113.

69. In his memoir, Mukhamet Shayakhmetov attests to the centrality of pastoral nomadism to his family's way of life on the eve of the famine (*The Silent Steppe*, trans. Jan Butler [London, 2006], 3–10).

70. Though empires also sought to deploy identity categories to manage diverse populations, the case of the nomadic Kazakhs perhaps most clearly illustrates the extraordinary emphasis that Moscow placed on its nation-making project. British imperial officials, for instance, explicitly rejected the idea that nationality could be built among the nomadic Bedouin. On this point, see Robert S. J. Fletcher, "Running the Corridor: Nomadic Societies and Imperial Rule in the Inter-War Syrian Desert," *Past and Present*, no. 220 (2013), 185–215.

71. There are a small number of works that depart from these two competing interpretations. Timothy Snyder argues that Stalin exploited the famine to settle two pressing problems, namely the "threat" of a war with Poland and a grain shortfall (*Sketches from a Secret War* [New Haven, 2005], chap. 5). Mark B. Tauger, rejecting the idea that the Ukrainian famine was manmade, argues that hunger was due to actual grain shortages brought about by a poor harvest in 1932 ("The 1932 Harvest and the Famine of 1933," *Slavic Review* 50, no. 1 [1991]: 70–89).

72. See Davies and Wheatcroft, *Years of Hunger*; and Shtefan Merl' [Stephan Merl], "Golod 1932–1933 godov—genotsid ukraintsev dlia oshushchestvleniia politiki rusifikatsii," *Otechestvennaia istoriia*, no. 1 (1995): 49–61.

73. There is a large literature on the Ukrainian famine, much of it in Ukrainian. The pioneering work on the topic is Robert Conquest's *Harvest of Sorrow*. See also Anne Applebaum, *Red Famine* (New York, 2017); Halyna Hryn, ed., *Hunger by Design* (Cambridge, MA, 2008); Wsevolod W. Isajiw, ed., *Famine-Genocide in Ukraine, 1932–33* (Toronto, 2003); S. V. Kul'chitskii, *Pochemu on nas unichtozhal?* (Kiev, 2007); and Frank Sysyn and Andrij Makuch, eds., *Contextualizing the Holodomor* (Toronto, 2015). Terry Martin argues that nationality was not a primary factor in the immediate origin of the famine but emerged out of the famine crisis, culminating in a nationalities terror against Ukraine and Kuban in 1933 (*Affirmative Action Empire*, 273–307).

74. On the link between nationality and territory in the Soviet context, see Madeleine Reeves, *Border Work* (Ithaca, 2014), chap. 2.

75. Terry Martin has argued: "The party leadership did not place their nationalities policy into a Bolshevik/non-Bolshevik framework, but rather one of hard-line and soft-line policies. Hard-line policies were the core Bolshevik tasks, whereas soft-line policies were designed to make those policies palatable to the larger population" (*Affirmative Action Empire*, 21).

76. Estimating that some 90 percent of Kazakhs practiced some form of stock raising, republic-level officials noted that the question of how to develop animal husbandry in the republic was not just an economic question, but a national one too. See *Materialy k otchetu Kazakskogo kraevogo komiteta VKP(b) na VII Vsekazakskoi partkonferentsii v Kraikom VKP(b)* (Alma-Ata, 1930), 6.

77. Recent works have stressed the participatory character of Soviet nation making, but they have not specifically treated the question of violence. See Adrienne Lynn Edgar, *Tribal Nation* (Princeton, 2004); Mayhill C. Fowler, "Mikhail Bulgakov, Mykola Kulish, and Soviet Theater: How Internal Transnationalism Remade Center and Periphery," *Kritika* 16, no. 2 (2015): 263–90; Adeeb Khalid, *Making Uzbekistan* (Ithaca, 2015); and O'Keeffe, *New Soviet Gypsies*. A partial exception is Martin, who has noted the role of "popular ethnic hostility" in border making (*Affirmative Action Empire*, chap. 8).

78. Here I am arguing against a literature that has tended to imply that Moscow's assaults on particular nationalities were carried out by outsiders, such as Russians or officials sent from Moscow. For a classic example of this approach, see Conquest, *Harvest of Sorrow*. The literature on the Soviet Union's use of violence against national groups has often had little to say about how such assaults were implemented locally. On the lack of attention to the issue of local-level implementation in the Ukrainian famine, see Himka, "Encumbered Memory," 424–25.

79. On efforts by the OGPU to bring the Red Army's sole Kazakh cavalry division into wider use, see APRK f. 141, op. 17, d. 465, l. 136; and V. Popov, "Pokhody dalekikh dnei," in *Chekisty Kazakhstana*, ed. N. I. Milovanov and A. F. Minaichev (Alma-Ata, 1971), 53; 61.

80. An argument first developed and explained by Pianciola, "Famine in the Steppe," 148–52.

81. On the worsening of the terms of trade between pastoralists and agriculturalists in the Ethiopian Famine of 1972–74, see Amartya Sen, *Poverty and Famines* (Oxford, 1981), chap. 7.

82. For the opposite view, see Matthew J. Payne, "Seeing Like a Soviet State: Settlement of Nomadic Kazakhs, 1928–1934," in *Writing the Stalin Era*, ed. Golfo Alexopoulous et al., (New York, 2011), 59–86.

83. A survey of the temperature and precipitation data for Kazakhstan in this period does not provide any evidence that the weather was a factor in the Kazakh famine, with the exception of summer 1931, when northeast Kazakhstan (an important grain-growing region) had very low rainfall. For further discussion of this issue, see chapter 4.

84. In 1928, a party health specialist noted that Kazakhstan's per capita expenditures on health were among the lowest in the Soviet Union. Should an epidemic hit Kazakhstan, he warned, it would have the makings of a "perfect storm" (M. M. Vilenskii, *Zdravookhranenie v Kazakstane* [Kzyl-Orda, 1928], 4).

85. On the linkage between disease and famine, see Sen, *Poverty and Famines*, 50.

86. On the rise of modern medical services as a factor in altering the nature of famine-related deaths, see Cormac Ó Gráda, *Famine* (Princeton, 2008), 108–28.

87. Both Payne and Pianciola have stressed this point. Payne argues that local cadres came to see Kazakh nomads as "superfluous people" once their livestock had been extracted from them ("Seeing Like a Soviet State," 70). Pianciola contends that Kazakh refugees occupied the lowest rung in the hierarchy of productive usefulness for the state ("Famine in the Steppe," 190). For the argument that the Stalinist regime constructed a "hierarchy of consumption," using food as a political tool to prioritize some groups and punish others, see E. A. Osokina, *Ierarkhiia potrebleniia: O zhizni liudei v usloviiakh Stalinskogo snabzheniia 1928–1935 gg* (Moscow, 1993).

88. For an account that emphasizes the importance of the "bloodlands," a region between Russia and Germany where Hitler and Stalin both held power, see Timothy Snyder, *Bloodlands: Europe Between Hitler and Stalin* (New York, 2010).

89. Stalin's visitors' book may not be a complete record of all Stalin's encounters, as records are fragmentary for the period 1924–27. But it indicates that the two men met twice during Goloshchekin's tenure as the republic party secretary, on July 28, 1928 and on September 17, 1932. Goloshchekin may also have met with Stalin during his visit to Siberia in 1928. Even so, the infrequency of Goloshchekin's meetings with Stalin is striking. For the records of Stalin's visitors' book, see A. A. Chernobaev, *Na prieme u Stalina* (Moscow, 2010).

90. *Sed'maia Vsekazakskaia konferentsiia VKP(b)* (Almaty, 1930), 48–49.

91. Focusing on the case of KarLag in central Kazakhstan, Steven A. Barnes argues that Gulag prisoners were the lowest priority in Soviet society (*Death and Redemption* [Princeton, 2011], 42).

92. Nicolas Werth has stressed the extraordinary weight of the manmade famines of the 1930s in the broader picture of Communist violence. See his "Keynote Address for the Holodomor Conference, Harvard Ukrainian Institute, 17–18 November 2008," in *After the Holodomor*, ed. Andrea Graziosi et al. (Cambridge, MA, 2013), xxx–xxi.

93. Shafik Chokin, *Chetyre vremeni zhizni* (Almaty, 1992, repr. 1998), 27.

94. Of the existing books on the Kazakh famine by Western scholars, the only one to make extensive use of the holdings at the Presidential Archives is Kindler's *Stalins Nomaden*. Though the 2014 publication of Kindler's book precedes my own, we conducted our research independently, and the completion of my 2010 dissertation, on which this book is in part based, preceded the completion of his 2012 dissertation.

95. US Commission on the Ukrainian Famine, *Investigation of the Ukrainian Famine, 1932–1933*.

96. An exception is the oral history accounts compiled in Khadbina, *Qïzïldar qïrghïnï* (1993), which were collected in 1991.

97. Some efforts to collect oral histories from survivors of the Kazakh famine began only in 2008. See TKN (Almaty, 2010).

98. There are only a handful of exceptions to this pattern. They include Chokin, *Chetyre vremeni zhizni*; and Mukhamet Shayakhmetov, *Sud'ba* (Almaty, 2002), later translated into English and published as *The Silent Steppe* (2006).

1. THE STEPPE AND THE SOWN

1. George J. Demko, *The Russian Colonization of Kazakhstan, 1896–1916* (New York, 1969), 2. Demko's study focuses on the steppe provinces of Akmolinsk, Semipalatinsk, Ural'sk, and Turgai and parts of Semirech'e and Syr-Daria, all of which would eventually become part of Soviet Kazakhstan.

2. Ibid., 139.

3. On this period of migration, see François-Xavier Coquin, *La Sibérie* (Paris, 1969); Willard Sunderland, *Taming the Wild Field* (Ithaca, 2004), chap. 5; and Donald W. Treadgold, *The Great Siberian Migration* (Princeton, 1957). For a broader overview of colonization and its place in Eurasian history, see the introduction to Nicholas B. Breyfogle et al., eds., *Peopling the Russian Periphery* (New York, 2007).

4. On peasant settlement of the Kazakh steppe, see Ian W. Campbell, *Knowledge and the Ends of Empire* (Ithaca, 2017), chap. 5; Demko, *Russian Colonization of Kazakhstan 1896–1916*; Gulnar Kendirbai, *Land and People* (Berlin, 2002); C. N. Maltusynov, *Agrarnyi vopros v Kazakhstane i Gosudarstvennaia duma Rossii 1906–1917 gg. (sotsiokul'turnyi podkhod)* (Almaty, 2006); Virginia Martin, *Law and Custom in the Steppe* (Surrey, 2001), chap. 3; and Ihor Stebelsky, "The Frontier in Central Asia," *Studies in Russian Historical*

Geography, vol. 1, ed. James H. Bater and R. A. French (London, 1983), 149–52. On the settlement of Russian Turkestan (parts of which would be joined to the steppe to form Soviet Kazakhstan), see Brower, *Turkestan and the Fate of the Russian Empire*; and Alexander Morrison, "Peasant Settlers and the Civilizing Mission in Russian Turkestan, 1865–1917," *Journal of Imperial and Commonwealth History* 43, no. 3 (2015): 387–417. The classic Soviet account is A. B. Tursunbaev, *Iz istorii krest'ianskogo pereseleniia v Kazakhstan* (Alma-Ata, 1950).

5. See, for instance, the declaration of the state counselor N. A. Kriukov: "Nomadism is an anachronism which the state should decisively end." See *Zhurnal soveshchaniia o zem-leustroistve kirgiz* (1907), 35–36; 113–21, republished in *Agrarnaia istoriia Kazakhstana (konets XIX–nachalo XX v.)*, ed. S. N. Maltusynov (Almaty, 2006), 119.

6. Nŭrbulat Masanov reaches similar conclusions, arguing that Russian imperial rule did not succeed in breaking apart the basic social and economic functions of Kazakh nomadic life (*Kochevaia tsivilizatsiia kazakhov,* 530–33).

7. Stebelsky, "Frontier in Central Asia," 158.

8. George Demko estimates that more than 22 percent of all settlers returned to European Russia (*Russian Colonization of Kazakhstan*, 203).

9. The first station to measure precipitation and temperature in the Kazakh steppe was Vernyi (present-day Almaty), where temperature and precipitation measurements began in 1879. Complete data for other stations in the Kazakh steppe, such as Fort Aleksandrovskii (present-day Fort Shevchenko) and Kazalinsk, followed only in 1891. Thus, it is very difficult to assess change over time, as well as regional differences in drought patterns in the Kazakh steppe for this period. For temperature and precipitation data for Central Asia, see M. W. Williams and V. G. Konovalov, *Central Asia Temperature and Precipitation Data, 1879–2003* (Boulder, 2008).

10. Historians of the Russian empire have devoted little attention to the ways in which borderland colonization changed native subsistence systems. These questions, however, have been explored extensively by US environmental historians focusing on Native American subsistence systems. Two classic studies are William Cronon, *Changes in the Land* (New York, 1983); and Richard White, *The Roots of Dependency* (Lincoln, 1983).

11. For examples of this approach, see Mike Davis, *Late Victorian Holocausts* (New York, 2002); Steven Serels, *Starvation and the State* (New York, 2013); and Michael Watts, *Silent Violence* (Berkeley, 1983).

12. This question has received little attention from scholars. The one exception is Pianciola, *Stalinismo di frontiera*, chaps. 1–2. In this chapter, I seek to build on Pianciola's observations, showing how the tools of environmental history might augment the economic approach that he utilizes in his study.

13. In its broadest definition, "Central Eurasia" comprises the land extending from the Ukrainian steppe in the west to the shores of the Pacific in the east. It is bounded in the north by the south edge of the Siberian forests and in the south by the Tibetan plateau. On the problems of defining "Central Eurasia," see the discussion in Peter C. Perdue, *China Marches West* (Cambridge, MA, 2005), 19.

14. See, for instance, Frachetti, *Pastoralist Landscapes and Social Interaction*. Frachetti's book is based on his archeological work in the Zunghar mountain region of Semirech'e, located in the southeast of present-day Kazakhstan.

15. Herodotus, *The Histories*, trans. Tom Holland (New York, 2014).

16. Yuri Bregel, *An Historical Atlas of Central Asia* (Boston, 2003), 2.

17. Frachetti, *Pastoralist Landscapes and Social Interaction*.

18. Nicola Di Cosmo, "Ancient Inner Asian Nomads," *Journal of Asian Studies* 54, no. 4 (1994): 1092–126.

19. Robert N. Taaffe, "The Geographic Setting," in *The Cambridge History of Early Inner Asia*, ed. Denis Sinor (Cambridge, 1990), 26. Taaffe prefers the term "Inner Asia" over "Central Eurasia." His definition of Inner Asia includes the Kazakh steppe.

20. Di Cosmo, for instance, uses his findings pertaining to Inner Asian agricultural practices to challenge the view that pastoral nomadic societies were inherently unstable, nonautarkic, and dependent on settled societies for basic necessities ("Ancient Inner Asian Nomads"). For the opposite view, that nomads of the Eurasian steppe were dependent on sedentary populations, see Anatoly Khazanov, *Nomads and the Outside World*, trans. Julia Crookenden (New York, 1983).

21. Philip Carl Salzman, *Pastoralists* (Boulder, 2004), 1.

22. Dale F. Eickelman, *The Middle East and Central Asia* (Upper Saddle River, 2002), 64–66.

23. Salzman, *Pastoralists*, 4.

24. Several scholars do not use the term "nomad" at all due to the misconception that this way of life was timeless, backward, and unchanging. The anthropologists Caroline Humphrey and David Sneath prefer the term "mobile pastoralism" (*The End of Nomadism?* [Durham, 1999]). In this book, I have chosen to use the term "pastoral nomadism," as I think it conveys what this way of life actually was more clearly than any other alterative. Throughout, I stress the adaptability and flexibility of pastoral nomadic life, rather than its supposedly stagnant and unchanging nature.

25. For critiques of this view, see Di Cosmo, "Ancient Inner Asian Nomads"; and Frachetti, *Pastoralist Landscapes and Social Interaction*.

26. For the argument that environmental and political changes during the Iron Age led pastoral nomads in Semirech'e to move from a "more pastoral orientation to a more intensive agricultural focus," see Arlene Miller Rosen et al., "Paleoenvironments and Economy of Iron Age Saka-Wusun Agro-Pastoralists in Southeastern Kazakhstan," *Antiquity* 70, no. 285 (2000): 611–23.

27. On the use of physical mobility as a political choice, see William Irons, "Nomadism as a Political Adaptation," *American Ethnologist* 1, no. 4 (1974): 635–58; and James C. Scott, *The Art of Not Being Governed* (New Haven, 2009).

28. Under the rule of Catherine the Great, St. Petersburg sought to promote Islam among the Kazakhs, believing that there was a connection between the development of what they saw as normative Islamic practices and sedentary life. See Robert D. Crews, *For Prophet and Tsar* (Cambridge, MA, 2006), chap. 4.

29. In his classic study of the shift from Indian to European dominance in colonial New England, the environmental historian William Cronon has offered similar cautions (*Changes in the Land*, 160–64).

30. Khazanov, *Nomads and the Outside World*, 46.

31. Ibid., 21; Humphrey and Sneath, *End of Nomadism*, 196.

32. Yuri Bregel, "Uzbeks, Qazaqs, and Turkmens," in *Cambridge History of Inner Asia*, 225 and Joo-Yup Lee, *Qazaqlïq* (Boston, 2015).

33. Due in part to the lack of sources from this period, it is difficult to date the formation of the three Kazakh hordes. The first mention of the three hordes by name in the sources appears in 1731, but most scholars date their formation to the late sixteenth century. See the discussion in Allen J. Frank, "The Qazaqs and the Russians," in *Cambridge History of Inner Asia*, 364–65.

34. Khazanov, *Nomads and the Outside World*, 146; Saulesh Yessenova, "Soviet Nationality, Identity, and Ethnicity in Central Asia," *Journal of Muslim Minority Affairs* 22, no. 1 (2002): 14.

35. On this expansion, see Michael Khodarkovsky, *Russia's Steppe Frontier* (Bloomington, 2002).

36. See, for instance, Michael Khodarkovsky, *Where Two Worlds Met* (Ithaca, 1992).

37. On the extensive contact between Siberian Cossacks and Kazakhs, see Yuriy Malikov, *Tsars, Cossacks, and Nomads* (Berlin, 2011). In 1867, St. Petersburg partitioned the Siberian Cossacks, creating an additional Cossack settlement (the Semirech'e Cossacks) much farther south in the Kazakh steppe.

38. Malikov emphasizes Russia's interest in trade, including securing safe passage for caravans through the Kazakh steppe, as well as the need to halt nomadic raids on Russian agricultural settlements behind the Siberian Line (*Tsars, Cossacks, and Nomads*, chap. 4). For a focus on the role that Kazakhs themselves played in facilitating and abetting this conquest, see Janet Kilian, "Allies and Adversaries," (PhD diss., George Washington University, 2013). For an overview of recent research on the conquest of Central Asia more generally, see Alexander Morrison, "Killing the Cotton Canard and Getting Rid of the Great Game," *Central Asian Survey* 33, no. 2 (2014): 131–42.

39. Population estimates for the three Kazakh hordes vary. In his account of Kazakh life, first published in 1832, the General Staff officer Aleksei Levshin estimated that the Elder Horde was the smallest of the three, with a total population of somewhere between 500,000 and 600,000 people, while the Little Horde had a population of 1,110,000 people. Levshin judged the Middle Horde to be the largest of the three hordes, with a population of 1,360,000. See A. I. Levshin, *Opisanie kirgiz-kazach'ikh, ili kirgiz-kaisatskikh, ord i stepei* (Almaty, 1833, repr. 1996), 288.

40. The text of this statute is republished in Maltusynov, *Agrarnaia istoriia Kazakhstana*, 25–28.

41. See Masanov, *Kochevaia tsivilizatsiia kazakhov*. For a critique of Masanov's work, see H. Alimbai et al., *Traditsionnaia kul'tura zhizneobespecheniia kazakhov* (Almaty, 1998). The authors critique Masanov for analyzing a society, Kazakhs, through its economic structure (nomadism), suggesting that he neglects the importance of spiritual and cultural practices. The geographer Owen Lattimore also adopted an approach rooted in cultural ecology, dividing Inner Asia into four environmental regions, each with its own process of cultural development (*Inner Asian Frontiers of China* [New York, 1940]).

42. I have adopted the classifications found in Taaffe, "Geographic Setting."

43. S. P. Suslov, *The Physical Geography of Asiatic Russia*, trans. Noah D. Gershevsky (San Francisco, 1961), 447–51.

44. Taaffe, "Geographic Setting," 30–31.

45. Ibid., 26.

46. Fahu Chen et al., "Humid Little Ice Age in Arid Central Asia Documented by Bosten Lake, Xinjiang China," *Science in China Series D: Earth Sciences* 49, no. 12: 1280–90.

47. Taaffe, "Geographic Setting," 28, 35–37.

48. Demko, *Russian Colonization of Kazakhstan*, 14.

49. Suslov, *Physical Geography of Asiatic Russia*, 427.

50. N. A. Zarudnyi, ed., *Strana svobodnykh zemel'* (St. Petersburg, 1908), 12.

51. Ibid., 29.

52. Ibid., 12.

53. Suslov, *Physical Geography of Asiatic Russia*, 514–16.

54. Zarudnyi, *Strana svobodnykh zemel'*, 13.

55. For an account of the challenges of traveling across this plateau, see E. Nelson Fell, *Russian and Nomad* (New York, 1916), 155–69.

56. Occasionally, commentators referred to this plateau as the *severnaia golodnaia step'*, or "The Northern Hungry Steppe," to differentiate it from another, smaller plain with the same name. The second Hungry Steppe, part of present-day Uzbekistan, is located between the city of Dzhizak and the Syr-Daria River.

57. See, for instance, A. Briskin, *Stepi Kazakskie (ocherki stepnogo Kazakstana)* (Kzyl-Orda, 1929), 4.

58. Thus, rather than a "natural" landscape, the treeless landscape of the steppe was to some extent a creation of human activity. On this point, see David Moon, *The Plough That Broke the Steppes* (Oxford, 2013), 7; and Salzman, *Pastoralists*, 2. For a discussion of Kazakh nomads' practice of burning, see Zarudnyi, *Strana svobodnykh zemel'*, 16.

59. F. Fiel'strur, "Skotovodstvo i kochevanie v chasti stepei zapadnogo Kazakhstana," *Kazaki*, ed. S. I. Rudenko (St. Petersburg, 1927), 104.

60. Some scholars have speculated that the two hazards are related, with a drought intensifying the effects of a zhŭt. See Troy Sternberg, "Tradition and Transition in the Mongolian Pastoral Environment," in *Modern Pastoralism and Conservation*, ed. Troy Sternberg and Dawn Chatty (Cambridge, 2013), 147.

61. On zhŭt, see Ian W. Campbell, "The Scourge of Stock Raising," in *Eurasian Environmental History* (forthcoming).

62. Aristov, *Na bor'bu s zasukhoi i dzhutom* (Petropavlovsk, 1927).

63. Martin, *Law and Custom in the Steppe*, 22.

64. Masanov, *Kochevaia tsivilizatsiia kazakhov*, 277–80.

65. Salzman, *Pastoralists*, 3.

66. Masanov, *Kochevaia tsivilizatsiia kazakhov*, 280.

67. Ibid., 240.

68. Yessenova, "Soviet Nationality, Identity, and Ethnicity," 17.

69. Martin, *Law and Custom in the Steppe*, 21.

70. Levshin, *Opisanie kirgiz-kazach'ikh*, 380.

71. Zarudnyi, *Strana svobodnykh zemel'*, 12.

72. Demko, *Russian Colonization of Kazakhstan*, 2.

73. Ihor Stebelsky, "Wheat Yields and Weather Hazards," 216. On the efforts of Russian naturalists and scientists to understand and alter the deterioration of the grasslands of European Russia, see Moon, *Plough That Broke the Steppes*.

74. In 1801, Russian authorities had removed a large group of Little Horde Kazakhs from the authority of their khan, renaming them the "Inner Horde," or "Bukei Horde." Members of the Inner Horde were then encouraged to migrate in the territory between the Volga and Ural Rivers, behind the Siberian Line. This territory was part of Astrakhan province. See Frank, "Qazaqs and the Russians," 371.

75. Demko, *Russian Colonization of Kazakhstan*, 114.

76. On the 1891 famine, see Richard G. Robbins, *Famine in Russia, 1891–1892* (New York, 1975).

77. Stebelsky, "The Frontier in Central Asia," 167–68.

78. Demko, *Russian Colonization of Kazakhstan*, 63.

79. Ibid., 13.

80. *Kratkii istoricheskii ocherk Semipalatinskogo kraia (do 1917 goda)* (Semipalatinsk, 1929), 33–34.

81. Orazgul Mŭkhatova, *Qazaqstandaghï XX-ghasïrdïng alghashqï onzhïldïq—tarïndaghï agrarlïq reformalar tarikhnamasï (1920–1929 zhïldar)* (Almaty, 1998), 3.

82. Lewis Siegelbaum, "Those Elusive Scouts," *Kritika* 14, no. 1 (2013): 31–58.

83. Demko, *Russian Colonization of Kazakhstan*, 120.

84. For a petition by the vice-governor of Akmolinsk province to close his region to colonization in 1906 and the refusal, see RGIA f. 391, op. 3, d. 105, ll. 5–6; and RGIA f. 391, op. 3, d. 105, l. 36, reprinted in Maltusynov, *Agrarnaia istoriia Kazakhstana*, 99–100. In 1902 in Turkestan, the governor-general begged the Ministry of Internal Affairs to cut off the flow of illegal settlers. See Brower, *Turkestan and the Fate of the Russian Empire*, 135.

85. The flies on the Kazakh steppe, as Vasilii Grigor'ev noted, "differed from the normal sort," and could enter into the eyes of people or animals, causing great pain or even blindness (*Narodopisanie* [1864], 41–42).

86. Ibid. For similar observations made by Russian travelers to the steppes of European Russia, see Moon, *Plough That Broke the Steppes*, chap. 1.

87. TsGARK f. 19, op. 1, d. 57, ll. 12–12ob. (Letter to the Committee for Assistance to the Starving from the Head of the Settlers' Affairs in Semirech'e Oblast', April 11, 1907).

88. TsGARK f. 64, op. 1, d. 4701, l. 27 (Letter to the Steppe administration of the Russian society of the Red Cross from a detachment of the Red Cross, April 6, 1907).

89. TsGARK f. 64, op. 1, d. 4752, l. 3–4. (Telegram from the Secretary of the Financial Committee in Omsk to the Minister of Trade and Industry, St. Petersburg. July 2, 1911.)

90. Demko, *Russian Colonization of Kazakhstan*, 174–75. The situation was similar farther south in Turkestan. There peasants in Semirech'e expanded their practice of stock raising to protect themselves in case of a bad harvest. See Brower, *Turkestan and the Fate of the Russian Empire*, 132–33.

91. A. S. Bezhkovich, "Zemledelie ukraintsev-pereselentsev iuzhnoi chasti Semipalatinskoi gubernii," in *Ukraintsy-pereselentsy Semipalatinskoi gubernii,* ed. S. I. Rudenko (Leningrad, 1930), 16.

92. Ibid., 103.

93. Martin, *Law and Custom on the Steppe*, 74–83.

94. K. A. Chuvelev, "O reorganizatsii kochevogo i polukochevogo khoziaistva," *Narodnoe khoziaistvo Kazakstana*, no. 2–3 (1928): 47.

95. Khazanov, *Nomads and the Outside World*, 46–49.

96. In Arakaraisk canton (Kustanai uezd), the number of cattle in Kazakhs' herds increased by 20 percent from 1898 to 1905 (*Vliianie kolonizatsii na kirgizskoe khoziaistvo* [St. Petersburg, 1907], 11). See also A. Iu Bykov, *Istoki modernizatsii Kazakhstana* (Barnaul, 2003), 208.

97. P. C. Shulkov, "Ob"em rynochnykh sviazei Kazakskogo khoziaistva," *Narodnoe khoziaistvo Kazakstana*, no. 11–12 (1928): 64–74.

98. Martin, *Law and Custom in the Steppe*, 66–67; Bykov, *Istoki modernizatsii Kazakhstana*, 200.

99. TsGARK f. 25, op. 1, d. 2822, ll. 213–214ob., reprinted in Maltusynov, *Agrarnaia istoriia Kazakhstana*, 109–11.

100. On the steppe trade, see Frank, "Qazaqs and Russia," 374–75; and T. K. Shcheglova, *Iarmarki Zapadnoi sibiri i stepnykh oblastei vo vtoroi polovine XIX veka* (Barnaul, 2002).

101. Demko, *Russian Colonization of Kazakhstan*, 186.

102. Kh. A. Argynbaev, *Istoriko-kul'turnye sviazi russkogo i kazakhskogo narodov* (Pavlodar, 2005), 66. Mohib Shahrani finds that Kirgiz pastoralists of the Afghan Pamirs made similar adaptations after the closure of the Soviet and Chinese frontiers. The region's animal population increased, as the Kirgiz responded to the growing possibilities for trade with settled groups. The Kirgiz then began to increase the numbers of sheep and yaks in their herds, while decreasing the number of camels and horses. See Shahrani, *The Kirghiz and Wakhi of Afghanistan* (Seattle, 1979), 224. Kazakhs' production of cattle for Russian markets was part of a broader shift. During the late nineteenth and twentieth centuries, as consumers began to eat more meat and distribution systems improved, the world's cattle population rose dramatically. See Otter, "Planet of Meat," 33–49.

103. Khodarkovsky, *Russia's Steppe Frontier*, 161.

104. V. Kuznetsov, *KKhAO*, vol. 1: *Kokchetavskii uezd* (St. Petersburg, 1909), 144. For further details on the Kuznetsov expedition and its place in discussions surrounding peasant settlement, see Campbell, *Knowledge and the Ends of Empire*, chap. 5 (I thank Ian Campbell for pointing me to this source).

105. Kuznetsov, *KKhAO*, 1:144.

106. Nurila Z. Shakanova, "The System of Nourishment among the Eurasian Nomads," in *Ecology and Empire*, ed. Gary Seaman (Los Angeles, 1989), 111–19; and G. E. Taizhanova, ed., *Kazakhi* (Almaty, 1995), 163–76.

107. On the Russian state's increasing interest in human nutritional needs, see Alison K. Smith, *Recipes for Russia* (DeKalb, 2008). On the development of food consumption surveys in the 1880s, see Stephen G. Wheatcroft, "Famine and Food Consumption Records in Early Soviet History, 1917–25," in *Food, Diet, and Economic Change Past and Present*, ed. Catherine Geissler and Derek J. Oddy (New York, 1993), 151–74. On the eighteenth-century grain trade in Russia, see Robert E. Jones, *Bread upon the Waters* (Pittsburgh, 2013).

108. The expedition found that individual consumption of meat declined from 8 poods, 32 funds per annum in 1896 to 3 poods, 15 funts per annum in 1907. Individual consumption of meat declined from 30.3 buckets per annum in 1896 to 19.5 buckets per annum in 1907. See Kuznetsov, *KKhAO*, 1:139.

109. Ibid., 145.

110. Demko, *Russian Colonization of Kazakhstan*, 200.

111. Ibid., 174.

112. On the relative absence of wars and its role in human and animal growth, see Martin, *Law and Custom in the Steppe*, 191.

113. Georgii Safarov, *Kolonial'naia revoliutsiia (opyt Turkestana)* (Alma-Ata, 1921, repr. 1996), 76.

114. Kuznetsov, in KKhAO, 1:12–13.

115. TsGARK f. 64, op.1, d. 4324, l. 34 (Letter from the Akmolinsk Governor to the Governor-General of the Steppe, June 30, 1890).

116. TsGARK f. 64, op. 1, d. 4752, 1. 121

117. Kuznetsov, *KKhAO*, 1:48.

118. Argynbaev, *Istoriko-kul'turnye sviazi russkogo i kazakhskogo narodov*, 58.

119. On the Turkestan famine, see Marco Buttino, *Revoliutsiia naoborot*, trans. from the Italian by Nikolai Okhotin (Moscow, 2007). On the Volga and Ural River famine, see Sergei Adamets, *Geurre civile et famine en Russie* (Paris, 2003); Bertrand M. Patenaude, *Big Show in Bololand* (Stanford, 2002); and Stephen Wheatcroft, "Soviet Statistics and Nutrition and Mortality during Times of Famine, 1917–22 and 1931–33," *Cahiers du monde russe* 30, no. 4 (1997): 525–57.

120. On 1916, see Brower, *Turkestan and the Fate of the Russian Empire*, especially chaps. 1 and 6; Happel, *Nomadische Lebenswelten und zarische Politik*; and Sokol, *Revolt of 1916 in Central Asia*.

121. Brower, *Turkestan and the Fate of the Russian Empire*, 164.

122. Demko, *Russian Colonization of Kazakhstan*, 180.

123. On the arrival of starving Kazakhs in Tashkent, see Jeff Sahadeo, *Russian Colonial Society in Tashkent, 1865–1923* (Bloomington, 2007), 200–207. The journey of starving refugees to Tashkent became immortalized in a popular fictional account, Aleksandr Neverov's *City of Bread*, published in the 1920s. During World War II, Tashkent became a popular destination for evacuees in part due to the idea that it was a "city of bread." See Rebecca Manley, *To the Tashkent Station* (Ithaca, 2009), 141–43.

124. Kŭramïsov composed his introduction in 1931, although the book itself was not published until 1932 (I. M. Kŭramïsov, "Introduction," in I. A. Zveriakov, *Ot kochevaniia k sotsializmu* [Almaty, 1932], 16).

125. Buttino, *Revoliutsiia naoborot*, 364.

126. Ibid., 365.

127. E. I. Mendeubaev, *Voennyi kommunizm v Kazakhstane* (Aktobe, 2003), 133.

128. Orazgul Mükhatova suggests that settlement was a concerted strategy by Kazakh nomads. Kazakhs settled to protect their lands from further peasant encroachment (*Qazaq-standaghï XX-ghasïrdïng alghashqï onzhïldïq*). Bykov speculates that nomads' growing consumption of grain could have promoted them to settle (*Istoki modernizatsii Kazakhstana*, 215). The large increases in the steppe's human and animal populations during the late Russian empire may have also resulted in the overgrazing of pasturelands, prompting some Kazakhs to settle.

129. Soviet sources classify most Kazakhs as "semi-nomadic" by the 1920s, 20–30 percent of Kazakhs as "settled" and a minority, usually less than 10 percent, of Kazakhs as "nomadic." For an analysis based on data from 1929, see Rodnevich, *Ot kolonial'nogo vyrozhdeniia k sotsialisticheskomu rastsvetu*, 15.

130. *Vsesoiuznaia perepis' naseleniia 17 dekabria 1926 g.*, 82.

131. Khazanov, *Nomads and the Outside World*, 21; Humphrey and Sneath, *End of Nomadism?*, 196.

2. CAN YOU GET TO SOCIALISM BY CAMEL?

1. On the joke, see D. A. Makhat, *Baspasöz* (Astana, 2007), 222. The joke also took other forms. In his 1932 work, *From Nomadism to Socialism*, I. A. Zveriakov sharply criticizes "Kazakh nationalists" for renaming his book, "From Camels to Socialism" (*Ot kochevaniia k sotsializmu*, 126).

2. On aspects of the "peasant question" in the NEP era, see James W. Heinzen, *Inventing a Soviet Countryside* (Pittsburgh, 2004); James Hughes, *Stalin, Siberia, and the Crisis of the New Economic Policy* (Cambridge, 2004); Tracy McDonald, *Face to the Village* (Toronto, 2011); and Olga Velikanova, *Popular Perceptions of Soviet Politics in the 1920s* (Basingstoke, 2013).

3. On the hunters and gathers of the Russian Far North, see Slezkine, *Arctic Mirrors*. On the Nivkhi, fishermen and hunters who lived on Sakhalin Island in the Russian Far East, see Bruce Grant, *In the Soviet House of Culture* (Princeton, 1995).

4. On this point, see also Alun Thomas, "Kazakh Nomads and the New Soviet State, 1919–1934" (PhD diss., University of Sheffield, 2015).

5. Other scholars have referred to this question as a "shepherd question." See Ernest Gellner, "Introduction," in Khazanov, *Nomads and the Outside World*, xvi; and M. P. Viatkin, *Batyr Srym* (Moscow, 1947). I prefer to call it a "nomad question." Technically, as Kazakhs pastured many types of animals, not just sheep, they were pastoral nomads rather than shepherds.

6. In 1924, the republic's People's Council of Commissars issued a ruling calling for more resources to support animal husbandry, heralding this way of life as the republic's major economic activity. On the ruling, see M. G. Sirius, "K voprosy o bolee ratsional'nom napravlenii sel'skogo khoziaistva v Severnom Kazakstane," *Narodnoe khoziaistvo Kazakstana*, no. 6–7 (1928): 16.

7. On this tendency in the Japanese empire, see Sakura Christmas, "The Cartographic Steppe" (PhD diss., Harvard University, 2016). See also Davis, *Arid Lands*, chap. 5.

8. Similar patterns were true for other parts of Central Asia during the NEP era. On the upheaval during the 1920s in Soviet Turkmenistan, see Edgar, *Tribal Nation*, chap. 6. In Kazakhstan, the onset of NEP was delayed. Due to outbreaks of rebellion and famine during the Civil War, NEP was not put into practice in many areas of the Kazakh steppe until the spring of 1923. See Mendeubaev, *Voennyi kommunizm v Kazakhstane*.

9. It is not clear why Kazakhstan did not immediately obtain the status of a full union republic. Kazakhstan's large ethnic Russian minority may have played a role in its initial classification within the boundaries of the RSFSR. Kirgizia, another republic with a large ethnic Russian minority, also was administered under the auspices of the RSFSR, before finally obtaining full union republic status in 1936.

10. Hirsch, "Soviet Union as a Work-in-Progress," 251–78.

11. Martin, *Affirmative Action Empire*, 59–67.

12. After the national delimitation, the Turkestan ASSR would be dissolved, and parts of its territory would be distributed to Kazakhstan. On the Politburo land reform process, see Genis, "Deportatsiia russkikh iz Turkestana."

13. Niccolò Pianciola, "Décoloniser L'Asie Centrale?," *Cahiers du monde russe* 49, no. 1 (2008): 101.

14. Ibid., 117.

15. TsGARK f. 74, op. 4, d. 254, l. 6 (Report to the Land Apportionment Department from Comrade Nurmukhamedov, the plenipotentiary for land apportionment in Semipalatinsk province).

16. Martin, *Affirmative Action Empire*, 64.

17. The sown field area declined from 640,000 desiatinas to 300,000 desiatinas and livestock numbers fell from 9.2 million to 2.6 million. See Genis, "Deportatsiia russkikh iz Turkestana," 57.

18. RGASPI f. 17, op. 85, d. 105, l. 23 (Letter from Serafimov to the All-Russian Central Executive Committee).

19. APRK f. 141, op. 1, d. 1038-b, ll. 1–8. (The Bureau of Kazkraikom on the results of the survey of the TsK committee of Dzhetisu province, October 3, 1927).

20. Ibid.

21. On the population of Kzyl-Orda, see V. Lan'ko, *Ves' Kazakstan* (Alma-Ata, 1931), 107.

22. APRK f. 811, op. 19, d. 238, l. 42 ("Vstrechis proshlym," unpublished memoir by Mikhail Riadnin). Riadnin's recollections, which were composed in 1978, are part of a special collection (fond 811) of unpublished memoirs at the Kazakh Presidential Archives entitled, "The Institute for Political Research of the Central Committee of the Communist Party of Kazakhstan." These memoirs were commissioned by the Communist Party to better understand the party's successes and failures.

23. A. P. Akachenok, ed., *Narymskaia ssylka (1906–1917 gg.)* (Tomsk, 1970), 338.

24. Slezkine, *Jewish Century*, 178–80.

25. RGASPI f. 17, op. 33, d. 484, ll. 108–9 (Letter from Goloshchekin to Molotov, August 17, 1926).

26. APRK f. 141, op. 1, d. 1040-a, ll. 48–49 (Kazkraikom ruling. "On priority in the allotment of land to unauthorized migrants to the KASSR prior to September 14, 1925 and measures against unauthorized migration to the KASSR after the indicated period").

27. Goloshchekin's assertion that "October passed by the aul" would spark an animated debate among later generations of Soviet historians. A. B. Tursunbaev argued that the aul was already fully Sovietized by 1917 (*Kazakhskii aul v trekh revoliutsiiakh*). For a similar perspective, see G. F. Dakhshleiger and K. Nurpeisov, *Istoriia krest'ianstva Sovetskogo Kazakhstana* (Alma-Ata, 1985). A. P. Kuchkin, by contrast, argues that the Kazakh aul was Sovietized during the period 1926–29 (*Sovetizatsiia kazakhskogo aula*).

28. APRK f. 141, op. 1, d. 1643, l. 134 (stenographic record of the meeting of the bureau of Kraikom).

29. On the elements of the campaign, see *Otchet kraevogo komiteta VI Vsekazakskoi partiinoi konferentsii* (Kzyl-Orda, 1928), 8.

30. For similar efforts to introduce "tribal parity" in Soviet Turkmenistan, see Edgar, *Tribal Nation*, chap. 6. The phrase "tribal parity" is Edgar's.

31. At the time, party members in Kazakhstan also likened the Sovietization of the Aul to the Face to the Village campaign. See *Otchet kraevogo komiteta VI Vsekazakskoi partiinoi konferentsii*, 8.

32. On the Face to the Village campaign in Riazan province, see McDonald, *Face to the Village*. McDonald argues that the failures of the Face to the Village campaign contributed to the regime's violent assault on the peasantry, with the onset of widespread collectivization in 1929.

33. V. G. Sokolovskii, *Kazakskii aul* (Tashkent, 1926).

34. A. E. Shmidt, *Materialy po rodovomu sostauv kazakskogo naseleniia iugo-zapadnoi chasti Shimkentskogo uezda* (Tashkent, 1927).

35. Sokolovskii, *Kazakskii aul*, 36. See also APRK f. 141, op. 1, d. 1041, l. 98.

36. See, for example, the study of P. S. Shulkov, which examines nomads who pasture sheep, "Optimal'nye razmery trudovogo pastbishchno-kochevogo ovtsevodcheskogo khoziaistva," *Narodnoe khoziaistvo Kazakstana*, no. 4–5 (1929): 63–78.

37. The scholar V. P. Voshchinin concluded that only Yakutia and Buriat-Mongolia exceeded Kazakhstan in the number of cattle per person (*SSSR po raionam* [Moscow, 1929], 31).

38. Sokolovskii, *Kazakhskii aul*, 4.

39. Ibid., 43–44.

40. *Spisok naselennykh punktov (v tom chisle i aulov-kstau) i skhematicheskaia 10-ti verstnaia karta Kazakstana* (Kzyl-Orda, 1928), vi–vii.

41. Sokolovskii, *Kazakskii aul*, 1.

42. Ibid. Similar claims are made in *Spisok naselennykh punktov*, vii.

43. Sokolovskii, *Kazakskii aul*, 2–3; Rodnevich, *Ot kolonial'nogo vyrozhdeniia k sotsialisticheskomu rastsvetu*, 20. Much of Sokolovskii's conclusions about the steppe came from a 1924–25 ethnographic expedition he co-led to the Aulie-Atinsk region. See TsGARK f. 1000, op. 1, d. 17, l. 127 (Report of Comrade Sokolovskii).

44. Briskin, *Stepi Kazakskie*, 12.

45. A. Nukhat, *"Iurty-kochevki": (K rabote zhenskikh "krasnykh iurt")* (Moscow, 1929), 6. For a more detailed explanation of the Red Yurt campaign, see Paula A. Michaels, *Curative Powers* (Pittsburgh, 2003), 154–64. Michaels notes that some 134 red yurts operated in Kazakhstan in 1929. The party adopted similar strategies to conduct party work with other hard-to-reach populations. Yuri Slezkine notes that the party used "red tents" with the hunters and gatherers of the Russian Far North (*Arctic Mirrors*, 229). In the highlands of Kirgizia, party members developed seasonal soviets. See Benjamin Loring, "Building Socialism in Kyrgyzstan," (PhD diss., Brandeis University, 2008), 184–88.

46. Briskin, *Stepi Kazakskie*, 6.

47. Nukhat, *"Iurty-kochevki,"* 6.

48. APRK f. 141, op. 1, d. 1643, l. 152 (Stenographic record of the meeting of the bureau of Kraikom).

49. On the party's struggles to implement land redistribution, see the meeting of Kraikom in APRK f. 141, op. 1, d. 1643, ll. 64–72. See also Kuchkin, *Sovetizatsiia kazakhskogo aula*, 185–90.

50. On these debates, see also Thomas, "Kazakh Nomads and the New Soviet State," chap. 6.

51. APRK f. 141, op. 1, d. 490, l. 42 (On the progress of the pre-election campaign, November 17, 1926).

52. On the organization and staffing of RSFSR Narkomzem and the challenges of integrating these "bourgeois specialists," see Heinzen, *Inventing a Soviet Countryside*. On the alliance between the Bolsheviks and liberal experts, including ethnographers, geographers and economists, see Hirsch, *Empire of Nations*, chap. 1.

53. Alexander Rabinowitch, *The Bolsheviks in Power* (Bloomington, 2008), 112–13.

54. S. P. Shvetsov, *Kazakskoe khoziaistvo v ego estestvenno-istoricheskikh i bytovykh usloviiakh*, (Leningrad, 1926), 100.

55. Ibid., 105. Shvetsov's warning is frequently invoked by contemporary Kazakhstani scholars of the famine. See, for instance, Abylkhozhin, *Traditsionnaia struktura Kazakhstana*, 221.

56. Evgenii Sh-Polochanskii, *Glavnye elementy ekonomicheskoi sviazi novykh gosudarstevennykh obrazovanii v Srednei Azii i zadachi Kirgizskoi respubliki po sel'skomu khoziaistvu* (Tashkent, 1925), 10.

57. Ibid., 11.

58. Aristov, *Na bor'bu s zasukhoi i dzhutom*, 24–26.

59. E. Timofeev, "Problema pustyni," *Narodnoe khoziaistvo Kazakstana*, no. 8–9 (1929), 70; E. A. Polochanskii, *Za novyi aul-kstau* (Moscow, 1926).

60. V. I. Skorospeshkin, "K voprosu o rekonstruktsii zhivotnovodcheskikh khoziaistv v KASSR," *Narodnoe khoziaistvo Kazakstana*, no. 8 (1928): 1–19.

61. Ibid., 1.

62. A. A. Rybnikov, "Perspektivy ratsionalizatsii i rekonstruktsii skotovodstva zasushlivogo tsentral'nogo Kazakhstana," *Narodnoe khoziaistvo Kazakstana*, no. 1 (1930): 1–22.

63. In 1922, Rybnikov had been arrested, along with several other specialists from RSFSR Narkomzem, and placed on a list of "anti-Soviet" figures scheduled to be deported from the country. But following a request by RSFSR Narkomzem, Rybnikov was removed from the list of those to be deported, and he immersed himself in scientific work, including the study of the Kazakh steppe. See Heinzen, *Inventing a Soviet Countryside*, 86–87.

64. Rybnikov, "Perspektivy ratsionalizatsii i reconstruktsii," 1–22.

65. For a comparative history of Russian and American efforts to manage native peoples (specifically, the Kazakhs and the Sioux) and transform arid lands, see Steven Sabol, *The Touch of Civilization* (Boulder, 2017).

66. M. G. Sirius, "K voprosu o bolee ratsional'nom napravlenii sel'skogo khoziaistva v Severnom Kazakstane," *Narodnoe khoziaistvo Kazakstana*, no. 6–7 (1928): 36.

67. On these debates under Russian imperial rule, see Campbell, *Knowledge and the Ends of Empire*, chap. 4; Saulesh Esenova, "Soviet Nationality, Identity, and Ethnicity in Central Asia," *Journal of Muslim Minority Affairs* 22, no. 1 (2002): 11–38; and Rottier, "Creating the Kazak Nation," chap. 4.

68. Akhmet Baitursynov, "Revoliutsiia i kirgizy," *Zhizn' natsional'nostei* (1919), in *Revoliutsiia v Srednei Azii glazami musul'manskikh bol'shevikov* (Oxford, 1985), 109–14. Under Russian imperial rule, Baytŭrsïnov had taken an intermediate position on sedentarization, arguing that it was suitable for some areas of the Kazakh steppe and not for others. See Campbell, *Ends of Empire*, 178.

69. Smagul Sadvakasov, "Voprosy narodnogo prosveshcheniia," *Izbrannoe*, ed. Kairgel'dy Akimbekov (Almaty, 1994), 124.

70. Moshe Lewin, *The Making of the Soviet System* (New York, 1985), 92.

71. Matthew J. Payne, *Stalin's Railroad* (Pittsburgh, 2001), 18.

72. Ibid.; A. Briskin, *Na iuzhturksibe* (Alma-Ata, 1930).

73. In his letter to Krzhizhanovskii, Goloshchekin proposed the creation of a special planning agency for Kazakhstan under the auspices of Gosplan, which would unify the various questions surrounding the development of the republic. Goloshchekin's request was never realized (APRK f. 141, op. 17, d. 356, l. 33 [Goloshchekin, letter to Krzhizhanovskii]). The letter itself is undated, but the context of the letter, as well as the other contents of the file, suggest that it is from 1929.

74. RGASPI f. 17, op. 113, d. 338, ll. 92–94 (Report to the Central Committee from the members of the bureau of Kraikom, October 22, 1927).

75. Chelintsev's speech was later republished as A. N. Chelintsev, "Perspektivy razvitiia sel'skogo khoziaistva Kazakstana," *Narodnoe khoziaistvo Kazakstana*, no. 4–5 (1928): 3.

76. Ibid., 33.

77. Martin, *Affirmative Action Empire*, 66.

78. Riadnin details how these experts unsuccessfully pleaded with Goloshchekin to be rehabilitated (APRK f. 811, op. 19, d. 238, l. 78).

79. "Ot redaktsii," *Narodnoe khoziaistvo Kazakstana*, no. 6–7 (1928): 37.

80. See, for instance, E. Fedorov, ed., *Kondrat'evshchina v Kazakstane* (Almaty, 1931).

81. Heinzen, *Inventing a Soviet Countryside*, 216.

82. Ibid., 217.

83. For the report, see RGASPI f. 17, op. 84, d. 586, ll. 38–48 (Iz doklada polnomochnogo predstavitelia GPU po KASSR I. D. Kashirina i nachal'nika sekretnogo otdela Iakubovskogo v Vostochnyi otdel GPU Ia. Kh. Petersu o sostoianii i deiatel'nosti Alash-Ordy i kazakskikh natsgruppirovok za vremia s 1 ianvaria po 1 marta 1923 g.), in *Rossiia i Tsentral'naia Aziia 1905–1925 gg.*, ed. D. A. Amanzholova (Karaganda, 2005), 376.

84. Ashimbaev, *Kto est' kto v Kazakhstane*, 171

85. RGAE f. 7486, op. 19, d. 10, ll. 237–38 (The project of the commission of Comrade Grin'ko).

86. A. N. Donich, "Problema 'novogo kazakskogo aula,'" *Narodnoe khoziaistvo Kazakstana*, no. 4–5 (1928): 144.

87. TsGARK f. 5, op. 19, d. 182a, l. 16 (Reasons for organizing the transition of nomadic and semi-nomadic households to a settled way of life).

88. TsGARK f. 5, op. 19, d. 182a, l. 3ob. (The file is untitled).

89. Zveriakov, *Ot kochevaniia k sotsializmu*, 29.

90. Ibid., 39. By the time of the First Five-Year Plan, many Soviet planners had come to see nature as an obstacle that needed to be "conquered." See Weiner, *Models of Nature*, 168–71.

91. Donich, "Problema 'novogo kazakskogo aula,'" 143; Thomas, "Kazakh Nomads and the New Soviet State," 57.

92. The potential existence of feudalism among nomads has been the subject of exhaustive investigation and debate by Soviet scholars. For an overview of many of these debates, see "The Social Structure of the Nomads of Asia and Africa," in *Studies on Central Asian History in Honor of Yuri Bregel*, ed. Devin DeWeese (Bloomington, 2001), 319–40; Gellner, "Introduction" to Khazanov, *Nomads and the Outside World*; and David Sneath, *The Headless State* (New York, 2007), 124–31.

93. For Toghzhanov's biographical details, see Ashimbaev, *Kto est' kto v Kazakhstane*, 1036.

94. G. Togzhanov, *Kazakskii kolonial'nyi aul* (Moscow, 1934), 36–89.

95. Ibid., 6.

96. Ibid., 31. See also Tursunbaev, *Pobeda kolkhoznogo stroia v Kazakhstane*, 3.

97. Terry Martin, *Affirmative Action Empire*, 12. Martin notes that Stalin's original formulation was "proletarian in content" (12n51).

98. One of the earliest examples of this argument is Donich, "Problema 'novogo Kazakskogo aula.'" See also Togzhanov, *Kazakskii kolonial'nyi aul*, 16; and Zveriakov, *Ot kochevaniia k sotsializmu*, 16.

99. Zveriakov, *Ot kochevaniia k sotsializmu*, 45, 59.

100. For examples of this argument, see Masanov, *Kochevaia tsivilizatsiia kazakhov*; and Abylkhozin, *Traditsionnaia struktura Kazakhstana*.

3. KAZAKHSTAN'S "LITTLE OCTOBER"

1. APRK f. 141, op. 1, d. 1675, ll. 124–25 (Telegram from a group of citizens in Semipalatinsk province to Stalin, July 28. 1928).

2. On the many uses of animals in Kazakh pastoral nomadic society, see S. Abashin, D. Arapov, and N. Bekmakhanova, eds., *Tsentral'naia Aziia v sostave Rossiiskoi imperii*

(Moscow, 2008), 188; Martin, *Law and Custom in the Steppe*, 23–24; and Masanov, *Kochevaia tsivilizatsiia kazakhov*, 449.

3. F. I. Goloshchekin, "Ocherednye zadachi VKP(b) v Kazakstane—doklad II plenumu kraevogo komiteta VKP(b), 1926 g," in *Partiinoe stroitel'stvo v Kazakstane (sbornik rechei i statei)* (Moscow, 1930), 72.

4. On the deveiling campaigns in Uzbekistan, see Gregory Massell, *The Surrogate Proletariat* (Princeton, 1974); Douglas Northrop, *Veiled Empire* (Ithaca, 2004); and Marianne Kamp, *The New Woman in Uzbekistan* (Seattle, 2006). On the Soviet regime's campaign against Islam in Uzbekistan, see Shoshana Keller, *To Moscow, Not Mecca* (Westport, 2001). On the assault on "tribalism" and efforts to "liberate" women in Turkmenistan, see Edgar, *Tribal Nation*, chaps. 6 and 8. On efforts to transform Kirgiz identity through the creation of Soviet culture clubs, see Ali Iğmen, *Speaking Soviet with an Accent* (Pittsburgh, 2012).

5. Shayakhmetov, *Silent Steppe*, 28–29.

6. APRK f. 141, op. 1, d. 2106, ll. 1–3, 62, 63, 116–22 (Iz obzora Kazkraikoma VKP(b) o sotsial'no-ekonomicheskom i politicheskom polozhenii respubliki, March 1928) in TKA, 1:20.

7. For this line of argumentation, see Conquest, *Harvest of Sorrow*; and Applebaum, *Red Famine*.

8. A point similarly demonstrated by Jan. T. Gross in his landmark work, *Revolution from Abroad* (Princeton, 1988). Scrutinizing how state power entered people's everyday lives in the case of Poland, Gross finds, "The fearsome, incapacitating quality of the Stalinist regime came from a myriad of minute, individual, spontaneous contributions" (232).

9. TsGARK f. 5, op. 21, d. 15, ll. 42–63 (Doklad pravitel'stva KASSR v TsK VKP(b) i VTsIK o provedenii i itogakh kampanii po konfiskatsii imushchestva i vyseleniiu krupnykh baev-polufeodalov, April 23, 1929), in TKA, 1:664. The original report listed 6,251 meetings with a total of 392,429 participants. The lowered numbers were added later in pencil.

10. In her study of ethnographic knowledge and its role in the making of the Soviet Union, Francine Hirsch has made a similar point, arguing that efforts to amalgamate nationalities did not signal a retreat from the regime's nationality policy. Rather, such efforts marked an attempt to further accelerate the revolution and speed the transition to Communism (*Empire of Nations*, 9).

11. On this system of "double oppression," see Rodnevich, *Ot kolonial'nogo vyrozhdeniia k sotsialisticheskomu rastsvetu*, 33; and Zveriakov, *Ot kochevaniia k sotsialismu*, 11.

12. N. Syrgabekov, "Sotsialisticheskoe zemledelie," in *15 let Kazakskoi ASSR, 1920–1935*, ed. N. I. Gusev and K. C. Pavlov (Alma-Ata, 1935), 86.

13. Sokolovskii, *Kazakskii aul*, 24.

14. See, for instance, the description of a bai given in GARF f. 3260, op. 10, d. 3, l. 13ob. (Report to the All-Russian Central Executive Committee on the conduct of the confiscation campaign in the KASSR, June 15, 1929).

15. Moshe Lewin, "Who Was the Soviet Kulak?," in *Making of the Soviet System*, 121–41; Lynne Viola, *The Unknown Gulag* (Oxford, 2007), 5–7.

16. On the idea of these exchanges as functioning as a kind of passport, see Maqash Tätimov, "Är Qazaqtïng terïnde tol shezhïresï ïlülï türghangha ne zhetsïn," *Zhüraghat*, nos. 9–10 (2006): 2–5.

17. Alfred E. Hudson, *Kazak Social Structure* (New Haven, 1964), 43–48. Members of a given clan, however, were not always close blood relatives. Over time, Kazakhs might shift the genealogies that they claimed in response to changing political and economic circumstances. See A. N. Kharuzin, *K voprosu o proiskhozhdenii kirgizskogo naroda* (Moscow, 1895), 59.

18. In contrast to some other Central Asian societies, such as the Turkmen, there was not a particularly strong or stable linkage between genealogy and social standing in

Kazakh society (with the partial exception of the Qïpchaq clan of the Middle Horde, who were reported to have been formed from ancient Turkic tribes long before the Kazakh khanate). In most cases, the status of a particular clan, lineage or sublineage shifted as the group became more or less politically powerful.

19. Hudson, *Kazak Social Structure*, 62; Frank, "Qazaqs and the Russians," 366.

20. In *The Headless State*, David Sneath argues that "aristocratic power and state-like process of administration" were fundamental to the organization of Inner Asian pastoral nomadic societies. He sees "egalitarian, kin-based structures" as something largely imposed by outsiders, as these societies came under colonial rule. By contrast, I see both elements—kinship and aristocratic power—as important organizing principles of Kazakh life, both prior to the Russian conquest of the Kazakh steppe and after. For reactions to Sneath's work, see the special forum, "Debating the Concepts of Evolutionist Social Theory: Responses to David Sneath," in *Ab Imperio*, no. 4 (2009).

21. Khazanov, *Nomads and the Outside World*, 146; Frank, "Qazaqs and the Russians," 366.

22. Frank, "Qazaqs and the Russians," 366.

23. Abashin, Arapov, and Bekmakhanova, *Tsentral'naia Aziia v sostave Rossiiskoi imperii*, 194–98; Virginia Martin, "Kazakh Chinggisids, Land, and Political Power in the 19th Century: A Case Study of Syrymbet," *Central Asian Survey* 29, no. 1 (2010): 79–102; and Masanov, *Kochevaia tsivilizatsiia kazakhov*, 446, 532.

24. Salzman, *Pastoralists*, 73–75.

25. Important studies on Kazakh Communists during the 1920s and 1930s include M. K. Koigeldiev, *Stalinizm i repressii v Kazakhstane 1920–1940-kh godov* (Almaty, 2009); Danagul Makhat, *Qazaq ziyälïlarïnïñ qasiretï* (Almaty, 2001); and Talas Omarbekov, *Qazaqstan tarikhïnïñ XX ghasïrdaghï özektï mäceleleri* (Almaty, 2003), chap. 1. Marysia Blackwood, a PhD student at Harvard, is currently completing a promising dissertation on the first generation of Kazakh Communists.

26. On the leading role of Middle Horde intellectuals in Kazakh culture during the nineteenth and early twentieth centuries, see Tomohiko Uyama, "The Geography of Civilizations: A Spatial Analysis of the Kazakh Intelligentsia's Activities, from the mid-19th to the Early 20th Century," in *Regions: A Prism to View the Slavic-Eurasian World*, ed. Kimitaka Matsuzato (Sapporo, 2000), 82.

27. Z. Golikova, P. Pakhmurnyi, and T. Pozniakova, *Kompartiia Kazakhstana za 50 let (1921–1971 gg.)* (Alma-Ata, 1972), 59.

28. Martin, *Affirmative Action Empire*, 145.

29. Amanzholova, *Na izlom*; Kendirbaeva, "'We Are Children of Alash. . . .'"

30. The tension between nationalism and socialism preoccupied native elites in other regions of the Soviet Union as well. On Uzbekistan, see Khalid, *Making Uzbekistan*.

31. Chernobaev, *Na prieme u Stalina*, 23.

32. Saduaqasülï, "Qazaqqa ne kerek?," *Örteng* (1922) in *Smaghül Saduaqasülï* (Almaty, 2003), 2:266.

33. Ibid., 267.

34. Saduaqasülï, "Zhastar siezïne," *Enbekshï Qazaq* (July 20, 1922), in ibid., 268.

35. Saduaqasülï, "Erïksïz zhaüap," *Enbekshï Qazaq* (March 8, 1924) in ibid., 293.

36. See, for instance, RGVA f. 33987, op. 2, d. 285, ll. 296–98 (Pis'mo A. T. Dzhangil'dina I. V. Stalinu o nesoglasii s pozitsiei rukovodstva KASSR v kadrovykh voprosakh i otnoshenii k byvshim deiateliam dvizheniia, April 24, 1925) in *Rossiia i Tsentral'naia Aziia 1905–1925 gg.*, 415–20.

37. Similar situations could be found in other Central Asian republics. On the regime's manipulation of factionalism in Kirgizia, see Loring, "Building Socialism in Kyrgyzstan," chap. 3.

38. Leon Trotsky, "National Aspects of Politics in Kazakhstan" (Letter to Grigori Sokolnikov, March 11, 1927), in *Leon Trotsky*, ed. Naomi Allen and George Saunders (New York, 1980), 213.

39. Ashimbaev, *Kto est' kto v Kazakhstane*, 905 (Säduaqasov) and 1117 (Qozhanov).

40. F. I. Goloshchekin, "Za sovetizatsiiu aula—doklad na kraevoi partkonferentsii o rabote kraikoma VKP(b) 1925," in *Partiinoe stroitel'stvo v Kazakstane*, 40.

41. F. I. Goloshchekin, "Protiv gruppovshchiny i 'vozhdizma': Doklad o vnutripartiinom polozhenii na 3 plenume kraegogo komiteta VKP(b) 1927," in *Partiinoe stroitel'stvo v Kazakstane*, 92–118.

42. Mambet Koigeldiev, "The Alash Movement and the Soviet Government: A Difference of Positions," in *Empire, Islam and Politics in Central Eurasia*, ed. Tomohiko Uyama (Sapporo, 2007), 168.

43. On Ezhov's tenure in Kazakhstan, see J. Arch Getty and Oleg. V. Naumov, *Yezhov* (New Haven, 2008), 57–67. In 1939, after being deposed as the head of the secret police, Ezhov confessed that he and Goloshchekin had been lovers while he was stationed in Kzyl-Orda. Ezhov's statement was made under duress, however, and no other accounts confirm it. For details of the Ezhov statement, see Marc Jansen and Nikolai Petrov, *Stalin's Loyal Executioner* (Stanford, 2002), 18.

44. The details of the Moscow meeting can be found in APRK f. 141, op. 1, d. 489. The meeting is also detailed in Payne, *Stalin's Railroad*, 22–23. In May 1926, Goloshchekin had introduced a new approach to indigenization, known as "functional korenizatsiia," which is likely to have further stoked Qozhanov and Mïngbaev's opposition. This policy curtailed the scope of indigenization, placing greater emphasis on hiring cadres who knew the local language, Kazakh, rather than simply cadres who were ethnically Kazakh. On this shift, see Martin, *Affirmative Action Empire*, 144.

45. APRK f. 141, op. 1, d. 502, l. 31 (letter from Goloshchekin to Stalin, Molotov, and Kosior, December 12, 1926) republished in Makhat, *Qazaq ziyälïlarïnïng qasiretï*, 222–23. Goloshchekin regularly reported to the Central Committee on the activities of leading Kazakh cadres. See, for instance, RGASPI f. 17, op. 33, d. 484, l. 109 (letter from Goloshchekin to Molotov, August 17, 1926).

46. APRK f. 811, op. 19, d. 238, l. 117. In a party deposition in 1928, Idris Mustambaev, chairman of the party's executive committee in the Syr-Daria region, also stressed Goloshchekin's uncompromising nature. Mustambaev, who had been accused of factionalism, stopped short of calling Goloshchekin a dictator but noted: "If you say that the bureau of kraikom numbers seven to eight people, then I will tell you that these are only arithmetic numbers, that almost all of the Kraikom is represented by Goloshchekin" (APRK f. 719, op. 1, d. 1046, l. 34 [Stenogram of the questioning of Comrade Mustambev]).

47. Ibid., 78.

48. Ibid., 115.

49. See, for instance, Mikhailov, *Khronika velikogo dzhuta*.

50. Goloshchekin, "Za sovetizatsiiu aula," 37.

51. Smagul Sadvakasov, "Ia ne soglasen s zaiavleniiami tovarishcha Goloshchekina. Vystuplenie S. Sadvakasova na VI konferentsii Kazkraikoma (1927 god. 15–23 noiabria)," in *Izbrannoe*, 66.

52. Smagul Sadvakasov, "O natsional'nostiakh i natsionalakh" (January 15, 1928), in *Smaghŭl Saduaqasŭlï*, 2:162–77.

53. See, for instance, the recollections of A. M. Kontorshchikov, "Darovanie vozhaka i tribuna," and F. A. Zhandosova (Sutiusheva), "Dvadtsatye gody: Tashkent i Kzyl-Orda," in *Qayran Oras*, ed. E. Zhandosov (Almaty, 1999), 102–5, 131–35.

54. Oraz Zhandosov, "Novyi etap v razreshenii national'nogo voprosa," *Sovetskaia step'*, May 29, 1928, in *Uraz Dzhandosov*, ed. M. K. Kozybaev (Almaty, 1999), 81–84.

55. APRK f. 719, op. 1, d. 1046, l. 49 (Resolution on the report of comrade Goloshchekin taken by a plenum of Kraikom and the Krai control commission, May 8–16, 1928).

56. See, for instance, G. Togzhanov, *O Baitursunove i baitursunovshchine* (Almaty, 1932).

57. On efforts to remove a group of "Trotskyists" from Leningrad and Moscow who were hiding in Kazakhstan, see APRK f. 719, op.1, d. 1049, l. 57 (Informatsionnaia svodka likvidatsii byvshei trotskistskoi oppozitsii v kazakstanskoi organizatsii VKP(b), Summary of the liquidation of the former Trotskyist opposition within the Kazakh party organization, April 15, 1928).

58. APRK f. 811, op. 19, d. 238, l. 79. Ernazarov also became chairman of the republic-level party committee charged with overseeing confiscation.

59. Riadnin recalls that Zhandosov played a leading role in the confiscation campaign: "The pioneer in this respect was him" (APRK f. 811, op. 19, d. 238, l. 68). For an example of Zhandosov's articles in the Kazakh-language press, see "'Äleumettïk toptar' attï maqala (Qazaqstan tŭrghndarïnïng," (*Qïzïl Qazaqstan*, May 1928), in *Uraz Dzhandosov*, 85–88.

60. Kozybaev, *Uraz Dzhandosov*, 272.

61. On the firing of Saduaqasov from his post in Tashkent, see APRK f. 141, op. 17, d. 255, ll. 8–12 (Correspondence between Goloshchekin and Aleksandr Zdobnov, the first secretary of the Tashkent regional committee, February 20–27, 1928).

62. The circumstances of Smaghŭl Säduaqasov's death remain unclear. Some historians maintain that he contracted typhus, while others argue that he died as the result of injuries sustained in an accident. See Gul'zhizhan Kasymzhanova, *Arkhiv pamiati* (Almaty, 2003), 200.

63. The historian Talas Omarbekov has argued that those Kazakh cadres who worked closely with Goloshchekin can be divided into three groups. The first group, which included Säduaqasov, was composed of those cadres who truly cared about Kazakhs and sought to speak their mind. The second group, which included Zhandosov, was composed of "bureaucrats." They did their job, but they failed to speak their mind. The third group, which included Isaev, was composed of those Kazakhs who were "careerists," or those who sought to use the opportunities provided by the party to advance themselves. See *Qazaqstan tarikhïnïng XX ghasïrdaghï özektï mäceleleri*, chap. 1.

64. Izvestiia TsK KPSS, 1991, no. 6, s. 202–3 (Telegramma I. V. Stalina iz Novosibirska v TsK VKP[b], January 20, 1928), in TSD, 1:157–58.

65. APRK f. 141, op. 1, d. 2087, ll. 47–46 (Iz svodki Kazkraikoma VKP[b] o meropriiatiakh v khode khlebozagotovok za vremia s 15 po 25 ianvaria 1928 g.), in TKA, 1:98. See also RTsKhIDNI f. 17, op. 3, d. 668, l. 7 (Iz protokola no. 5 zasedaniia Politbiuro TsK VKP[b], January 12, 1928), in TSD, 1:146. A number of Kazakhstani historians argue that Goloshchekin then traveled to Krasnoiarsk, where he met with Stalin in early February 1928, though they do not provide conclusive evidence. See G. Khalidullin, *Politika sovetskogo gosudarstva v otnoshenii kazakhskikh sharua (1917–1940 gg.)* (Almaty, 2001), 86.

66. APRK f. 141, op. 1, d. 1696, ll. 291–324 (Zakrytoe pis'mo sekretaria Dzhetysuiskogo gubkoma v TsK VKP[b] o polozhenii gubernii, January 29, 1928), in TKA, 1:103–34.

67. APRK f. 141, op. 1, d. 1043, ll. 29–35 (Meeting of the secretariat of Kazkraikom, June 23, 1927).

68. RGASPI f. 17, op. 33, d. 420, ll. 63–64 (Report of Massive Livestock Deaths in Semipalatinsk Province, May 8, 1928).

69. Historians have accorded the Ural-Siberian method a central place in the conjuncture between NEP and the First Five-Year Plan. See Davies, *Socialist Offensive*.

70. APRK f. 141, op. 1, d. 1867, ll. 90–93 (Instruktivnoe pis'mo Aktiubinskogo GK VKP[b] vsem upolnomochennym gubkoma, sekretariam ukomov i volkomov VKP[b] o forsirovanii khlebozagotovok, February 26, 1928) in TKA, 1:151.

71. APRK f. 141, op. 1, d. 1696, ll. 291–324, in TKA, 1:107.

72. APRK f. 141, op. 1. d. 4577, l. 22 (Material for the report of the Kraikom commission on migration).

73. Allen J. Frank and Mirkasym A. Usmanov, eds., *Materials for the Islamic History of Semipalatinsk* (Berlin, 2001), 1.

74. RGASPI f. 17, op. 33, d. 420, l. 69 (On the events in Semipalatinsk on May 15 and 16, June 25, 1928).

75. Payne, *Stalin's Railroad,* 134–36.

76. RGASPI f. 94, op. 1, d. l, l. 661 (Meeting of the Bolshevik faction of the presidium of the All-Russian Central Executive Committee September 24, 1928).

77. Ibid., l. 676.

78. Ibid., l. 674.

79. Ibid., l. 670.

80. Ibid., l. 591.

81. Ibid., l. 636.

82. Ibid., l. 679.

83. In February 1929, a year after the Semipalatinsk affair, a representative from Kazakhstan's Commissariat of Justice visited the province. He noted that work for restitution was "far from being accomplished." Those charged with carrying out restitution did not even have any records of what they had done. See TsDNIVKO f. 15, op. 2, d. 1, l. 4ob. (Letter to the People's Commissariat of Justice of the RSFSR from N. Zhalnin, representative from Kaznarkomiusta, February 14, 1929).

84. RGASPI f. 94, op. 1, d. l, l. 578 (Report by the chairman of the Kiselev commission, September 22, 1928).

85. TsDNIVKO f. 578, op. 1, d. 240, l. 16 (Report "On confiscation in the Chingistaiskii district," undated, probably 1929).

86. Several scholars have either stated or implied that the Semipalatinsk affair was an attack by "Russians" against Kazakhs. See, for instance, Martin, *Affirmative Action Empire,* 66; and Pianciola, "Famine in the Steppe," 148–52. By contrast, I am arguing that the campaign relied heavily on the participation of Kazakhs themselves, a strategy that was designed to tear apart the very fabric of Kazakh life.

87. TsDNIVKO f. 1, op. 1, d. 1583, l. 42 (Telegram, Karkaralinsk ukom to Semipalatinsk, May 21, 1928).

88. Ibid., l. 43 (Telegram from Semipalatinsk to Karkaralinsk, undated, probably 1928).

89. TsDNIVKO f. 3, op. 1, d. 22, l. 33 (Report on Aiaguzsk district, signed by the plenipotentiary for the district, November 27, 1928).

90. Ibid.

91. Ibid.

92. This quote comes from a decision in which Stalin instructs Aleksandr Smirnov, the vice-chairman of Sovnarkom RSFSR, to tell Sheverdin, the public prosecutor for the high court of the RSFSR who was investigating the violence in Semipalatinsk, that the Politburo had in fact authorized an early start to the bai confiscation campaign. See RGASPI f. 558, op. 11, d. 63, l. 38 (Telegram from Goloshchekin to Molotov, June 8, 1928, with decision by Stalin to A. P. Smirnov on June 9, 1928), in SDA.

93. See, for instance, a meeting of the bureau of the republic's party committee about the Semipalatinsk affair, where considerable attention was paid to the issue of the Chinese border and economic concerns. See APRK f. 141, op. 1, d. 1650, ll. 18–26 (Stenogram of a meeting of the bureau of Kazkraikom, September 9, 1928).

94. Lynne Viola has argued that Moscow used investigations at a tool, intervening only when scapegoating an individual served a particular political purpose or, alternately, when developments on the periphery threatened to undermine the regime's long-term economic interests. The Semipalatinsk affair appears to fit this pattern (*Unknown Gulag,* chap. 5).

95. See, for instance, TsDNIVKO f. 1, op. 1, d. 1583 (Correspondence between Bekker and Aleksandr Zvonarev, first party secretary of the Pavlodar region, March 10, 1928).

96. Ashimbaev, *Kto est' kto v Kazakhstane*, 204.

97. An argument first developed and explained in Pianciola, "Famine in the Steppe," 148–52.

98. See, for instance, RGASPI f. 94, op. 1, d. l, l. 567 (Report by the chairman of the Kiselev commission, September 22, 1928).

99. On the worsening of the terms of trade between pastoralists and agriculturalists in the Ethiopian Famine of 1972–74, see Sen, *Poverty and Famines*, chap. 7.

100. That fall, confiscation campaigns were also launched in several other nomadic societies, including Kyrgyzstan and Buryatia. On the campaign in Kirgizia, see Loring, "Building Socialism in Kyrgyzstan," chap. 6.

101. "Iz postanovleniia TsIK i SNK KazASSR 'o konfiskatsii baiskikh khoziastv'" (August 27, 1928) in *Nasil'stvennai kollektivizatsiia i golod v Kazakhstane 1931–1933 gg.*, 28.

102. APRK f. 141, op. 1, d. 1842, ll. 231–41 (Dokladnaia zapiska Kazkraikoma VKP[b] v TsK VKP[b] "O konfiskatsii sredstv i orudii proizvodstva u krupnykh baiskikh khoziaistv i lits iz byvshikh privilegirovannykh soslovii i rodovykh grupp," May 15, 1928), in TKA, 1:353.

103. APRK f. 141, op. 1, d. 1687, ll. 42–42ob. (Pis'mo sekretaria Kazkraikoma F. Goloshchekina v TsK VKP[b] V. Molotovu, September 22, 1928) in TKA, 1:473.

104. APRK f. 141, op. 1, d. 2067, ll. 1–5 (Postanovlenie TsK VKP[b] o konfiskatsii khoziastv i vysylke naibolee krupnykh skotovodov, August 9, 1928), in TKA, 1:361.

105. APRK f. 141, op. 1, d. 1688, ll. 34–35 (Protokol no. 1 zasedaniia Partiinoi komissii po provedeniiu konfiskatsii, August 16, 1928), in TKA, 1:376.

106. A point made in Ohayon, *Sédentarisation des Kazakhs*, 57. For the decree, see TsGARK f. 30, op. 1, d. 813, ll. 106–14 (SNK KASSR ruling on the establishment of nomadic, semi-nomadic and settled districts in Kazakhstan, August 30, 1928).

107. TsGARK f. 5, op. 21, d. 15, ll. 4–7 (Protokol ob"edinennogo zasedaniia TsIK i SNK KASSR ob utverzhdenii proekta dekreta o konfiskatsii i vyselenii krupneishikh baiskikh khoziaistv, August 27, 1928) in TKA, 1:390. Animals were also tallied in various ways: five sheep, for instance, were regarded as equivalent to one cow.

108. APRK f. 141, op. 1, d. 1687, l. 17 (Vypiska iz protokola no. 5 zasedaniia Partiinoi komissii po konfiskatsii pri KazTsIK o poriadke rassmotreniia spiskov baev, August 25, 1928), in TKA, 1:389.

109. See APRK f. 141, op. 1, d. 1688, ll. 34–35 (Protokol no. 1 zasedaniia Partiinoi komissii po provedeniiu konfiskatsii, August 16, 1928) in TKA, 1:376; and TsGARK f. 30, op. 1, d. 813, l. 115 (Postanovlenie SNK KASSR ob opredelenii raionov vyseleniia lits, podlezhashchikh vyseleniiu po postanovleniiu TsIK i SNK Kazakskoi ASSR ot 27 avgusta 1928, August 30, 1928), in TKA, 1:404–5.

110. TsGARK f. 5, op. 21, d. 15, ll. 4–7, in TKA, 1:390.

111. TsGARK f. 135, op. 1, d. 4, ll. 72–76 (Telegrafnoe soobshchenie Semipalatinskoi okrkomissii v TsK KASSR o khode kampanii po konfiskatsii, October 9, 1928), in TKA, 1:551.

112. See, for instance, the documents pertaining to the fate of Baikadam Karaldin, especially APRK f. 141, op. 1, d. 2056, ll. 118–19 (Protokol zakrytogo zasedaniia biuro kustanaiskogo OK VKP[b] po voprosu priostanovleniia konfiskatsii imushchestva B. Karaldina, October 3, 1928) in TKA, 1:447.

113. Shayakhmetov, *Silent Steppe*, 51.

114. TsGARK f. 135, op. 1, d. 4, l. 90 (Report by the chairman of SNK KASSR to the Krai commission for confiscation, August 10, 1928).

115. APRK f. 141, op. 17, d. 233, l. 17 (Report by the Eastern section plenipotentiary representative of the OPGU for the KASSR on the progress of the confiscation campaign October 15, 1928).

116. TsGARK f. 135, op. 1, d. 1, ll. 22–25 (Zapros upolnomochennogo Kazkraikoma po Aktiubinskomu okrugu v kraevuiu komissiiu o zaiavleniakh chlenov semei konfiskuemykh baev o razdele imushchestva, September 29, 1928), in TKA, 1:497.

117. TsGARK f. 135, op. 1, d. 8, l. 76 (Pis'mo upolnomochennogo KazTsIK po Syr-Dar'inskomu okrugu v Kraevuiu komissiiu o massovykh zhalobakh baev na nepravomernost' ikh konfiskatsii, October 17, 1928), in TKA, 1:567.

118. TsGARK f. 135, op. 1, d. 1, l. 66 (Telegrafnoe ukazanie predsedatelia SNK KASSR vsem okrispolkomam o presechenii mer po iskusstvennomu ob"edineniiu khoziaistv s tsel'iu ikh konfiskatsii, October 6, 1928), in TKA, 1:540. The Kiselev Commission found that similar issues surfaced during the Semipalatinsk affair. See RGASPI f. 94, op. 1, d. 1, l. 569.

119. TsGARK f. 135, op. 1, d. 1, l. 108 (Telegrafnoe ukazanie predsedatelia KazTsIK vsem okrispolkomam, September 20, 1928), in TKA, 1:431.

120. TsGARK f. 135, op. 1, d. 8, l. 76, in TKA, 1:567.

121. Saule Zhakisheva estimates that approximately 94 percent of those identified as bais were men ("Bai-'polufeodaly' v Kazakhstane na rubezhe 20–30kh godov XX v." [Candidate of Sciences diss., Institut istorii i etnologii im. Ch. Ch. Vaikhanova, 1996], 179). It is difficult to find out much information about the handful of women who were arrested as bais. Iiulia Kaimulina, named as a bai, petitioned the authorities for her release. See APRK f. 719, op. 5, d. 45, l. 1, December 9, 1929. On the draft, see Pianciola, "Famine in the Steppe," 147.

122. Shayakhmetov, *Silent Steppe*, 59–60.

123. GARF P-1235, op. 141, d. 305, l. 15ob. (Petition from Zeineb Mametova to the republic's public prosecutor, January 31, 1929). In the file, it is noted that the conviction of Mametova's husband was upheld.

124. Isabelle Ohayon provides fascinating evidence to illustrate this point, showing how some women petitioned the regime for a divorce by claiming that they were forced into marriage through the practice of qalïm (*Sédentarisation des Kazakhs*, 98).

125. GARF P-1235, op. 141, d. 305, l. 19ob.

126. TsGARK f. 135, op. 1, d. 4, l. 55 (Telegram from Semipalatinsk province to TsK KASSR, October 13, 1928).

127. TsGARK f. 135, op. 1, d. 374, ll. 4–4ob. (Zhaloba Ibragimova Turagula, vyslannogo iz Semipalatinskogo v Syr-Dar'inyskii okrug, v TsIK KASSR, January 25, 1929), in TKA, 1:692.

128. For a sense of the scope of the campaign, read Seisen Mŭqtarŭlï, ed., *Kĕmpeske* (Almaty, 1997), which catalogues all the people who were named as bais, the family members who were deported with them, and their eventual fate.

129. TsGARK f. 135, op. 1, d. 564, ll. 60–60ob. (Zaiavlenie byvshego zaveduiushchego Lepsinskoi shkoloi-kommunoi Dzhetysuiskoi gubernii I. Mamanova v presidium VTsIK o bedstvennom polozhenii ego sem'i v meste vysylki, January 1, 1929), in TKA 1:690.

130. TsGARK f. 135, op. 1, d. 374, ll. 4–4ob. in TKA, 1:692. The fate of Ibragimov is detailed in a footnote appended by the editors of TKA.

131. TsGARK f. 135, op. 1, d. 1, ll. 29, 42, 44 (Telegrammy KazTsIK i SNK KASSR vsem okruzhnym komissiiam o zapreshchenii konfiskatsii ukrashenii i predmetov domashnego obikhoda, September 30, 1928) in TKA, 1:500–501.

132. TsGARK f. 135, op. 1, d. 1, ll. 60–61 (Pis'mo Zamnarkoma prosveshcheniia v TsIK KASSR o peredache starinnykh rukopisei i drugikh predmetov, iavliaiushchikhsia istoricheskimi tsennostiami, v fond Tsentral'nogo kraevogo muzeia Kazakstana, October 9, 1928), in TKA, 1:547–48.

133. Shayakhmetov, *Silent Steppe*, 50–51.

134. GARF f. 3260, op. 1, d. 3, ll. 8–8ob. (Report to the All-Russian Central Executive Committee on the conduct of the confiscation campaign in the KASSR, June 15, 1929).

135. On the use of physical mobility as a political choice, see Irons, "Nomadism as a Political Adaptation."

136. See, for instance, TsGARK f. 135, op. 1, d. 1, l. 65 (Telegrafnoe ukazanie predsedatelia SNK KASSR vsem okrispolkomam o konfiskatsii khoziaistv perekochevavshikh v drugie okrugi baev, October 2, 1928) in TKA, 1:516. On the formation of internal borders, which was known as *raionirovanie* (regionalization), see Martin, *Affirmative Action Empire*, 34, 65. Kazakhstan began the process relatively late, toward the end of 1927.

137. TsGARK f. 135, op. 1, d. 4, ll. 72–76 (Telegrafnoe soobshchenie Semipalatinskoi okrkomissii v TsK KASSR o khode kampanii po konfiskatsii, October 9, 1928), in TKA, 1:552.

138. APRK f. 141, op. 17, d. 299, l. 26 (Letter to the Central Committee on the conduct of the confiscation campaign in the KASSR, March 5, 1929).

139. TsGARK f. 5, op. 21, d. 15, ll. 42–63 (Doklad pravitel'stva KASSR v TsK VKP[b] i VTsIK o provedenii i itogakh kampanii po konfiskatsii imushchestva i vyseleniiu krupnykh baev-polufeodalov, April 23, 1929), in TKA, 1:672.

140. APRK f. 141, op. 17, d. 299, l. 18.

141. Ibid., l. 15.

142. GARF f. 3260, op. 1, d. 3, l. 8ob. Some Kazakhstani historians argue that more than a thousand bais were expropriated during the campaign. See, for instance, Khalidyllin, *Politika sovetskogo gosudarstva*, 76.

143. Khalidyllin, *Politika sovetskogo gosudarstva*, 76.

144. TsGARK f. 5, op. 21, d. 15, ll. 42–63, in TKA, 1:669.

145. By contrast, those educated Kazakhs who were opposed to the Alash movement and who became early supporters of the Bolsheviks were largely non-Arghïns. Säken Seyfullin, an Arghïn, was one of the few exceptions to this model. Seyfullin initially supported Alash Orda but later broke with them, joining the Bolsheviks in 1918, prior to Alash Orda's surrender. See Uyama, "Geography of Civilizations," 87.

146. Ashimbaev, *Kto est' kto v Kazakhstane*, 116.

147. Äuezov's ancestry is disputed. He was regarded as a qozha but also as a member of the Arghïn tribe of the Middle Horde. See Uyama, "Geography of Civilizations," 96.

148. APRK f. 141, op. 1, d. 2407, l. 121.

149. According to the recollections of some of Äuezov's contemporaries, Äuezov earned his release by publishing a letter "confessing" to his sins in the republic's newspaper. This confessional letter, however, provoked some of his old colleagues within the Kazakh elite to regard him with disgust. For a discussion of the episode, see L. D. Kuderina, *Genotsid v Kazakhstane* (Moscow, 1994), 52–53.

150. APRK f. 141, op. 1, d. 2058, ll. 58–67 (Spetssvodka Semipalatinskogo OO OGPU o khode konfiskatsii, October 20, 1928) in TKA, 1:592.

151. Ashimbaev, *Kto est' kto v Kazakhstane*, 1040.

152. A point also made in Ohayon, *Sédentarisation des Kazakhs*, 57.

153. James C. Scott, *Seeing Like a State* (New Haven, 1998), especially chap. 9.

4. NOMADS UNDER SIEGE

1. For the perspective that the regime's own economic decisions, especially an "incoherent grain price policy," served to undermine NEP, see Lewin, *Making of the Soviet System*, chap. 4. Other scholars place emphasis on the party's increasing prioritization of heavy industry due to national security concerns. See E. H. Carr, *The Russian Revolution from Lenin to Stalin, 1917–1929* (New York, 2004); Davies, *Socialist Offensive*, 36, 403;

and Alec Nove, *An Economic History of the USSR 1917–1991* (New York, 1992), 117–18. Revisionists, by contrast, have argued that popular participation contributed to the downfall of NEP and lent social support to the sweeping changes of the First Five-Year Plan. On the Moscow working class, see William Chase, *Workers, Society, and the Soviet State* (Chicago, 1987). On the development of a new class of Soviet bureaucrats invested in the transformation, see Sheila Fitzpatrick, ed., *Cultural Revolution in Russia, 1928–1931* (Bloomington, 1977). Oleg Khlevniuk focuses attention on the competing interests of different agencies within the Stalinist system in *Master of the House* (New Haven, 2009).

2. For one of the earliest articulations of this idea, see "Rezoliutsii i postanovleniia V plenuma Kazakhskogo kraevogo komiteta VKP(b) 11–16 dekabria 1929," in KSKK, 268.

3. See Ĭzmŭkhan Kŭramïsov, introduction to Zveriakov, *Ot kochevaniia k sotsializmu*, v.

4. In 1930, 26,400 settlers arrived in the republic. See APRK f. 141, op. 1, d. 2474, l. 39 (report on migration to the KASSR in 1929/1930).

5. The party planned to construct a total of 360 state farms in the republic, with 270 state farms focused on animal rearing, 70 state farms devoted to grain cultivation, and 20 state farms devoted to rice or cotton cultivation. See K. P. Kamenskii, "Piatiletnii plan razvitiia i rekonstruktsii sel'skogo khoziaistva Kazakstana," *Narodnoe khoziaistvo Kazakstana* no. 5–6 (1930): 43.

6. The party planned to construct combines in several Kazakh cities close to railway lines, including Semipalatinsk, Sergiopol', Aktiubinsk, Pavlodar and Alma-Ata (TsGARK f. 5, op. 9, d. 178, ll. 32–33).

7. RGAE f. 7486, op. 19, d. 10, l. 19 (Conclusion of Narkomzem SSR on a plan for the development of agriculture in Kazakhstan in the remaining years of the first Five-Year Plan, probably 1930).

8. "Rezoliutsii i postanovleniia V plenuma Kazakhskogo kraevogo komiteta VKP(b) 11–16 dekabria 1929," in KSKK, 263.

9. TsGARK f. 1179, op. 1, d. 87 (Speech of Kŭramïsov at meeting for sedentarization, probably 1930).

10. In their *Peasants under Siege* (Princeton, 2011), Gail Kligman and Katherine Verdery stress the ways that the party-state was not a fully formed social actor at the time of collectivization. The case of Kazakhstan offers a particularly extreme variation on this point: not only was the party-state not a fully formed social actor, but in many areas of the republic the party-state bureaucracy did not even exist beyond the provincial level at the time of collectivization.

11. The entirety of Kustanai and Petropavlovsk provinces, as well as twelve districts from Syr-Daria, Semipalatinsk, Aktiubinsk, Alma-Atinsk, Ural'sk, and Pavlodar provinces, were slated for full collectivization. See "Rezoliutsii i postanovleniia V plenuma Kazakhskogo kraevogo komiteta VKP(b) 11–16 dekabria 1929," in KSKK, 273.

12. R. W. Davies finds that Soviet officials vacillated several times on the date by which these regions would complete collectivization. But in April 1930, Stalin indicated that they should complete collectivization by the spring of 1931 (*Socialist Offensive*, 202).

13. TsGARK f. 1179, op. 1, d. 1, l. 6 (On the question of the release of funds for events connected with the transition of 84,000 nomadic households to settled life, March 4, 1930).

14. APRK f. 141, op. 1, d. 2926, ll. 91–92 (Postanovlenie Kazkraikoma VKP[b] ob osedanii kochevogo i polukochevogo kazakhsogo naseleniia, January 19, 1930), in KSKK, 276.

15. In a letter to Goloshchekin after the completion of the first collectivization drive, Isaev wrote: "As you know, neither Gosplan nor Narkomzem have considered questions of economic regionalization. Because of this, we don't have the data that could characterize the condition and perspective of individual districts." See APRK f. 141, op. 17, d. 467, ll. 125–26 (Letter from Isaev to Goloshchekin, September 30, 1930). As Lynne Viola has

argued, Stalinist policy was often contingent and reactive, creating the conditions for a state of perpetual crisis (*Unknown Gulag,* 188–89).

16. See, for instance, the speech by F. I. Goloshchekin, which called for strengthening the grain supply to nomadic regions. See "Kazakstan na pod"eme: Rech' na vi s"ezde VKP(b) 29 iiulia 1930 g.," *Narodnoe khoziaistvo Kazakstana,* no. 5–6 (1930): 20.

17. APRK f. 141, op. 17, d. 254, l. 183 (Report on questions related to the grain-forage balance in Petropavlovsk and Akmolinsk okrugs, October 3, 1928). Using data from the last decades of the Russian empire, in 1928 the republic's state statistical commission had determined that a Russian peasant consumed 15.1 poods of grain per year; an urban dweller, twelve poods; and a Kazakh, eight poods.

18. RTsKhIDNI f. 17, op. 85, d. 333, ll. 2–35 (Pis'mo M. I. Frumkina v TsK i TsKK VKP(b) o polozhenii v sel'skom khoziaistve i vzaimootnosheniiakh s krest'ianstvom, May 11, 1928) in TSD, 1:451.

19. As of December 1929, only 15 of the republic's 156 districts had collectivization rates above 50 percent. See RGAE f. 7486, op. 37, d. 40, ll. 211–206 (Svedeniia NKZema SSR o khode kollektivizatsii po okrugam i kraiam SSSR na 15 dekabria 1929 g., sostavlennye po soobshcheniiam sekretarei okruzhkomov VKP[b]), in TSD, 2:53.

20. Prior to the first collectivization drive, the Central Committee did not provide any concrete instructions as to how collective farms should be organized. In the absence of central directives, local activists often took the initiative to implement more stringent forms of collective farms. See R.W. Davies, *The Industrialization of Soviet Russia,* vol. 2: *Soviet Collective Farm 1929–1930* (London, 1980), 172–74.

21. APRK f. 141, op. 1, d. 2969, ll. 4–4ob. (Protokol zasedaniia troiki pri Kazkraikome VKP[b] o poriadke vyseleniia i rasseleniia kulatskikh khoziaistv, January 23, 1930), in IIDK, 50.

22. RGAE f. 7446, op. 1, d. 12, l. 51 (Svedeniia Narkomzema RSFSR o khode kollektivizatsii v RSFSR na 1 marta 1930 g., March 7, 1930), in TSD, 2:289.

23. On the importance of sedentarization, see APRK f. 141, op. 1, d. 2896, ll. 1–5, 22 (Iz doklada aul'no-derevenskogo otdela Kazkraikoma VKP[b] "Osedanie kochevogo i polukochevogo naseleniia," December 1929), in TKA, vol. 2.

24. Ibid., 5. Those being sedentarized were supposed to contribute 99,123,400 rubles to the project. On the lack of state funds for sedentarization, see also Pianciola, "Famine in the Steppe," 155.

25. APRK f. 141, op. 1, d. 5071, ll. 1–20 (Kratkii obzor o khode osedaniia po dannym raionov i kraevykh organizatsii na 20 maia s. g., May 30, 1931) in TKA, vol. 2.

26. TsGARK f. 1179, op. 1, d. 2, l. 13 (Report on the progress of work for sedentarization, 1931).

27. TsGARK f. 1179, op. 1, d. 2 (Letter from Sïrghabekov to Isaev, 1931).

28. TsGARK f. 1179, op.1, d. 2, ll. 75–75ob. (Letter from Toqtabaev to Narkomzem soiuza, February 17, 1931).

29. TsGARK f. 1179, op. 6, d. 10, l. 87 (Letter from Sïrghabekov to Goszemtrest, June 13, 1931).

30. P. Abramichev, "Nam ne k spekhu—my ne kochuem: Plan osedaniia pod ugrozoi sryva. Razbit' kosnost' i biurokratizm apparata!" *Sovetskaia step',* 1930; E. Ernasarov, "Itogi i perspektivy osedaniia—iz doklada tov. E. Ernasova na vsekazaksom s"ezde sovetov," *Sovetskaia step',* 21 February 1931.

31. TsGARK f. 1179, op. 1, d. 2, l. 13 (Report on the progress of world for sedentarization, 1931).

32. Abramichev, "Nam ne k spekhu—my ne kochuem."

33. APRK f. 141, op. 17, d. 471, ll. 92–93 (Letter from Chelkarsk district to Lev Roshal' [third secretary of kraikom from 1930 to 1931], March 23, 1930).

34. APRK f. 141, op. 1, d. 2968, ll. 1–3ob., 18ob.–24 (Iz doklada [sekretaria KazTsIKa A.A. Asylbekova] v Kazkraikom VKP[b] o poezdke v Sarysuiskii i Talasskii raiony dlia vyiasneniia sostoianiia del v sviazi s kollektivizatsiei, April 26, 1930), in IIDK, 251.

35. Lev Kopelev served as a 25,000er in Soviet Ukraine, later becoming a Soviet dissident. An engrossing account of his experiences as a 25,000er can be found in his essay "Last Grain Collection (1933)," in *Education of a True Believer* (New York, 1980), 224–86.

36. On the number of 25,000ers sent to Kazakhstan, see Viola, *Best Sons of the Fatherland*, 40. Activists sent to the republic's grain-growing regions struggled to fulfill the party's directives, and an OGPU report noted their "despondent mood" and "persistent desire to return back to the factory." See APRK f. 719, op. 2, d. 125, ll. 74–75 (Svodka PP OPGU po KASSR v Kazkrai KK-Narkomatu RKI o rabote i nastroenii prislannykh v Kazakhstan "dvadtsatipiatitysiachnikov," prior to April 23, 1930), in IIDK, 240–42.

37. APRK f. 141, op. 1, d. 2968, ll. 1–3ob., 18ob.–24, in IIDK, 252.

38. Chokin, *Chetyre vremeni zhizni*, 6–9.

39. Ibid., 26.

40. Ibid., 25.

41. Ibid., 40.

42. Ghalym Akhmedov, "Sol bïr auïr zhïldarda," *Qïzïldar qïrghïnï*, 25.

43. GAAO f. 1, op. 15, d. 56, ll. 19–20, 26 (Iz pis'ma rabotnika Alma-atinskogo obkoma VKP[b] pervomu sekretariu obkoma t. Kuramysovu, February 1, 1933), in TKN, 239–40.

44. TsGARK f. 44, op. 12, d. 494, l. 2 (Counter-revolutionary organization controlling the leadership of the district, October 1, 1931).

45. Shayakhmetov, *The Silent Steppe*, 56–57.

46. APRK f. 719, op. 5, d. 108, l. 144 (Report on the condition of Karmakchinsk district and several statistics from Kazalinsk and Alamesekskii districts in Kzyl-Orda okrug).

47. APRK f. 141, op. 1, d. 3297, ll. 109–11a ob. (Pis'mo predsedatelia TsIK KASSR E. Ernazarova sekretariu Kazkraikoma VKP[b] F. I. Goloshchekinu o khode proverki ispravleniia peregibov kollektivizatsii, April 21, 1930), in IIDK, 232–33.

48. "Kak stroit' pereselencheskie kolkhozy," *Sovetskaia step'*, January 31, 1930, 2.

49. A. G. Zvonarev, "O kollektivizatsii aula (Kazakskii kolkhoz v aul, kak on est')," *Bol'shevik Kazakstana*, no. 5 (1931): 24; "Kak svesti auly v krupnye kolkhozy," *Sovetskaia step'*, March 12, 1930, 2.

50. TsGANKh f. 7446, op. 13, d. 47, ll. 57–62 (Iz vystypleniia predstavitelia Kazakhstana na soveshchanii massovogo sektora TsK VKP[b] s predstaviteliami natsional'nykh respublik i oblastei po voprosam razvitiia zhivotnovodstva, November 26, 1931), in KSKK, 384–85.

51. Here I draw on the work of Caroline Humphrey, who showed in an analysis of the Buriat collective farm during the 1960s and 1970s how the institution of the collective farm served to maintain some of the very features of Buriat culture that Moscow sought to eliminate (*Marx Went Away—but Karl Stayed Behind* [Ann Arbor, 2001]).

52. TsGARK f. 30, op. 7, d. 100, ll. 174–80 (Doklad upolnomochennogo Kazkraikoma VKP[b] i nachal'nika ekspeditsii po skotozagotovkam v Sary-Suiskom raione v Kazkraikom VKP[b], KazTsIK, KasSNK, Kazklebzhivsoiuz i Kazkontoru Soiuzmiaso, February 11, 1931), in TKA, vol. 2. Later generations of Soviet historians criticized the emergence of these "nomadic collective farms." See Tursunbaev, *Pobeda kolkhoznogo stroia v Kazakhstane*, 149, 206–7.

53. TsGARK f. 247, op. 1, d. 644, ll. 35–39 (Iz protokola zasedaniia pravleniia Kazkraikolkhozsoiuza o bor'be s rodovymi perezhitkami v kolkhoznom stroitel'stve, February 12, 1931) in KSKK, 384–85.

54. APRK f. 719, op. 5, d. 108, l. 146 (Report on the condition of Karmakchinsk district and several statistics from Kazalinsk and Alamesekskii districts in Kzyl-Orda okrug).

55. APRK f. 141, op. 1, d. 3297, ll. 109–11a ob., in IIDK, 234.
56. Zeitïn Aqïshev, "Bïlïsin münï ürpaktar," in Qïzïldar qïrghïnï, 13.
57. Ibid., 14.
58. On the number of livestock in Kazakhstan, see APRK f. 141, op. 1, d. 2870, ll. 124–27 (Iz obzora Kazkraikoma VKP[b] "Sostoianie zhivotnovodstva v KASSR v 1927/1928 gg. i perspektivy ego razvitiia v tekushuiu piatiletku," December 1929), in TKA, 2:2.
59. APRK f. 141, op. 1, d. 5059, ll. 12–20 (Spetssvodka no. 2 o khode skotozagotovitel'noi kampanii 1930/1931 gg. po KSSR po materialam INFO PP OGPU po KSSR na 10 fevralia 1931 g.), in TKA, 2:17, 18.
60. Ibid., 16–17.
61. Shayakhmetov, Silent Steppe, 106.
62. GAAO f. 1, op. 15, d. 56, ll. 19–20, 26 (Iz pis'ma rabotnika Alma-atinskogo obkoma VKP[b] pervomu sekretariu obkoma t. Kuramysovu, February 1, 1933), in TKN, 239–40.
63. RGASPI f. 17, op. 162, d. 8, ll. 94–101 (Postanovlenie Politbiuro TsK VKP[b] "O kollektivizatsii i bor'be s kulachestvom i natsional'nykh ekonomicheski otstalykh raionakh," February 20, 1930) in TSD, 2:251–56.
64. Ibid., 253.
65. Ibid., 254. In Kazakhstan, this Central Committee directive was then followed by a local decree prohibiting animal slaughter in nomadic regions. See TsGARK f. 5, op. 11, d. 80, l. 7 (Ruling of KTsIK and SNK on measures to prevent the slaughter of livestock in nomadic and semi-nomadic districts, March 21, 1930).
66. See, for instance, the speech of Comrade Kurmanbaev (TsGANKh f. 7446, op. 13, d. 47, ll. 57–62, in KSKK, 472).
67. K. S. Aldazhumanov, "Krest'ianskoe dvizhenie soprotivleniia kollektivizatsii i politicheskie repressii v Kazakhstane," in Narod ne bezmolvstvuet, ed. M. I. Pomarev (Almaty, 1996), 13.
68. I. V. Stalin, "Dizzy with Success: Concerning Questions of the Collective-Farm Movement," Pravda, March 2, 1930, in The War against the Peasantry, 1927–1930, ed. Lynne Viola et al., trans. Steven Shabad (New Haven, 2005), 277–78.
69. Collectivization rates for Kazakhstan in 1930: January (24.5 percent), February (26 percent), March (45 percent), April (51.5 percent). See Sed'maia Vsekazakskaia konferentsiia VKP(b), 101. Alec Nove offers similar, though not identical, figures for collectivization rates in Kazakhstan: March 1 (37.1 percent), March 10 (47.9 percent), April 1 (56.6 percent), May 1 (44.4 percent). See Nove, Economic History of the USSR, 171.
70. APRK f. 719, op. 2, d. 123, l. 61 (Excerpts from the minutes of a meeting of the bureau of Kazkraikom on March 21, 1930).
71. APRK f. 141, op. 1, d. 3297, ll. 109–111a ob., in IIDK, 233. The party's struggle to implement "Dizzy with Success" was complicated by a reshuffling of the middle, provincial layer (known as okrug and later as oblast), of the republic's bureaucracy during 1930–32. While this reorganization was ongoing, some districts (raiony) did not have provincial oversight. Rather, they reported directly to the republican center in Alma-Ata.
72. Like elsewhere in the Soviet Union, most officials charged with committing "distortions" during the first collectivization drive were not fired. They were simply transferred to work in other areas of the republic. See APRK f. 141, op. 17, d. 607, ll. 1–14 (Letter from Isaev to Stalin, August 1932) in TKN, 209.
73. Sed'maia Vsekazakskaia konferentsiia VKP(b), 74.
74. TsA FSB RF f. 2, op. 8, d. 744, ll. 103–5 (Informationnaia zapiska polnomochnogo predstavitel'stva OGPU po Kazakhskoi ASSR v informatsionnyi otdel OGPU SSSR po voprosu prodovol'stvennykh zatrudnenii na 5 iiulia 1930 g.), in GVS, vol. 1, book 1:216–18.
75. APRK f. 141, op. 1, d. 2948, ll. 19a–20 (Pis'mo sekretaria Kazkraikoma VKP[b] F. I. Goloshchekina narkomu vneshnei i vnutrennei torgovli SSSR A. I. Mikoianu ob otsutstvii

khleba i faktakh goloda v Kazakhstane, April 19, 1930), in IIDK, 223. The letter was also circulated to Molotov.

76. RGASPI f. 17, op. 167, d. 28, l. 159 (Shifrotelegramma V. M. Molotova pervomu sekretariu kazakhskogo kraikoma VKP[b] F. I. Goloshchekinu ob otkochevkakh kazakhov na sredniuiu Volgu, August 20, 1930), in GVS, vol. 1, book 1:262–63.

77. Soviet ethnographers concluded that most Adai were Kazakhs, although members of the Adai clan might also be found among another ethnicity—the Kara-Kalpaks, Turkic-speaking nomads who inhabited the republic's nearby Karakalpak Autonomous Region (KAO). See Mukhamedzhan Tynyshpaev, "Genealogiia kirgiz-kazakhskikh rodov" (1925), reprinted in *Istoriia kazakhskogo naroda*, ed. A.Takenov and B. Baigaliev (Almaty, 2002), 103, 106.

78. TsGARK f. 5, op. 9, d. 23, l. 16 (Report on the existence of the Adai okrug, 1929).

79. Turganbek Allaniiazov and Amangel'dy Taukenov, *Poslednii rubezh zashchitnikov nomadizma* (Almaty, 2008), 334.

80. TsGARK f. 5, op. 9, d. 23, l. 11 (Report on the existence of the Adai okrug 1929). The report cites I. V. Larin, ed., *Osobennosti sel'skogo khoziastva Adaevskogo uezda* (Alma-Ata, 1928) as the original author of this quote.

81. V. N. Semevskii, "O sud'bakh Adaia (k probleme tsentral'nogo Kazakstana)," *Narodnoe khoziaistvo Kazakstana* no. 9–10 (1930): 41.

82. APRK f. 141, op. 1, d. 1694, ll. 32–40 (Doklad o polozhenii v okruge i zadachakh po sovetskomu stroitel'stvu, March 1928) in TKA, 1:184.

83. A report found that 47 percent of the nomads in the Adai okrug migrated more than a thousand kilometers per year, with 65 percent of this group carrying out migrations that exceeded two thousand kilometers per year. See TsGARK f. 5, op. 9, d. 23, l. 10 (Report on the existence of the Adai okrug KSSR, 1929).

84. M. S. Tursunova, *Kazakhi Mangyshlaka vo vtoroi polovine XIX veka* (Alma-Ata, 1977), 4.

85. TsGARK f. 5, op. 9, d. 23, l. 12 (Report on the existence of the Adai okrug KSSR, 1929).

86. See, for instance, the report on the Adai by Kul'dzhanov in TsGARK f. 1000, op. 1, d. 31, l. 144 (Report no. 1, January 25, 1929).

87. Ohayon, *Sédentarisation des Kazakhs*, 160. For an example of the use of the term, "Central Kazakhstan," see N. I. Maslov, "Puti ispol'zovaniia tsentral'nogo Kazakhstana," *Narodnoe khoziaistvo Kazakstana*, no. 4–5 (1929): 79–87.

88. See, for instance, V. N. Semevskii, "O sud'bakh Adaia," 40.

89. TsGARK f. 5, op. 9, d. 23, l. 14 (Report on the existence of the Adai okrug KSSR 1929).

90. APRK f. 141, op. 1, d. 1694, l. 32 (Doklad o polozhenii v okruge i zadachakh po sovetskomu stroitel'stvu, March 1928), in TKA, 1:185.

91. Izturgan Sariev, "Krovavoe poboishche," in *Stepnaia tragediia*, trans. Zhumaliev Bakytzhan (from the Kazakh) (Almaty, 2010), 77–130.

92. APRK f. 141, op. 17, d. 325b, l. 25 (Report of the PP OGPU for Kazakhstan on counter-revolutionary groups in Aktiubinsk and Gur'ev okrugs and the KAO, December 10, 1929), 25.

93. APRK f. 141, op. 1, d. 1694, l. 32 (Doklad o polozhenii v okruge i zadachakh po sovetskomu stroitel'stvu, March 1928), in TKA, 1:186.

94. Ibid.

95. On the linkage between Älniyäzŭlï and this incident, see the recollections of Mikhail Riadnin in APRK f. 811, op. 19, d. 238, l. 81. On the incident itself, see M. Omarov, *Rasstreliannaia step'* (Almaty, 1994), 10–16; and Sariev, "Krovavoe poboishche," 138–40.

96. APRK f. 141, op. 1, d. 1694, ll. 32–40 (Doklad o polozhenii v okruge i zadachakh po sovetskomu stroitel'stvu, March 1928), in TKA, 1:187.

97. Allaniiazov and Taukenov, *Poslednii rubezh zashchitnikov nomadizma*, 335.

98. TsGARK f. 1000, op. 1, d. 32, l. 35 (Osnovnye polozheniia operatsionnogo na 29/30 god i piatiletnego planov meropriiatii po vnutrirespublikanskomu pereseleniiu v Kazakstane, 1929). In contrast to the more limited mandate of Osedkom, however, the Migration Bureau, which was created in 1929, also oversaw the settlement of the Kazakh steppe by settlers from European Russia.

99. TsGARK f. 30, op. 6, d. 28, l. 71 (Letter from Goloshchekin and Isaev to Mikoian, March 29, 1929).

100. TsGARK f. 1000, op. 1, d. 68, l. 3.

101. Semevskii, "O sud'bakh Adaia," 43.

102. Ibid., 40.

103. TsGARK f. 1000, op. 1, d. 68, l. 39ob. (Letter from a plenipotentiary to the Migration Bureau, April 14, 1930).

104. TsGARK f. 1000, op. 1, d. 31, ll. 211–14 (Report by a plenipotentiary to Aktiubinsk okrug May 10, 1930).

105. APRK f. 141, op. 17, d. 325b, l. 25.

106. TsA FSB RF f. 2, op. 8, d. 3, ll. 194–96 (Zapis' soobshcheniia po priamomu provodu PP OGPU po Srednei Azii V. A. Karutskogo E. G. Evdokimovu o politicheskom sostoianii raionov Srednei Azii, not earlier than February 11, 1930), in SDG, vol. 3, book 1:165.

107. *Stepnaia tragediia*, 259.

108. APRK f. 141, op. 1. d. 2948, ll. 7, 9–11, 41–46 (Iz zakrytogo pis'ma sekretaria Kazkraikoma VKP[b] F. I. Goloshchekina sekretariu TsK VKP[b] I. V. Stalinu o politiko-ekonomicheskom sostoianii Kazakhstana, March 5, 1930), in IIDK, :144.

109. RGASPI f. 17, op. 167, d. 28, l. 108 (Shifrotelegramma sekretaria TsK VKP[b] P. P. Postysheva na mesta o sryve snabzheniia Moskvy miasom, July 22, 1930), in GVS. vol. 1, book 1:258.

110. On this point, see also Omarbekov, *20–30 zhïldardaghï Qasaqstan*, 62–81; and Pianciola, "Towards a Transnational History of Great Leaps Forward in Pastoral Central Eurasia."

111. GARF f. R-5674, op. 9, d. 19, ll. 21–22 (Postanovlenie no 202s sto SSSR "O snabzhenii Moskvy i Leningrada," September 28, 1931), in GVS, vol. 1, book 1:620.

112. RGASPI f. 558, op. 11, d. 63, l. 72 (Cable from Mikoian to the Central Committee, January 20, 1931), in SDA.

113. APRK f. 141, op. 1, d. 5062, l. 195 (Telegramma Kazkraikoma VKP[b] sekretariam iany-kurganskogo, karatal'skogo, talasskogo, suzakskogo, chelkarskogo raikomov, July 1931)/ in TKA, 2:35–35.

114. APRK f. 141, op. 1, d. 5062, l. 332 (Telegramma Kazkraikoma VKP[b] sekretariu leningradskogo OK VKP[b] Chudovu, oblsnabotdelu Ziminu, August 24, 1931), in TKA, 2:39–40. Before reaching Leningrad, this livestock was processed in several Western Siberian meat-packing combines.

115. Allaniiazov and Taukenov, *Poslednii rubezh zashchitnikov nomadizma*, 335.

116. "Zhurnal 'Partiinaia zhizn' Kazakhstana,'" 1990, no. 10, s. 76–84 (Dokladnaia zapiska zamestitelia predsedatelia SNK RSFSR T. R. Ryskulova v SK VKP[b]—I. V. Stalinu, 28. 9. 1932)." in NKG, 184.

117. Later generations of Soviet historians criticized this decision. See Tursunbaev, "Introduction," in KSKK, 14. In part, these shifts toward larger and more restrictive forms of collective farms were taking place across the Soviet Union. See Wheatcroft and Davies, *Years of Hunger*, 322.

118. APRK f. 141, op. 1, d. 5116, ll. 102–10 (Pis'mo sekretaria Kazkraikoma VKP[b] chlenam biuro Kazkraikoma i prezidiuma KraiKK VKP[b], July 6, 1931), in TKA, 2:30.

119. RGASPI f. 82, op. 2, d. 61, ll. 1–39 (Iz stenogrammy soveshchaniia v TsK VKP[b] po khlebozagaotovkam, September 14, 1930), in TSD, 2:619.

120. APRF f. 3, op. 40, d. 77, ll. 32–39 (Dokladnaia zapiska pervogo sekretaria VTsSPS N. M. Shvernika I. V. Stalinu o poezdke v Kazakhstan na khlebozagatovki, March 12, 1931), in GVS, vol. 1, book 1:366.

121. RGASPI f. 17, op. 167, d. 31, l. 124 (Shifrotelegramma I. V. Stalina pervomu sekretariu kazakhskogo kraikoma VKP[b] F. I. Goloshchekinu o vyvoze khleba iz glubinnykh punktov, July 1, 1931), in GVS, vol. 1, book 1:408.

122. APRK f. 141, op. 1, d. 5062, l. 214 (Telegramma Kazkraikoma VKP[b] sekretariu Aksuiskogo raikoma VKP[b] o vyvoze glubinnogo khleba, July 3, 1931), in TKA, 2:65.

123. In an indication of the severity of the drought, the average precipitation for Semipalatinsk in June for the period 1921–31 was 32.3 millimeters and the average precipitation for Semipalatinsk in July for the period 1921–31 was 38.3 millimeters. For further information, see the data on precipitation levels contained in the appendix.

124. TsGARK f. 30, op. 6, d. 85, l. 34 (Letter from Roshal' to Kakhiani and Isaev, July 17, 1931)

125. APRF f. 3, op. 40, d. 77, ll. 139–40 (Pis'mo chlenov kazakhskogo kraikoma VKP[b] M. I. Kakhiani, I. M. Kuramysova, U. D. Isaeva I. V. Stalinu o nevozmozhnosti vypolneniia plana khlebozagotovok, no later than July 30, 1931), in GVS, vol. 1, book 1:467.

126. Viola, *Unknown Gulag*, 195–96.

127. Ibid.

128. TsA FSB RF f. 2, op. 2, d. 20, ll. 181–83 (O vyselennykh i pereselennykh kulakakh v Kazakhstane, May 4, 1931), in SDG, vol. 3, book 1:668–69.

129. Nikolai Boldyrev, "Kogo prizvat' k otvetu," in *Narod ne bezmolvstvuet*, 55.

130. Zoia Alekseeva, "Khvatili likha," in ibid., 27.

131. APRK f. 141, op. 17, d. 477, ll. 43–45 (Telegram from Goloshchekin to Stalin, Molotov, and Kaganovich, 1930).

132. Barnes, *Death and Redemption*, 31.

133. Ibid., 34.

134. On KarLag, see Barnes, *Death and Redemption*; and Wladislaw Hedeler and Meinhard Stark, *Das Grab in der Steppe* (Paderborn, 2008).

135. TsGARK f. R-30, op. 7, d. 46, l. 68 (Protokol zasedaniia SNK KASSR ob otvode lageriam osobogo naznacheniia OGPU v Kazakhstane zemel'nogo massiva, May 13, 1930), in IIDK, 262–63.

136. N. O. Dulatbekov, ed., *Qarlag* (Karaganda, 2010), 2:255. In 1937, Zhurgenov was shot as an enemy of the people, and Ermekova spent eight years in Alzhir, the labor camp for "wives of the traitors of the motherland." On Ermekova's distinguished career as a doctor, see Michaels, *Curative Powers*, 1–3.

137. Michael Ellman, for instance, has classified drought and the weather as "exogenous, non-policy related factors" in his analysis of the Soviet collectivization famines. See "The Role of Leadership Perceptions and of Intent in the Soviet Famine of 1931–1934," *Europe-Asia Studies* 57, no. 6 (2005): 834.

138. In *Works in Progress* (Yale, 2014), Jenny Leigh Smith offers a revisionist view of Soviet agriculture, arguing that it was the state's inability to understand, anticipate and respond to the natural environment rather than "socialism" or "totalitarianism" that thwarted "rural progress." Smith does not consider the case of the Kazakh famine, but it would seem to contradict her claim that famine due to collectivization began only in 1932.

5. VIOLENCE, FLIGHT, AND HUNGER

1. TsGARK f. 44, op. 12, d. 492, l. 53.

2. An increase in the amount of small livestock for sale in regional markets was often one indication that residents were preparing for flight. See, for instance, a report from the northeast region of Semipalatinsk in 1928 (TsDNIVKO f. 3, op. 1, d. 25, l. 25).

3. TsGARK f. 44, op. 12, d. 492, ll. 54, 58.

4. Ibid., 54.

5. Ibid., 53.

6. Ibid., 54–54ob.

7. According to several secret police reports circulated among top party officials, more than one thousand people were shot while trying to cross the border in 1930. See APRK f. 141, op. 1, d. 4577, ll. 1–2; this data is confirmed by a second report, see APRK f. 141, op. 1, d. 4577, l. 72. There are countless individual archival examples of shootings and border violence throughout 1931, while the total number of those fleeing to Xinjiang in 1931 doubled in comparison with 1930. Though I did not uncover cumulative data on border deaths for 1931, I am convinced that the level of violence was similar to, if not greater than, that in 1930.

8. Estimates for the numbers who fled to China vary. Robert Conquest estimates that 200,000 people fled to China during the Kazakh famine (Robert Konkvest, "Zhatva skorbi," *Voprosy istorii*, no. 4 [1990], 88). Talas Omarbekov argues that sixty thousand ethnic Kazakhs relocated to Xinjiang during this period 1930–33 (*Qazaqstan tarikhïnïng XX ghasïrdaghï*, 272).

9. For a detailed analysis of an uprising in Karakalpak Autonomous Oblast, then part of Kazakhstan, see Turganbek Allaniiazov, *"Konttrevoliutsiia" v Kazakhstane* (Almaty, 1999). The other two uprisings took place in Bostandyk district (Syr-Daria province) and Batbakkarinsk district (Kustanai province).

10. APRK f. 141, op. 1, d. 5052, ll. 315–19 (Spravka o bandvosstaniiakh i bandvystupleniiakh na territorii Kazakhstana v period 1929–1931 godov), in Allaniiazov and Taukenov, *Poslednii rubezh zashchitnikov nomadizma*, 419.

11. Ibid., 358, 423.

12. APRK f. 141, op. 1, d. 3336, ll. 7–10 (Iz telegrafnoi zapiski upolnomochennykh OGPU polnomochnym predstaviteliam OGPU v Srednei Azii i Kazakhstane Bel'skomu i Vollenbergu o Suzakskom vosstanii i polozhenii v raione, February 18, 1930), in NKG, 62.

13. Omarbekov, *Zobalang (küshtep üzhumdastïrugha karsïlïq)*, 269 (citing OGPU documents).

14. See, for instance, the discussion in APRK f. 141, op. 17, d. 452a (Stenogram of closed session of the bureau of Kazkraikom, January 2, 1930). Kazakhstani scholars have debated many of these issues. In *Zobalang (küshtep üzhumdastïrugha karsïlïq)*, Talas Omarbekov argues that the uprisings represented "national liberation" revolts and identifies common features between these uprisings and the revolt of 1916. By contrast, Turganbek Allaniiazov and Amangel'dy Taukenov argue that the revolts were not "national liberation" revolts. In their assessment, protestors had divergent aims. See *Poslednii rubezh zashchitnikov nomadizma*.

15. In an analysis of the 1930 Suzak uprising, Niccolò Pianciola argues that the Russian empire, which set up the administrative system of volosts in the Kazakh steppe, provided the geographical framework, or "grammar," in which these rebellions were articulated. He notes that few rebel leaders were able to mobilize participants beyond the boundaries of their former volosts. See "Interpreting an Insurgency in Soviet Kazakhstan: The OGPU, Islam and Qazaq 'Clans' in Suzak, 1930," in *Islam, Society and States across the Qazaq Steppe (18th–Early 20th Centuries)*, ed. Niccolò Pianciola and Paolo Sartori (Vienna, 2013), 333.

16. APRK f. 141, op. 17, d. 325b, l. 21 (Report of the PP OGPU for Kazakhstan on the counter-revolutionary groups in Aktiubinsk and Gur'ev okrugs and the KAO, December 10, 1929); APRK f. 141, op. 17, d. 325b, l. 39 (Brief information on the Kara-Kum ishan, probably 1929).

17. V. Popov, "Pokhody dalekikh dnei," 54, 59.

18. Ibid., 54.

19. For one such report, see APRK f. 141, op. 17, d. 471, l. 206 (OGPU report on a band in the Kara-Kum desert, April 13, 1930). On the British empire's use of "air control" to police Iraq, see Priya Satia, "The Defense of Inhumanity," *American Historical Review* 111, no. 1 (2006): 16–51. The number of planes in Kazakhstan was limited, however, and the OGPU seems to have deployed air power intermittently.

20. In one such aerial bombardment, in Alma-Ata province in 1930, fifteen to twenty rebels were killed. See APRK f. 141, op. 17, d. 471, l. 271.

21. APRK f. 141, op. 17, d. 465, l. 136.

22. Popov, "Pokhody dalekikh dnei," 53, 61. On Mendeshev's mandate, see TsGARK f. 135, op. 1, d. 3, ll. 8–9 (Telegramma U. Isaeva i F. Goloshchekina S. Mendeshevu v sviazi s likvidatsieii vosstaniia v byvshem Adaevskom okruge, April 5, 1931), in NKG, 83.

23. Allaniiazov and Taukenov argue that major conflict came to an end in Mangyshlak in the fall of 1931 (*Poslednii rubezh zashchitnikov nomadizma,* 358), while other studies claim that the party did not end fighting in the peninsula until the summer of 1932 (NKG, 83–84).

24. On the practice of taxation and conscription by rebel groups, see Pianciola, "Interpreting an Insurgency in Soviet Kazakhstan," 331.

25. Focusing primarily on the western borderlands, Terry Martin charts a shift in policy, from an interest in exploiting cross-border ethnic ties to project Soviet influence abroad (what he terms "The Piedmont Principle"), to a preoccupation with cross-border ties as an instrument of foreign influence inside the Soviet Union (*Affirmative Action Empire,* chap. 8). For other accounts that focus either exclusively or primarily on the western borderlands during the First Five-Year Plan, see Snyder, *Sketches from a Secret War,* chap. 5; Kate Brown, *A Biography of No Place* (Cambridge, MA, 2004), chap. 3; and Andrea Chandler, *Institutions of Isolation* (Montreal, 1998), chap. 5.

26. The regime's administrative definition of the "border strip" (*pogranichnye polosy*), as well as the benefits and punitive measures accorded to this area changed over time. At times, the border strip extended not only to those raions immediately adjacent to the border but also to the interior districts that abutted them. See Andrey Shlyakhter, "Smugglers and Commissars" (PhD diss., University of Chicago, forthcoming). I thank Andrey Shlyakhter for allowing me to read portions of his dissertation. See also Martin, *Affirmative Action Empire,* chap. 8.

27. Martin, *Affirmative Action Empire,* 322.

28. Several Kazakhstani scholars have examined the role of the Sino-Kazakh border during the Kazakh famine. See Omarbekov, *20–30 zhïldardaghï Qasaqstan qasïretï,* 272–81; and Omarbekov, *Qazaqstan tarikhïnïng XX ghasïrdaghï,* 271–82 (Omarbekov is one of the few Kazakhstani scholars who have been given access to the former secret police archives in Kazakhstan). See also Mendikulova, *Kazakhskaia diaspora,* 132–36; and N. N. Ablazhei, *Kazakhskii migratsionnyi maiatnik "Kazakhstan-Sin'tszian"* (Novosibirsk, 2015), 34–45. There are also a handful of memoir accounts, including Shayakhmetov, *Silent Steppe,* 39–44; and V. I. Petrov, *Miatezhnoe "serdtse" Azii* (Moscow, 2003), 324–35. Little scholarly attention has been paid to the borders of Central Asia during the First Five-Year Plan. One exception is Adrienne Edgar's account of the Turkmen-Afghan border in *Tribal Nation,* 213–20. There does not appear to have been a similar level of violence on the Turkmen-Afghan border, perhaps reflecting Kazakhstan's far more desperate economic plight.

29. Owen Lattimore, *Pivot of Asia* (Boston, 1950).

30. In 1940, Andrew D. W. Forbes calculates that Muslim nationalities in Xinjiang numbered 3,439,000, while Han Chinese settlers numbered 200,000. Of these Muslim groups, Uyghurs were estimated at 2,941,000, while Kazakhs numbered 319,000 and Kirgiz 65,000 (*Warlords and Muslims in Chinese Central Asia* [Cambridge, 1986], 6).

31. Under the warlord Sheng Shicai in the early 1930s and in a departure from Guomindang ideology, Xinjiang recognized fourteen ethnic categories, including Kazakhs, Uyghurs, and Taranchi (the people of northern Xinjiang, who are now also known as Uyghur). Sheng Shicai also adopted several strategies that resembled the Soviet Union's policy of indigenization (*korenizatsiia*), including the promotion of ethnic elites, as well as the sponsorship of education and publications in native languages. See James A. Millward, *Eurasian Crossroads* (London, 2007), 207–9. On the construction of Uyghur identity by Chinese officials, see Justin Jon Rudelson, *Oasis Identities* (New York, 1997), 4–7. In the debates surrounding the compilation of the 1926 Soviet census, Uyghurs were not immediately recognized as a nationality. Originally put on a list of "questionable" nationalities for the 1926 census (groups Soviet ethnographers believed to be of "mixed origins"), they were later given official recognition as a nationality in the final version of the list (Hirsch, *Empire of Nations*, 131, 133).

32. Millward, *Eurasian Crossroads*, ix.

33. Frank and Usmanov, *Materials for the Islamic History of Semipalatinsk*, 1.

34. Millward, *Eurasian Crossroads*, 170–77.

35. *Zapiski Semipalatinskogo otdela obshchestva izucheniia Kazakstana* (Semipalatinsk, 1929), 10.

36. Aleksandr Igorevich Pylev, *Basmachestvo v Srednei Azii* (Bishkek, 2006), 174.

37. James Millward and Nabijian Tursun, "Political History and Strategies of Control," in *Xinjiang: China's Muslim Borderland*, 75–80.

38. From 1689 to 1727, parts of this border were demarcated with similar results. See Andrey V. Ivanov, "Conflicting Loyalties," *Journal of Early Modern History* 13, no. 5 (2009): 333–58.

39. Scholars in Kazakhstan have represented the 1881 treaty as the moment when a "united Kazakh people" was divided into "Russian Kazakhs" and "Chinese Kazakhs." See, for example, Fy Chzhen-Kun, *Istoricheskie sviazi i sovremennye otnosheniia mezhdu Kitaem i Kazakhstanom* (Almaty, 2001). In his memoir, Mukhamet Shayakhmetov, a survivor of the Kazakh famine of the 1930s, suggests that many Kazakhs continued to retain their Chinese identities throughout the Soviet period (*Sud'ba*, 19). Kazakhs living in China numbered over 1.1 million in 1990, constituting the largest Kazakh diaspora community. See Linda Benson and Ingvar Svanberg, *China's Last Nomads* (Armonk, NY, 1998), 110.

40. Mendikulova, *Kazakhskaia diaspora*, 119.

41. Estimates for flight from Central Asia into Xinjiang for the period 1916–20 vary. Archival sources estimate that one hundred thousand Kazakhs and Kirgiz fled during the period (TsGARK f. 938, op. 1, d. 51, l. 13). Mendikulova estimates that 150,000 ethnic Kazakhs fled beginning in January 1917 (*Kazakhskaia diaspora,* 122).

42. On the White Army officers, see Millward, *Eurasian Crossroads*, 185. On the flight of Dungans, see Safarov, *Kolonial'naia revoliutsiia*, 94.

43. RGASPI f. 94, op. 1, d. 1, l. 661.

44. TsDNIVKO f. 338-P, op. 1, d. 188, ll. 75, 75 ob., in *Pod grifom sekretnosti,*, ed. O. V. Zhandabekov (Ust-Kamenogorsk, 1998), 16–18.

45. On clan ties and their role in cross-border flight, see APRK f. 141, op. 1, d. 1650, l. 69. On agents engaged in trafficking, see ibid., 43–44.

46. Ibid., 18.

47. RGASPI f. 94, op. 1, d. 1, l. 632.

48. APRK f. 141, op. 1, d. 1650, l. 20.

49. Yet as of October 1929, officials in Moscow claimed they had no data on exactly how many households had returned (GARF f. r-1235, op. 140, d. 1053, l. 73).

50. APRK f. 141, op. 1, d. 4577, l. 13.

51. Ibid., 73.

52. APRK f. 141, op. 17, d. 465, l. 93.

53. Omarbekov, *Qazaqstan tarikhïnïng XX ghasïrdaghï*, 284.

54. Talas Omarbekov argues that the majority of those who fled to China were ethnic Kazakhs followed by Uyghurs, Russians, and Dungans (ibid., 272).

55. APRK f. 141, op. 17, d. 465, l. 203.

56. APRK f. 141, op. 3, d. 185, l. 1.

57. APRK f. 141, op. 1, d. 4577, l. 74.

58. APRK f. 141, op. 17, d. 465, l. 205. On a shortage of manufactured goods in border districts, as well as tea, see also APRK f. 719, op. 3, d. 91, l. 45.

59. RGASPI f. 17, op. 42, d. 34, ll. 65–72, in TSD, 3:210–11.

60. The term "kishlak" is often used to refer to non-Slavic settled communities in Central Asia, such as the households of the Uzbeks, Dungans, or Uyghurs.

61. APRK f. 141, op. 1, d. 4577, l. 77.

62. APRK f. 719, op. 5, d. 108, l. 133.

63. There are numerous documents from regional archives detailing this pattern in *Pod grifom sekretnosti*, 56–66.

64. APRK f. 141, op. 17, d. 465, l. 203.

65. TsGARK f. 44, op. 12, d. 492, l. 55.

66. APRK f. 141, op. 17, d. 465, l. 17. Many local historians maintain that Soviet officials practiced preventive shootings in Kazakhstan, slaughtering individuals or even entire groups simply on the rumor that they were preparing to flee to China. See, for instance, Maqash Tätimov, "Goloshcheekindik genotsid nemese Qazaqstandaghï 'qïzïl' qïrghïn qïrsïqtarï," *Zan Gazetï*, May 29, 1996, 5; and Kh. M. Gabzhalilov, "XX ghasïrdïng 30-shï zhïldarïngdaghï Qazaqstandaghï ashtïq demografiiasïnïng zerttelŭi turalï," *QazÜU khabarshïsï*, no. 38, 12. These authors, however, do not provide archival evidence to back up their claims. Yet given that some archival documentation on the period still remains closed, it is possible that violence was more widespread than currently available archival evidence would indicate.

67. APRK f. 141, op. 17, d. 465, l. 191.

68. APRK f. 141, op. 1, d. 4577, l. 13.

69. Ibid., 72.

70. Using data from the secret police archives, Talas Omarbekov has revealed a regime highly preoccupied with the problem of cross-border flight and the social composition of emigrants (*Qazaqstan tarikhïnïng XX ghasïrdaghï*, 272). In October 1931, a Soviet secret police report estimated that over 80 percent of those who fled were of modest means (RGASPI f. 17, op. 42, d. 34, ll. 65–72, in TSD, 3:209).

71. See, for instance, APRK f. 141, op. 1, d. 4577, l. 13.

72. APRK f. 141, op. 14, d. 465, l. 204.

73. APRK f. 719, op. 3, d. 185, l. 5.

74. APRK f. 141, op. 17, d. 465, ll. 96–97.

75. Regime officials often noted the problem of cross-border kinship connections. See APRK f. 141, op. 1, d. 4577, l. 21 and l. 75 and APRK f. 719, op. 3, d. 185, l. 1.

76. On Chernenko's service on the Sino-Kazakh border, see B. Gh. Aiagana [Ayäghan], ed., *1932–1933 zhïldardaghï aharshïlïq aqiqatï* (Almaty, 2012), 290.

77. TsDNIVKO f. 788, op. 1 d. 35, ll. 107–16, in *Pod grifom sekretnosti*, 24–32.

78. TsDNIVKO f. 788, op. 1, d. 41, l. 27, in *Pod grifom sekretnosti*, 39.

79. TsDNIVKO f. 788, op. 1, d. 35, ll. 10–116, in *Pod grifom sekretnosti*, 31. Kazakhs did not have a "prince" (*kniaz'*). Kazakhs did, however, have sultans, members of a hereditary elite who claimed to trace their ancestry back to Chinghis Khan.

80. APRK f. 719, op. 2, d. 126, l. 180.

81. APRK f. 141, op. 17, d. 465, ll. 43–44ob.

82. See, for example, the numerous instances of armed violence detailed in APRK f. 141, op. 17, d. 465, ll. 307–38.

83. Ibid., 150, 186.

84. Secret police reports sent to Goloshchekin in May 1930 detailed the numbers of people starving, as well as the specific regions affected by hunger (APRK f. 719, op. 5, d. 108, l. 141).

85. APRK f. 141, op. 1, d. 4577, l. 73.

86. For a description of one such counterrevolutionary organization, see TsDNIVKO f. 1-P, op. 2, d. 4981, ll. 79–80, in *Pod grifom sekretnosti*, 65–66.

87. TsGARK f. 44, op. 2, d. 492, l. 53.

88. TsGARK f. 44, op. 2, d. 492, ll. 53–55ob.

89. TsGARK f. 44, op. 2, d. 492, ll. 57–58.

90. In 1928, Stalin severed diplomatic relations, only to resume them in 1932. During the entire time, however, Soviet officials maintained consulates in Xinjiang. See Jonathan Haslam, *The Soviet Union and the Threat from the East, 1933–1941* (Pittsburgh, 1992); and D. B. Slavinskii, *Sovetskii Soiuz i Kitai* (Moscow, 2003)

91. Allen S. Whiting and Sheng Shih-ts'ai, *Sinkiang* (East Lansing, MI, 1958), xii. Whiting attributes this description to Wendell Willkie, who met Sheng when he visited Xinjiang in 1942. From 1941 to 1951, Soviet, Chinese, and Anglo-American policy makers again competed for influence in Xinjiang. See Justin Jacobs, "The Many Deaths of a Kazak Unaligned," *American Historical Review* 115, no. 5 (2010): 1291–315.

92. Selçuk Esenbel, "Japan's Global Claim to Asia and the World of Islam," *American Historical Review* 109, no. 4 (2004): 1161–62.

93. APRK f. 141, op. 1, d. 4577, l. 1.

94. APRK f. 141, op. 1, d. 4577, l. 62.

95. GAAO f.173, op. 4, d. 9, l. 3.

96. See, for instance, "Anglo-iaponskoe sopernichestvo v Sin'tsziane," *Kazakstanskaia pravda*, April 16, 1933; and "Idet podgotovka k imperialisticheskomy zakhvaty Srednei Azii," *Kazakstanskaia pravda*, August 20, 1933.

97. APRK f. 141, op. 1, d. 4577, l. 2. For a description of one such "stakeout" and chase, see Shayakhmetov, *Silent Steppe*, 41–43.

98. APRK f. 141, op. 1, d. 4577, ll. 4–5.

99. Ibid., 8.

100. Ibid., 9.

101. Ibid., 6.

102. Ibid., 2. Using materials from the secret police archives in Kazakhstan, Talas Omarbekov has done considerable work on Sino-Soviet extradition programs from Xinjiang during the 1930s. In his recounting, refugee work was further complicated by Soviet officials' refusal to accept the extradition of those considered to be bais, kulaks, and other counter-revolutionary figures (*Qazaqstan tarikhïnïng XX ghasïrdaghï*, 284). In 1946, the Soviets resumed efforts to return refugees from the Kazakh famine still residing in Xinjiang, granting returnees citizenship and passports while foregoing the intense scrutiny of who was returning (*bai* or *bedniak*) that had accompanied repatriation efforts in the 1930s. By the end of 1956, more than 150,000 Kazakhs had been returned to Kazakhstan under this program (*Pod grifom sekretnosti*, 10). See also Bruce F. Adams, "Reemigration from Western China to the USSR, 1954–1962," in *Migration,*

Homeland, and Belonging in Eurasia, ed. Cynthia J. Buckley and Blair A. Ruble (Washington, DC, 2008), 183–203.

103. RGASPI f. 558, op. 11, d. 40, l. 87 (Cable from Stalin and Molotov to Eliava, February 13, 1931), in SDA.

104. APRK f. 141, op. 1, d. 4577, ll. 61–63.

6. KAZAKHSTAN AND THE POLITICS OF HUNGER, 1931–34

1. Duysen Asanbaev, "Kösh songïnda köz büldïrap," in *Qïzïldar qïrghïnï*, 23.

2. Sëden Mëlïmülï, "Amaldap zhürïp zhan baqtïq," in ibid., 143–44.

3. Zeitïn Aqïshev, "Bïlïsin münï ürpaktar," in ibid., 17.

4. APRK f. 141, op. 1, d. 5192, ll. 129–31 (Sovet narodnykh komissarov g. Moskva, tt. Molotovu, Sulimovu, Grin'ko, Iakovlevoi. Dokladnaia zapiska. "O neobkhodimykh finansovykh meropriiatiiakh v sviazi s nedorodami, otkochevkami i pereseleniiami khoziaistv, May 11, 1932) in TKN, 174.

5. GARF f. 6985, op. 1, d. 3, l. 30 (Stenogramma besedy tov. Kiseleva s raionnymi rabotnikami KASSR, June 18, 1934)

6. F. I. Goloshchekin, "Eshche raz o putiakh razvitiia zhivotnovodstva i ob opportunistakh na etom fronte," *Narodnoe khoziaistvo Kazakstana,* no. 8–9 (1931): 28.

7. On the turn to police repression to cope with the rising social disorder provoked by the collectivization, see Paul Hagenloh, *Stalin's Police* (Washington, DC, 2009); and David R. Shearer, *Policing Stalin's Socialism* (New Haven, 2009).

8. In 1928, a party health specialist noted that Kazakhstan's per capita expenditures on health were among the lowest in the Soviet Union. Should an epidemic hit Kazakhstan, he warned, it would have the makings of a "perfect storm." See Vilenskii, *Zdravookhranenie v Kazakstane,* 4. On public health campaigns in Kazakhstan under Stalin, see Michaels, *Curative Powers.*

9. TsGARK f. 30, op. 6, d. 207, l. 2.

10. On the national territorial delimitation as the point at which the normative relationship between ethnicity and territory became institutionalized, see Reeves, *Border Work,* chap. 2.

11. GARF f. R-1235, op. 141, d. 1007, l. 4 (Report on the condition of animal husbandry in the Kazakh ASSR, November 28, 1931). Specifically, the commission calculated that meat procurements and the flight of Kazakhs and their animals across borders accounted for no more than 11.28 million of these losses, with the remaining 17.5 million losses due to the errors of local officials and razbazarivanie.

12. Ibid., 3.

13. Asanbaev, "Kösh songïnda köz büldïrap," 19.

14. Dëmetken Shotbaev, "Ölgender kömusiz zhata beretïn," *Angïz adam* 64, no. 4 (2013).

15. TsGARK f. 30, op. 7, d. 108, ll. 58–60ob. (Dokladnaia zapiska kraevogo prokurora Sibiri sekretariu Zapsibrkraikoma VKP[b] R. I. Eikhe 'O stikhiinom pereselenii v predely Zapadno-Sibirskogo kraia kazakhov iz KazASSR i polozhenii pereselivshikhsia v krae,' March 29, 1932), in NKG, 127.

16. RGAE f. 7486, op. 37, d. 154, l. 158 (Pis'mo zaveduiushchei zhensektorom Kliuchevskogo raiona Zapadno-Sibirskogo kraia Biriukovoi v kraiispolkom o golodaiushchikh bezhentsakh iz Kazakhstana, March 1932), in GVS, vol. 1, book 2:132.

17. TsGARK f. 44, op. 14, d. 549, ll. 156–59 (Dokladnaia zapiska S. Mendesheva v Kazkraikom VKP[b] i SNK KazSSR o polozhenii otkochevnikov v Karakalpakii, October 1933), in NKG, 251.

18. APRK f. 141, op. 1, d. 5233, ll. 8–9 (Zaiavlenie politicheskikh ssyl'nykh V. A. Iogansena, Iu. N. Podbel'skogo, O. V. Selikhovoi, P. P. Semenin-Tkachenko, A. F. Flegontova v Presidium Tsentral'nogo ispolnitel'nogo komiteta SSSR, February 1, 1932), in KSKK, 109.

19. APRK f. 141, op. 1, d. 5217, ll. 84–88 (Sekretariu kraikoma Mirzoianu: Otryvok iz doklada zav. Sektorom partraboty v tsvetnoi promyshlennosti narskogo July 3, 1933), in *Noveishaia istoriia Kazakhstana,* ed. K. Karazhanov and A. Takenov (Almaty, 1998), 1:267–68.

20. Kamil Ikramov, *Delo moego ottsa* (Moscow, 1991), 97.

21. Victor Serge, *Memoirs of a Revolutionary,* trans. from French by Peter Sedgwick with George Paizis (New York, 1951, repr. 2012), 349–50.

22. RGAE f. 7486, op. 37, d. 154, l. 158, in GVS, vol. 1, book 2:131–32.

23. Pianciola, "Famine in the Steppe," 164 (citing GARF f. 6985, op. 1, d. 7, ll. 101–99).

24. At the end of 1932, a report concluded that the work to sedentarize the republic's nomadic population was far from completion. See TsGARK f. 1179, op. 1, d. 37, ll. 1–25 (Iz proizvodstvenno-finansovogo otcheta Kaznarkomzema 'O provedennykh meropriiati-iakh po osedaniiu trudiashchegosia kochevogo i polukochevogo naseleniia Kazakhstana za 1932 god,' after December 31, 1932), in KSKK, 562–64.

25. *Kazakstanskaia pravda,* May 15, 1933, 3.

26. APRK f. 141, op. 17, d. 465, l. 150 (Letter to Kazkraikom VKP[b] Roshal' from the head of the SOU PP OGPU, April 1930).

27. Allaniiazov and Taukenov, *Poslednii rubezh zashchitnikov nomadizma,* 358.

28. See, for instance, David Arnold, *Famine* (New York, 1988), 85–86; and Ó Gráda, *Famine,* 52–56.

29. APRK f. 141, op. 1, d. 5192, ll. 21–21ob. (Pis'mo sekretaria Zapadno-Sibirskogo kraikoma VKP[b] Zaitseva M. sekretariu Kazkraikoma VKP[b] Goloshchekinu F. o tiazhelom polozhenii kazakhskikh otkochevshchikov, August 2, 1932), in TKN, 365–66.

30. APRK f. 141, op. 1, d. 5208, ll. 15–16 (Doklad prokuratury i narsuda Maksimo-Gor'kovskogo raiona o prichinakh sokrashcheniia pogolov'ia skota za 1931 g., massovom begstve naseleniia i prodovol'stvennykh zatrudneniiakh v raione, January 31, 1932), in TKA, 2:51.

31. Later generations of Soviet historians reiterated this explanation, portraying the flight of starving Kazakhs as a "political act" spearheaded by "bais." See Tursunbaev, *Pobeda kolkhoznogo stroia v Kazakhstane,* 144.

32. TsGARK f. 30, op. 7, d. 108, ll. 58–60ob., in NKG, 128–29.

33. Nicholas Werth, *Cannibal Island,* trans. from French Steven Rendall (Princeton, 2007), 33.

34. TsGARK f. 30, op. 7, d. 108, ll. 58–60ob., in NKG, 129. Similarly, in the Middle Volga, where many Kazakhs fled, there were instances where Kazakhs were prohibited from entering cafeterias or clubs or blocked from receiving their salaries. See APRK f. 141, op. 1, d. 5192, l. 107 (Iz pis'ma S. Mendesheva sekretariu Kazkraikoma VKP[b] F. I. Goloshchekinu predsedateliu Sovnarkoma U. I. Isaevu, March 26, 1932), in NKG, 123.

35. GANO f. 3p, op. 2, d. 205, ll. 72–73 (Dokladnaia zapiska predstavitelia Vostochno-Kazakhstanskogo obkoma VKP[b] Zapsibkraikomu i Aleiskomu raikomu partii o nasil'stvennom vozvrashchenii otkochevnikov iz Zapadnoi Sibiri v Kazakhstan, March 31, 1932), in IIVTK, 19.

36. Ibid., 20.

37. TsDNI VKO f. 15p, op. 1, d. 1, l. 52–54ob. (Iz protokola no. 4 zasedaniia biuro Vostochno-Kazakhstanskogo obkoma VKP[b] o vozvrashchenii obratno otkochevnikov, March 11, 1932) in ibid., 14.

38. GANO f. 1353, op. 3, d. 49, l. 179 (Otnoshenie zapsibkraizdrava upravleniiu Oms-koi zheleznoi dorogi s trebovaniem vypolnit' postanovlenie kraiispolkoma ob organizatsii izoliatsionno-propusknykh punktov, February 22, 1932), in *Gonimye golodom,* ed. V. S. Poznanskii (Almaty, 1995), 52.

39. On Eikhe's biography, see Werth, *Cannibal Island,* 28–29.

40. APRK f. 141, op. 1, d. 5192, ll. 17–20 (Pis'mo pervogo sekretaria Kazakhskogo kraikoma VKP[b] F. I. Goloshchekina pervomu sekretariu Zapadno-Sibirskogo kraikoma VKP[b] R. I. Eikhe o vozvrashchenii kazakhskogo naseleniia, otkochevavshego v zapadnuiu Sibir', March 20, 1932), in GVS, vol. 1, book 2:271–72.

41. APRK f. 141, op. 17, d. 465, l. 330 (Letter to Goloshchekin from the PP OGPU for the KASSR Danilovskii, August 27, 1931).

42. APRK f. 141, op. 17, d. 465, l. 41 (Letter to Goloshchekin from the vice PP OGPU for the KASSR Al'shanskii, June 5, 1930).

43. Ohayon, *Sédentarisation des Kazakhs*, 291–93.

44. Ibid., 286.

45. APRK f. 141, op. 1, d. 5192, ll. 42–43 (Pis'mo sekretaria Zapadno-Sibirskogo kraikoma VKP[b] Eikhe sekretariu Kazakhskogo kraikoma VKP[b] F. I. Goloshchekinu, September 3, 1932), in NKG, 117–18.

46. APRK f. 141, op. 1, d. 5192, ll. 45–46 (Iz dokladnoi zapiski upolnomochennogo Izenbaeva Vostochno-Kazakhstanskomu obkomu VKP[b] i oblastnomu ispolnitel'nomu komitetu ob otkochevnikakh v Sibiri, March 29, 1932), in NKG, 133.

47. APRK f. 141, op. 17, d. 605, l. 95 (Goloshchekin to Eikhe, undated, probably March 1932).

48. APRK f. 141, op. 1, d. 5192, l. 39 (Protokol no. 97 zasedaniia biuro Kazkraikoma VKP[b]), in NKG, 134–35.

49. Ohayon, *Sédentarisation des Kazakhs*, 167. In December 1932, Soviet authorities took further steps to regulate population movement, introducing an internal passport system. See David R. Shearer, "Elements Near and Alien: Passportization, Policing, and Identity in the Stalinist State, 1932–1952," *Journal of Modern History* 76, no. 4 (2004): 835–81.

50. RGASPI f. 17, op. 42, d. 34, ll. 85–86 (Protokol no. 107 [osobaia papka] zasedaniia biuro Kazakhskogo kraikoma VKP[b] o tiazhelom prodovol'stvennom polozhenii v riade raionov Kazakhstana, July 2, 1932), in GVS, vol. 1, book 2:275.

51. APRK f. 141, op. 1, d. 5192, ll. 27–28 (Postanovlenie biuro Karagandinskogo gorkoma VKP[b] "O bor'be s epidemicheskimi zabolevaniiami," September 15, 1932), in IIDK, 524–26.

52. On the processing of special settlers, see Werth, *Cannibal Island*, 173.

53. Medical practitioners' efforts to help starving Kazakhs were hampered by the fact that medical research on the effects of starvation was not possible in the Soviet Union in the early 1930s. In the Soviet Union, hunger became a legitimate area of research only in World War II, when medical practitioners began to explore how to identify the victims of hunger and treat them. On this point, see Rebecca Manley, "Nutritional Dystrophy," in *Hunger and War*, ed. Wendy Z. Goldman and Donald Filtzer (Bloomington, 2015), 206–64.

54. TsDNIVKO f. 15p, op. 4, d. 110, ll. 133–69, 180–84, 186 (Akt, sostavlennyi brigadoi Vostochno-Kazakhstanskoi oblastnoi KK RKI po itogam obsledovaniia ustroistva otkochevnikov, ikh obsluzhivaniia, bor'by s bezprizornost'iu, October 26, 1932), in IIVTK, 70.

55. TsGARK f. 1179, op. 1, d. 47, ll. 157–59 (Dokladnaia zapiska v SNK KazASSR ob ustroistve vozvrativshikhsia bezhentsev v Karagandinskoi oblasti, September 3, 1932), in NKG, 173–74.

56. RGASPI f. 17, op. 3, d. 880, l. 7 (Iz protokola no. 96 zasedaniia Politburo TsK VKP[b] ob okazanii pomoshchi kazakhskim khoziastvam, vozvrashchaiushchimsia iz drugikh raionov, April 16, 1932), in GVS, vol. 1, book 2:272. From February to July 1932, the Politburo authorized a total of 320,000 tons of grain for food to regions including Ukraine, the North Caucasus, and Kazakhstan. See Wheatcroft and Davies, *Years of Hunger*, 214–15.

57. TsDNIVKO f. 15p, op. 4, d. 110, ll. 28–29 (Svodka Vostochno-Kazakhstanskogo oblastnogo otdela zdravookhraneniia o medobsledovanii otkochevnikov, June 3, 1932), in IIVTK, 50.

58. TsDNIVKO f. 578, op. 1, d. 17, ll. 14–20 (Iz proekta rezoliutsii prezidiuma Vostochno-Kazakhstanskoi oblastnoi KK RKI po voprosu neudovletvoritel'noi organizatsii priema otkochevnikov-vozvrashchentsev, not before May 13, 1932), in IIVTK, 23.

59. APRK f. 719, op. 4, d. 69, l. 130 (Report on the progress of the settlement of otkochevniki in East Kazakhstan oblast, May 20, 1932).

60. TsGARK f. 5s, op. 21s, d. 95, ll. 51–54 (Dokladnaia zapiska instruktora VTsIK Kushaevu KazTsIKu o rezul'tatakh proverki raboty sovetov v Aktiubinskoi oblasti po vozvrashcheniiu i khoziaistvennomu ustroistvu otkochevavshikh khoziaistv, August 27, 1932), in NKG, 171.

61. APRK f. 141, op. 1, d. 5757, l. 8 (Postanovlenie biuro Kazkraikoma VKP[b] "O spetspereselentsakh," March 31, 1933), in IIDK, 577.

62. RGASPI f. 17, op. 42, d. 34, ll. 5–7 (Protokol no. 195 [osobaia papka] zasedaniia sekretariata Kazakhskogo kraikoma VKP[b] o prodovol'stvennykh zatrudneniiakh v nekotorykh raionakh kraia, February 5, 1932), in GVS, vol. 1, book 2:208.

63. RGASPI f. 17, op. 42, d. 34, ll. 85–86 (Postanovlenie biuro Kazakhskogo kraikoma VKP[b] o massovom golode v Kazakhstane, June 2, 1932), in TSD, 3:404–6.

64. TsGARK f. 30, op. 6, d. 34, l. 59 (On the state of animal husbandry in Kazakhstan and necessary measures, July 8, 1932).

65. On Stalin's relative lack of attention to livestock matters, see R. W. Davies, "Stalin as Economic Policy Maker," in *Stalin*, ed. Sarah Davies and James Harris (Cambridge, 2006), 121–39.

66. APRK f. 141, op. 17, d. 605, l. 111 (Goloshchekin to the Central Committee and Stalin, December 31, 1932).

67. Pitirim Sorokin, *Man and Society in Calamity* (New York, 1942, repr. 1968), 68.

68. Shayakhmetov, *Silent Steppe*, 163.

69. GAAO f. 1, op. 13, d. 82, ll. 7–8 (Informatsiia ob ustroistve otkochevnikov poselka Burlo-Tiube, April 1933), in TKN, 299.

70. Köken Belgïbaev, "Taghdïr tälkeghï," in *Qïzïldar qïrghïnï*, 84.

71. Aqïshev, "Bïlïsin mŭnï ŭrpaktar," 15.

72. L. S. Aktaeva, "Dokumenty o tragicheskoi stranitse Kazakhskogo naroda v fondakh Tsentral'nogo gosudarstvennogo arkhiva respubliki Kazakhstan," in *Sbornik materialov*, ed. B. G. Aiagana (Astana, 2012), 312–13.

73. TsGARK f. 30, op. 7, d. 108, ll. 58–60ob. (Dokladnaia zapiska kraevogo prokurora Sibiri sekretariu Zapsibrkraikoma VKP[b] R. I. Eikhe "O stikhiinom pereselenii v predely Zapadno-Sibirskogo kraia kazakhov iz KazASSR i polozhenii pereselivshikhsia v krae," March 29, 1932), in NKG, 127.

74. Serge, *Memoirs of a Revolutionary*, 350.

75. Vera Rikhter, "Puteshestvie iz g. Karkaralinska v. g. Moskvu," in TKN, 140.

76. Ibid., 141.

77. See, for instance, GANO f. R-47, op. 5, d. 174, ll. 184–87 (Dokladnaia zapiska organov iustitsii Zapadno-Sibirskogo kraia o bor'be s proiavleniiami velikoderzhavnogo shovinizma v otnoshenii kazakhov-migrantov, March 25, 1933) in GVS, 2:583–86.

78. GAAO f. 1, op. 15, d. 60, ll. 2–7 (Iz dokladnoi zapiski zamestiteliu predsedatelia Komissii ispolneniia pri SNK KazASSR tov. Egorovy "O polozhenii v Chuiskom raione," March 12, 1933), in TKN, 277.

79. I borrow the terms "survivor cannibalism" and "murder cannibalism" from the work of Cormac Ó Gráda. See *Eating People Is Wrong, and Other Essays on Famine, Its Past, and Its Future* (Princeton, 2015), 15.

80. TsA FSB f. 2, op. 11, d. 551, ll. 36–38 (Iz spetssvodki Operativnogo otdela Glavnogo upravleniia raboche-krest'ianskoi militsii pri OGPU SSSR "O liudoedstve i ubiistvakh s tsel'iu liudoedstva," March 31, 1933), in GVS, 2:424.

81. Ghalym Akhmedov, "Sol bïr auïr zhïldarda," in Qïzïldar qïrghïnï, 32. References to cannibalism are particularly prevalent in oral history accounts of the Kazakh famine. See the oral histories collected in Qïzïldar qïrghïnï and Angïz adam 64, no. 4 (2013).

82. See, for example, Nŭrsŭltan Äbdïghanŭlï, "Qïzïl qïrghïn qasïretï," in Qïzïldar qïrghïnï, 38; and Shayakhmetov, Silent Steppe, 163.

83. D. Äuelbekov, "Tïshqan etïn zhegïzgen," in Qïzïldar qïrghïnï, 75.

84. This bread recalls the "famine bread" often eaten by Russian peasants during times of hunger. Famine bread was commonly formed by mixing a weed, goosefoot (lebeda), with other ingredients including clay or rye. See Robbins, Famine in Russia, 1891–1892, 12.

85. GAAO f. 1, op. 15, d. 60, ll. 2–7, in TKN, 277.

86. GARF f. 1235, op. 141, d. 1533, ll. 265–68 (Doklad chlena VTsIK, zamestitelia predsedatelia SNK KASSR Kulumbetova, predsedateliu VTsIK Kalininu M. I. o sostoianii pomoshchi besprizornym detiam, October 1, 1933), in IIVTK, 237.

87. TsGARK f. 509, op. 1, d. 181, l. 173.

88. APRK f. 141, op. 1, d. 5233, ll. 8–9 (Zaiavlenie politicheskikh ssyl'nykh V. A. Iogansena, Iu. N. Podbel'skogo, O. V. Selikhovoi, P. P. Semenin-Tkachenko, A. F. Flegontova v Presidium Tsentral'nogo ispolnitel'nogo komiteta SSSR, February 1, 1932), in KSKK, 108.

89. Mëlïmŭlï, "Amaldap zhürïp zhan baqtïq," 144.

90. On child abandonment as "a kind of brutal group survival strategy," see Ó Gráda, Famine, 61–62.

91. Some accounts suggest that many Kazakh families chose to abandon their daughters while keeping their sons. As a result, young women may have fared worse in the disaster than young men. See Mikhailov, Khronika velikogo dzhuta, 159.

92. APRK f. 141, op. 1, d. 5233, ll. 8–9, in KSKK, 108.

93. TsGARK f. 509, op. 1, d. 206, l. 145 (May 19, 1933).

94. Serge, Memoirs of a Revolutionary, 350.

95. GAAO f. 1, op. 15, d. 60, ll. 2–7, in TKN, 275–76.

96. TsGARK f. 1179, op. 5, d. 8, ll. 29–29ob. (Letter to Kazkraikom secretary comrade Goliudov from the road-transportation department, February 25, 1933).

97. The image of the arba occurs frequently in the oral history accounts collected in Qïzïldar qïrghïnï. In her study of famine in North China, the historian Kathryn Edgerton-Tarpley refers to such images as "icons of starvation," tropes that reappear as people try to make sense of the disaster (Tears from Iron [Berkeley, 2008]).

98. See, for instance, Äbdïghanŭlï, "Qïzïl qïrghïn qasïretï," 40. On the importance of burial rituals to the Kazakhs, see Bruce G. Privratsky, Muslim Turkistan (Richmond, 2001), 96.

99. GAAO f. 1, op. 15, d. 60, ll. 2–7, in TKN, 275–76.

100. Aqïshev, "Bïlïsin münï ŭrpaktar," 16.

101. RGAE f. 8043, op. 11, d. 59, l. 24 (Zapiska po priamomu provodu zamestitelia Narkoma tiazheloi promyshlennosti SSSR A. P. Serebrovskogo i predsedatelia TsK Soiuza rabochikh dobychi i obrabotki metallov SSSR S. V. Vasil'eva v TsK VKP[b] o neudovletvoritel'nom pitanii rabochikh Balkhashstroia, June 17, 1932), in GVS, vol. 1, book 2:134.

102. Agnessa Mironova-Korol, Agnessa (Bloomington, 2012), 49.

103. Ibid., 51.

104. Soviet historians accorded the September 17th decision a central role in their retelling of collectivization, lauding it as a "historic" ruling that helped right the errors

of previous policies. See Sh. Khasanov, "Pervye pobedy," in *Karagandinskaia oblast' k 15-i godovshchine Kazakstana* (Petropavlovsk, 1935), 11.

105. RGASPI f. 17, op. 162, d. 13, ll. 116–17 (Postanovlenie Politburo TsK VKP[b] "O sel'skom khoziaistve i, v chastnosti, zhivotnovodstve Kazakhstana," September 17, 1932), in TSD, 3, 483–84.

106. See, for instance, Kŭramïsov, "Introduction," in Zveriakov, *Ot kochevaniia k sotsializmu*, vii. In his introduction, Kŭramïsov offers up some corrections to Zveriakov's views of sedentarization (composed a few months earlier), including a critique of the "Sedentarization on the Basis of Full Collectivization" slogan.

107. APRK f. 141, op. 1, d. 5235, ll. 139–40.

108. On how the kraikom modeled this campaign after the Kuban, see APRF f. 30, op. 40, d. 83, ll. 139–139ob. (Shifrotelegramma sekretaria Kazakhskogo kraikoma VKP[b] M. I. Kakhiani I. V. Stalinu o neobkhodimosti izbiratel'no primeniat' repressivnye mery v Iuzhnom Kazakhstane, November 20, 1932) in GVS, 2:219.

109. RGASPI f. 558, op. 11, d. 45, l. 31 (Shifrotelegramma Stalina I. V. v Alma-Atu, November 21, 1932), in SDA.

110. On the number of districts blacklisted, see TsA FSB f. 2, op. 10, d. 514, ll. 295–98 (Spetssvodka Sekretno-politicheskogo otdela OGPU SSSR o khode khlebozagotovok i otkochevkakh v Kazakhstane, December 7, 1932), in GVS, 2:246.

111. TsA FSB RF f. 2, op. 10, d. 514, ll. 403–6 (Spetssoobshchenie no. 7 Sekretno-politicheskogo otdela OGPU ob itogakh vyseleniia iz raionov Kubani, December 31, 1932), in TSD, 3:612–13. On the Kuban deportations, see also Martin, *Affirmative Action Empire*, 325–26.

112. "Ot"ezd t. F. I. Goloshchekina," *Kazakstanskaia pravda*, February 8, 1933.

113. "O no. 7 Bol'shevika Kazakstana," *Kazakstanskaia pravda*, August 1, 1933. (This article also discussed efforts to correct errors in a recent issue of the republic's party journal. Hence the title.)

114. Yuri Slezkine, *The House of Government: A Saga of the Russian Revolution* (Princeton, 2017), 435.

115. Isaev, "Pis'mo Stalinu,"*Partiinaia zhizn' Kazakstana*, no. 6 (1990): 83–89, republished in NKG, 162.

116. RGASPI f. 81, op. 3, d. 419, ll. 55–57 (Letter from Goloshchekin to Stalin and Molotov, August 4, 1933), in *Sovetskoe rukovodstvo. Perepiska, 1928–1941*, ed. Franco Venturi (Moscow, 1999), 245.

117. Ibid., 247. For Goloshchekin's second letter, see RGASPI f. 81, op. 3, d. 419, ll. 55–57 (Letter from Goloshchekin to Molotov, September 20, 1933) in *Sovetskoe rukovodstvo. Perepiska, 1928–1941*, 258–59.

118. Culled from LMK and Panza Altïnbekov, *Aqiqat pen qasïret (1933–1938 zhzh.)* (Astana, 2001).

119. APRK f. 141, op. 1, d. 5827, ll. 17–22 (Letter from Mirzoian to Kaganovich, February 24, 1933) in LMK, 24.

120. Ibid., 23.

121. APRK f. 141, op. 1, d. 5827, ll. 44–47 (Iz dokladnoi zapiski I. V. Stalinu, L. M. Kaganovichu o khode posevnoi v Alma-Atinskoi i Vostochno-Kazakhstanskoi oblastiakh, April 21, 1933) in LMK, 39.

122. See, for example, Altïnbekov, *Aqiqat pen qasïret*. Zh. Abylkhozhin is one of the few Kazakhstani historians to note Mirzoian's brutality. See his article, "Inertsiia mifotvorchestva v osveshchenii sovetskoi i postsovetskoi istorii Kazakhstana," in *Nauchnoe znanie i mifotvorchestvo v sovremennoi istoriografii Kazakhstana*, ed. N. E. Masanov, Zh. B. Abylkhozin, and I. V. Erofeeva (Almaty, 2007), 251–52.

123. APRK f. 141, op. 1, d. 5827 ll. 17–22, in LMK, 22.

124. APRK f. 141, op. 1, d. 5827, ll. 44–47, in LMK, 40. In the original letter, "teary telegrams" is in all capital letters.

125. TsGARK f. 1179, op. 5, d. 8, l. 253.

126. TsDNI VKO f. 578, op. 1, d. 8, l. 51 (Letter from the kraikom to all provinces and districts, April 19, 1933).

127. TsGARK f. 1179, op. 1, d. 14, l. 10.

128. TsGARK f. 30, op. 6, d. 207, l. 2 (Stenogram of a meeting of the Rïsqŭlov commission, February 22, 1933).

129. Ibid., l. 19.

130. APRK f. 141, op. 1, d. 5724, l. 209 (Letter from Mirzoian to Bauman, Sredazbiuro, March 12, 1933), in Altïnbekov, *Aqiqat pen qasrïret (1933–1938 zhzh.)*, 191.

131. APRK f. 141, op. 1, d. 5724, l. 25 (Letter from Mirzoian to Ural'sk and Petropavlovsk provinces, March 12, 1933), in Altïnbekov, *Aqiqat pen qasrïret (1933–1938 zhzh.)*, 192.

132. APRK f. 141, op. 1, d. 5877, ll. 33–38.

133. The issue of how Kazakh refugees were treated in neighboring republics has been the subject of lively debate among Kazakhstani scholars. In "Asïra sïlteu saldarï," *Aqtandaqtar aqiqatï*, 53–55. Kiikbai Zhaulin argues that officials in Soviet Uzbekistan worked to poison the children of Kazakh refugees during the famine. The treatment of Kazakh refugees in Western Siberia has received mixed reviews. Some allege discrimination, while others praise the "heroic" actions of those who labored to assist Kazakh refugees despite the difficult economic conditions in Western Siberia. For the former view, see "Introduction," IIVTK. For the latter view, see M. P. Mal'sheva and V.S. Poznanskii, *Kazakhi-bezhentsy ot goloda v Zapadnoi Sibiri (1931–1934 gg.)* (Almaty, 1999).

134. TsGARK f. 1179, op. 5, d. 7, l. 3.

135. RGASPI f. 62, op. 2, d. 3135, l. 42 (Ryskulov to TsK KP Uzbekistana t. Ikramov, with copy to Sr. Azbiuro TsK VKP[b] T. Bauman, July 3, 1933).

136. GARF P-1235, op. 141, d. 1533, l. 138ob.

137. APRK f. 141, op. 1, d. 5828, ll. 81–85 (Dokladnaia zapiska I. V. Stalinu o zhivotnovodstve, December 17, 1933), in LMK, 63.

138. TsGARK f. 1179, op. 5, d. 9, l. 6 (Letter to Kazpredstavitel'stvo Toktabaev from Sovnarkom [Sluchak], Narkomfin [Bezsonov], and Predkomissii [Egorov], March 22, 1933).

139. GARF f. 6985, op. 1, d. 3, ll. 117–20 and 254 (Stenogram of VTsIK Commission for Sedentarization, 1934). By 1935, party officials proudly trumpeted the increase in smallpox vaccinations in Kazakhstan as a "great victory." See Gusev and Pavlov, *15 let Kazakskoi ASSR, 1920–1935*, 103.

140. APRK 141, op. 1, d. 5827, ll. 181–88 (Pis'mo ot Mirzoiana k Stalinu i Kaganovichu. "O rabote plenuma Kazkraikoma VKP[b]," July 30, 1933), in LMK, 47.

141. GARF f. 6985, op. 1, d. 3, l. 21 (Stenogram of VTsIK Commission for Sedentarization, 1934).

142. TsGARK f. 30, op. 6, d. 175, l. 7 (Stenogram of a meeting of the Rïsqŭlov Commission, February 22, 1933).

143. Ibid., l. 1.

144. Ibid., l. 37.

145. GARF f. R-5446, op. 18, d. 469, ll. 192–93 (Postanovlenie SNK SSSR no. 1239/277ss "O zakupke skota dlia Kazakhstana," June 17, 1933), in GVS, 2:639.

146. TsGARK f. 74, op. 11, d. 219, l. 4.

147. TsGARK f. 74, op. 11, d. 218, ll. 85ob.–86 (Report on the work for the organization of the return of Kazakh otkochevniki, July 13, 1935).

148. RGASPI f. 62, op. 2, d. 3135, l. 66ob. (Ryskulov to TsK KP Uzbekistana t. Ikramov, with copy to Sr. Azbiuro TsK VKP (b) T. Bauman, July 3, 1933).

CONCLUSION

1. Ibragim Khisamutdinov, "Prizvanie-pedagog," in *Stranitsy tragicheskikh sudeb*, ed. L. D. Degitaeva et al. (Almaty, 2002), 300.

2. Mëlïmülï, "Amaldap zhürïp zhan baqtïq," 143–44.

3. Nurtazina, "Great Famine of 1931–1933 in Kazakhstan," 116.

4. For statistics, see TsA FSB RF f. 2, op. 11, d. 1050, ll. 53–56, in TSD, 3:811.

5. Roy H. Behnke, Jr., "Reconfiguring Property Rights and Land Use," in *Prospects for Pastoralism in Kazakstan and Turkmenistan*, 76.

6. Out of 118 districts, only 48 had direct telephone connections with provincial centers. See APRK f. 141, op. 1, d. 5827, l. 32 (Dokladnaia zapiska I. V. Stalinu, L. M. Kaganovichu, V. M. Molotovu o sviazi, February 3, 1933 [from Mirzoian and Isaev]), in LMK, 32.

7. APRK f. 141, op. 1, d. 5827, ll. 17–22, in LMK, 24.

8. For the argument that the Soviet Union carried out a "striking leap" in state capacity and mobilization during the interwar period, see Kotkin, "Modern Times," 132.

9. RGASPI f. 82, op. 2, d. 670, ll. 11–14ob., in TSD, 3:508.

10. T. B. Balakaev, *Kolkhoznoe krest'ianstvo Kazakhstana v gody Velikoi Otechestvennoi voiny 1941–1945 gg.* (Alma-Ata, 1971).

11. O. A. Korbe, "Kul'tura i byt kazakhskogo kolkhoznogo aula (k 30-letiiu Kazakhskoi SSR)," *Sovetskaia etnografiia*, no. 4 (1950): 75.

12. Sarah Robinson and E. J. Milner-Gulland, "Contraction in Livestock Mobility Resulting from State Farm Reorganization," in *Prospects for Pastoralism in Kazakstan and Turkmenistan*, 133.

13. Korbe, "Kul'tura i byt kazakhskogo kolkhoznogo aula," 67–91.

14. According to the 1959 census, there were 753,600 "herders and shepherds" in the Soviet Union, although it did not break down this data by republic. See Elizabeth E. Bacon, *Central Asians under Russian Rule* (Ithaca, 1966), 120.

15. "Kolkhoz ornaghannan song," in *Qïzïldar qïrghïnï*, 83.

16. In 1926, just 2 percent of Kazakhs lived in cities, but by 1939 16 percent did. From 1926 to 1939, urbanization rates in Kazakhstan as a whole jumped from 9 percent to 28 percent, one of the highest rates in the USSR. See Robert J. Kaiser, *The Geography of Nationalism in Russia and the USSR* (Princeton, 1994), 122.

17. APRK f. 141, op. 1, d. 5828, ll. 81–85, in LMK, 63.

18. There are challenges to further investigations into the death toll for the Kazakh famine. The flight of starving refugees was far more extensive in the Kazakh famine than in other Soviet collectivization famines, and an accurate assessment of the Kazakh famine's death toll hinges on detailed work with population data in other Soviet republics, as well as in Xinjiang (where the first population census was conducted only in 1953). Some Kazakhstani scholars also allege that the 1926 Soviet census, the first systematic attempt to count the steppe's nomads, underestimated the republic's Kazakh population. Remembering the brutality of the 1916 conscription order, some Kazakhs sought to evade being counted (Talas Omarbekov, personal communication). Finally, the vital statistics registration system, which would provide data such as annual births and deaths crucial to an accurate tally of famine dead, was still in its infancy in the second half of the 1920s in Kazakhstan. On recent efforts to break down the death toll within Ukraine, see Serhii Plokhy, "Mapping the Great Famine" http://gis.huri.harvard.edu/images/pdf/MappingGreatUkrainianFamine.pdf.

19. See Asanbaev, "Kösh songïnda köz büldïrap," 19; Duysebek Säülebekülï, "Bastan qalay ötkïzdïkï," in *Qïzïldar qïrghïnï*, 196; and Nurtazina, "Great Famine of 1931–1933 in Kazakhstan," 124–25.

20. See, for instance, the plan to resettle thirteen thousand refugee households in south Kazakhstan province in TsGARK f. 30, op. 6, d. 227, l. 85 (Protokol zasedaniia Prezidiuma Iuzhno-kazakstanskogo oblastnogo ispolnitel'nogo komiteta, April 4, 1933).

21. On this point with reference to KarLag, see Kate Brown, "Gridded Lives," *American Historical Review* 106, no. 1 (2001): 17–48.

22. On the size of KarLag, see Barnes, *Death and Redemption*, 21–22.

23. Michael H. Westren, "Nations in Exile" (PhD diss., University of Chicago, 2012).

24. Nurtazina, "Great Famine of 1931–1933 in Kazakhstan," 116.

25. Ibid., 122.

26. Shayakhmetov, *Silent Steppe*, 250–51.

27. Roberto Carmack, "'A Fortress of the Soviet Home Front'" (PhD diss., University of Wisconsin, 2015).

28. The Kazakhstani scholar Nurbulat Masanov also identifies the famine as a turning point, arguing that at this moment the Kazakhs abandoned an identity based on household type and moved toward an understanding of being Kazakh rooted in ethnicity ("Mifologizatsiia problem etnogeneza kazakhskogo naroda i kazakhskoi nomadnoi kul'tury," in *Nauchnoe znanie i mifotvorchestvo*, 104).

29. Gabit Musrepov, "An Ethnographic Tale," in *The Stories of the Great Steppe: The Anthology of Modern Kazakh Literature,* ed. Rafis Abazov (2013), 26.

30. For Müsïrepov's biographical details, see Ashimbaev, *Kto est' kto v Kazakhstane*, 745.

31. For statistics on flight during the famine, see APRK f. 725, op. 1, d. 1268, l. 2 (Report on steps connected with the return of otkochveniki and their settlement in the Kazakh ASSR during the year 1933).

32. Korbe, "Kul'tura i byt kazakhskogo kolkhoznogo aula," 86. For the argument that Soviet rule reduced Kazakh clan identity to its instrumental aspect, see Edward Schatz, *Modern Clan Politics* (Seattle, 2004), chap. 3.

33. Nurtazina, "Great Famine of 1931–1933 in Kazakhstan," 113–14, 123–24.

34. Claudia Chang, "The Study of Nomads in the Republic of Kazakhstan," in *The Ecology of Pastoralism,* ed. P. Nick Nardulias (Boulder, 2015), 17–40.

35. On how the Nazarbayev regime uses archeology in the service of its goals, see Claudia Chang, *Rethinking Prehistoric Central Asia: Shepherds, Farmers, and Nomads* (London, 2018), 127–30.

36. Iu. Abdrakhmanov, *1916 Dnevniki. Pis'ma k Stalinu* (Frunze, 1991), 185.

37. In Kirgizia, 39,200 people are estimated to have perished due to famine. See Sh. D. Batyrbaeva, "Golod 1930-kh gg. v Kyrgyzstane," in *Sovetskie natsii i natsional'naia politika v 1920–1950-e gody*, ed. N. A. Volynchik (Moscow, 2014), 224.

38. There have been few studies of the collectivization of Central Asia by Western scholars. On Uzbekistan, see Marianne Kamp and Russell Zanca, "Recollections of Collectivization in Uzbekistan: Stalinism and Local Activism," *Central Asian Survey* 63, no. 1 (2017): 55–72.

39. On this pattern in Kirgizia, see Loring, "Building Socialism in Kyrgyzstan," 329–31.

40. Melissa Chakars, *The Socialist Way of Life in Siberia* (Budapest, 2014), 72.

41. Kenneth E. Linden, "Representations and Memory of the Collectivization Campaigns in the Mongolian People's Republic, 1929–1960" (MA thesis, Indiana University, 2015), 40.

42. By 1933, Kirgizia had just 22 percent of the livestock it had in 1929 (Loring, "Building Socialism in Kyrgyzstan," 338).

43. On population flight in Mongolia, see Linden, "Representations and Memory," 41. On Turkmenistan, see Edgar, *Tribal Nation*, 216. On Kirgizia, see Loring, "Building Socialism in Kyrgyzstan," 346–47. On Buriat-Mongolia, see Chakars, *Socialist Way of Life in Siberia*, 66–67.

44. Tsedendambyn Batbayar, "Stalin's Strategy in Mongolia, 1932–1936," *Mongolian Studies* 22 (1999): 1–17.

45. Daniel Rosenberg, "The Collectivization of Mongolia's Pastoral Production," *Nomadic Peoples*, no. 9 (1981): 23–39.

46. Niccolò Pianciola, "Stalinist Spatial Hierarchies," *Central Asian Survey* 36, no. 1 (2017): 73–92.

47. US Commission on the Ukrainian Famine, *Investigation of the Ukrainian Famine, 1932–1933: Report to Congress* (Washington, DC, 1998), 136.

48. For the text of the resolution, see Parliamentary Assembly, "Commemorating the Victims of the Great Famine (Holodomor) in the Former USSR," http://assembly.coe.int/nw/xml/XRef/Xref-XML2HTML-en.asp?fileid=17845&lang=en.

49. There is considerable confusion on this point in the literature. Anne Applebaum argues that certain decrees were directly solely at Ukraine, including border closures and the blacklisting of dozens of collective farms and villages (*Red Famine*, 353). In his study of Stalinist crimes, Norman Naimark asserts that "Kazakhs were not prevented from escaping famine-struck regions or seeking aid in the cities or towns" (*Stalin's Genocides*, 76). But these statements are not correct: border closures, blacklisting, the expulsion of famine refugees, and a host of other brutal tactics were used against starving Kazakhs.

50. Terry Martin argues that the closure of the Ukrainian and North Caucasus borders in January 1933 "clearly shows that Ukraine and Kuban were singled out for special treatment specifically because of the national interpretation of the famine" (*Affirmative Action Empire*, 307). But this action did not constitute a distinctive break from previous policy: Moscow had adopted similar (and more brutal) tactics toward starving Kazakh refugees in 1931 and 1932, blocking them from crossing into the RSFSR and slaughtering thousands of them on the Sino-Kazakh border.

51. For this argument, see Martin, *Affirmative Action Empire*, chap. 7.

52. Raphael Lemkin, *Axis Rule in Occupied Europe* (Washington, DC, 1944).

53. See United Nations Human Rights, Office of the High Commissioner, "Convention on the Prevention and Punishment of the Crimes of Genocide," http://www.ohchr.org/EN/ProfessionalInterest/Pages/CrimeOfGenocide.aspx.

54. Naimark, *Stalin's Genocides*, 21–24.

EPILOGUE

1. Nurtazina, "Great Famine of 1931–1933 in Kazakhstan," 127.

2. Chingiz Aitmatov, *The Day Lasts More Than a Hundred Years* (Bloomington, 1983).

3. For a discussion of how the term "mankurt" has been used in Kazakhstan, see Bhavna Dave, *Kazakhstan* (New York, 2007), chap. 3.

4. Contrast, for instance, with the Kirgiz, another former pastoral nomadic group, where just 36.9 percent claimed Russian proficiency (Kaiser, *Geography of Nationalism*, 270–71).

5. In 1989, the proportion of mixed families in Kazakhstan was 23.9 percent. For this statistic as well as cautions on how to interpret the figure, see Saule K. Ualiyeva and Adrienne L. Edgar, "In the Laboratory of Peoples' Friendship: Mixed People in Kazakhstan from the Soviet Era to the Present," in *Global Mixed Race*, ed. Rebecca C. King-O'Riain et al. (New York, 2014), 72.

6. Central Intelligence Agency, *The World Factbook* (2017 figures), https://www.cia.gov/library/publications/the-world-factbook/geos/kz.html.

7. Unfortunately, A. V. Grozin's study of "the memory politics" of the Kazakh famine, *Golod 1932–1933 godov i politika pamiati v respublike Kazakhstan* (Moscow, 2014), is disappointing. It does not discuss key elements of the question, such as how Kazakhs remembered the famine privately, and it is based solely on published Russian-language sources.

8. For similar tensions in the Nazarbayev regime's portrayal of nuclear testing during the Soviet period in Kazakhstan, see Cynthia Werner and Kathleen Purvis-Roberts, "Cold War Memories and Post-Cold War Realities," in *Ethnographies of the State in Central Asia*, ed. Madeline Reeves et al. (Bloomington, 2013), 285–309.

9. *Karavan-Blitz*, October 16, 1994, 4.

10. I attended this May 2012 conference, as did numerous other experts on the Kazakh famine.

11. Nazarbayev noted: "But we should be wise in interpreting history and not allow the politicization of this theme" ("Vystuplenie Prezidenta Respubliki Kazakhstan N. A. Nazarbaeva na otkrytii monumenta pamiati zhertv goloda 1932–1933 godov," in *Sbornik materialov*, 9).

12. In 2013, Kazakhstan's Ministry of Culture published a seven-hundred-page document collection devoted to the Kazakh famine, *Tragediia kazakhskogo aula 1928–1934* (The Tragedy of the Kazakh Aul, 1928–1934). Several more volumes are planned, and the project is extensive, combining documents from state, party, and regional archives. The Presidential Archives has begun a project to tally the names of the famine dead. Information about the project can be found at http://asharshylyq.kz/?page_id=104&lang=ru. On efforts to uncover burial sites in Pavlodar province, see "V Pavlodare obnaruzheny novye mesta zakhoroneniia zhertv golodomora," *TengriNews*, May 30, 2012, http://ten-grinews.kz/kazakhstan_news/v-pavlodare-obnarujenyi-novyie-mesta-zahoroneniya-jertv-golodomora-215057/.

13. See Antipova, *Golod v SSSR: 1930–1934 gg.*; Kondrashin, *Golod 1932–1933 godov*; and Kondrashin, *Golod v SSSR 1929–1934*.

14. See, for instance, L. S. Aktaeva, "Dokumenty o tragicheskoi stranitse kazakhskogo naroda v fondakh Tsentral'nogo gosudarstvennogo arkhiva respubliki Kazakhstan," in *Sbornik materialov*, 312–13.

15. See "Astana Declaration of the OSCE Parliamentary Assembly and Resolutions Adopted at the Seventeen Annual Session," https://www.oscepa.org/documents/all-documents/annual-sessions/2008-astana/declaration-7/256-2008-astana-declaration-eng/file (the text of the resolution can be found on page 44).

16. For an example of one such critique, see A. Sadvakasov, "Paradoksy parlamentskoi assamblei OBSE," July 9, 2008, http://www.neweurasia.info/cgi-bin/datacgi/database.cgi?file=News&report=SingleArticleRu2005&ArticleID=0015270.

17. For the text of the resolution, see Parliamentary Assembly, "Commemorating the Victims of the Great Famine (Holodomor) in the former USSR," http://assembly.coe.int/nw/xml/XRef/Xref-XML2HTML-en.asp?fileid=17845&lang=en.

18. Zhasulan Kuzhekov, "Astana, nakonets, predlagaet otmechat' pamiat' o Golode, no 'bez politizatsii,'" May 20, 2010, https://rus.azattyq.org/a/Famine_Kazakhstan_/2047107.html.

19. See, for example, M. Mïrzakhmetov, *Qazaq qalay orïstandïrïldï* (Almaty, 1993). The book is titled "How the Kazakhs Were Russified."

20. Kuzhekov, "Astana, nakonets, predlagaet otmechat' pamiat'."

21. Talas Omarbekov, interview with author, Almaty, Kazakhstan, October 2007.

22. M. Kh. Asylbekov et al., eds., *Istoriia Kazakhstana s drevneishikh vremen do nashikh dnei*, 5 vols. (Almaty, 2010).

23. "Baibek v Almaty otkryl pamiatnik zhertvam golodomora," *TengriNews*, May 31, 2017, https://tengrinews.kz/kazakhstan_news/baybek-v-almatyi-otkryil-pamyatnik-jertvam-golodomora-319198/?_utl_t=fb.

24. For the figure of twenty-five million, see Tätimov and Aliev, *Derbestïmïz-demo-grafiiada*, 216. For similar argumentation, see Taldïbaev, "Ashtïqtan kelgen demografiialïq

apat." In 2017, the US Central Intelligence Agency estimated Kazakhstan's population at 18.5 million. See https://www.cia.gov/library/publications/the-world-factbook/geos/kz.html.

25. This repatriation project ran from 1991 to 2011, when it was terminated. See Anna Genina, "Claiming Ancestral Homelands" (PhD diss., University of Michigan, 2015); and Alexander C. Diener, *One Homeland or Two?* (Washington, DC, 2009).

26. In 2017, the Nazarbayev government announced plans for a "gradual transition" from the Cyrillic alphabet to the Latinate alphabet, concluding in 2025.

27. Genina, "Claiming Ancestral Homelands," 60.

Bibliography

I. UNPUBLISHED ARCHIVAL SOURCES

The Center for the Documentation of New History, Eastern Kazakhstan Oblast (TsDNIVKO). Semey

f. 1, Semipalatinskoi gubernskii komitet
f. 3, Semipalatinskoi okruzhnoi komitet
f. 15, Vostochno-Kazakhstanskii obkom VKP(b)
f. 17, Raboche-krest'ianskaia inspektsiia (Vostochno-Kazakhstanskaia oblKK RKP[b]-RKI)
f. 73, Semipalatinskii gubernskii ispolnitel'nyi komitet
f. 578, Vostochno-Kazakhstanskaia oblastnaia kontrol'naia komissiia
f. 598, Semipalatinskaia raionnaia komissiia po uluchsheniiu zhizni detei

Central State Archive of the Republic of Kazakhstan (TsGARK). Almaty

f. 5, Tsentral'nyi ispolnitel'nyi komitet Kirgizskoi (Kazakhskoi) ASSR
f. 19, Zaveduiushchii pereselencheskim upravleniem Semirechenskoi oblasti Glavnogo upravleniia zemleustroistva i zemledeliia
f. 30, Sovet narodnykh komissarov Kazakhskoi ASSR (Sovnarkom, SNK)
f. 44, Narodnyi komissariat raboche-krest'ianskoi inspektsii Kazakhskoi ASSR (NK RKI)
f. 64, Stepnoe general-gubernatorstvo
f. 74, Narodnyi komissariat zemledeliia Kazakhskoi ASSR (Narkomzem, NKZ)
f. 82, Narodnyi komissariat zdravookhraneniia Kazakhskoi ASSR
f. 135, Tsentral'naia komissiia po konfiskatsii imushchestva baev i polufeodalov
f. 247, Kazakhskii kraevoi kolkhoztsentr (Kazkraikolkhoztsentr)
f. 509, Tsentral'naia detskaia komissiia po uluchsheniiu zhizni detei pri TsIK Kazakhskoi ASSR (Kazdetkomissiia)
f. 698, Tsentral'noe statisticheskoe upravlenie Kazakhskoi ASSR
f. 938, Osobaia komissiia po zemleustroistvu iuzhnykh gubernii Kazakhskoi ASSR i Kirgizskoi ASSR pri VTsIK RSFSR (Osobkomzem)
f. 962, Gosudarstvennaia planovaia komissiia (Gosplan) pri Sovete narodnykh komissarov Kazakhskoi ASSR (1921–36)
f. 1000, Pereselencheskoe upravlenie pri Sovete narodnykh komissarov Kazakhskoi ASSR
f. 1179, Komitet po osedaniiu kochevogo i polukochevogo Kazakhskogo naseleniia pri Sovete narodykh komissarov Kazakhskoi ASSR
f. 1380, Narodnyi komissariat iustitsii Kazakhskoi ASSR (Narkomiust KazASSR)
f. 1431, Narodnyi komissariat snabzheniia Kazakhskoi ASSR (Narkomsnab KazASSR)

The President's Archive of the Republic of Kazakhstan (APRK). Almaty

f. 141, Tsentral'nyi komitet VKP(b) Kazakhskoi ASSR
f. 719, Narodnyi komissariat raboche-krest'ianskoi inspektsii KazASSR
f. 725, Upolnomochennyi komissii partiinogo kontrolia (1934–37) (UpolKPK pri TsiK VKP)
f. 811, Institut istorii partii pri TsK KPK

Russian State Archive of the Economy (RGAE). Moscow
f. 7486, Ministerstvo sel'skogo khoziaistva SSSR

Russian State Archive of Sociopolitical History (RGASPI). Moscow
f. 17, Tsentral'nyi komitet VKP(b)
f. 62, Sredneaziatskoe biuro TsK VKP(b) (Sredazbiuro)
f. 94, Fraktsiia RKP(b), VKP(b) vo Vserossiiskom tsentral'nom ispolnitel'nom
    komitete (VTsIK), na s″ezdakh Sovetov, v Prezidiume TsIK SSSR
f. 112, Politsektor upravleniia upolnomochennogo Narkomzema SSSR v Srednei Azii
f. 558, Stalin, Josef (1878–1953)
f. 607, Biuro po delam RSFSR pri TsK VKP(b)
f. 613, Tsentral'naia kontrol'naia komissiia VKP(b) (TsKK)

State Archive, Almaty Oblast (GAAO). Almaty
f. 142, Alma-Atinskoe okruzhnoe zemel'noe upravlenie
f. 591, Alma-Atinskaia okruzhnaia komissiia po konfiskatsii baiskikh khoziaistv pri
    Prezidiume Okrispolkoma
f. 374, Tsentral'naia kontrol'naia komissiia VKP(b)-Narodnyi komissariat raboche-
    krest'ianskoi inspektsii SSSR
f. 393, Narodnyi komissariat vnutrennikh del RSFSR
f. 3260, Federal'nyi komitet po zemel'nomu delu pri Prezidiume Vserossiiskogo
    tsentral'nogo ispolnitel'nogo komiteta
f. 1235, Vserossiiskii tsentral'nyi ispolnitel'nyi komitet RSFSR
f. 3316, Tsentral'nyi ispolnitel'nyi komitet SSSR
f. 6985, Komissia VTsIK po voprosam osedaniia kochevogo i polukochevogo naseleniia

II. PUBLISHED PRIMARY SOURCES

a) Newspapers
Kazakstanskaia pravda
Sovetskaia step'

b) Journals and Serials
Bol'shevik Kazakstana
Narodnoe khoziaistvo Kazakstana

c) Books, Stenograms, Articles
Abdairaeiymov, S., ed. *Golod v kazakhskoi stepi: Pis'ma trevogi i boli*. Almaty, 1991.
Abdrakhmanov, Iu. *1916. Dnevniki. Pis'ma k Stalinu*. Frunze, 1991.
Aitmatov, Chingiz. *The Day Lasts More Than a Hundred Years*. Bloomington, 1983.
Akachenok, A. P., ed. *Narymskaia ssylka (1906–1917 gg.): Sbornik dokumentov i materi-
    alov o ssyl'nykh bol'shevikakh*. Tomsk, 1970.
Amazholova, D. A., ed. *Rossiia i Tsentral'naia Aziia 1905–1925 gg. (sbornik dokumentov)*.
    Karaganda, 2005.
Antipova, O., ed. *Golod v SSSR: 1930–1934 gg*. Moscow, 2009.
Aristov, *Na bor'bu s zasukhoi i dzhutom*. Petropavlovsk, 1927.
Baitursynov, Akhmet [Akhmet Baytürsïnov]. "Revoliutsiia i kirgizy." In *Revoliutsiia v
    Srednei Azii glazami musul'manskikh bol'shevikov*, 109–14 (Oxford, 1985).
Berelovich, A., and V. Danilov, eds. *Sovetskaia derevnia glazami VChK-OGPU-NKVD:
    Dokumenty i materialy*. 4 vols. Moscow, 2003.
Bezhkovich, A. S. "Zemledelie ukraintsev-pereselentsev iuzhnoi Semipalatinskoi gubernii."
    In *Ukraintsy-pereselentsy*, ed. S. I. Rudenko, 99–178. Leningrad, 1930.

Boranbaeva, S. I., ed. *Tragediia Kazakhskogo naroda: Sbornik dokumentov i materialov: golod 20-kh, 30-kh godov XX veka v Kazakhstane*. Almaty, 2010.

Briskin, A. *Na iuzhturksibe (ocherki turksiba)*. Alma-Ata, 1930.

Briskin, A. *Stepi kazakskie (ocherki stepnogo Kazakstana)*. Kzyl-Orda, 1929.

Briskin, A. *V strane semi rek*. Moscow, 1926.

Chokin, Shafik [Shapïq Shokin]. *Chetyre vremeni zhizni: Vospominaniia i razmyshleniia*. Almaty, (1992) 1998.

Danilov, V., R. Manning, and L. Viola, eds. *Tragediia sovetskoi derevni: Kollektivizatsiia i raskulachivanie. Dokumenty i materialy 1927–1939*. 5 vols. Moscow, 1999–2006.

Degitaeva, L. D. *Levon Mirzoian v Kazakhstane: Sbornik dokumentov i materialov (1933–1938 gg.)*. Almaty, 2001.

Degitaeva, L. D., et al. *Stranitsy tragicheskikh sudeb: Sbornik vospominanii zhertv politicheskikh repressii v SSSR v 1920–1950-e gg*. Almaty, 2002.

Dulatbekov, N. O., ed. *Qarlag: Näubet zhïldardïng zhazïlmas zharasï (estelïktep)/Karlag: Vechnaia vol' surovykh vremen (vospominaniia)*. Karaganda, 2010.

Elübaev, Smaghŭl. *Aqboz üy*. Alma-Ata, 1989.

Fedorov, E., ed. *Kondrat'evshchina v Kazakstane: Sbornik*. Almaty, 1931.

Fell, E. Nelson. *Russian and Nomad: Tales of the Kirgiz Steppes*. New York, 1916.

Fiel'strur, F. "Skotovodstvo i kochevanie v chasti stepei Zapadnogo Kazakstana." In *Kazaki. Antropologicheskie ocherki, sbornik II*, ed. S. I. Rudenko. St. Petersburg, 1927.

Grigor'ev, V. *Narodopisanie: Orenburgskie kirgizy—ikh chestnost' i umen'e v torgovom dele*. 1864.

Gusev, N. I., and K. C. Pavlov, eds. *15 let Kazakskoi ASSR, 1920–1935*. Alma-Ata, 1935.

Herodotus. *The Histories*. Translated by Tom Holland. New York, 2014.

Ikramov, Kamil. *Delo moego ottsa: Roman-khronika*. Moscow, 1991.

Karagandinskaia oblast' k 15-i godovshchine Kazakstana: Sbornik statei. Petropavlovsk, 1935.

Karazhanov, K., and A. Takenov. *Noveishaia istoriia Kazakhstana: Sbornik dokumentov i materialov*. Almaty, 1998.

Khabdina, B., ed. *Qïzïldar qïrghïnï*. Almaty, 1993.

Kharuzin, A. N. *K voprosu o proiskhozhdenii kirgizskogo naroda*. Moscow, 1895.

Klid, Bohdan, and Alexander J. Motyl, eds. *The Holodomor Reader: A Sourcebook on the Famine of 1932–33 in Ukraine*. Edmonton, 2012.

Koigeldiev, M. K., et al., eds. *Krasnyi terror: Politicheskaia istoriia Kazakhstana (sbornik dokumental'nykh materialov politicheskikh repressii 20–50-kh godov XX veka)*. Almaty, 2008.

Kondrashin, Viktor, ed. *Golod v SSSR 1929–1934*. 3 vols. Moscow, 2011.

Kopelev, Lev. *Education of a True Believer*. New York, 1980.

Kozybaev, M. K., ed. *Nasil'stvennaia kollektivizatsiia i golod v Kazakhstane 1931–33 gg.: Sbornik dokumentov i materialov*. Almaty, 1998.

Kozybaev, M. K., ed. *Uraz Dzhandosov: Dokumenty i publitsistika (1918–1937 gg.)*. 2 vols. Almaty, 1999.

Kratkii istoricheskii ocherk Semipalatinskogo kraia (do 1917 goda). Semipalatinsk, 1929.

Krymov, D. B. *Zhivye bogatstva Kazakstana*. Moscow, 1928.

Kuznetsov, V. K., ed. *Kirgizskoe khoziaistvo v Akmolinskoi oblasti*. 5 vols. St. Petersburg, 1909–10.

Lan'ko, V. *Ves' Kazakstan: Spravochnaia kniga 1931 god*. Alma-Ata, 1931.

Larin, I. V. *Osobennosti sel'skogo khoziastva Adaevskogo uezda*. Alma-Ata, 1928.

Leonov, N. I. *V stepnykh prostorakh: Kak zhivut i chem promyshliaiut kirgizy (kazaki)*. Moscow, 1927.

Levshin, A. I. *Opisanie kirgiz-kazach'ikh, ili kirgiz-kaisatskikh, ord i stepei*. Almaty, (1833) 1996.

Maltusynov, S. N., ed. *Agrarnaia istoriia Kazakhstana (konets XIX–nachalo XX v.):*
Sbornik dokumenov i materialov. Almaty, 2006.
Materialy k otchetu Kazakskogo kraevogo komiteta VKP(b) na VII Vsekazakskoi partkon-
ferentsii v Kraikom VKP(b). Alma-Ata, 1930.
Mekebaev, Adam. *Kŭpiyä koima.* Alma-Ata, 1979.
Mŭqtarŭlï, Seisen, ed. *Kĕmpeske.* Almaty, 1997.
Musrepov, Gabit [Ghabit Müsïrepov]. "An Ethnographic Tale." In *The Stories of the*
Great Steppe: The Anthology of Modern Kazakh Literature, ed. Rafis Abazov,
15–27. San Diego, 2013.
Nukhat, A. *"Iurty-kochevki": (K rabote zhenskikh "krasnykh iurt")* Moscow, 1929.
Nurtazina, Nazira, ed. "Great Famine of 1931–1933 in Kazakhstan: A Contemporary's
Reminiscences." *Acta Slavica Iaponica* 32 (2012): 105–29.
Otchet kraevogo komiteta VI Vsekazakskoi partiinoi konferentsii. Kzyl-Orda, 1928.
Partiinoe stroitel'stvo v Kazakstane (sbornik rechei i statei). Moscow, 1930.
Petrov, V. I. *Miatezhnoe "serdtse" Azii: Sin'tszian. Kratkaia istoriia narodnykh dvizhenii i*
vospominaniia. Moscow, 2003 [reprint].
Polochanskii, E. A. *Za novyi aul-kstau.* Moscow, 1926.
Pomarev, M. I., ed. *Narod ne bezmolvstvuet.* Almaty, 1996.
Popov, V. "Pokhody dalekikh dnei." In *Chekisty Kazakhstana*, ed. N. I. Milovanov and
A. F. Minaichev, 37–62. Alma-Ata, 1971.
Poznanskii, V. S., ed. *Gonimye golodom: Dokumenty o sud'be desiatkov tysiach kazakhov*
bezhavshikh v Sibir' v nachale 30-kh godov. Almaty, 1995.
Qïdïrbekŭlï, Balghabek. *Alataü.* Alma-Ata, 1986.
Rudenko, S. I., ed. *Kazaki: Antropologicheskie ocherki, sbornik 2.* St. Petersburg, 1927.
Rodnevich, A. *Ot kolonial'nogo vyrozhdeniia k sotsialisticheskomu rastsvetu: O Kazak-*
stane. Moscow, 1931.
Ryskulov, T. R. [Tŭrar Rïsqŭlov]. *Sobranie sochinenii.* 3 vols. Almaty, 1997.
Saduaqasŭlï, Smaghŭl. *Ekĭ tomdïq shĭgharmalar zhinaghï.* Edited by M. Kŭl-Mŭkhammed.
2 vols. Almaty, 2003.
Sadvakasov, Smagul [Smaghŭl Saduaqasŭlï]. *Izbrannoe.* Edited by Kairgel'dy Akim-
bekov. Almaty, 1994.
Safarov, Georgii. *Kolonial'naia revoliutsiia (opyt Turkestana).* Alma-Ata, 1921.
Reprinted 1996.
Sed'maia Vsekazakskaia konferentsiia VKP(b): Stenograficheskii otchet. Alma-Ata, 1930.
Serge, Victor. *Memoirs of a Revolutionary.* Translated by Peter Sedgwick with George
Paizis. New York, 1951. Reprinted 2012.
Sh-Polochanskii, Evgenii. *Glavnye elementy ekonomicheskoi sviazi novykh gosudarstven-*
nykh obrazovanii v Srednei Azii i zadachi kirgizskoi respubliki po sel'skomu khozi-
aistvu. Tashkent, 1925.
Shaiakhmetov, Mukhamet [Mukhamet Shayakmetov]. *Sud'ba: Dokumental'naia*
povest'. Almaty, 2002.
Shayakhmetov, Mukhamet. *The Silent Steppe: The Story of a Kazakh Nomad under Sta-*
lin. Translated by Jan Butler. London, 2006.
Shepel', V. N., ed. *Iz istorii deportatsii Kazakhstan 1930–1935 gg.: Sbornik dokumentov.*
Almaty, 2012.
Shmidt, A. E. *Materialy po rodovomy sostavy kazakskogo naseleniia iugo-zapadnoi chasti*
Shimkentskogo uezda. Tashkent, 1927.
Shvetsov, S. P. *Kazakskoe khoziastvo v ego estestvenno-istoricheskikh i bytovykh uslovi-*
iakh. Leningrad, 1926.
Sokolovskii, V. G. *Kazakskii aul: K voprosu o metodakh ego izucheniia gosudarstvennoi*
statistikoi na osnove reshenii V-i Vsekazakskoi partkonferentsii i 2-go plenuma
Kazkraikoma VKP(b). Tashkent, 1926.

Spisok naselennykh punktov (v tom chisle i aulov-kstau) i skhematicheskaia 10-ti verst-naia karta Kazakstana. Kzyl-Orda, 1928.

Takenov, A., and B. Baigaliev, eds. *Istoriia Kazakhskogo naroda.* Almaty, 2002.

Togzhanov, G. [G. Toghzhanov]. *Kazakskii kolonial'nyi aul.* Moscow, 1934.

Togzhanov, G. [G. Toghzhanov]. *O Baitursunove i baitursunovshchine.* Almaty, 1932.

Trotsky, Leon. "National Aspects of Politics in Kazakhstan." In *Leon Trotsky: The Challenge of the Left Opposition (1926–1927),* ed. Naomi Allen and George Saunders, 210–14. New York, 1980.

Tursunbaev, A. B., ed. *Kollektivizatsiia sel'skogo khoziaistva Kazakhstana (1926 iiun'–1941 g.).* Almaty, 1967.

Venturi, Franco, ed. *Sovetskoe rukovodstvo. Perepiska, 1928–1941.* Moscow, 1999.

Vilenskii, M. M. *Zdravookhranenie v Kazakstane.* Kzyl-Orda, 1928.

Viola, Lynne, V. P. Danilov, N. A. Ivnitskii, and Denis Kozlov, eds. *The War against the Peasantry, 1927–1930.* Translated by Steven Shabad. New Haven, 2005.

Vladimirtsov, I. *Obshchestvennyi stroi Mongolov: Mongol'skii kochevoi feodalizm.* Leningrad, 1934.

Vliianie kolonizatsii na kirgizskoe khoziaistvo. St. Petersburg, 1907.

Voshchinin, V. P. *SSSR po raionam: Kazakhstan.* Moscow, 1929.

Vsekazakskaia konferentsiia VKP(b): Stenograficheskii otchet. Almaty, 1930.

Vsesoiuznaia perepis' naseleniia 17 dekabria 1926 g.: Kratkie svodki. Narodnost' i rodnoi iazyk naseleniia SSSR. Moscow, 1927.

Williams, M. W., and V. G. Konovalov. *Central Asia Temperature and Precipitation Data, 1879–2003.* Boulder, 2008.

Zapiski Semipalatinskogo otdela obshchestva izucheniia Kazakstana. Semipalatinsk, 1929.

Zarudnyi, N. A., ed. *Strana svobodnykh zemel'.* St. Petersburg, 1908.

Zhandabekov, O. V., ed. *Pod grifom sektretnosti: Otkochevki kazakhov v Kitai v period kollektivizatsii. Reemigratsiia, 1928–1957 gg. Sbornik dokumentov.* Ust-Kamenogorsk, 1998.

Zhandosov, E., ed. *Qayran Oras: Oraz Zhandosov zamandastar közǐmen/Legendarnyi Oras: Uras Dzhandosov glazami sovremennikov.* Almaty, 1999.

Zhaugashty, Nabie, ed. *Stepnaia tragediia: Adaiskoe vosstanie 1929–1931 gg.* Translated by Zhumaliev Bakytzhan. Almaty, 2010.

Zulkasheva, A. C., ed. *Tragediia kazakhskogo aula: 1928–1934. Sbornik dokumentov.* Vol. 1. Almaty, 2013.

Zveriakov, I. A. *Ot kochevaniia k sotsializmu.* Alma-Ata, 1932.

III. SECONDARY SOURCES: BOOKS AND ARTICLES

Abashin, S., D. Arapov, and N. Bekmakhanova, eds. *Tsentral'naia Aziia v sostave Rossiiskoi imperii.* Moscow, 2008.

Ablazhei, N. N. *Kazakhskii migratsionnyi maiatnik "Kazakhstan-Sin'tszian": Emigratsiia, repatriatsiia, integratsiia.* Novosibirsk, 2015.

Abylkhozhin, Zh. B. "Inertsiia mifotvorchestva v osveshchenii sovetskoi i postsovetskoi istorii Kazakhstana." In *Nauchnoe znanie i mifotvorchestvo v sovremennoi istoriografii Kazakhstana,* eds. N. E. Masanov, Zh. B. Abylkhozin, and I. V. Erofeeva, 11–51. Almaty, 2007.

Abylkhozhin, Zh. B. *Traditsionnaia struktura Kazakhstana: Sotsial'no-ekonomicheskie aspekti funktsionirovaniia i transformatsii.* Almaty, 1991.

Abylkhozhin, Zh. B., M. Kozybaev, and M. B. Tatimov. "Kazakhstanskaia tragediia." *Voprosy istorii,* no. 7 (1989): 53–71.

Adamets, Sergei. *Guerre civile et famine en Russie: Le pouvoir bolchevique et la population face à la catastrophe démographique, 1917–1923.* Paris, 2003.

Adams, Bruce F. "Reemigration from Western China to the USSR, 1954–1962." In *Migration, Homeland and Belonging in Eurasia*, ed. Cynthia J. Buckley and Blair A. Ruble, 183–203. Washington, DC, 2008.

Aiagana [Ayäghan], B. G., ed. *1932–1933 zhïldardaghï aharshïlïq aqiqatï/Pravda o golode 1923–1933 godov.* Almaty, 2012.

Aiagana [Ayäghan], B. G. *Sbornik materialov Mezhdunarodnoi nauchnoi konferentsii "Golod v Kazakhstane. Tragediia naroda i uroki istorii."* Astana, 2012.

Alimbai, H., M. C. Mukhanov, and Kh. Argynbaev. *Traditsionnaia kul'tura zhizneobe-specheniia kazakhov: Ocherki teorii i istorii.* Almaty, 1998.

Allaniiazov, Turganbek. *"Kontrrevoliutsiia" v Kazakhstane: Chimbaiskii variant.* Almaty, 1999.

Allaniiazov, Turganbek. *Krest'ianskie vystupleniia 1929–1932 gg. v Kazakhstane: Opyt i problemy izucheniia.* Almaty, 2002.

Allaniiazov, Turganbek, and Amangel'dy Taukenov. *Poslednii rubezh zashchitnikov nomadizma: Istoriia vooruzhennykh vystuplenii i povstancheskikh dvizhenii v Kazakhstane (1929–1931 gody).* Almaty, 2008.

Altïnbekov, Panza. *Aqiqat pen qasïret (1933–1938 zhzh.): Derekname.* Astana, 2001.

Amanzholova, D. A. *Na izlome: Alash v etnopoliticheskoi istorii Kazakstana.* Almaty, 2009.

Applebaum, Anne. *Red Famine: Stalin's War on Ukraine.* New York, 2017.

Argynbaev, Kh. A. *Istoriko-kul'turnye sviazi russkogo i kazakhskogo narodov.* Pavlodar, 2005.

Arnold, David. *Famine: Social Crisis and Historical Change.* New York, 1988.

Ashimbaev, Daniiar, ed. *Kto est' kto v Kazakhstane: Biograficheskaia entsiklopediia.* Almaty, 2010.

Asylbekov, M. Kh., et al., eds. *Istoriia Kazakhstana s drevneishikh vremen do nashikh dnei.* 5 vols. Almaty, 2010.

Bacon, Elizabeth E. *Central Asians under Russian Rule: A Study in Culture Change.* Ithaca, 1966.

Balakaev, T. B. *Kolkhoznoe krest'ianstvo Kazakhstana v gody Velikoi Otechestvennoi voiny 1941–1945 gg.* Alma-Ata, 1971.

Barnes, Steven A. *Death and Redemption: The Gulag and the Shaping of Soviet Society.* Princeton, 2011.

Batbayar, Tsedendambyn. "Stalin's Strategy in Mongolia, 1932–1936." *Mongolian Studies* 22 (1999): 1–17.

Batyrbaeva, S. D. "Golod 1930-kh gg. v Kyrgyzstane: Novye materialy, novye podkhody." In *Sovetskie natsii i natsional'naia politika v 1920–1950-e gody: Materialy VI mezhdunarodnoi nauchnoi konferentsii, Kiev, 10–12 oktiabria 2013 g.*, ed. N. A. Volynchik, 222–30. Moscow, 2014.

Benson, Linda, and Ingvar Svanberg. *China's Last Nomads: The History and Culture of China's Kazaks.* Armonk, 1998.

Bregel, Yuri. *An Historical Atlas of Central Asia.* Boston, 2003.

Bregel, Yuri. "Uzbeks, Qazaqs and Turkmens." In *The Cambridge History of Inner Asia*, ed. Nicola Di Cosmo et al., 221–36. Cambridge, 2009.

Breyfogle, Nicholas B., Abby Schrader, and Willard Sunderland, eds. *Peopling the Russian Periphery: Borderland Colonization in Eurasian History.* New York, 2007.

Brower, Daniel R. *Turkestan and the Fate of the Russian Empire.* New York, 2003.

Brown, Kate. *A Biography of No Place: From Ethnic Borderland to Soviet Heartland.* Cambridge, MA, 2004.

Brown, Kate. "Gridded Lives: Why Kazakhstan and Montana Are Nearly the Same Place." *American Historical Review* 106, no. 1 (2001): 17–48.

Bruno, Andy. *The Nature of Soviet Power: An Arctic Environmental History.* Cambridge, 2016.

Buttino, Marco. *Revoliutsiia naoborot: Sredniaia Aziia mezhdu padeniem tsarskoi impe-rii i obrazovaniem SSSR*. Translated by Nikolai Okhotin. Moscow, 2007.

Bykov. A. Iu. *Istoki modernizatsii Kazakhstana* (Barnaul, 2003).

Campbell, Ian W. *Knowledge and the Ends of Empire: Kazak Intermediaries and Russian Rule on the Steppe, 1731–1917*. Ithaca, 2017.

Campbell, Ian W. "The Scourge of Stock Raising: Zhüt, Limiting Environments and the Economic Transformation of the Steppe." In *Eurasian Environmental History*, ed. Nicholas B. Breyfogle (forthcoming).

Carmack, Roberto. "'A Fortress of the Soviet Home Front': Mobilization and Ethnicity in Kazakhstan during World War II." PhD diss., University of Wisconsin, 2015.

Carr, E. H. *The Russian Revolution from Lenin to Stalin, 1917–1929*. New York, 2004.

Chakars, Melissa. *The Socialist Way of Life in Siberia: Transformation in Buryatia*. Budapest, 2014.

Chandler, Andrea. *Institutions of Isolation: Border Controls in the Soviet Union and Its Successor States, 1917–1993*. Montreal, 1998.

Chang, Claudia. *Rethinking Prehistoric Central Asia: Shepherds, Farmers, and Nomads*. London, 2018.

Chang, Claudia. "The Study of Nomads in the Republic of Kazakhstan." In *The Ecology of Pastoralism*, ed. P. Nick Nardulias, 17–40. Boulder, 2015.

Chase, William. *Workers, Society, and the Soviet State: Labor and Life in Moscow, 1918–1929*. Chicago, 1987.

Chen Fahu, Xiaozhong Huang, Jianwu Zhang, J. A. Holmes, and Jianhui Chen. "Humid Little Ice Age in Arid Central Asia Documented by Bosten Lake, Xin-jiang China." *Science in China Series D: Earth Sciences* 49, no. 12: 1280–90.

Cherfas, Teresa. "Reporting Stalin's Famine: Jones and Muggeridge. A Case Study in Forgetting and Rediscovery." *Kritika: Explorations in Russian and Eurasian History* 14, no. 4 (2013): 775–804.

Chernobaev, A. A., ed. *Na prieme u Stalina: Tetrady (zhurnaly) zapisei lits, priniatykh I. V. Stalinym (1924–1953 gg.)*. Moscow, 2010.

Christmas, Sakura. "The Cartographic Steppe: Mapping Environment and Ethnicity in Japan's Imperial Borderlands." PhD diss., Harvard University, 2016.

Chzhen-Kun, Fy. *Istoricheskie sviazi i sovremennye otnosheniia mezhdu Kitaem i Kazakhstanom*. Almaty, 2001.

Conquest, Robert. *The Harvest of Sorrow: Soviet Collectivization and the Terror-Famine*. New York, 1986.

Coquin, François-Xavier. *La Sibérie: Peuplement et immigration paysanne au 19e siècle*. Paris, 1969.

Crews, Robert D. *For Prophet and Tsar: Islam and Empire in Russia and Central Asia*. Cambridge, MA, 2006.

Cronin, Stephanie. *Tribal Politics in Iran: Rural Conflict and the New State, 1921–1941*. London, 2007.

Cronon, William. *Changes in the Land: Indians, Colonists, and the Ecology of New England*. New York, 1983.

Dakhshsleiger, G. F., and K. Nurpeisov. *Istoriia krest'ianstva Sovetskogo Kazakhstana*. Almaty, 1985.

Dave, Bhavna. *Kazakhstan: Ethnicity, Language, and Power*. New York, 2007.

Davies, R. W. *The Industrialisation of Soviet Russia 2: The Soviet Collective Farm, 1929–1930*. London, 1980.

Davies, R. W. *The Socialist Offensive: The Collectivisation of Soviet Agriculture, 1929–1930*. London, 1980.

Davies, R. W. "Stalin as an Economic Policy Maker: Soviet Agriculture, 1931–1936." In *Stalin A New History*, eds. Sarah Davies and James Harris, 121–36. Cambridge, 2006.

Davies, R. W., and Stephen G. Wheatcroft. "Stalin and the Soviet Famine of 1932–33: A Reply to Ellmann." *Europe-Asia Studies* 58, no. 4 (2006): 625–33.

Davis, Diana K. *The Arid Lands: History, Power, Knowledge.* Cambridge, MA, 2016.

Davis, Mike. *Late Victorian Holocausts: El Niño Famines and the Making of the Third World.* New York, 2002.

Diener, Alexander C. *One Homeland or Two? The Nationalization and Transnationalization of Mongolia's Kazakhs.* Washington, DC, 2009.

Demko, George J. *The Russian Colonization of Kazakhstan, 1896–1916.* New York, 1969.

DeWeese, Devin, ed. *Studies on Central Asian History in Honor of Yuri Bregel.* Bloomington, 2001.

Di Cosmo, Nicola. "Ancient Inner Asian Nomads: Their Economic Basis and Its Significance in Chinese History." *Journal of Asian Studies* 54, no. 4 (1994): 1092–126.

Edgar, Adrienne Lynn. *Tribal Nation: The Making of Soviet Turkmenistan.* Princeton, 2004.

Edgerton-Tarpley, Kathryn. *Tears from Iron: Cultural Responses to Famine in Nineteenth-Century China.* Berkeley, 2008.

Eickelman, Dale F. *The Middle East and Central Asia: An Anthropological Approach.* Upper Saddle River, 2002.

Elie, Marc. "Desiccated Steppes: Droughts, Erosion, Climate Change and the Crisis of Soviet Agriculture, 1960s–1980s." In *Eurasian Environmental History,* ed. Nicholas B. Breyfogle (forthcoming).

Ellman, Michael. "The Role of Leadership Perceptions and of Intent in the Soviet Famine of 1931–1934." *Europe-Asia Studies* 57, no. 6 (2005): 823–41.

Esenbel, Selçuk. "Japan's Global Claim to Asia and the World of Islam: Transnational Nationalism and World Power, 1900–1945." *American Historical Review* 109, no. 4 (2004): 1140–70.

Esenova, Saulesh. "Soviet Nationality, Identity, and Ethnicity in Central Asia: Historic Narratives and Kazakh Ethnic Identity." *Journal of Muslim Minority Affairs* 22, no. 1 (2002): 11–38.

Fitzpatrick, Sheila, ed. *Cultural Revolution in Russia, 1928–1931.* Bloomington, 1977.

Fitzpatrick, Sheila. *Stalin's Peasants: Resistance and Survival in the Russian Village after Collectivization.* Oxford, 1994.

Fletcher, Robert S. J. *British Imperialism and "The Tribal Question": Desert Administration and Nomadic Societies in the Middle East, 1919–1936.* Oxford, 2015.

Fletcher, Robert S. J. "Running the Corridor: Nomadic Societies and Imperial Rule in the Inter-War Syrian Desert." *Past and Present,* no. 220 (2013): 185–215.

Forbes, Andrew D. W. *Warlords and Muslims in Chinese Central Asia: A Political History of Republican Sinkiang, 1911–1949.* Cambridge, 1986.

Fowler, Mayhill C. "Mikhail Bulgakov, Mykola Kulish, and Soviet Theater: How Internal Transnationalism Remade Center and Periphery." *Kritika: Explorations in Russian and Soviet History* 16, no. 2 (2015), 263–90.

Frachetti, Michael D. *Pastoralist Landscapes and Social Interaction in Bronze Age Eurasia.* Berkeley, 2008.

Frank, Allen J. "The Qazaqs and the Russians." In *The Cambridge History of Inner Asia,* ed. Nicola Di Cosmo et al., 363–79. Cambridge, 2009.

Frank, Allen J., and Mirkasym A. Usmanov, eds. *Materials for the Islamic History of Semipalatinsk.* Berlin, 2001.

Gabzhalilov, Kh. M. "Xx ghasïrdïng 30-shï zhïldarïngdaghï Qazaqstandaghï ashtïq demografiiasïnïng zerttelui turalï." *QazÜU khabarshïsï. Tarikh seriiasï* 3, no. 38 (2005): 12–15.

Genina, Anna. "Claiming Ancestral Homelands: Mongolian Kazakh Migration in Inner Asia." PhD diss., University of Michigan, 2015.

Genis, V. L. "Deportatsiia russkikh iz Turkestana v 1921 gody ('Delo Safarova')." *Voprosy istorii*, no. 1 (1998): 44–58.

Getty, J. Arch, and Oleg V. Naumov. *Yezhov: The Rise of Stalin's "Iron Fist."* New Haven, 2008.

Golikova, Z., P. Pakhmurnyi, and T. Pozniakova. *Kompartiia Kazakhstana za 50 let (1921–1971 gg.)*. Alma-Ata, 1972.

Goriachev, Iu. V., ed. *Tsentral'nyi komitet KPSS, VKP(b), RKP(b), RSDRP(b) 1917–1991: Istoriko-biograficheskii spravochnik*. Moscow, 2005.

Grant, Bruce. *In the Soviet House of Culture: A Century of Perestroikas* (Princeton, 1995).

Graziosi, Andrea. *The Great Soviet Peasant War: Bolsheviks and Peasants, 1917–1933*. Cambridge, MA, 1996.

Graziosi, Andrea, Lubomyr A. Hajda, and Halyna Hryn, eds. *After the Holodomor: The Enduring Impact of the Great Famine on Ukraine*. Cambridge, MA, 2013.

Gross, Jan T. *Revolution from Abroad: The Soviet Conquest of Poland's Western Ukraine and Western Belorussia*. Princeton, 1988.

Grozin, A. V. *Golod 1932–1933 godov i politika pamiati v respublike Kazakhstan*. Moscow, 2014.

Hagenloh, Paul. *Stalin's Police: Public Order and Mass Repression in the USSR, 1926–1941*. Washington, DC, 2009.

Happel, Jörn. *Nomadische Lebenswelten und zarische Politik: Der Aufstand in Zentralasien 1916*. Stuttgart, 2010.

Haslam, Jonathan. *The Soviet Union and the Threat from the East, 1933–1941: Moscow, Tokyo, and the Prelude to the Pacific War*. Pittsburgh, 1992.

Hedeler, Wladislaw, and Meinhard Stark. *Das Grab in der Steppe: Leben im GULAG. Die Geschichte eines sowjetischen "Besserungsarbeitslagers" 1930–1959*. Paderborn, 2008.

Heinzen, James W. *Inventing a Soviet Countryside: State Power and the Transformation of Rural Russia, 1917–1929*. Pittsburgh, 2004.

Himka, John-Paul. "Encumbered Memory: The Ukrainian Famine of 1932–33." *Kritika: Explorations in Russian and Eurasian History*, 14, no. 2 (2013): 411–36.

Hirsch, Francine. *Empire of Nations: Ethnographic Knowledge and the Making of the Soviet Union*. Ithaca, 2005.

Hirsch, Francine. "The Soviet Union as a Work-In-Progress: Ethnographers and the Category Nationality in the 1926, 1937, and 1939 Censuses." *Slavic Review* 56, no. 2 (1997): 251–78.

Hryn, Halyna, ed. *Hunger by Design: The Great Ukrainian Famine and Its Soviet Context*. Cambridge, MA, 2008.

Hudson, Alfred E. *Kazak Social Structure*. New Haven, 1964.

Hughes, James. *Stalin, Siberia, and the Crisis of the New Economic Policy*. Cambridge, 2004.

Humphrey, Caroline. *Marx Went Away—but Karl Stayed Behind*. Ann Arbor, 2001.

Humphrey, Caroline, and David Sneath. *The End of Nomadism? Society, State, and the Environment in Inner Asia*. Durham, 1999.

Iğmen, Ali. *Speaking Soviet with an Accent: Culture and Power in Kyrgyzstan*. Pittsburgh, 2012.

Irons, William. "Nomadism as a Political Adaptation: The Case of the Yomut Turkmen." *American Ethnologist* 1, no. 4 (1974): 635–58.

Isajiw, Wsevolod W., ed. *Famine-Genocide in Ukraine, 1932–33: Western Archives, Testimonies, and New Research*. Toronto, 2003.

Ivanov, Andrey V. "Conflicting Loyalties: Fugitives and 'Traitors' in the Russo-Manchurian Frontier, 1651–1689." *Journal of Early Modern History* 13, no. 5 (2009): 333–58.

Jacobs, Justin. "The Many Deaths of a Kazak Unaligned: Osman Batur, Chinese Decolonization and the Nationalization of a Nomad." *American Historical Review* 115, no. 5 (2010): 1291–315.

Jansen, Marc, and Nikolai Petrov. *Stalin's Loyal Executioner: Nikolai Ezhov, 1895–1940*. Stanford, 2002.

Jones, Robert E. *Bread upon the Waters: The St. Petersburg Grain Trade and the Russian Economy, 1703–1811*. Pittsburgh, 2013.

Jungbluth, Frauke, and Tjaart Schillhorn Van-Veen. *Kazakhstan's Livestock Sector: Supporting Its Revival*. Washington, DC, 2004.

Kaiser, Robert J. *The Geography of Nationalism in Russia and the USSR*. Princeton, 1994.

Kamp, Marianne. *The New Woman in Uzbekistan: Islam, Modernity, and Unveiling under Communism*. Seattle, 2006.

Kamp, Marianne, and Russell Zanca, "Recollections of Collectivization in Uzbekistan: Stalinism and Local Activism." *Central Asian Survey* 63, no. 1 (2017): 55–72.

Kasymzhanova, Gul'zhizhan. *Arkhiv pamiati*. Almaty, 2003.

Keller, Shoshana. *To Moscow, Not Mecca: The Soviet Campaign against Islam in Central Asia, 1917–1941*. Westport, 2001.

Kendirbaeva, Gulnar [Gulnar Kendirbai], "'We are Children of Alash . . .'" *Central Asian Survey* 18, no. 1 (1999): 5–36.

Kendirbai, Gulnar. *Land and People: The Russian Colonization of the Kazak Steppe*. Berlin, 2002.

Kerven, Carol, ed. *Prospects for Pastoralism in Kazakstan and Turkmenistan: From State Farms to Private Flocks*. New York, 2003.

Khalid, Adeeb. *Making Uzbekistan: Nation, Empire and Revolution in the Early USSR*. Ithaca, 2015.

Khalidyllin, G. *Politika sovetskogo gosudarstva v otnoshenii kazakhskikh sharua (1917–1940 gg)*. Almaty, 2001.

Khazanov, Anatoly M. *Nomads and the Outside World*. Translated by Julia Crookenden. New York, 1983.

Khlevniuk, Oleg. *Master of the House: Stalin and His Inner Circle*. Translated by Nora Seligman Favorov. New Haven, 2009.

Khodarkovsky, Michael. *Russia's Steppe Frontier: The Making of a Colonial Empire, 1500–1800*. Bloomington, 2002.

Khodarkovsky, Michael. *Where Two Worlds Met: The Russian State and the Kalmyk Nomads 1660–1771*. Ithaca, 1992.

Kilian, Janet. "Allies and Adversaries: The Russian Conquest of the Kazakh Steppe." PhD diss., George Washington University, 2013.

Kindler, Robert. *Stalins Nomaden: Herrschaft und Hunger in Kasachstan*. Hamburg, 2014.

Kligman, Gail, and Katherine Verdery. *Peasants under Siege: The Collectivization of Romanian Agriculture, 1949–1962*. Princeton, 2011.

Koigeldiev, M. K. "The Alash Movement and the Soviet Government: A Difference of Positions." In *Empire, Islam and Politics in Central Eurasia*, ed. Tomohiko Uyama, 153–84. Sapporo, 2007.

Koigeldiev, M. K. *Stalinizm i repressii v Kazakhstane 1920–1940-kh godov*. Almaty, 2009.

Kondrashin, Viktor. *Golod 1932–1933 godov: Tragediia Rossiiskoi derevni*. Moscow, 2008.

Kondrashin, Viktor, and Diana Penner. *Golod: 1932–1933 gody v sovetskoi derevne (na materialakh Povolzh'ia, Dona i Kubani)*. Samara, 2002.

Konkvest, Robert [Robert Conquest]. "Zhatva skorbi." *Voprosy istorii*, no. 4 (1990): 83–100.

Korbe, O. A. "Kul'tura i byt kazakhskogo kolkhoznogo aula (k 30-letiiu Kazakhskoi SSR)." *Sovetskaia etnografiia*, no. 4 (1950): 67–91.

Kosicki, Piotr H. "Forests, Families, and Films: Polish Memory of Katyń, 1943–2015." *East European Politics and Societies and Cultures* 29, no. 4 (2015): 730–60.

Kotkin, Stephen. "Modern Times: The Soviet Union and the Interwar Conjuncture." *Kritika: Explorations in Russian and Eurasian History* 2, no. 1 (2001): 111–64.

Kuchkin, A. P. *Sovetizatsiia kazakhskogo aula*. Moscow, 1962.

Kuderina, L. D. *Genotsid v Kazakhstane*. Moscow, 1994.

Kul'chitskii, S. V. *Pochemu on nas unichtozhal? Stalin i ukrainskii Golodomor*. Kiev, 2007.

Lattimore, Owen. *Inner Asian Frontiers of China*. New York, 1940.

Lattimore, Owen. *Pivot of Asia: Sinkiang and the Inner Asian Frontiers of China and Russia*. Boston, 1950.

Lee, Joo-Yup. *Qazaqlïq, or Ambitious Brigandage, and the Formation of the Qazaqs: State and Identity in Post-Mongol Central Eurasia*. Boston, 2016.

Lee, Paula Young, ed. *Meat, Modernity, and the Rise of the Slaughterhouse*. Durham, NH, 2008.

Lemkin, Raphael. *Axis Rule in Occupied Europe: Laws of Occupation, Analysis of Government, Proposals for Redress*. Washington, 1944.

Lewin, Moshe. *The Making of the Soviet System: Essays in the Social History of Interwar Russia*. New York, 1985.

Lewin, Moshe. *Russian Peasants and Soviet Power: A Study of Collectivization*. New York, 1968.

Linden, Kenneth E. "Representations and Memory of the Collectivization Campaigns in the Mongolian People's Republic, 1929–1960." MA thesis, Indiana University, 2015.

Loring, Benjamin. "Building Socialism in Kyrgyzstan: Nation-Making, Rural Development and Social Change, 1921–1932." PhD diss., Brandeis University, 2008.

Makhat, D. A. *Baspasöz: Stalinshïldïktïng Qazaqstanda ornïghülï (1925–1956 zh. zh.)*. Astana, 2007.

Makhat, Danagul. *Qazaq ziyälïlarïnïng qasiretï*. Almaty, 2001.

Malikov, Yuriy. *Tsars, Cossacks, and Nomads: The Formation of a Borderland Culture in Northern Kazakhstan in the 18th and 19th Centuries*. Berlin, 2011.

Maltusynov, C.N. *Agrarnyi vopros v Kazakhstane i Gosudarstvennaia duma Rossii 1906–1917 gg. (sotsiokul'turnyi podkhod)*. Almaty, 2006.

Mal'sheva, M. P., and V. S. Poznanskii. *Kazakhi-bezhentsy ot goloda v Zapadnoi Sibiri (1931–1934 gg.)*. Almaty, 1999.

Manley, Rebecca. "Nutritional Dystrophy: The Science and Semantics of Starvation in World War II." In *Hunger and War: Food Provisioning in the Soviet Union during World War II*, ed. Wendy Z. Goldman and Donald Filtzer, 206–64. Bloomington, 2015.

Manley, Rebecca. *To the Tashkent Station: Evacuation and Survival in the Soviet Union at War*. Ithaca, 2009.

Martin, Terry. *The Affirmative Action Empire: Nations and Nationalism in the Soviet Union, 1923–1939*. Ithaca, 2001.

Martin, Virginia. "Kazakh Chinggisids, Land, and Political Power in the 19th Century: A Case Study of Syrymbet." *Central Asian Survey* 29, no. 1 (2010): 79–102.

Martin, Virginia. *Law and Custom in the Steppe: The Kazakhs of the Middle Horde and Russian Colonialism in the Nineteenth Century*. Richmond, 2001.

Masanov, Nurbulat. *Kochevaia tsivilizatsiia kazakhov: Osnovy zhiznedeiatel'nosti nomadnogo obshchestva*. Almaty, 1995. Reprinted 2011.

Masanov, N.E. "Mifologizatsiia problem etnogeneza kazakhskogo naroda i kazakhskoi nomadnoi kul'tury." In *Nauchnoe znanie i mifotvorchestvo v sovremennoi istoriografii Kazakhstana*, ed. N. E. Masanov, Zh. B. Abylkhozin and I. V. Erofeeva, 52–131. Almaty, 2007.

Massell, Gregory. *The Surrogate Proletariat: Muslim Women and Revolutionary Strategies in Central Asia, 1919–1929*. Princeton, 1974.

McDonald, Tracy. *Face to the Village: The Riazan Countryside under Soviet Rule, 1921–1930*. Toronto, 2011.

McGuire, Gabriel. "By Coin or By Kine? Barter and Pastoral Production in Kazakhstan." *Ethnos* 81, no. 1 (2016): 53–74.

Mendeubaev, E. I. *Voennyi kommunizm v Kazakhstane: Politika, praktika, ideologiia (1918–1921 gg.)*. Aktobe, 2003.

Mendikulova, Gul'nara. *Kazakhskaia diaspora: Istoriia i sovremennost'*. Almaty, 2006.

Merl, Stephan. *Bauern unter Stalin: Die Formierung des sowjetischen Kolchossystems 1930–1941*. Berlin, 1990.

Merl', Shtefan [Stephan Merl]. "Golod 1932–1933 godov-genotsid ukraintsev dlia osushchestvleniia politiki rusifikatsii." *Otechestvennaia istoriia*, no. 1 (1995): 49–61.

Michaels, Paula A. *Curative Powers: Medicine and Empire in Stalin's Central Asia*. Pittsburgh, 2003.

Mikhailov, Valerii. *The Great Disaster: Genocide of the Kazakhs*. Translated by Katherine Judelson. London, 2014.

Mikhailov, Valerii. *Khronika velikogo dzhuta*. Almaty, 1990. Reprinted 1996.

Millward, James A. *Eurasian Crossroads: A History of Xinjiang*. London, 2007.

Millward, James A., and Nabijan Tursun. "Political History and Strategies of Control." In *Xinjiang: China's Muslim Borderland*, ed. S. Frederick Starr, 63–100. Armonk, 2004.

Mironova-Korol, Agnessa. *Agnessa: From Paradise to Purgatory. A Voice from Stalin's Russia*. Translated by Rose Glickman. Bloomington, 2012.

Mïrzakhmetov, M. *Qazaq qalay orïstandïrïldï*. Almaty, 1993.

Moon, David. *The Plough That Broke the Steppes: Agriculture and Environment on Russia's Grasslands, 1700–1914*. Oxford, 2013.

Morrison, Alexander. "Killing the Cotton Canard and Getting Rid of the Great Game: Rewriting the Russian Conquest of Central Asia, 1814–1895." *Central Asian Survey* 33, no. 2 (2014): 131–42.

Morrison, Alexander. "Peasant Settlers and the Civilizing Mission in Russian Turkestan, 1865–1917." *Journal of Imperial and Commonwealth History* 43, no. 3 (2015): 387–417.

Mŭkhatova, Orazgul. *Qazaqstandaghï XX-ghasïrdïng alghashqï onzhïldïq—tarïndaghï agrarlïq reformalar tarikhnamasï (1920–1929 zhïldar)*. Almaty, 1998.

Naimark, Norman M. *Stalin's Genocides*. Princeton, 2010.

Naumkin, Vitalii, Kenneth Shapiro, and Anatoly Khazanov, eds. *Pastoralizm v Tsentral'noi Azii*. Moscow, 1997.

Northrop, Douglas. *Veiled Empire: Gender and Power in Stalinist Central Asia*. Ithaca, 2004.

Nove, Alec. *An Economic History of the USSR, 1917–1991.* New York, 1992.

Ó Gráda, Cormac. *Eating People Is Wrong, and Other Essays on Famine, Its Past, and Its Future.* Princeton, 2015.

Ó Gráda, Cormac. *Famine: A Short History.* Princeton, 2009.

Ohayon, Isabelle. *La sédentarisation des Kazakhs dans l'URSS de Staline: Collectivisation et changement social (1928–1945).* Paris, 2006.

O'Keefe, Brigid. *New Soviet Gypsies: Nationality, Performance, and Selfhood in the Soviet Union.* Toronto, 2013.

Olcott, Martha Brill. "The Collectivization Drive in Kazakhstan." *Russian Review* 40, no. 2 (1981): 122–42.

Omarbekov, Talas. *20–30 zhïldardaghï Qasaqstan qasïretï.* Almaty, 1997.

Omarbekov, Talas. *Qazaqstan tarikhïnïng XX ghasïrdaghï özektï mäceleleri: Kömekshïoqu qûralï.* Almaty, 2003.

Omarbekov, Talas. *Zobalang (küshtep üzhumdastïrugha karsïlïq): Oqu qûralï.* Almaty, 1994.

Omarov, M. *Rasstreliannaia step': Dokumental'noe povestvovanie.* Almaty, 1994.

Osokina, E. A. *Ierarkhiia potrebleniia: O zhizni liudei v usloviiakh stalinskogo snabzheniia 1928–1935 gg.* Moscow, 1993.

Otter, Chris. "Planet of Meat: A Biological History." In *Challenging (the) Humanities,* ed. Tony Bennett, 33–49. Melbourne, 2013.

Patenaude, Bertrand M. *Big Show in Bololand: The American Relief Expedition to Soviet Russia in the Famine of 1921.* Stanford, 2002.

Payne, Matthew J. "Seeing Like a Soviet State: Settlement of Nomadic Kazakhs, 1928–1934." In *Writing the Stalin Era: Shelia Fitzpatrick and Soviet Historiography,* ed. Golfo Alexopoulous, Julie Hessler, and Kiril Tomoff, 59–86. New York, 2011.

Payne, Matthew J. *Stalin's Railroad: Turksib and the Building of Socialism.* Pittsburgh, 2001.

Penner, D'Ann R. "Stalin and the Ital'ianka of 1932–1933 in the Don Region." *Cahiers du monde russe* 39, no. 1–2 (1998): 27–67.

Perdue, Peter C. *China Marches West: The Qing Conquest of Central Eurasia.* Cambridge, MA, 2005.

Peyrouse, Sebastian. *The Russian Minority in Central Asia: Migration, Politics, and Language.* Washington, DC, 2008.

Pianciola, Niccolò. "Décoloniser L'Asie Centrale? Bolcheviks et colons au Semireč'e (1920–1922)." *Cahiers du monde russe* 49, no. 1 (2008): 101–43.

Pianciola, Niccolò. "Famine in the Steppe: The Collectivization of Agriculture and the Kazak Herdsmen, 1928–1934." *Cahiers du monde russe* 45, no. 1–2 (2004): 137–92.

Pianciola, Niccolò. *Stalinismo di frontiera: Colonizzazione agricola, sterminio dei nomadi e costruzione statale in Asia centrale, 1905–1936.* Rome, 2009.

Pianciola, Niccolò. "Stalinist Spatial Hierarchies: Placing the Kazakhs and Kyrgyz in Soviet Economic Regionalization." *Central Asian Survey* 36, no. 1 (2017): 73–92.

Pianciola, Niccolò. "Towards a Transnational History of Great Leaps Forward in Pastoral Central Eurasia." *East/West: Journal of Ukrainian Studies* 3, no. 2 (2016): 75–116.

Pianciola, Niccolò, and Paolo Sartori, eds. *Islam, Society and States across the Qazaq Steppe (18th–Early 20th Centuries).* Vienna, 2013.

Pohl, Michaela. "The Virgin Lands between Memory and Forgetting: People and Transformation in the Soviet Union, 1954–1960." PhD diss., Indiana University, 1999.

Privratsky, Bruce G. *Muslim Turkistan: Kazak Religion and Collective Memory.* Richmond, 2001.

Pylev, Aleksandr Igorevich. *Basmachestvo v Srednei Azii: Etnopoliticheskii srez (vzgliad iz XXI veka)*. Bishkek, 2006.

Quandïqov, Esenghazï. *Süreng salghan sürqiyä sayäsat: Ghïlïmi maqalalar men zertteuler*. Almaty, 1999.

Rabinowitch, Alexander. *The Bolsheviks in Power: The First Years of Soviet Power in Petrograd*. Bloomington, 2008.

Reeves, Madeleine. *Border Work: Spatial Lives of the State in Rural Central Asia*. Ithaca, 2014.

Robbins, Richard G. *Famine in Russia, 1891–1892: The Imperial Government Responds to a Crisis*. New York, 1975.

Rosen, Arlene Miller, Claudia Chang, and Fedor Pavlovich Grigoriev. "Paleoenvironments and Economy of Iron Age Saka-Wusun Agro-Pastoralists in Southeastern Kazakhstan." *Antiquity* 70, no. 285 (2000): 611–23.

Rosenberg, Daniel. "The Collectivization of Mongolia's Pastoral Production." *Nomadic Peoples*, no. 9 (1981): 23–39.

Rottier, Pete. "Creating the Kazak Nation: The Intelligentsia's Quest for Acceptance in the Russian Empire, 1905–1920." PhD diss., University of Wisconsin, 2005.

Rudelson, Justin Jon. *Oasis Identities: Uyghur Nationalism along China's Silk Road*. New York, 1997.

Rudnytskyi, Omelian, et al., "Famine Losses in Ukraine in 1932 and 1933 within the Context of the Soviet Union." In *Famines in European Economic History*, ed. Declan Curry et al., 192–222. New York, 2015.

Sabol, Steven. *Russian Colonization and the Genesis of Kazak National Consciousness*. New York, 2003.

Sabol, Steven. *"The Touch of Civilization": Comparing American and Russian Internal Colonization*. Boulder, 2017.

Sahadeo, Jeff. *Russian Colonial Society in Tashkent, 1865–1923*. Bloomington, 2007.

Salzman, Philip Carl. *Pastoralists: Equality, Hierarchy, and the State*. Boulder, 2004.

Sariev, Izturgan. "Krovavoe poboishche." In *Stepnaia tragediia: Adaiskoe vosstanie 1929–1931 gg.* ed. Nabie Zhaugashty. Translated by Zhumaliev Bakytzhan, 11–256. Almaty, 2010.

Satia, Priya. "The Defense of Inhumanity: Air Control and the British Idea of Arabia." *American Historical Review* 111, no. 1 (2006): 16–51.

Schatz, Edward. *Modern Clan Politics: The Power of "Blood" in Kazakhstan and Beyond*. Seattle, 2004.

Scott, James C. *The Art of Not Being Governed: An Anarchist History of Upland Southeast Asia*. New Haven, 2009.

Scott, James C. *Seeing Like a State: How Certain Schemes to Improve the Human Condition Have Failed*. New Haven, 1998.

Sen, Amartya. *Poverty and Famines: An Essay on Entitlement and Deprivation*. Oxford, 1981.

Serels, Steven. *Starvation and the State: Famine, Slavery, and Power in Sudan, 1883–1956*. New York, 2013.

Shahrani, Mohib. *The Kirghiz and Wakhi of Afghanistan: Adaptation to Closed Frontiers*. Seattle, 1979.

Shakanova, Nurila Z. "The System of Nourishment Among the Eurasian Nomads: The Kazakh Example." In *Ecology and Empire: Nomads in the Cultural Evolution of the Old World*, ed. Gary Seaman, 111–17. Los Angeles, 1989.

Shcheglova, T. K. *Iarmarki Zapadnoi Sibiri i stepnykh oblastei vo vtoroi polovine XIX veka: Iz istorii rossiisko-aziatskoi torgovli*. Barnaul, 2002.

Shearer, David R. "Elements Near and Alien: Passportization, Policing, and Identity in the Stalinist State, 1932–1952." *Journal of Modern History* 76, no. 4 (2004): 835–81.

Shearer, David R. *Policing Stalin's Socialism: Repression and Social Order in the Soviet Union, 1924–1953.* New Haven, 2009.

Shlyakhter, Andrey. "Smugglers and Commissars: The Making of the Soviet Border Strip, 1917–1939." PhD diss., University of Chicago, forthcoming.

Siegelbaum, Lewis. "Those Elusive Scouts: Pioneering Peasants and the Russian State, 1870s–1950." *Kritika: Explorations in Russian and Eurasian History* 14, no. 1 (2013): 31–58.

Slavinskii, D. B. *Sovetskii Soiuz i Kitai: Istoriia diplomaticheskikh otnoshenii 1917–1937 gg.* Moscow, 2003.

Slezkine, Yuri. *Arctic Mirrors: Russia and the Small Peoples of the North.* Ithaca, 1994.

Slezkine, Yuri. *The House of Government: A Saga of the Russian Revolution.* Princeton, 2017.

Slezkine, Yuri. *The Jewish Century.* Princeton, 2006.

Slezkine, Yuri. "The USSR as a Communal Apartment, or How a Socialist State Promoted Ethnic Particularism." *Slavic Review* 53, no. 2 (1994): 414–52.

Smith, Alison K. *Recipes for Russia: Food and Nationhood under the Tsars.* DeKalb, 2008.

Smith, Jenny Leigh. *Works in Progress: Plans and Realities on Soviet Farms, 1930–1963.* New Haven, 2014.

Sneath, David. *The Headless State: Aristocratic Orders, Kinship Society, and Misrepresentations of Nomadic Inner Asia.* New York, 2007.

Snyder, Timothy. *Bloodlands: Europe Between Hitler and Stalin.* New York, 2010.

Snyder, Timothy. *Sketches from a Secret War: A Polish Artist's Mission to Liberate Soviet Ukraine.* New Haven, 2005.

Sokol, Edward D. *The Revolt of 1916 in Central Asia.* Baltimore, 1953.

Sorokin, Pitirim. *Man and Society in Calamity: The Effects of War, Revolution, Famine, Pestilence upon Human Mind, Behavior, Social Organization, and Cultural Life.* New York, 1942. Reprinted 1968.

Stebelsky, Ihor. "The Frontier in Central Asia." In *Studies in Russian Historical Geography,* ed. James H. Bater and R. A. French, 1:143–73. London, 1983.

Stebelsky, Ihor. "Wheat Yields and Weather Hazards in the Soviet Union." In *Interpretations of Calamity from the Viewpoint of Human Ecology,* ed. K. Hewitt, 202–18. Winchester, 1983.

Sternberg, Troy. "Tradition and Transition in the Mongolian Pastoral Environment." In *Modern Pastoralism and Conservation: Old Problems, New Challenges,* ed. Troy Sternberg and Dawn Chatty, 141–59. Cambridge, 2013.

Sunderland, Willard. *Taming the Wild Field: Colonization and Empire on the Russian Steppe.* Ithaca, 2004.

Suny, Ronald Grigor. *The Revenge of the Past: Nationalism, Revolution, and the Collapse of the Soviet Union.* Stanford, 1993.

Suslov, S. P. *The Physical Geography of Asiatic Russia.* Translated by Noah D. Gershevsky. San Francisco, 1961.

Sysyn, Frank, and Andrij Makuch, eds. *Contextualizing the Holodomor: The Impact of Thirty Years of Ukrainian Famine Studies.* Toronto, 2015.

Taaffe, Robert N. "The Geographic Setting." In *The Cambridge History of Early Inner Asia,* ed. Denis Sinor, 19–40. Cambridge, 1990.

Taizhanova, G. E., ed. *Kazakhi: Istoriko-etnograficheskoe issledovanie.* Almaty, 1995.

Taldïbaev, Zhetpïs. "Ashtïqtan kelgen demografiialïq apat." *Abai*, no. 1 (2000): 28–33.

Tätimov, Maqash. "Är Qazaqtïng terïnde tol shezhïresï ïlülï tŭrghangha ne zhetsïn." *Zhŭraghat*, no. 9–10 (2006): 2–5.

Tätimov, Maqash, and Zh. Aliev. *Derbestïmïz-demografiiada*. Almaty, 1999.

Tauger, Mark B. "The 1932 Harvest and the Famine of 1933." *Slavic Review* 50, no. 1 (1991): 70–89.

Thomas, Alun. "Kazakh Nomads and the New Soviet State, 1919–1934." PhD diss., University of Sheffield, 2015.

Tolybekov, S.E. *Obshchestvenno-ekonomicheskii stroi kazakhov v XVII–XIX vekakh*. Almaty, 1959.

Treadgold, Donald W. *The Great Siberian Migration: Government and Peasant in Resettlement from Emancipation to the First World War*. Princeton, 1957.

Tursunbaev, A. B. *Iz istorii krest'ianskogo pereseleniia v Kazakhstan*. Alma-Ata, 1950.

Tursunbaev, A.B. *Kazakhskii aul v trekh revoliutsiiakh*. Almaty, 1967.

Tursunbaev, A. B. *Pobeda kolkhoznogo stroia v Kazakhstane*. Almaty, 1957.

Tursunova, M. S. *Kazakhi Mangyshlaka vo vtoroi polovine XIX veka*. Alma-Ata, 1977.

Ualiyeva, Saule K., and Adrienne L. Edgar. "In the Laboratory of Peoples' Friendship: Mixed People in Kazakhstan from the Soviet Era to the Present." In *Global Mixed Race*, ed. Rebecca C. King-O'Riain et al., 68–90. New York, 2014.

US Commission on the Ukrainian Famine. *Investigation of the Ukrainian Famine, 1932–1933: Report to Congress*. Washington, DC, 1998.

Uyama, Tomohiko. "The Geography of Civilizations: A Spatial Analysis of the Kazakh Intelligentsia's Activities, from the Mid-19th to the Early 20th Century." In *Regions: A Prism to View the Slavic-Eurasian World*, ed. Kimitaka Matsuzato, 70–99. Sapporo, 2000.

Vallin, Jacques, France Meslé, Serguei Adamets, and Serhii Pyrozhkov. "A New Estimate of Ukrainian Population Losses during the Crises of the 1930s and 1940s." *Population Studies* 56, no. 3 (2002): 249–64.

Velikanova, Olga. *Popular Perceptions of Soviet Politics in the 1920s: Disenchantment of the Dreamers*. Basingstoke, 2013.

Viatkin, M. P. *Batyr Srym*. Moscow, 1947.

Viola, Lynne. *The Best Sons of the Fatherland: Workers in the Vanguard of Soviet Collectivization*. New York, 1987.

Viola, Lynne. *Peasant Rebels under Stalin: Collectivization and the Culture of Peasant Resistance*. New York, 1996.

Viola, Lynne. *The Unknown Gulag: The Lost World of Stalin's Special Settlements*. Oxford, 2007.

Watts, Michael. *Silent Violence: Food, Famine, and Peasantry in Northern Nigeria*. Berkeley, 1983.

Weiner, Douglas R. *Models of Nature: Ecology, Conservation, and Cultural Revolution in Soviet Russia*. Pittsburgh, 2000.

Werner, Cynthia, and Kathleen Purvis-Roberts. "Cold War Memories and Post-Cold War Realities: The Politics of Memory and Identity in the Everyday Life of Kazakhstan's Radiation Victims." In *Ethnographies of the State in Central Asia: Performing Politics*, ed. Madeline Reeves et al., 285–309. Bloomington, 2013.

Werth, Nicholas. *Cannibal Island: Death in a Siberian Gulag*. Translated by Steven Rendall. Princeton, 2007.

Werth, Nicholas. "La Famine au Kazakhstan 1931–1933: Le rapport à Staline du 9 mars 1933." *Communisme*, no. 74/75 (2003): 9–18.

Westren, Michael H. "Nations in Exile: The 'Punished Peoples' in Soviet Kazakhstan, 1941–1961." PhD diss., University of Chicago, 2012.

Wheatcroft, Stephen G. "Famine and Food Consumption Records in Early Soviet History, 1917–25." In *Food, Diet, and Economic Change Past and Present,* ed. Catherine Geissler and Derek J. Oddy, 151–74. New York, 1993.

Wheatcroft, Stephen G. "Soviet Statistics and Nutrition and Mortality during Times of Famine, 1917–22 and 1931–33." *Cahiers du monde russe* 30, no. 4 (1997): 525–57.

Wheatcroft, Stephen G., and R. W. Davies. *The Years of Hunger: Soviet Agriculture, 1931–1933.* New York, 2009.

White, Richard. *The Roots of Dependency: Subsistence, Environment, and Social Change among the Choctaws, Pawnees, and Navajos.* Lincoln, 1983.

Whiting, Allen S., and Sheng Shih-ts'ai. *Sinkiang: Pawn or Pivot?* East Lansing, 1958.

Yessenova, Saulesh. "Soviet Nationality, Identity, and Ethnicity in Central Asia: Historic Narratives and Kazakh Ethnic Identity." *Journal of Muslim Minority Affairs* 22, no. 1 (2002): 12–36.

Zhakisheva, Saule. "Bai-'polufeodaly' v Kazakhstane na rubezhe 20–30-kh godov XX v.: Istoriko-istochnikovedcheskii analiz problem." Candidate of Sciences diss., Institut istorii i etnologii im. Ch. Ch. Vaikhanova, 1996.

Zhaulin, Kiïkbai. "Asïra sïlteu saldarï: Mangghïstau öngïrïngdegiï 1931–32 zhïldardaghï asharshïlïq turalï ne bïlemïz?" *Aqtandaqtar aqiqatï* (2003): 53–55.

Index

Page numbers followed by letters *f*, *m*, and *t* refer to figures, maps, and tables, respectively.

CPSIA information can be obtained
at www.ICGtesting.com
Printed in the USA
LVHW111953071118
596314LV00006B/61/P